Education Policy in Developing Countries

Education Policy in Developing Countries

Edited by Paul Glewwe

The University of Chicago Press :: Chicago and London

Paul Glewwe is professor in the Department of Applied Economics at the University of Minnesota and for thirteen years before that was a research economist at the World Bank. He is the author or coeditor of several books, most recently *Economic Growth, Poverty, and Household Welfare in Vietnam*.

The University of Chicago Press, Chicago 60637
The University of Chicago Press, Ltd., London
© 2014 by The University of Chicago
All rights reserved. Published 2014.
Printed in the United States of America

23 22 21 20 19 18 17 16 15 14   1 2 3 4 5

ISBN-13: 978-0-226-07868-7 (cloth)
ISBN-13: 978-0-226-07871-7 (paper)
ISBN-13: 978-0-226-07885-4 (e-book)
DOI: 10.7208/chicago/9780226078854.001.0001

Library of Congress Cataloging-in-Publication Data

Education policy in developing countries / edited by
Paul Glewwe.
    pages cm
  Includes bibliographical references and index.
  ISBN 978-0-226-07868-7 (cloth : alkaline paper)
  ISBN 978-0-226-07871-7 (paperback : alkaline paper)
  ISBN 978-0-226-07885-4 (e-book)
    1. Education and state—Developing countries.   I. Glewwe, Paul,
1958– editor
  LC98.E33 2014
  379.172'4—dc23

                                                  2013016603

Contents

1

Overview of Education Issues in Developing Countries

Paul Glewwe (Department of Applied
Economics, University of Minnesota)

During this century, education, skills, and other knowledge have become crucial determinants of a person's and a nation's productivity. One can even call
the twentieth century the Age of Human Capital in the sense that the primary
determinant of a country's standard of living is how well it succeeds in developing and utilizing the skills, knowledge, health, and habits of its population.
Gary Becker (1995)

Most, if not almost all, economists agree with Gary Becker
on the importance of human capital in determining a
country's standard of living, and that formal education
is a large, and perhaps the largest, component of human
capital. This consensus reflects the fact that economists
and other researchers have accumulated a vast amount of
evidence that education increases workers' productivity
and thus increases their incomes. They have also shown
that education leads to improvements in health and many
other types of nonmonetary benefits.

While economists and other researchers may lament
that many of their research findings are routinely ignored
by policymakers, this does not appear to be the case for
education. International organizations fully endorse the
importance of education for economic and social development. For example, two of the eight Millennium

Development Goals (MDGs) adopted at the United Nations Millennium Summit in September 2000 focus on education. Even more important, policymakers in developing countries also generally agree that there are important benefits from investment in human capital. One consequence of this consensus is that policymakers have greatly increased their funding of education; governments in developing countries now spend about $700 billion *each year* on education, and parents' expenditures on their children's education are likely to be on the same order of magnitude.[1]

Have these investments in education increased the stock of human capital in developing countries? There has certainly been substantial progress in terms of increases in school enrollment rates and completion rates. For example, the World Bank (2012) estimates that 87% of children in developing countries finish primary school, and the gross enrollment rate for secondary school in these countries in 2010 was on average 64%, which is a large improvement over the rate of 41% in 1980.

Yet it is still the case that 13% of children in developing countries do not finish primary school, and over one-third do not enroll in secondary school. Even more worrisome is the large amount of evidence that students in developing countries learn far less than do students in developed countries. In an international comparison conducted in 2009, 58.1% of U.S. fifteen-year-old students attained a literacy score of Level 3 or higher, where Level 3 corresponds to "capable of reading tasks of moderate complexity" (OECD 2010, p. 51). In contrast, the corresponding figures for fifteen-year-old students in many developing countries were much lower: 23.3% for Brazil, 12.2% for Indonesia, 20.1% for Jordan, and 13.1% for Peru. Results for mathematics Level 3 proficiency, which is defined as being able to "execute clearly described procedures, including those that require sequential decisions," reveal an even larger gap: 52.2% for the United States, yet only 11.9% for Brazil, 6.4% for Indonesia, 11.9% for Jordan, and 9.5% for Peru.

While spending even more money may increase enrollment and learning to some extent, most developing countries face serious budget constraints that will make it difficult for them to devote significantly larger amounts of money to education. This raises the question of whether current spending could be allocated more efficiently, and more generally whether education policies could be improved in ways that increase both enrollment and learning at little additional cost. Economists and other researchers have conducted a large amount of research on education in developing countries in the last two decades, but their findings are scattered in many different academic journals and other types of publications.

The importance of education in determining countries' and individuals' standards of living, combined with the low levels of learning in many developing countries despite the hundreds of billions of dollars devoted each year to education in those countries, underscores the urgent need to find policies that will lead to better education outcomes in those countries. Fortunately, there has been a large increase in research on education in developing countries in the last two decades, which presents an unprecedented opportunity to assess how this research can be used to improve education policies in developing countries. In response to this opportunity, this volume has three goals: to take stock of what this recent research has found; to present the implications of this research for education policies in developing countries; and, finally, to set priorities for future research on education in those countries. These goals are accomplished in the remaining chapters of this book. This chapter lays out the broad issues and highlights some of the most important findings in the chapters that follow.

Broadly speaking, the factors that determine how many years children are enrolled in school, and how much they learn while they are in school, can be divided into child and family characteristics, and school and teacher characteristics. Child and family characteristics are often difficult to change through government policies, though some policies, such as those aimed at improving child health, can have important effects. In contrast, since most children in developing countries are enrolled in publicly operated schools, government policies can have direct (and indirect) impacts on school and teacher characteristics. Thus a reasonable place to begin when reviewing the evidence on the impact of government policies on students' education outcomes is to focus on school and teacher characteristics. Indeed, while students' characteristics and backgrounds can have important effects on how much they learn, careful research has shown that schools and teachers can also make a substantial difference.[2]

Almost every parent would like his or her child to attend a "high-quality" school, but it is not necessarily clear which schools are of high quality. By definition, a "high-quality school" is a school whose students are more likely to achieve or exceed the learning goals set by the educational system, compared to similar students in other schools. Similarly, a "low-quality school" is one whose students are less likely to attain those goals, again compared to similar students in other schools. But what makes some schools (and teachers) "high quality" and others "low quality"? The role of basic school and teacher characteristics in determining students' educational outcomes is reviewed in chapter 2, by Glewwe, Hanushek, Humpage and Ravina. This chapter systematically reviews the research done in the last two decades to assess what has been learned about the causal impact of basic school and teacher characteristics—such as class size (student-teacher ratio), teacher education, availability of textbooks and desks, teacher training, and pedagogical methods used—on students' educational attainment (years of schooling) and learning. To the extent that certain teacher or school characteristics have strong positive impacts on students' educational outcomes, funding for education should be reallocated toward policies that promote those characteristics and away from interventions that focus on characteristics that appear to have little or no effect.

The findings of this chapter are sobering. The studies that are deemed to be of the highest quality yield only a few unambiguous results, and those results are not particularly surprising. The clearest findings are that having a fully functioning school—one with better quality roofs, walls or floors, with desks, tables, and chairs, and with a school library—appears conducive to student learning. These findings are little more than common sense, and even the impacts of these attributes may not be causal; perhaps the true causal factor is an interest in, and a commitment to, providing a quality education. On the personnel side, the most consistent results are positive impacts of having teachers with greater knowledge of the subjects they teach, having a longer school day, and providing tutoring. An additional, and again unsurprising, finding is that it matters whether the teacher shows up for work; teacher absence has a clear negative effect on learning. Again, these findings regarding teachers offer little more than what common sense would predict.

One immediate implication of these research findings is that countries that are interested in improving student outcomes should ensure that these common-sense solutions to increase their students' performance are in fact being implemented. Remarkably, many countries around the world fail to provide a basic institutional structure that promotes student achievement. Yet these findings do *not* imply that common sense can serve as a reliable guide for education policies, because many other policies that may also appear to be common sense, such as reducing class size, are not supported by recent research.

Perhaps most important, the analysis in chapter 2 suggests that progress in improving students' educational outcomes in developing countries will require going beyond a narrow focus on basic school and teacher characteristics. Several possible directions could be pursued, and they can be divided into three broad types: policies that alter student characteristics before they begin primary school (and perhaps while they are in school), policies that are designed to alter student and parent behavior, and policies that attempt to change the way that schools are operated in terms of both the management structure and the incentives faced by teachers and school administrators. These three types of policies are systematically reviewed in chapters 3–7.

Consider first policies that attempt to change student characteristics before they even enroll in primary school. The two main avenues to change child characteristics in the first years of life are early childhood development programs, especially preschools, and child health and nutrition programs. The former are examined in chapter 3, and the latter are reviewed in chapter 4.

In developed countries, most children attend preschool before entering primary school, and preschools are becoming increasingly common in developing countries. The potential role that preschools could play in raising students' progress in primary and secondary school in developing countries is examined by Behrman, Engle and Fernald in chapter 3. They find evidence from a small number of high-quality studies that preschools can have strong, positive effects on children's long-run educational and income-earning outcomes.

Yet preschools can vary in many dimensions, and the evidence to date is insufficient to determine what aspects of preschools are most important for boosting student outcomes and outcomes during adulthood. In addition, there are many unanswered questions regarding how preschool services should be provided. For example, should developing country governments establish a nationwide system of preschools, or should they offer subsidies that families can use to enroll their children in privately operated preschools? Chapter 3 concludes with priorities for future research, including specific recommendations for the types of research methods and data-collection efforts that are most promising.

Any comprehensive analysis of education in developing countries must address the relationship between students' educational progress and their health and nutritional status. The need for a comprehensive analysis of this relationship reflects two fundamental facts: (1) Many children in developing countries suffer from malnutrition and other conditions of poor health; and (2) there is strong evidence that malnutrition and poor health, both during the first years of life and while in school, can have negative impacts on students' educational outcomes. This analysis is provided by Alderman and Bleakley in chapter 4.

After a conceptual overview of the impact of poor health on education outcomes in developing countries, Alderman and Bleakley focus on

two specific dimensions of poor health: malnutrition and parasitic infections. They highlight the findings that improvements in these two dimensions have the potential not only to increase years of schooling but
also to increase learning per year of school, the latter of which is consistent with an emphasis on improving the quality of education. Interventions that reduce early childhood malnutrition and parasitic infections
have economic returns that greatly exceed their costs. Alderman and
Bleakley also point out that both of these dimensions are characterized
by the presence of externalities; diarrheal infections that lead to early
childhood malnutrition and parasitic infections that affect children during their school-going years are easily spread from one child to another,
which implies that private investments in child health are below socially
optimal levels. In addition, public interventions to improve child health
lead not only to increased economic efficiency by addressing the above-
mentioned externalities but also reduce inequality, since efforts to improve child health tend to benefit the poor more than they benefit higher-
income households.

A final point regarding the impact of child health on schooling outcomes is that some successful interventions will require cooperation
among two separate government ministries, the Ministry of Health and
the Ministry of Education, that have had relatively little interaction in
the past in many countries. This could lead to administrative conflicts;
for example, some activities of the Ministry of Education that are not
particularly effective in improving students' outcomes should have their
funding reduced, and those funds may better contribute to education
outcomes if they are used to fund health programs administered by the
Ministry of Health.[3] This is consistent with the more general point made
above that parts of the institutional structure in many developing countries impede more effective policies and thus inhibit better results.

Policies that attempt to improve students' education outcomes by
changing teacher and school characteristics are, in effect, policies that
focus on the supply side of schooling. Yet there may be policies that are
more effective by focusing on the demand side. This leads to the second
type of policies that go beyond attempts to change school and teacher
characteristics: policies that change the incentives faced by students and
parents. The potential for such policies is explored by Behrman, Parker,
and Todd in chapter 5. This chapter is particularly timely because such
incentive programs, especially conditional cash-transfer programs, have
become much more common in developing countries in the past one to
two decades (see World Bank 2009).

Programs that provide incentives for students and their parents can take several forms. Chapter 5 reviews the evidence on four types of incentive programs: (1) Conditional cash-transfer programs, which provide parents monthly payments conditional on their children attending school regularly; (2) payments to students based on academic performance, such as scores on exams; (3) school-voucher programs that provide funds that parents can use to enroll their children in either public or private schools; and (4) "food-for-education" programs that provide children with meals at school or supply their families with staple foods to be consumed at home. The authors find that many of these programs lead to increases in school enrollment, although there is less evidence on whether they lead to increased student learning as measured by performance on academic tests.

While incentive programs seem to be a promising avenue for increasing students' educational outcomes, further research is needed to understand the circumstances that make these programs particularly effective. Given the variation in country and education system characteristics across developing countries, it is not clear that a program that worked well in one country will also be effective in another country with very different characteristics. Another important issue is cost-benefit ratios. Some incentive programs, such as conditional cash-transfer programs, are quite expensive, and there may be other policies that can raise students' educational progress at a much lower cost. On the other hand, when assessing the costs of those programs it is important to note that, from the perspective of society as a whole, transfers are simply a redistribution of resources from one group of households (taxpayers) to another (program participants) and thus these transfers should not be counted as a cost of the program to society as a whole (although raising taxes to pay for any program does entail a social cost, namely the deadweight cost of raising government revenue).

The third and final type of policies that go beyond attempts to change basic school and teacher characteristics is those that focus on the ways that schools, and more generally school systems, are organized. Such policies focus on the supply side of the education sector, but also on how that supply can be made more responsive to the demand for education. These types of policies can be divided into those that focus on how public schools are managed, and those that foster competition between (and among) both public and private schools. These two types of policies are examined in chapters 6 and 7 respectively.

Many observers argue that the focus of supply-side efforts pertaining to public schools should not be on their basic characteristics; instead it may be that the way schools are organized and managed may be much more important for increasing students' educational progress. One startling symptom of poor management is that teacher absences are quite common in developing countries; averaging over six countries, Chaudhury et al. (2006) find that on any given day 19% of teachers are absent. Organizational and management issues, and the recent research on them, are reviewed by Galiani and Perez-Truglia in chapter 6. They focus on three specific issues that have received particular attention in developing countries: school decentralization, tracking, and teacher incentives.

School decentralization is the delegation of the management of educational resources to lower levels of public administration, the lowest of which is the school. While this policy has been widely advocated since the 1990s, until recently there was little research on its impact in developing countries. Galiani and Perez-Truglia conclude that the most credible studies find that, on average, school decentralization policies increase students' learning and time in school. Unfortunately, these average impacts do not appear to be evenly spread across all students; the few studies that examine the impacts for different groups of students find that the poorest students do not seem to benefit, which implies that such policies lead to a more unequal distribution of educational outcomes unless other policies are adopted that can raise educational progress among the poor.

The evidence on tracking by student ability in developing countries is quite sparse. The best study to date, from Kenya, finds benefits to all students from tracking, but more research is needed in other contexts to see whether this finding can be generalized to other countries and educational systems.

There is somewhat more evidence on teacher incentives. Most, but not all, of the teacher-incentive schemes studied found positive impacts in terms of reducing teacher absenteeism and improving students' performance, though the compensations systems should be designed to discourage teaching to the test. A more specific type of teacher incentive program is the increasing use of contract teachers, who are less-qualified, locally hired teachers who have little job security (a typical contract is for one year) and receive relatively low pay. The best studies to date indicate that such teachers can raise student learning, although again additional research is needed to determine whether these findings generalize to many different settings.

Discussion of school-management issues sooner or later leads to the question of the role that could be played by private schools, and more generally the role of competition in promoting effective delivery of education services. In general, economists favor competition as a means to increase efficiency in a wide variety of settings, and it is not surprising that many economists advocate a greater role for private schools and for other policies that promote competition among schools, such as vouchers. These issues are considered MacLeod and Urquiola in chapter 7.

These authors begin with a review of the empirical evidence. While many economists would expect that competition in the provision of education would lead to an unambiguous improvement in education outcomes, they argue that this is not the case. First, they examine whether private schools are more efficient than public schools, focusing on studies from Colombia and India, which have the strongest research designs. The evidence for both countries is mixed. They then turn to the question of whether increased competition among both public and private schools improves students' educational outcomes, focusing on evidence from Chile and Pakistan, which have the highest-quality studies of this type. These results are also mixed. A final point is that evidence from several of these countries shows that increased competition, especially in the form of an increase in the share of students enrolled in private schools, leads to greater social stratification and inequality in education outcomes.

Given these results, which may be surprising to many economists, MacLeod and Urquiola present a broad theoretical discussion of the nature of competition in education services, drawing on theoretical models of incentives and contracts (particularly models of incomplete contracts). They conclude that the theoretical arguments for increased competition in education are mixed. The crux of the problem is that students' academic performance depends not only on school quality, however defined, but also on students' ability and effort, and it is difficult for parents, or more generally the market, to distinguish between these effects. For example, in many countries students who attend private schools perform better on academic tests than do students in public schools, but it is unclear whether this difference reflects that private schools are of higher quality or that the students in those schools have higher ability and more parental support. In such situations, where asymmetric information problems are pervasive, economic theory does not assure that increased competition will increase students' educational progress. Thus the mixed empirical findings should not be seen as particularly surprising.

Taken as a whole, the findings in chapters 2–7 provide substantial guidance regarding what policies are most promising for improving students' educational outcomes in developing countries, but clearly more research is needed. Yet once one has fairly reliable results concerning the impacts of several policy options on students' years of schooling and learning, one has only half of the information needed to choose from among those options; information is also needed on the costs of each of the options. In theory, the different policy options need to be compared using cost-benefit analysis. Yet the wisdom of this approach is questioned by Dhaliwal, Duflo, Glennerster and Tulloch in chapter 8. They argue that cost-effectiveness analysis is a more useful guide for policy decisions.

Cost-benefit analysis attempts to compare the monetary value of the costs of a program to the monetary value of all of the outcomes brought about by that program. In contrast, cost-effectiveness analysis compares the monetary costs of a program to the "amount" of the outcomes, which in the case of education projects are years in school, skills learned, and perhaps other educational outcomes. This has the advantage that there is no need to calculate the monetary value of the outcomes, which can be very complicated and may require assumptions that could be incorrect. On the other hand, cost-effectiveness analysis has the disadvantage that one can compare only programs with similar outcomes, while in principle cost-benefit analysis can be used to compare *any* types of programs for which cost-benefit calculations can be made, for example comparing the relative merits of a given education program to a hydropower project or an anticorruption program.

Dhaliwal et al. argue that many, if not most, education decisions can be made on the basis of cost-effectiveness analysis. While this has the benefit that it requires fewer assumptions than cost-benefit analysis, it is still the case that cost-effectiveness analysis is not always straightforward, so the authors provide detailed advice in how best to implement it. Difficulties regarding the calculation of the impacts include obtaining credible estimates of those impacts (the main focus of chapters 2–7), comparisons when programs have multiple impacts, statistical imprecision in the estimated impacts, spillover effects, and aggregation issues. Complications that arise in calculating costs include calculating the marginal costs of a program, determining the value of goods and services that are obtained at little or no cost, calculating (direct and indirect) costs incurred by beneficiaries, and deciding how to treat income and other transfers (which involve redistribution of resources but perhaps little cost to the economy as a whole), management costs, and issues involved in scaling up a pilot program.

Considered together, the chapters in this book summarize the current state of knowledge regarding the policy options available to developing countries that are most promising for increasing the stock of human capital of their youth. While much has been learned in the past ten to twenty years, much more remains to be learned. Fortunately, economists and other researchers currently are doing a large amount of high-quality research on education in developing countries. They use a wide variety of methods, but this is a strength, rather than a weakness, of this research (Rosenzweig 2010). Future work should, when possible, involve interaction of innovative empirical work with new theoretical work (as recommended by Banerjee and Duflo [2010]). Given that policymakers in developing countries and international development agencies do heed the advice that economists and other researchers offer on education policy, the results of new research will not be of merely academic interest but have the potential to increase the quantity and quality of education of hundreds of millions of children in the developing world.

A final point is that much of the research by economists and other researchers looks at the impact of specific programs and policies. A bigger task would be to develop a decisionmaking structure that countries can use in a systematic way to maintain and expand those programs that are successful while eliminating those that are not. Unfortunately, this important issue is often overlooked. The running story throughout this book is that some programs that appear to be quite efficacious are not necessarily the ones most often implemented. In addition to building a database about the success and failure of individual policies, future research should also focus on the decisionmaking process of both developed and developing countries.

Notes

1. See chapter 2 by Glewwe et al. on figures for government expenditures on education, as well as references regarding economists' support for education.

2. For example, two recent studies using US data (Carrell and West 2010; Rivkin, Hanushek, and Kain 2005) show strong impacts of individual teachers on student learning.

3. Bundy et al. (2009) provide a discussion, and examples, of how to improve collaboration between the Ministry of Education and the Ministry of Health in developing countries.

References

Banerjee, Abhijit, and Esther Duflo. 2010. "Giving Credit Where It Is Due." *Journal of Economic Perspectives* 24 (3): 61–79.

Becker, Gary. 1995. "Human Capital and Poverty Alleviation." Human Resources Development and Operations Policy Working Paper 52. Washington, DC: World Bank.

Bundy, Donald, et al. 2009. Rethinking School Feeding: Social Safety Nets, Child Development and the Education Sector. Washington, DC: World Bank.

Carrell, Scott, and James West. 2010. "Does Professor Quality Matter? Evidence from Random Assignment of Students to Professors." *Journal of Political Economy* 118 (3): 409–32.

Chaudhury, Nazmul, Jeffrey Hammer, Michael Kremer, Karthik Muralidharan, and F. Halsey Rogers. 2006. "Missing in Action: Teacher and Health Worker Absence in Developing Countries." *Journal of Economic Perspectives* 20 (1): 91–116.

OECD. 2010. *PISA 2009 Results: What Students Know and Can Do*. Paris: Organization for Economic Cooperation and Development.

Rivkin, Steven, Eric Hanushek, and John Kain. 2005. "Teachers, Schools, and Academic Achievement." *Econometrica* 73 (2): 417–58.

Rosenzweig, Mark. 2010. "Microeconomic Approaches to Development: Schooling, Learning and Growth." *Journal of Economic Perspectives* 24 (3): 81–96.

World Bank. 2009. "Conditional Cash Transfers: Reducing Present and Future Poverty." World Bank Policy Research Report. Washington, DC: World Bank.

———. 2012. *World Development Indicators 2012*. Washington, DC: World Bank.

2

School Resources and Educational Outcomes in Developing Countries: A Review of the Literature from 1990 to 2010

Paul Glewwe (University of Minnesota)
Eric A. Hanushek (Stanford University)
Sarah Humpage (University of Minnesota)
Renato Ravina (University of Minnesota)

2.1. Introduction and Motivation

As explained in chapter 1, economists and other research-ers have accumulated a large amount of evidence that ed-ucation increases workers' productivity and thus increases their incomes.[1] There are also many nonmonetary benefits of education, such as improved health status and lowered crime (Lochner 2011). Finally, at the country level there is also a large amount of evidence that education increases the rate of economic growth (Hanushek and Woessmann 2008). These analyses all highlight the value of improving a country's human capital and provide the motivation for developing countries to invest in the skills of their popula-tions. They do not, however, indicate which types of spe-cific investments should be pursued.

Chapter 1 also pointed out that policymakers in devel-oping countries have quite generally accepted the message of these benefits from improved human capital and have greatly increased their funding of education. As seen in table 2.1, since 1980 real government expenditures on education more than doubled in Latin America, almost tripled in the Middle East and Sub-Saharan Africa, and increased by more than fivefold in East Asia and by about sevenfold in South Asia. International development agencies have also called for greater resources to be devoted to education, and have increased their levels of assistance for education projects in recent years, as shown in table 2.2.

The most consistent focus of investment has been on increasing primary and secondary school enrollment rates, with the ultimate goal of higher levels of educational attainment. The increases in enrollment over the past three decades, particularly at the primary level, have been quite dramatic. From 1980 to 2010 primary and secondary enrollment rates have increased in all regions of the developing world (table 2.3), so that by 2010 gross primary enrollment rates were at or above 100% in all regions, and gross secondary enrollment rates were above 50% in all regions except Sub-Saharan Africa.[2] Similarly, table 2.4 shows that primary school completion rates increased in all regions from 1991 to 2010, and in the latter year were near 90% or higher in all regions except Sub-Saharan Africa.

Much of the increased funding for education, particularly in the earlier periods, took the form of building and staffing schools in areas

Table 2.1 Public expenditures on education in developing countries, 1980–2010 (millions of 2000 US dollars)

Region	1980	1996	2010
East Asia and Pacific	78,923	197,804	435,982
Latin American and Caribbean	51,931	70,067	130,500
Middle East and North Africa	26,326	41,915	68,486
South Asia	4,315	14,972	30,195
Sub-Saharan Africa	9,332	13,089	27,405

Sources: World Bank 1999, 2008, 2012.

Table 2.2 Official development assistance for education, 1980–2010 (millions of constant 2010 US dollars)

	1980	1990	2000	2010
All donors	7,400	10,986	7,619	13,412
DAC (OECD Dev. Assist. Comm.) Countries	7,400	8,631	5,522	9,420
Multilateral	—	2,355	2,097	3,652
Non-DAC countries	—	—	—	340

Source: OECD, International Development Statistics (www.oecd.org/dac/stats/idsonline).

Table 2.3 Primary and secondary gross enrollment rates, 1980–2010

Region	Primary			Secondary		
	1980	1995	2010	1980	1995	2010
East Asia and Pacific	111	115	111	43	65	76
Latin American and Caribbean	106	111	117	42	53	90
Middle East and North Africa	87	97	102	42	64	72
South Asia	76	99	110	27	49	55
Sub-Saharan Africa	78	75	100	14	27	36

Sources: World Bank 1998, 2012.

Table 2.4 Primary school completion rates, 1991 and 2010

Region	1991	2010
East Asia and Pacific	101	97
Latin American and Caribbean	84	102
Middle East and North Africa	77	88
South Asia	62	86
Sub-Saharan Africa	51	67

Sources: World Bank 2002, 2012.

where no school previously existed, reflecting the rather obvious fact that it is hard to go to school if no school exists. Moreover, there is ample evidence that enrollment increases when the distance to the nearest school decreases. When increased spending on existing schools makes them more attractive, either by reducing school fees and other direct costs of schooling or by improving the quality of the educational opportunities they provide, one would expect that enrollment would increase further.[3]

More recently, however, attention has begun to swing toward the quality of schools and the achievement of students—and here the evidence on outcomes is decidedly more mixed. Over the past decade, it has become possible to follow changes in student performance on tests offered by the Programme for International Student Assessment (PISA). While student learning appears to be increasing in several countries, this tendency is not universal. More specifically, table 2.5 presents evidence on learning among 15-year-old students in 12 developing countries (of which 7 are in Latin America). Examining trends from 2000 to 2009, 5 countries show clear upward trends (Chile, Colombia, Peru, Tunisia, and Turkey), while the other 7 show either mixed or even decreasing trends. At the aggregate level, it may simply be that expanded enrollment brings in progressively less able and less qualified students, who then

Table 2.5 Scores on internationally comparable tests for 15-year-old students, 2000–2009

Country	Subject	2000	2003	2006	2009
Argentina	Reading	418		374	398
	Mathematics			381	388
Brazil	Reading	396	403	393	412
	Mathematics		356	370	386
Chile	Reading	410		442	449
	Mathematics			411	421
Colombia	Reading			385	413
	Mathematics			470	481
Indonesia	Reading	371	382	393	402
	Mathematics		360	381	371
Jordan	Reading			401	405
	Mathematics			384	387
Mexico	Reading	422	400	410	425
	Mathematics		385	406	419
Peru	Reading	327			370
Thailand	Reading	431	420	417	421
	Mathematics		417	417	419
Tunisia	Reading		375	380	404
	Mathematics		359	365	371
Turkey	Reading		375	380	404
	Mathematics		423	424	445
Uruguay	Reading		434	413	426
	Mathematics		422	427	427

Sources: OECD 2000, 2003, 2006, 2009.
Note: Peru has a math score for 2009, but not for any of the previous years. Since the main purpose of this table is to compare changes over time in test scores, Peru's math score in 2009, which was 365, is not included in this table.

pull down the average score. Yet some countries with mixed or declining trends did not show large increases in school enrollment, and were increasing real expenditures per student on education. For example, in Argentina the gross secondary school enrollment rate has been about 85% from 1998 to 2007, and spending per pupil was somewhat higher in 2004–6 than in 1998–2000; yet test scores in 2007 were lower than in 2000. Similarly, Brazil's progress has been uneven at best, yet it experienced only a moderate increase in secondary school enrollment (7–13 percentage points) from 2000 to 2007, and real spending on education steadily increased over time.[4]

The concern about quality becomes more significant in analyses of the impact on student learning (achievement) of demand-side programs that stimulate increased enrollment. A recent survey of high-quality analyses of currently popular demand-side programs—fee reductions, conditional cash transfers, and school nutrition programs—found that the higher enrollment induced by these programs was not accompanied by increased achievement (Hanushek 2008).[5] It is natural to think that bringing students into school must certainly increase their learning and achievement, but this impact may be limited to new students who were not previously in school, with no effect (or even a negative effect) on current students.

This discussion is related to a substantial body of literature, particularly for developed countries, that suggests that money alone is not the answer to increase student learning. Specifically, for developed countries there is substantial research indicating that overall expenditures, and common school initiatives funded by those expenditures such as lower class sizes or more educated teachers, are not closely related to student outcomes.[6] Similar findings, although not as strong, come from the research on schools in developing countries (Fuller and Clarke 1994; Hanushek 1995; Harbison and Hanushek 1992).

In response to findings that increased educational spending has had little effect on student performance, many policymakers and researchers in both developed and developing countries have advocated changing the way that schools are run—such as changing the incentives faced by teachers (and by students) and, more generally, changing the way that schools are organized. The evidence on whether such policies have been effective is reviewed in chapters 5, 6 and 7 of this book.

Yet it is still possible that spending that changes basic school and teacher characteristics, if properly directed, could play a role in improving students' educational outcomes in developing countries. Thus it is useful to review the more recent literature on school spending and resources, extending the prior reviews that covered studies through the early 1990s. Indeed, significant numbers of new studies have appeared since 1990.

More important, many of the newer studies employ much stronger research designs than were previously used. The appreciation of researchers for the difficulty of obtaining clear estimates of causal impacts has grown considerably over the past two decades. The sensitivity to these issues, along with more care about the underlying methodological approach, suggests that the new studies may in fact yield conclusions different from those drawn on the older research.

In response to this need for an up-to-date assessment of this research, this chapter examines both the economics literature and the education literature published in the last two decades to assess the extent to which school and teacher characteristics have a causal impact on student learning and enrollment. More specifically, this chapter reviews the literature that attempts to estimate the impact of school infrastructure and pedagogical materials (such as electricity, condition of the building, desks, blackboards and textbooks), teacher characteristics (education, training, experience, sex, subject knowledge, and ethnicity), and school organization (pupil-teacher ratio, teaching methods, decentralized management, and teacher contracts and working conditions) on student enrollment and learning.

The remainder of this chapter is organized as follows. The next section describes a simple interpretive framework. This is followed by a description of the parameters of this review and of the method used to select studies for inclusion in it. Finally, the chapter presents the results of this review and draws conclusions about priorities for future research.

2.2. Interpreting the Research on Basic Education Inputs

The overarching conceptual framework employed here considers schools as "factories" that produce "learning" using various school and teacher characteristics as "inputs." This is the production function approach introduced early in microeconomics courses. However, the actual application and interpretation in education differ from the simple textbook treatment.

The reasoning underlying this conceptual framework is that the process by which cognitive skills are learned is determined by many different factors, and production functions are expressions, in simple terms, of this process. The relationship can be very flexible, allowing for almost any learning process. In this sense, an education production function always exists, although its existence does not guarantee that one can estimate it.

In the ideal case, if one can estimate this relationship, one can then use information on the costs of school characteristics, classroom materials, and even teacher characteristics to select the combination of these that is most effective in increasing enrollment and/or student performance (e.g., increase in test scores per dollar spent) given a limited budget. In theory, this could also apply to pedagogical practices, which have implementation costs. The details of how to use data on costs to assess the cost-effectiveness of various interventions are explained by Dhaliwal and others in chapter 8.

2.2.1. Relationships of Interest. To interpret the research results presented later in this chapter, it is useful to step back to consider what relationships are of interest and how those relationships interact with households' behavior. The theory of the firm, where analyses of production functions are generally introduced, takes the perspective of a decisionmaker who optimally chooses the combination of inputs for his or her firm. But this perspective ignores a key reality of education: students and parents—both important inputs into achievement—also make their own decisions in response to the school decisionmaker's choices.

To begin, assume that the parents of the child maximize, subject to constraints, a (life-cycle) utility function. The main arguments in the utility function are consumption of goods and services (including leisure) at different points in time, and each child's years of schooling and learning. The constraints faced are the production function for learning, the impacts of years of schooling and of skills obtained on the future labor incomes of children, a life-cycle budget constraint, and perhaps some credit constraints or an agricultural production function (for which child labor is one possible input). Following Glewwe and Kremer (2006), the production function for learning (a structural relationship) can be depicted as:

$$(1) \qquad\qquad A = a(S, \mathbf{Q}, \mathbf{C}, \mathbf{H}, \mathbf{I})$$

where A is skills learned ("achievement"), S is years of schooling, $\mathbf{Q}$ is a vector of school and teacher characteristics (inputs that raise school "quality"), $\mathbf{C}$ is a vector of child characteristics (including "innate ability"), $\mathbf{H}$ is a vector of household characteristics, and $\mathbf{I}$ is a vector of school inputs under the control of parents, such as children's daily attendance and purchases of textbooks and other school supplies. Although children acquire many different skills in school, for the purpose at hand little is lost by treating A as a single variable.

Assume that all elements in the vectors $\mathbf{C}$ and $\mathbf{H}$ (which include parental tastes for schooling, parental education, and children's "ability") are exogenous, that is, they cannot be changed by children or their parents. Some child characteristics that affect education outcomes (such as child health) may be endogenous; they can be treated as elements of $\mathbf{I}$, all of which are endogenous (i.e., can be influenced by children and/or parents).

In the simplest scenario, only one school is available and parents can do nothing to change that school's characteristics. Thus all variables in $\mathbf{Q}$ are exogenous to the household. Parents choose S and $\mathbf{I}$ (subject to the above-mentioned constraints) to maximize household utility, which implies that years of schooling S and schooling inputs $\mathbf{I}$ can be expressed as general functions of the four vectors of exogenous variables:

$$(2) \qquad\qquad S = f(\mathbf{Q}, \mathbf{C}, \mathbf{H}, \mathbf{P})$$

$$(3) \qquad\qquad \mathbf{I} = g(\mathbf{Q}, \mathbf{C}, \mathbf{H}, \mathbf{P})$$

where prices related to schooling (such as tuition, other fees, and prices of textbooks and uniforms), which are also exogenous, are denoted by the vector **P**.

Inserting (2) and (3) into (1) gives the reduced-form equation for (A):

(4) $$A = h(\mathbf{Q}, \mathbf{C}, \mathbf{H}, \mathbf{P})$$

This reduced-form equation is a causal relationship, but it is not a textbook production function because it reflects household preferences and includes prices among its arguments.

The more realistic assumption that households can choose from more than one school implies that **Q** and **P** are endogenous even if they are fixed for any given school. In this scenario, households maximize utility with respect to each schooling choice, and then choose the school that leads to the highest utility. Conditional on choosing that school, they choose S and **I**, as in the case where there is only one school from which to choose.

Policymakers are primarily concerned with the impact of school and teacher characteristics (**Q**) and prices related to schooling (**P**) on years of schooling (S) and eventual academic achievement (A). For example, reducing class size can be seen as a change in one element of **Q**, and changing tuition fees can be seen as altering one component of **P**. Equations (2) and (4) show how changes in the **P** variables would affect S and A. In addition, equation (2) also shows how changes in school and teacher quality (**Q**) affect students' years of schooling (S).

Turning to the impact of school-quality variables (**Q**) on student learning, there are two distinct relationships. To see this, consider a change in one element of **Q**, call it Q_i. Equation (1) shows how changes in Q_i affect A when all other explanatory variable are held constant, and thus provides the *partial* derivative of A with respect to Q_i. In contrast, equation (4) provides the *total* derivative of A with respect to Q_i because it allows for changes in S and **I** in response to the change in Q_i.[7] Parents may respond to higher school quality by increasing their provision of educational inputs such as textbooks. Alternatively, if they consider higher school quality a substitute for those inputs, they may decrease those inputs.

The fact that parental actions may reduce or reinforce school decisions may help to explain a portion of the prior inconsistencies in estimates of the impacts of school resources. Indeed, different studies could obtain different estimates of the impacts of the **Q** variables on student learning because some studies estimate the production function, that is equation (1), while others estimate the reduced-form relationship in equation (4), and it is quite possible that impacts of the **Q** variables will be different in these two equations.

When examining the impact of school quality (**Q**) on academic skills (A), are the impacts in equation (1) or equation (4) most useful for policy purposes? Equation (4) is useful because it shows what will actually happen to A after a change in one or more element in **Q**. In contrast, equation (1) will not show this because it does not account for changes in S and I in response to changes in **Q** and **P**. Yet the impact in equation (1) is also of interest because it may better capture overall welfare effects. Intuitively, if parents respond to an increase in Q_i by, for example, reducing purchases of inputs I, they will be able to raise household welfare by purchasing more of some other good or service that raises utility. The impact of **Q** on A in equation (4) (i.e., the total derivative) reflects the drop in A due to the reduction in I, but it does not account for the increase in household welfare from the increased purchase of other goods or services. In contrast, the structural impact measured in equation (1) ignores both effects. Since these two effects have opposing impacts on household welfare, they tend to cancel each other out, so the overall welfare effect is reasonably approximated by the change in A measured in equation (1). This is explained more formally in Glewwe, Kremer, Moulin, and Zitzewitz (2004).

2.2.2. Estimation Problems and Potential Solutions. Many published studies in both the economics literature and the education literature attempt to estimate the impact of school and teacher characteristics on enrollment and learning, but these attempts face a number of serious estimation challenges.

Consider estimation of a simple linear specification of the production function in equation (1):

(1′)
$$A = \beta_0 + \beta_1 S + \beta_{Q1} Q_1 + \beta_{Q2} Q_2 + \ldots + \beta_{C1} C_1 + \beta_{C2} C_2 + \ldots$$
$$+ \beta_{H1} H_1 + \beta_{H2} H_2 + \ldots + \beta_{I1} I_1 + \beta_{I2} I_2 + \ldots + u_A$$

where each variable in **Q, C, H,** and **I** is shown explicitly.[8] An "error term," u_A, is added, for several reasons. First, data never exist for all variables in **Q, C, H,** and **I**, so u_A accounts for all unobserved variables. Second, u_A indicates that (1′) is only a linear approximation of (1). Third, observed test scores (A) may measure actual skills with error, so u_A includes measurement errors in the "true" A. Finally, the explanatory variables in (1′) may also have measurement errors, which are also included in u_A (when the values of these variables in (1) are the observed values, not the "true" values).

The causal impacts of the *observed* variables in (1′) on learning, the β coefficients, can be consistently estimated by ordinary least squares (OLS) *only if u_A is uncorrelated with ALL the observed "explanatory" variables*. Unfortunately, under a range of circumstances, u_A is likely to be correlated with those variables.

The potential pitfalls of statistical analysis aimed at uncovering the causal impact of various factors on achievement are now fairly well understood. They are the subject of graduate courses in evaluation methods as well as critiques of existing research. For detailed discussions, see Glewwe (2002) and Glewwe and Kremer (2006); the rest of this section summarizes both the problems and the potential solutions.

The most common generic concerns are omitted variable bias, sample selection, endogenous program placement, and measurement errors. Turning to the first concern, if major inputs to achievement are omitted from the estimation of equation (1′), they will end up in u_A. If these omitted factors are correlated with the included variables, bias is introduced, with the bias being proportional to the importance of the omitted factors (their coefficient in equation (1′)) and their correlation with the included factors. Similarly, school and teacher factors often affect which children attend school and how their parents make decisions about their schooling (see, e.g., Hanushek, Lavy, and Hitomi 2008). School quality could also be correlated with u_A if governments improve schools that have unobserved education problems (Pitt, Rosenzweig, and Gibbons 1993). Governments may also raise school quality in areas with good education outcomes, if those areas have political influence (World Bank 2001). The former causes underestimation of school quality variables' impacts on learning, while the latter causes overestimation.[9] Finally, measurement error—a ubiquitous problem that can be particularly severe in developing countries—can bias estimates, often pushing estimates toward zero and so making estimated impacts appear insignificant.

Considerable effort has now gone into how to deal with these problems. Besides better measurement to correct errors in variables, the essential thrust has been to develop estimation methods that ensure that u_A is uncorrelated with the variables of interest. Most significant in recent decades has been the design of experiments that work to ensure this, that is, the use of randomized control trials (RCTs) (see, e.g., Kremer 2003). But other methods, such as regression discontinuity (RD) designs and panel data methods, have also been pursued to achieve the same goal. While these are the subject of considerable current research, there are also good reviews and discussions of them elsewhere (e.g., Blundell and Dias 2009;

Imbens and Wooldridge 2009). The important fact for our purposes is that these approaches have begun to appear in the literature on achievement in developing countries. And we explicitly include this literature in our review below.

2.3. Scope of Review

We now move to the heart of this chapter—reviewing relevant research on the determinants of student achievement and time in school in developing countries. This review is, however, more limited than that statement might suggest. First, it focuses on studies from 1990 to 2010 and does not return to prior studies that have been reviewed elsewhere. Second, it focuses only on primary and secondary education, and thus it does not include preprimary, vocational, or postsecondary education (see chapter 3, by Behrman, Engle and Fernald, for a review of the evidence on preprimary education). Third, the primary outcome of interest is student learning (usually measured in terms of test scores), although we also consider school enrollment (including related phenomena such as daily attendance and years of schooling attained).[10] Finally, this chapter will not examine school policies related to child health (since it is covered by Alderman and Bleakley in chapter 4), incentives for students and parents (covered by Behrman, Parker, and Todd in chapter 5), school organization and management (covered by Galiani and Perez-Truglia in chapter 6), and the relative performance of private and public schools (covered by MacLeod and Urquiola in chapter 7).

The rest of this section explains how the vast literatures in economics and education were searched. The objective of the review process was to identify as many relevant, high-quality papers as possible. The strategy was to search a wide variety of sources, and then systematically eliminate papers that do not meet a series of criteria for relevance and quality. The first step was to conduct the search for journal articles published between 1990 and 2010 using two search engines that cover the economics and education literatures, respectively: EconLit and the Education Resources Information Center (ERIC). The search was conducted during October and November of 2010; for this reason, papers that were not yet available at that time are not included in this review. The authors searched for papers that listed both "education" as a key word, and any one of a list of 72 educational inputs as keywords (see appendix 2A for this list). Because of the overwhelming number of papers found in ERIC using these search terms (over half a million), the search was limited to papers that also included the name of at least one developing country or the term "developing country" or "developing countries" in the abstract. Developing countries are defined as in the International Monetary Fund's list of emerging and developing countries, as found in its *World Economic Outlook Report*, published in April 2010.

This search yielded a total of about 9,000 articles. Two of the authors reviewed each of the 9,000 articles individually, selecting those that looked potentially relevant based on the information found in the abstract (and, in some cases, looking at the introduction or conclusion of the paper). Based on reviews of the abstracts only, papers that did not focus on developing countries or that did not estimate the impact of a school-level (or teacher-level) variable on students' educational outcomes were eliminated. Papers selected by either of these two authors were included in the next phase of the review; this winnowing process reduced the total number of papers to 307.[11]

In addition to published papers, the authors also searched several prominent series of working papers in economics: National Bureau of Economic Research (NBER) working papers; World Bank Policy Research working papers; the Institute for the Study of Labor (IZA); the Center for Economic and Policy Research (CEPR); and the CESIfo Research Network. Papers listed as education papers on the Abdul Latif Jameel Poverty Action Lab's website were also searched. Working papers published before 2005 were not included, as it was assumed that high-quality working papers written before 2005 should have been published by 2010. When the same paper appears both as a working paper and as a journal article, only the journal article was included. Using this process, 29 working papers were added to the 307 published articles. All four authors reviewed the abstracts of this large group of papers and narrowed the sample to 253 by eliminating duplicate papers and papers that did not focus on one or more of the following factors that affect students' educational outcomes: school infrastructure and pedagogical materials; teacher (and principal) characteristics; and school organization.

In the second phase, the authors read each of the 253 papers (in contrast to first phase, when only abstracts were read) to obtain further information about each study. During this phase, additional papers were eliminated for lack of relevance. These fell into three categories: (1) The paper's focus was not on a developing country (this was not clear in the abstracts of some papers); (2) the paper focused on an education policy unrelated to school infrastructure and pedagogical materials, teacher (and principal) characteristics, and school organization; and (3) the pa-

Table 2.6 Steps used to select papers used in the literature review

Review phase	Procedures used	Number of papers
1	Search EconLit and ERIC databases.	~9,000
	Review abstracts of all results.	307
	Add 29 working papers written after 2004.	336
	Review abstracts again; eliminate duplicate papers and papers that did not estimate the impacts of school or teacher characteristics.	253
2	Review full papers; eliminate papers based on lack of relevance, lack of quantitative analysis.	112
3	Eliminate papers based on methodology or lack of basic covariates. These 79 papers are the full sample.	79
4	Exclude papers that used OLS only on cross-sectional data. The remaining 43 papers are the "high quality" sample.	43

per did not include quantitative analysis of the impact of a school or teacher characteristic on students' educational outcomes. A little more than half of the 253 papers chosen in the first stage were eliminated at this stage, which reduced the studies considered to 112.

In a third phase, the remaining 112 papers were reviewed for their quality, considering both the econometric methodology used and, when appropriate, covariates included in the analysis. All articles that were based on an RCT were retained, as these studies avoid, or at least minimize, many of the estimation problems discussed in section 2.2. Further, estimates based on a difference in differences (DD) regression, regression discontinuity design (RDD), or matching methods were also included. Finally, papers that used other, simpler quantitative methods (e.g., OLS) *and* included at least one general family background variable (e.g., parental schooling or household income) and school expenditure per pupil, or one family background variable, one teacher variable, and at least one additional school variable, were included. By excluding papers that did not meet these criteria, the sample was reduced to 79 papers (listed in appendix 2B).

A fourth and final phase of the review made further quality distinctions. We examined further all papers that did not use an RCT, DD, or RDD estimation method. Of these, 36 papers that relied on ordinary least squares analysis of cross-sectional data failed to employ any more sophisticated methodology to control for potential omitted variable or endogeneity bias (such as instrumental variables or selection bias correction methods) and these were deemed to be of lower quality. While results are presented for all 79 studies, a separate analysis is also done for the 43 papers considered to be "high quality" by this more stringent methodological criterion. The evolution of the sample is summarized in table 2.6.

2.4. What Have We Learned from Studies of Education in Developing Countries since 1990?

This section focuses on three sets of results that examine student learning as measured by test scores. In subsection 2.4.1, the results of all 79 studies are summarized. In 2.4.2, the results of the 43 studies that passed the higher-quality bar are separately reviewed. Subsection 2.4.3 shows only results from 13 RCTs. Finally, 2.4.4 examines studies that investigate the determinants of time in school (enrollment, years of schooling, and daily attendance) outcomes.

Obviously, there is an inevitable tradeoff between raising the standard one sets for a study to be credible and the number of studies one has for drawing general conclusions. In particular, when the review is limited to studies that used RCTs, only 13 studies examined school and teacher characteristics, while there are dozens of school and teacher characteristics (including pedagogical practices) in which one may be interested. A related issue is how many studies of a particular school or teacher characteristic are needed to be included in the summary tables. We have set a low limit of requiring only two studies, which some readers may argue is too low; yet it is easy for any reader to exclude some of the rows in the summary tables that are deemed to have too few studies. The exception to this rule is the subsection that focuses on RCTs; all studies are included, even when only one study examined a particular school or teacher characteristic.

Our review of the literature falls into the general category of "meta-analysis," or the systematic combining of results from multiple studies. These techniques have been employed for over a century, with the most intense work found in reviews of medical research. More recently, however, various forms of meta-analysis have been applied to education research; see, for example, Hedges and Olkin (1985) for an early application to the education literature. Meta-analysis can be used for many different purposes, including generalizing to wider populations, understanding the heterogeneity of effects, and improved statistical power. Here we do not undertake any formal statistical analyses of the study results because we are interested in the simplest issue: do studies find consistent impacts of school resources and pedagogical factors on student achievement?

The general literature on meta-analysis does, however, raise one potentially serious issue related to our review, that of "publication bias." In particular, if authors tend to submit studies with positive (or negative) findings more frequently than those with null findings, or if editors and journals are more likely to publish articles with significant results, our review of the published work may overstate the statistical significance of any particular factor.

This problem may be less important in our review than in other areas for meta-analysis, but in the end we are unable to assess its importance. The reason for potentially less impact here is that many of the statistical studies reviewed here attempt to estimate the impacts of multiple factors—such as pupil-teacher ratios along with the impacts of textbooks and teacher experience. Thus, a given publication can easily contain a mixture of significant and insignificant factors, whereas a medical publication that addresses a single effect (e.g., the treatment outcome related to a specific drug) will be more focused on the significance or insignificance of that single parameter. Nonetheless, we do not present any quantitative analysis of how publication bias may affect our review.

2.4.1. Summary Results from All 79 Studies. This section casts the widest possible net, examining the impacts of over 30 school and teacher characteristics on student test scores. It is convenient to divide these school and teacher characteristics into three broad types: (1) School infrastructure and pedagogical supplies; (2) teacher (and principal) characteristics; and (3) school organization. In some cases, one could debate whether a particular characteristic belongs in one category or another (e.g., contract teachers could be thought of as a teacher characteristic or a school organization characteristic); in such cases an admittedly somewhat arbitrary assignment is made, but of course the conclusions drawn regarding any particular school or teacher characteristic do not depend on which of these three categories it has been assigned.

Table 2.7 summarizes the findings of the 79 studies in terms of the impact of the first broad type of variables on students' test scores. Within this broad type, the variables in the table are ordered by the number of estimates available from these 79 studies, starting with those with the largest number of estimates. Note that many studies present multiple estimates of the impact of the same variable, because of multiple estimation methods or multiple subsamples. In general, different estimation methods or estimations based on different subgroups (e.g., boys and girls, or different grades) were counted as separate estimates, but adding or removing a few variables for the same estimation method (or a

Table 2.7 Summary of impacts on test scores of school infrastructure and pedagogical supplies (all 79 studies)

	Negative		Zero, or insignificant and no sign given	Positive		Total studies
	Significant	Insignificant		Insignificant	Significant	
Textbooks/workbooks	4 (3)	13 (8)	7 (5)	10 (7)	26 (10)	21
Desks/tables/chairs	0 (0)	0 (0)	13 (1)	7 (5)	8 (4)	8
Computers/ electronic games	1 (1)	9 (5)	1 (1)	8 (3)	7 (4)	8
Electricity	0 (0)	3 (2)	0 (0)	6 (5)	6 (2)	6
School infrastructure index	0 (0)	1 (1)	7 (1)	1 (1)	13 (4)	6
Blackboard/flip chart	0 (0)	2 (2)	13 (1)	3 (3)	7 (3)	6
Library	1 (1)	3 (2)	7 (1)	1 (1)	10 (5)	6
Roof/wall/floor	0 (0)	1 (1)	0 (0)	3 (2)	2 (1)	4

Note: Figures are number of estimates; figures in parentheses are number of papers/studies. Table includes all school infrastructure characteristics with at least two separate papers/studies.

similarly minor change) was not counted as a separate estimate. In cases in which an author presents results from multiple estimations, but argues that one is a more reliable set of estimates than the others, only the author's preferred set of estimates is included. This is likely to result in an overrepresentation of results from studies that present multiple estimation methods and do not indicate which method is the preferred one. In order to allow the reader to give equal weight to studies (i.e., not to give a large weight to a single study that produced many different estimates of the impact of the same variable), the numbers in parentheses in table 2.7 show how many separate publications found a particular impact. Finally, note that for any given estimate, there are five possible classifications: significantly negative, insignificantly negative, zero (or insignificant but sign not reported), insignificantly positive, and significantly positive. A 10% significance-level cutoff was used; while this relatively generous definition of statistical significance will classify more findings as significant, it is possible that some results that would have fit this criterion are omitted from the analysis since some authors may not have presented results that are significant only at the 10% level.

2.4.1.1. School Infrastructure and Pedagogical Materials. Turning to the results, table 2.7 summarizes the findings for eight different school infrastructure and pedagogical material variables. By far the most commonly estimated impact is that for textbooks and workbooks; there are 60 estimates from 21 different studies. (The numbers in parentheses add up to 33, but this reflects the fact that some studies found different effects

using different estimation methods or different subsamples, and thus a single study can appear in parentheses in more than one column; the last column in the table gives the total number of studies.) Although these studies are not unanimous in their estimates, most of them (36) find positive effects, and most of these (26) are significantly positive. This is what almost anyone would expect, and the number of estimates that are negative and significant is quite small (4 estimates from 3 studies).[12] Thus this evidence strongly suggests that textbooks and similar materials (workbooks, exercise books) increase student learning.

The next most commonly estimated impacts are those of basic furniture (desks, tables, and chairs) and of computers and electronic games. The evidence in table 2.7 suggests that adequate amounts of desks, tables, and chairs raise student test scores, as common sense would suggest. More specifically, of the 28 estimates from eight studies, none is negative and 15 are positive (of which 8 are significantly positive). The evidence is even stronger if one counts studies instead of individual estimates (the 13 estimates of zero impact are all from a single study); all but one study finds a positive impact, and four of the eight find significantly positive impacts. In contrast, the results for computers and related materials are less clear; 18 of the 26 estimates are statistically insignificant (and they are almost evenly divided between negative and insignificant and positive and insignificant), while 7 are significantly positive and 1 is significantly negative. Given that computers can be relatively expensive, this suggests caution when deciding whether scarce funds for education should be used to purchase computers and related products.

Another commonly estimated school characteristic is electricity.[13] One would expect a positive effect, since electric lighting should help students read and see the blackboard, and it may also help by providing power for other useful items (e.g., fans to keep the classroom cooler). Of the 15 estimates in table 2.7, only 3 are negative (and none is significantly negative) while 12 are positive (of which 6 are significantly positive). A similar result holds if one counts the number of studies with these results; of the 6 studies only 2 find negative impacts (neither of which is significant) while 5 find positive but insignificant impacts and 2 find significantly positive impacts. Thus the evidence gives some support to the proposition that providing electricity to schools increases student learning.

Similarly positive effects are found for general indices of school "infrastructure" and for blackboards and other visual aids.[14] Again, this is what one would expect. Turning to a more costly school characteristic, school libraries also appear to have generally positive impacts on student learning as measured by test scores; this is particularly the case when each study is given equal weight (5 of the 6 studies found a significantly positive effect, while only 1 found a significantly negative effect). Finally, it is also the case that high-quality walls, roofs, and floors appear to lead to better outcomes: 5 of the 6 estimates are positive, and 2 of the 5 are significantly positive (the sole negative estimate is not significant).

2.4.1.2. Teacher (and Principal) Characteristics. Table 2.8 summarizes the findings from the 79 studies for teacher and principal characteristics. The most commonly examined characteristic is the teacher's level of education; there are 72 separate estimates from 24 distinct studies. Of these estimates, 46 found a positive impact on student learning, and 24 of these were significantly positive. In contrast, only 15 estimates were negative, and only 4 of these were significantly negative. Counting the number of studies (as opposed to distinct parameter estimates) in each category gives similar results; only 3 studies found significantly negative effects while 11 found significantly positive effects. Thus, as one would expect, the results generally support the proposition that providing more educated teachers raises students' test scores. Similarly, teacher experience seems to have a positive effect, but the evidence is not quite as strong. More specifically, 43 of the 63 estimates found no statistically significant impact, although of the 20 that did almost all (17) found a significantly positive effect.[15]

A more direct measure of teacher competence is teachers' knowledge of the subjects that they teach. The 79 studies include 33 estimates of the impact of teacher knowledge, as measured by teacher test scores, on student learning. Almost all (29 out of 33) found positive effects, and most of these positive effects (18) were statistically significant. The evidence is not quite as strong if one examines number of studies instead of number of estimates (7 studies found significantly positive effects while only 2 studies' findings were significantly negative), but it is still strong and thus supports the common-sense notion that teachers who better understand the subjects they teach are better at increasing their students' learning.

One teacher characteristic that has more ambiguous effects is whether the teacher is female. There are 39 estimates, of which 13 are negative (and 6 of these are significant) and 24 are positive (and 12 are significant). While positive impacts are more common than negative ones, when one counts the number of studies the results are even more ambiguous: 4 found significant negative effects, while 5 found significantly positive effects. Overall, there is little support for any systematic difference in teacher effectiveness by gender.[16]

Table 2.8 Summary of impacts on test scores of teacher and principal characteristics (all 79 studies)

	Negative		Zero, or insignificant and no sign given	Positive		Total studies
	Significant	Insignificant		Insignificant	Significant	
Teachers						
Education level	4 (3)	11 (9)	11 (3)	22 (11)	24 (11)	24
Experience	3 (3)	16 (11)	1 (1)	26 (13)	17 (7)	20
Knowledge (test)	2 (2)	2 (2)	0 (0)	11 (5)	18 (7)	9
Female teachers	6 (4)	7 (5)	2 (1)	12 (7)	12 (5)	11
Training (in service)	1(1)	10 (6)	0 (0)	7 (5)	11 (6)	11
Quality index	0 (0)	0 (0)	8 (1)	0 (0)	6 (2)	2
Teaching degree	0 (0)	2 (1)	2 (1)	0 (0)	2 (1)	2
Principals						
Experience	0 (0)	1 (1)	0 (0)	3 (2)	2 (2)	2
Education	2 (1)	1 (1)	1 (1)	1 (1)	1 (1)	2

Note: Figures are number of estimates; figures in parentheses are number of papers/studies. Table includes all teacher and principal characteristics with at least two separate papers/studies.

The next most common teacher variable in the 79 studies is in-service teacher training. Of the 29 estimates, 17 are insignificant (10 are negative and 7 are positive) while 11 are significantly positive and only 1 is significantly negative. Giving each study equal weight leads to a similar conclusion. Overall, in-service teacher training appears to have a strong positive impact on student learning.

The last two teacher variables are a general index of teacher quality and whether the teacher has a teaching degree (as opposed to a general degree).[17] Of the 14 estimates of indices of teacher quality, none is negative, 8 are zero (or insignificant but of unknown sign), and 6 are significantly positive. A similar result holds if one gives each study equal weight, although there are only two studies. This suggests that indices of teacher quality have strong positive impacts on student learning. In contrast, the two studies that considered whether a teacher had a teaching degree yield less-clear conclusions. Of the 6 estimates from the two studies, 2 are insignificantly negative, 2 have point estimates close to zero, and 2 have significantly positive impacts. The same distribution holds if one gives each study equal weight.

Two principal characteristics were examined in several different studies: years of experience and level of education, and their impacts appear to be different. In particular, years of experience had a positive impact in 5 of the 6 estimates, and of the 5 positive estimates 2 were statistically significant (the sole negative estimate was not significant). Giving each study equal weight does not change this finding. In contrast, of the 6 estimates of the impact of the principal's level of education, 2 were significantly negative, 1 was significantly positive, and the other 3 were not statistically significant (and the same general result holds if each study is given equal weight). Thus principal experience appears to lead to increased student learning, but there is no clear evidence that the same is true of principal education.

2.4.1.3. School Organization. Table 2.9 examines the third general category of school and teacher variables, school organization. These variables focus on how schools are organized, as opposed to the basic characteristics of schools and teachers. By far the most common variable of this type in the literature is class size, that is, the pupil-teacher ratio; there were 101 separate estimates from 29 different studies.[18] Intuitively, one would expect the pupil-teacher ratio to have a negative effect on student learning, and that was the case in 59 of the 101 estimates, although only 30 of the 59 were statistically significant. Another 39 estimates had an unexpected positive sign, but only 15 of these were statistically significant. In terms of numbers of studies instead of numbers of estimates, 26 studies found a negative impact, of which 13 were significantly negative, and 21 found a positive impact, of which 9 were significantly positive.

Overall, these estimates suggest that increases in class size usually have negative impacts on student learning, as one would expect, but the finding that 9 of the 29 studies found a significantly positive effect suggests caution. These positive effects could reflect either random chance or estimation problems; an example of the latter is that schools that are of high quality due to unobserved characteristics will attract more students, raising the pupil-teacher ratio and thus leading to a positive correlation between that ratio and student test scores. Nonetheless, the frequency of "unexpected" positive impacts, even in developing countries where pupil-teacher ratios can be very large, is similar to the findings for developed countries (Hanushek 2003).

Clearer results are seen in the next two variables: teacher absenteeism and teacher assigns homework. As one would expect, for teacher absenteeism 13 of the 15 estimates are negative, and 7 of the 13 are significantly negative. None of the 15 estimates is positive, although 2 are insignificant and of unknown sign (the paper did not report the signs of the insignificant results). In contrast, but also as expected, teacher assignment of homework generally has positive impacts on students' test scores. Of the 16 estimates, 12 are significantly positive and only 4 are negative (and none is significantly negative). The main caveat is that these findings are less strong when each of the 5 studies is given equal weight: 3 are significantly positive and 2 are insignificantly negative.

Table 2.9 Summary of impacts on test scores of school organization (all 79 studies)

	Negative		Zero, or insignificant and no sign given	Positive		Total studies
	Significant	Insignificant		Insignificant	Significant	
Pupil-teacher ratio	30 (13)	29 (13)	3 (2)	24 (12)	15 (9)	29
Teacher absenteeism	7 (4)	6 (3)	2 (1)	0 (0)	0 (0)	5
Teacher assigning homework	0 (0)	4 (2)	0 (0)	0 (0)	12 (3)	5
School providing meals	4 (1)	3 (2)	0 (0)	0 (0)	6 (3)	4
Multigrade teaching	4 (1)	0 (0)	10 (1)	5 (2)	2 (2)	4
Hours of school day	1 (1)	1 (1)	0 (0)	2 (1)	4 (2)	4
Tutoring	1 (1)	0 (0)	0 (0)	2 (1)	2 (1)	3
Salaried teacher	0 (0)	0 (0)	0 (0)	4 (1)	2 (2)	3
Contract teacher	1 (1)	0 (0)	0 (0)	1 (1)	4 (1)	2
Expenditure/pupil	2 (2)	0 (0)	0 (0)	0 (0)	1 (1)	2
Cost of attending	1 (1)	1 (1)	0 (0)	4 (2)	0 (0)	2
Total school enrollment	2 (1)	0 (0)	2 (1)	1 (1)	1 (1)	2
Group work	0 (0)	4 (1)	0 (0)	5 (1)	4 (2)	2
Teacher giving examples	2 (1)	0 (0)	0 (0)	2 (1)	3 (1)	2
Student attendance	0 (0)	0 (0)	0 (0)	0 (0)	8 (2)	2

Note: Figures are number of estimates; figures in parentheses are number of papers/studies. Table includes all school organization variables with at least two separate papers/studies.

School provision of meals has been used in many developing countries to achieve two distinct goals: improved child health and increased student learning. Four of the 79 studies examined the impact of school meals on student test scores, producing 13 distinct estimates. The evidence is inconclusive; 7 estimates are negative, of which 4 are significantly negative, while 6 estimates are positive (all of which are statistically significant). Considering the number of studies gives a somewhat more positive impact; only 1 found a significantly negative impact, while 2 found insignificantly negative impacts and 3 found significantly positive impacts. Even so, the evidence does not provide strong support for this intervention, at least as a means to raise student learning, and school meal programs have the disadvantage that they can be relatively expensive. Further discussion, with similar results, is found by Alderman and Bleakley in chapter 4 and by Behrman, Parker, and Todd in chapter 5.

The next two school organization practices yield contrasting results. The first is one that is unavoidable in small, rural schools: multigrade teaching, where one teacher teaches more than one grade in the same classroom. There are 21 estimates of its impact, although they are based on only four distinct studies. Four estimates (all from the same study) show a significantly negative effect, while 7 estimates yield positive effects (of which 2, from two different studies, are statistically significant). Overall, these results are decidedly ambiguous, and the actual impact may vary given other factors, such as class size and teacher characteristics. In contrast, results are relatively unambiguous, and in the expected direction, for hours of the school day; 6 of the 8 estimates are positive, and 4 are significantly positive (although when studies are given equal weight the distribution of the findings is less clear cut).

The results for tutoring are also rather ambiguous, which is somewhat counterintuitive. In particular, while 4 of the 5 estimates are positive, and 2 of these 4 are significantly positive, when studies are equally weighted 2 of the 3 studies show a positive effect, of which one is significant, but the third shows a significantly negative effect. While one would think that tutoring should help, and would not have any negative effects, it could be that the tutors are simply the students' teachers, who may be curtailing effort during the school day to obtain paying students for their tutoring classes (for a general discussion see Dang and Rogers 2008). Participation in tutoring may also be an indicator that the student needs extra help, that is, that low achievement is causing tutoring rather than the other way around.

The next two school organization variables focus on teacher pay: teacher salary and whether the teacher is a contract teacher. There are only six estimates of the impact of teacher salary, but all are positive and two are significantly positive, which may indicate that higher salary raises teacher morale or leads to better selection into teaching. The findings for contract teachers, however, indicate a possible contradiction. These teachers are hired on short-term contracts and, in general, have relatively low qualifications, less experience, little or no benefits, and lower salaries, a combination that might superficially suggest that these teachers would be less effective.[19] Yet five of the six estimates yield positive impacts, and four of them are significantly positive (although the results are more ambiguous when each study is given equal weight). The counterbalancing force behind the positive impact of contract teachers, according to several researchers, is that they have much stronger incentives to perform well than regular teachers, who are insulated from performance concerns by civil services rules. Thus, even with lower salaries, they are induced to perform well in school (perhaps so that they can subsequently get a regular teaching position with its higher salary and greater job security). Overall, the teacher salary results are consistent with pay inducing more teacher effort or leading to better selection into teaching, although the interpretation is ambiguous because much of the variation in salaries comes from pay for different characteristics rather than identifying the impact of increasing or decreasing the overall salary schedule for teachers.

There are only three estimates in table 2.9 regarding the impact of overall school expenditures per pupil, but the results are somewhat puzzling; in two of the three cases, the estimated effect is significantly negative (an unexpected effect), while in the other it is significantly positive. This measure is somewhat difficult to interpret. It could simply reflect compensatory funding—that is, schools that are doing poorly get additional funds. It is also possible that the estimated negative effects arise because other school characteristics are included in the regression; in both studies from which these estimates come (Du and Hu 2008; Nannyonjo 2007) several other school and teacher characteristics are included in the regression. Again, however, there is little overall evidence to support a strong positive impact of school expenditures, a repeated finding in a wide range of reviews for developed countries (Hanushek 2003).

The next two school variables have rather inconclusive results. The cost of enrolling in school could have a negative effect if it interferes with schooling (a child may be excluded from school until fees are paid) or if it leads to a reduction in home-supplied pedagogical materials, but the evidence in table 2.9 is inconclusive. Similarly, the overall size of the school has no clear tendency, and it is not clear a priori what the sign of the effect should be.

The next two variables focus on specific elements of pedagogical style: group work and whether the teacher gives examples in class. Overall, group work seems to have a positive impact on students' test scores. In contrast, teachers giving examples in class is more ambiguous (5 estimates are positive, of which 3 are significantly positive, but 2 are significantly negative).

The last school organization variable in table 2.9 is student attendance. All eight estimates from the two studies that examined student attendance are significantly positive. This, of course, is quite plausible, and it shows that for a few variables the results are clear and unambiguous.

2.4.2. Summary Results from 43 Higher-Quality Studies. This section repeats the analysis of the last section but drops 36 studies that were deemed to be of lower quality because they used simple OLS on cross-sectional data without attempting to use any of the more sophisticated methods to address the potential estimation problems. As in the previous subsection, results are shown only if the same school or teacher characteristic was examined in two or more separate studies.

2.4.2.1. School Infrastructure and Pedagogical Materials. The first panel in table 2.10 shows summary results for seven different school infrastructure

Table 2.10 Summary of impacts on test scores of school variables (43 high-quality studies)

	Negative		Zero, or insignificant and no sign given	Positive		Total studies
	Significant	Insignificant		Insignificant	Significant	
School Infrastructure						
Textbooks/workbooks	1 (1)	8 (4)	3 (1)	6 (4)	3 (2)	8
Desks/tables/chairs	0 (0)	0 (0)	0 (0)	4 (3)	3 (2)	4
Computers/elec. games	1 (1)	9 (5)	0 (0)	8 (3)	4 (3)	6
Electricity	0 (0)	3 (2)	0 (0)	3 (2)	0 (0)	3
Blackboard/flip chart	0 (0)	2 (2)	0 (0)	2 (2)	2 (1)	3
Library	0 (0)	1 (1)	0 (0)	1 (1)	4 (2)	3
Roof/wall/floor	0 (0)	1 (1)	0 (0)	3 (2)	2 (1)	4
Teacher Characteristics						
Education level	1 (1)	5 (5)	0 (0)	5 (4)	2 (1)	6
Experience	1 (1)	10 (6)	0 (0)	12 (7)	5 (2)	9
Knowledge (test)	0 (0)	0 (0)	0 (0)	7 (3)	13 (4)	5
Female teachers	1 (1)	1 (1)	0 (0)	5 (2)	1 (1)	2
Training (in-service)	0 (0)	3 (3)	0 (0)	0 (0)	3 (2)	3
School Organization						
Pupil-teacher ratio	14 (5)	18 (9)	1 (1)	10 (6)	3 (3)	14
Teacher absenteeism	4 (2)	2 (2)	0 (0)	0 (0)	0 (0)	2
School providing meals	0 (0)	1 (1)	0 (0)	0 (0)	2 (1)	2
Multigrade teaching	4 (1)	0 (0)	0 (0)	5 (2)	1 (1)	2
Hours of school day	0 (0)	0 (0)	0 (0)	0 (0)	4 (2)	2
Tutoring	0 (0)	0 (0)	0 (0)	2 (1)	2 (1)	2
Contract teacher	1 (1)	0 (0)	0 (0)	1 (1)	4 (1)	2

Note: Figures are numbers of estimates; figures in parentheses are number of papers/studies. Table includes all school or teacher characteristics with at least two separate papers/studies.

and pedagogical material variables (the school infrastructure index was dropped because it was considered by only 1 of the 43 studies). As in subsection 2.4.1, the most common estimated effect is that for textbooks and workbooks; there are 21 estimates from 8 different studies. While intuitively one would expect that these items would increase student learning, the estimated effects are far from unanimous: slightly less than half of the estimates (9 out of 21) find positive effects, but only 3 of these are significantly positive (and one is significantly negative). Thus, after dropping less rigorous studies, the evidence that textbooks and similar materials (workbooks, exercise books) increase student learning is quite weak.

In contrast to textbooks and workbooks, the evidence in table 2.10 supports much more strongly the hypothesis that desks, tables, and chairs raise student test scores. More specifically, all 7 estimates are positive, and 3 of them are significantly positive. On the other hand. the results for computers and related materials are at best only weakly supportive: 17 of the 22 estimates are statistically insignificant (and they are almost evenly divided between negative and insignificant and positive and insignificant), but of the 5 that are statistically significant 4 are significantly positive. These results suggest caution when advocating the introduction of computers and similar devices, especially if they are relatively expensive.

The next most commonly estimated school characteristic is electricity. While the evidence when all 79 studies were examined strongly supported the proposition that providing electricity to schools increases student learning, this finding completely disappears when less rigorous studies are dropped: all 6 estimates are insignificant, of which 3 are negative and 3 are positive. This result is somewhat counterintuitive, but it suggests that the impact of providing electricity (or, more generally, better school facilities) may not be very strong.

The findings for blackboards (and other visual aids) are generally positive, but based on limited evidence. More specifically, while 4 of the 6 estimates are positive, and 2 are significantly positive, the 2 significantly positive results are from a single study. The results for libraries are almost unanimous: 4 of the 6 estimates are significantly positive, and none is significantly negative.

The last school infrastructure variable is the quality of the school's walls, roofs, and ceilings. When all 79 studies were considered, they offered strong support that improvements in these school characteristics raised students' test scores. The evidence in table 2.10, based on only the higher-quality studies, also strongly supports this conclusion (since all of the estimates in table 2.7 are still in table 2.10).

2.4.2.2. Teacher Characteristics. The second panel of table 2.10 summarizes the findings from the 43 higher-quality studies for teacher characteristics. (There are no results for principal characteristics because none had more than one higher-quality study.) The first characteristic, the teacher's level of education, has ambiguous results; of the 13 estimates 10 are statistically insignificant (and evenly divided between insignificantly positive and insignificantly negative), and while 2 of the other 3 are significantly positive the third is significantly negative. Counting the number of studies in each category gives similarly ambiguous results. These results stand in sharp contrast to those when all 79 studies were included; once lower-quality studies are eliminated there is little evidence that teachers' level of education has any impact on student test scores. There is some evidence that teacher experience has a positive effect; 17 of the 28 estimates found positive effects, and 5 of the 17 are significantly positive (and only 1 is significantly negative). Yet with 22 of the 28 estimates being statistically insignificant (and these are almost evenly split between insignificantly negative and insignificantly positive), there is only weak evidence that teacher experience has a beneficial effect, especially when one focuses on the number of studies (the numbers in parentheses).

In contrast to teachers' education and experience, more direct measures of their competence, their knowledge of the subjects that they teach, shows very strong positive effects. More specifically, of the 20 estimates of the impact of teacher knowledge (as measured by test scores) on student learning, *all* are positive and 13 are significantly positive, which provides very strong support to the hypothesis that teacher knowledge plays a very large role in student learning.

As when all 79 studies are examined, teacher gender has an ambiguous impact within the 43 highest-quality studies. There are 8 estimates: 6 are statistically insignificant (although 5 of these are positive and only 1 is negative), 1 is significantly negative, and 1 is significantly positive. Looking at the counts of studies does not alter the ambiguous results.

The last teacher characteristic in the middle panel of table 2.10 is in-service teacher training. Of the 6 estimates of its impact, 3 are significantly positive and 3 are negative but insignificant. Thus the evidence at best provides only moderate support to the hypothesis that in-service teacher training has a positive impact on students' test scores.

2.4.2.3. School Organization.

The third panel of table 2.10 examines 7 school organization variables (9 of the variables that were in table 2.7 have been dropped because they were not included in 2 or more high-quality studies). As in subsection 2.4.1, by far the most commonly estimated impact is that of the pupil-teacher ratio; there are 46 separate estimates from 14 different studies. As with the 79 studies examined above, most of the estimates are negative, with 32 (70%) of the 46 showing a negative impact, which is a higher percentage than when the 79 studies were examined (58%). In addition, 14 of the 32 are significantly negative, while only 3 are significantly positive. In terms of numbers of studies, however, the results are not as decisive. In particular, 5 studies found significantly negative effects while 3 studies found a significantly positive effect. Overall, these results again suggest that increases in class size usually have negative impacts on student learning, as one would expect, but this is not always the case. Another interpretation is that the effect is negative but it is quite small, so that random variation in estimates often yield positive point estimates, which on occasion are significantly positive.

In contrast, the results for teacher absenteeism are clearly negative. Of the 6 different estimates, all are negative and 4 are significantly negative. This finding also holds when each study is given equal weight.

Turning to school meals, the evidence is scarce and remains ambiguous. In particular, there are only 3 estimates from 2 studies; 1 study presents 2 estimates that are significantly positive but the other study finds only an insignificantly negative impact.

The next school organization variable is multigrade classrooms; there are 10 estimates of its impact, although they are based on only 2 distinct studies. Four estimates (all from the same study) show a significantly negative effect, while 6 find positive effects, although only 1 of the 6 is significantly positive. Overall, these results are decidedly ambiguous, as was the case when all 79 studies were examined.

The next two variables in table 2.10, hours of the school day and tutoring, have unambiguous results. Regarding the former, all 4 estimates (from 2 different studies) are significantly positive. The results for tutoring are almost as unambiguous and equally plausible: all 4 estimates are positive and 2 are significantly positive. This is less ambiguous than was the case when all 79 studies were examined.

Finally, for contract teachers, the results are identical to those in table 2.7 because all the 79 studies that examined the impact of contract teachers were found to be sufficiently rigorous to be in the 43 higher-quality studies. Again, if one gives equal weight to each estimate, contract teachers appear to have strong positive impacts on students' test scores, but if one gives equal weight to studies, the results are more ambiguous.

2.4.3. Results from 13 Randomized Control Trials. This subsection presents the results from 13 RCTs that altered school characteristics. As noted above, the RCT methodology is best suited for analysis of specific programs or resources that can be identified and manipulated easily within an experiment. Thus, the evidence in this section focuses on a more limited set of inputs; indeed, there are no results for teacher or principal characteristics, which are difficult to randomize. Unlike the previous subsections, results are shown even if there is only one study for a given school or teacher characteristic, since there are very few RCTs available.

2.4.3.1. School Infrastructure and Pedagogical Materials. The first three rows in table 2.11 show results for three different general school infrastructure

Table 2.11 Summary of impacts on test scores of school variables (13 RCT studies)

	Negative		Zero, or insignificant and no sign given	Positive		Total studies
	Significant	Insignificant		Insignificant	Significant	
School Infrastructure						
Textbooks/workbooks	0 (0)	1 (1)	3 (1)	0 (0)	0 (0)	2
Computers/elec. games	1 (1)	7 (4)	0 (0)	8 (3)	4 (3)	5
Blackboard/flip chart	0 (0)	1 (1)	0 (0)	0 (0)	0 (0)	1
School organization						
Pupil-teacher ratio	3 (1)	2 (1)	0 (0)	0 (0)	0 (0)	1
School providing meals	0 (0)	1 (1)	0 (0)	0 (0)	0 (0)	1
Tutoring	0 (0)	0 (0)	0 (0)	0 (0)	2 (1)	1
Contract teachers	0 (0)	0 (0)	0 (0)	0 (0)	4 (1)	1
Community information campaign	0 (0)	4 (1)	5 (1)	4 (1)	1 (1)	1
Merit-based scholarship	0 (0)	0 (0)	0 (0)	1 (1)	1 (1)	1

Note: Figures are number of estimates; figures in parentheses are number of papers/studies.

and pedagogical material characteristics that have been analyzed using randomized trials: textbooks, computers, and flipcharts. Two studies examined textbooks, one in the Philippines (Tan, Lane, and Lassibille 1999) and one in Kenya (Glewwe, Kremer, and Moulin 2009). Overall, the results suggest no impact of providing textbooks; none of the four estimates is positive, and none is statistically significant. This is consistent with the weak results found above (subsection 2.4.2) for the 43 higher-quality studies.

The next variable in table 2.11 is the availability of computers and related electronic pedagogical devices (e.g., Internet connections, educational videogames). Five different RCTs have examined the use of these types of materials. The results are rather mixed, which is consistent with the findings of the 43 high-quality studies. Of the 20 separate estimates, 8 were negative (but only 1 significantly so) and 12 have been positive (of which 4 were significantly positive).

To understand the variation in results, it is useful to examine each of these five studies. Banerjee, Cole, Duflo, and Linden (2007) evaluate an intervention in Indian primary schools in which schoolteachers received training on how to use educational mathematics software in the classroom. In treatment schools, students used the software for two hours a week. After two years of the treatment, students in treatment schools were found to score significantly higher on math tests than students in the control group, but there was no significant difference in language scores. In contrast, Barrera-Osorio and Linden (2009) evaluated the Computers for Education program in Colombia and found less positive results. In this program, teachers receive computers as well as eight months of training on how to use the computers in the classroom. In the schools in their sample, teachers were trained on how to use the computers to support language education. Pooling results across grades 3 through 9, there were no significant results of the intervention on any of the eight math and language skills evaluated. Disaggregated by grade, there are significant positive effects in grade 9 and significantly negative effects in grade 8.

Linden (2008) evaluated a computer-assisted learning program in India and also found mixed results. When students used computers instead of interacting with classroom teachers for part of the day, the intervention had a significant negative effect on test outcomes. Students who used the computer program after school as a complement to their classroom experience, however, showed some (albeit insignificant) improvement. In another study conducted in India, Inamdar (2004) evaluated a program that consisted on installing "Minimally Invasive Education kiosks" in rural Indian schools. These kiosks have Internet-connected computers installed where children can explore without any adult direct intervention. Students in the experimental group obtained better results in the grade 8 computers examination. Note, however, that the sample size of this investigation is quite small, collecting information for a total of only 103 students.

Finally, Rosas et al. (2003) evaluated the effects of introducing educational videogames in a sample of primary schools in disadvantaged areas of Chile. These videogames cover basic mathematics and reading comprehension, and they were designed for first- and second-grade students. The results indicate the children in the experimental group performed better in mathematics, Spanish, and spelling.

The last RCT that examined a school infrastructure variable is that of Glewwe, Kremer, Moulin, and Zitzewitz (2004), who examined the impact of flipcharts in Kenya. As seen in table 2.11, the results were disappointing, with a negative but statistically insignificant impact. Note that this result does not necessarily contradict the results in the previous subsection for the 43 high-quality studies. In particular, recall that only 2 of the 6 estimates were significantly positive.

2.4.3.2. School Organization. Several RCTs have been conducted that examine the ways in which schools are organized. Muralidharan and

Sundararaman (2008) examine the impact of class size on achievement in India. In this paper, class size is reduced in schools that were randomly assigned to receive an extra contract teacher. That paper presents 5 estimates of the impact of class size on student achievement; 3 are significantly negative while 2 are negative but not significant. More specifically, the effect of class size on combined math and language test scores is significantly negative in grades 1 through 3, but not in grades 4 and 5. While these findings are consistent with what one would expect, the authors cannot separate out the class-size effect from the contract-teacher effect. Moreover, it is only one study, and thus it is hard to generalize.

One RCT has considered the impact of providing school meals. Tan, Lane, and Lassibille (1999) found a negative but insignificant effect of this type of program in the Philippines. Tutoring has also been examined by a randomized trial, the study of the *Balsakhi* tutoring program in India by Banerjee, Cole, Duflo, and Linden (2007). That study found that providing tutors to children who are falling behind in the curriculum greatly increased their test scores.

Turning to contract teachers, Muralidharan and Sundararaman (2008) present 4 estimates of the impact of contract teachers on student performance, and all 4 are significantly positive. This is somewhat more positive than the average over the 43 high-quality studies. However, recall from the discussion of this paper above that the contract teacher was an "extra" teacher. For this reason, the effect that is found could also be, at least in part, a class-size effect.

Another RCT conducted in India (Pandey, Goyal, and Sundararaman 2009) examined the impact of community information campaigns on students' test scores. The study presents 14 different estimates of impacts on reading, writing, and math tests, varying by grade and state, but all are statistically insignificant except for one that is significantly positive. Overall, there is little evidence that these campaigns had sizable effects on students' test scores.

A final school organization variable is the provision of merit-based scholarships. The single RCT study, conducted by Kremer, Miguel, and Thornton (2009), provides 2 estimates, both of which are positive with 1 being statistically significant.

2.4.4. Impact of School and Teacher Variables on Time in School. Almost all (69) of the 79 studies examined above focused on student test scores as the outcome of interest. Yet 18 of these studies also examined time-in-school variables, such as daily attendance, current enrollment, and years in school. This subsection reviews the findings of these 18 studies

Table 2.12 Summary of impacts of school and teacher variables on time in school (all 79 studies)

	Negative		Zero, or insignificant and no sign given	Positive		Total papers
	Significant	Insignificant		Insignificant	Significant	
School Infrastructure						
Textbooks/workbooks	0 (0)	2 (2)	1 (1)	2 (1)	2 (2)	4
Library	0 (0)	0 (0)	0 (0)	0 (0)	2 (2)	2
Roof/wall/floor	0 (0)	1 (1)	0 (0)	0 (0)	1 (1)	2
Building new schools	0 (0)	0 (0)	0 (0)	1 (1)	4 (3)	3
School quality index	0 (0)	0 (0)	0 (0)	1 (1)	4 (2)	2
Teacher Characteristics						
Education level	0 (0)	2 (2)	0 (0)	2 (2)	1 (1)	4
Experience	1 (1)	0 (0)	0 (0)	4 (3)	2 (2)	5
Training (in service)	1 (1)	2 (2)	0 (0)	0 (0)	0 (0)	2
School Organization						
Pupil-teacher ratio	0 (0)	3 (2)	0 (0)	2 (1)	2 (1)	3
Cost of attending	0 (0)	5 (3)	0 (0)	1 (1)	0 (0)	4
Merit based scholarship	0 (0)	1 (1)	0 (0)	2 (2)	0 (0)	2

Note: Figures are number of estimates; figures in parentheses are number of papers/studies. Table includes all school or teacher characteristics with at least two separate papers/studies.

on these time-in-school variables. It is of course necessary to interpret these studies with added caution, because a variety of programs aimed directly at enrollment and attainment—such as many conditional cash-transfer programs—have failed to lead to added learning (see the review in Hanushek 2008). Simply increasing time in school without commensurate additions to learning and achievement is likely to have little value (Hanushek and Woessmann 2008).

2.4.4.1. All 79 Studies. Table 2.12 summarizes the findings when all 79 studies are examined (of which 18 examined time in school), for all school or teacher variables found in at least two separate studies. The first five lines examine school infrastructure and pedagogical material variables. The first examines textbooks and workbooks, for which there are seven estimates from four distinct studies. These 7 estimates yielded only 2 significant results: textbooks/workbooks lead to increased time in school. While this is intuitively plausible, the other 5 estimates are insignificant, of which 2 are negative and 2 are positive (and 1 is insignificant but of unknown sign). Thus it appears that textbooks do not have a consistent effect on students' time in school.

The next two school infrastructure variables are whether the school has a library and the condition of its roof, walls, and floors. There are only 2 estimates, from 2 distinct studies, for school libraries, but they are both statistically significant, in the same direction, and intuitively plausible: school libraries increase the time the students spend in school. Only 2 separate studies examined the impact of the quality of the physical building (roof, wall, and floor) on students' time in school. Of these, 1 found a significantly positive effect while the other found an insignificantly negative effect. This lack of agreement, as well as the small number of studies, prevents any general conclusions from being drawn.

The following infrastructure variable, building new schools, has a more consistent set of findings. Of the 5 distinct estimates, all are positive and 4 are significantly positive. A similar finding holds when one gives each of the 3 studies from which these estimates come equal weight. All 3 had at least one set of estimates with a significantly positive impact, and only 1 had a positive but insignificant impact. Of course, this finding is of little surprise; building new schools (which in effect reduces the distance to the nearest school, and may also reduce capacity constraints) should increase enrollment and thus eventual years of completed schooling.

Finally, a general school-quality index was used in two separate studies. Together there are 5 sets of estimates. All 5 show positive effects, and 4 of the 5 are statistically significant. Yet the evidence is somewhat less strong if one gives each study equal weight; one study's estimates were significantly positive while the other study's results had a significantly positive impact and an insignificantly positive impact. More important, the school-quality index in one paper is composed of several different variables, so it is unclear which variables are the most important, and in the other paper school quality is a school fixed effect from a previous estimation, which also does not indicate what school characteristics determine school quality.

Table 2.12 presents results for three teacher characteristics: education level, experience, and in-service teacher training. For teachers' level of education there are five estimates from four distinct studies that point to ambiguous results: only one of the five is statistically significant. While that one significant estimate is in the expected direction—more educated teachers lead students to spend more time in school—the other four are statistically insignificant, with two negative and two positive.

The findings for teacher experience are puzzling. While on the one hand six of the seven estimates are positive and two are significantly positive, the one that is negative is significantly negative, so that when one considers only the estimates that are statistically significant one is negative and two are positive. Thus there seems to be a positive impact, but it may be prudent to examine only the studies that are of higher quality (which is done below).

The 3 estimates of the impact of in-service teacher training are similar but give an unexpected result: all 3 are negative and 1 is significantly negative. Given that there are only 2 studies, one cannot draw a strong conclusion. Yet one can conclude that the small amount of evidence that exists provides no support for the conjecture that in-service teacher training leads to increased student time in school.

The last 3 variables in table 2.12 focus on school organization. For the first, the pupil-teacher ratio, 5 of the 7 estimates are statistically insignificant (of which 3 are negative and 2 are positive). The 2 that are significant, which are from the same study, show a positive impact. At first glance, this is an unexpected result; a higher pupil-teacher ratio would have a negative effect on learning and so would make time in school less valuable. On the other hand, schools that are attractive for unobserved reasons will increase student enrollment and years of schooling, which will lead to a positive correlation between time in school and the pupil-teacher ratio that is not necessarily a causal effect. This makes it difficult for any study (with the possible exception of a randomized trial) to determine the impact of the pupil-teacher ratio on time spent in school.

The cost of enrolling in school (e.g., tuition) should have little direct effect on learning, but other things being equal it should reduce time spent in school. Of the 6 estimates shown in table 2.12, 5 are negative while only 1 is positive. However, all 6 of the estimates are statistically insignificant, so there is not strong evidence that a higher cost of enrolling in school will lead to lower enrollment and reduced years of completed schooling. As with the pupil-teacher ratio, there could be serious estimation problems; schools that are more expensive may be attractive in unobserved ways, which will lead to upward bias of the impact of the cost of attending school.

Finally, 2 studies examined merit based scholarships, producing 3 sets of estimates. Two estimates are positive while 1 is negative, yet none of the estimates is statistically significant. Thus there is no clear impact of merit scholarships on time spent in school.

2.4.4.2. The 43 High-Quality Studies. Table 2.13 also examines the impacts of school and teacher variables on students' time in school, but it considers only the 43 high-quality studies, of which 14 examined the impacts of those variables on time in school. Turning to school infrastructure and pedagogical materials, the results are identical to those in table 2.12

Table 2.13 Summary of impacts of school and teacher variables on time in school (43 high quality studies)

	Negative		Zero, or insignificant and no sign given	Positive		Total papers
	Significant	Insignificant		Insignificant	Significant	
School Infrastructure						
Textbooks/workbooks	0 (0)	2 (2)	1 (1)	2 (1)	2 (2)	4
Roof/wall/floor	0 (0)	1 (1)	0 (0)	0 (0)	1 (1)	2
Building new schools	0 (0)	0 (0)	0 (0)	1 (1)	4 (3)	3
Teacher Characteristics						
Education level	0 (0)	2 (2)	0 (0)	2 (2)	1 (1)	4
Experience	1 (1)	0 (0)	0 (0)	4 (3)	1 (1)	4
Training (in service)	1 (1)	2 (2)	0 (0)	0 (0)	0 (0)	2
School Organization						
Pupil-teacher ratio	0 (0)	3 (2)	0 (0)	2 (1)	2 (1)	3
Cost of attending	0 (0)	5 (3)	0 (0)	1 (1)	0 (0)	4
Merit based scholarship	0 (0)	1 (1)	0 (0)	2 (2)	0 (0)	2

Note: Figures are number of estimates; figures in parentheses are number of papers/studies. Table includes all school or teacher characteristics with at least two separate papers/studies.

for textbooks and workbooks, roof, walls, and floors, and building new schools, because for those categories all of the studies were of high quality. In contrast, neither library nor school quality index appears because neither had two or more high-quality studies.

The results pertaining to teacher characteristics in table 2.13 are also almost identical to those in table 2.12; of the three types of teacher characteristics considered (teacher education, teacher experience, and teacher in-service training), almost all of the studies are high-quality studies. The only exception is teacher experience, yet even here 4 of the 5 studies from the full set of 79 are high-quality studies; for these 4 studies the impact of teacher experience on time in school is mixed, with 1 study finding a significant positive effect, another finding a significant negative effect, and 3 finding positive but insignificant effects.

Finally, for the three school organization variables (pupil-teacher ratio, cost of attending, and merit-based scholarships) the results in table 2.13 are identical to those in table 2.12 since all of the studies for each of those variables are classified as high-quality studies.

2.4.4.3. The 13 Randomized Control Trials. Table 2.14 examines six RCTs that have estimated impacts of school and teacher variables on students' time in school. Two of these studies examined the impact of providing textbooks or workbooks; 2 of the 3 estimates in these 2 studies found significantly positive effects. There were also 2 studies of the impact of

Table 2.14 Summary of impacts of school and teacher variables on time in school (13 RCTs)

	Negative		Zero, or insignificant and no sign given	Positive		Total papers
	Significant	Insignificant		Insignificant	Significant	
School Infrastructure						
Textbooks/workbooks	0 (0)	0 (0)	1 (1)	0 (0)	2 (2)	2
Building new schools	0 (0)	0 (0)	0 (0)	1 (1)	3 (2)	2
School Organization						
School provides meals	0 (0)	0 (0)	0 (0)	1 (1)	0 (0)	1
Merit based scholarship	0 (0)	1 (1)	0 (0)	1 (1)	0 (0)	1

Note: Figures are number of estimates; figures in parentheses are number of papers/studies.

building new schools; both found significantly positive impacts on time in school. In contrast, there is no significant impact of merit-based scholarships, with one estimate insignificantly negative and the other insignificantly positive. Similarly, the one estimate of school-provided meals is statistically insignificant.

2.5. Conclusion and Priorities for Future Research

By describing the results sequentially by specific items and quality of studies, it is difficult to see the overall picture. The results across this review of the literature from 1990 to 2010 are summarized in tables 2.15 and 2.16. Table 2.15 does this for the results of studies that focus on students' learning, as measured by test scores, while table 2.16 does the same for the results for students' time in school.

Table 2.15 summarizes the impacts of 35 different school and teacher variables on student learning. When all 79 studies are examined, about half of these variables seem to have clear negative or positive impacts on student learning. However, when the evidence is limited to the 43 high-quality studies, only a few inputs appear to have unambiguous results.

Perhaps the clearest finding is that having a fully functioning school— one with better-quality roofs, walls, or floors, with desks, tables, and chairs, and with a school library—appears conducive to student learning. Of course, these attributes may partially be signaling an interest in, and commitment to, providing a quality education. On the personnel side, the most consistent results reflect having teachers with greater knowledge of the subjects they teach, having a longer school day, and providing tutoring. Additionally, and again unsurprising, it makes a difference if teachers show up for work; teacher absence has a clear negative effect on learning.

Table 2.15 Overall summary of estimated achievement impacts from tables 2.7–2.11

Teacher/School Variable	All 79 studies	43 high-quality studies	RCTs
School Infrastructure			
Textbooks/workbooks	Mostly positive (21)[a]	Inconclusive (8)	No significant effect (2)
Desks/tables/chairs	Almost all positive (11)	All positive (4)	—
Computers/elec. games	Mostly positive (8)	Positive?/Ambiguous (6)	Inconclusive (5)
Electricity	Mostly positive (6)	No significant effect (3)	—
School infrastructure index	Mostly positive (6)	—	—
Blackboard/flip chart	Mostly positive (6)	Positive?/Ambiguous (3)	No significant effect (1)
Library	Mostly positive (6)	Mostly positive (3)	—
Roof/wall/floor	Mostly positive (4)	Mostly positive (4)	
Teacher Characteristics			
Education level	Mostly positive (24)	Inconclusive (6)	—
Experience	Positive?/Ambiguous (20)	Positive?/Ambiguous (9)	—
Knowledge (test)	Mostly positive (9)	All positive (5)	—
Female teachers	Inconclusive (11)	Inconclusive (2)	—
Training (in service)	Mostly positive (11)	Positive?/Ambiguous (3)	—
Quality index	Mostly positive (2)	—	—
Teaching degree	Positive?/Ambiguous (2)	—	—
Principal experience	Mostly positive (2)	—	—
Principal education	Inconclusive	—	—
School Organization			
Pupil-teacher ratio	Negative?/Ambiguous (29)	Negative?/Ambiguous (14)	Negative (1)
Teacher absenteeism	Almost all negative (5)	All negative (2)	—
Teacher assigning homework	Mostly positive (5)	—	—
School provides meals	Positive?/Ambiguous (4)	Positive?/Ambiguous (2)	No significant effect (1)
Multigrade teaching	Inconclusive (4)	Inconclusive (2)	—
Hours of school day	Positive?/Ambiguous (4)	All positive (2)	—
Tutoring	Positive?/Ambiguous (3)	All positive (2)	Positive (1)
Teacher salary	Almost all positive (3)	—	—
Contract teacher	Positive?/Ambiguous (2)	Positive?/Ambiguous (2)	Positive (1)
Expenditure/pupil	Inconclusive (2)	—	—
Cost of attending	Inconclusive (2)	—	—
Total school enrollment	Inconclusive (2)	—	—
Group work	Mostly positive (2)	—	—
Teacher giving examples	Inconclusive (2)	—	—
Student attendance	All positive (2)	—	—
Parent follow-up	Mostly positive (2)	—	—
Commun. Inform. Campaign	—	—	Positive?/Ambiguous (1)
Merit-based scholarship	—	—	Positive (1)

[a] Number of studies in parentheses

Randomized trials arguably provide the most rigorous evidence, but for most variables there is either no study at all or at most one study. Thus, it is currently difficult to draw general conclusions from the available results. Somewhat surprisingly, however, for the two variables with more than one RCT (textbooks/workbooks and computers), no clear results have been found.

On the other hand, perhaps the most useful conclusion to draw for policy is that there is little empirical support for a wide variety of school and teacher characteristics that some observers may view as priorities for school spending. While one could argue that the absence of strong results simply reflects insufficient data (low statistical power) to detect systematic effects, it could also be the case that most of the effects are themselves small. Quite plausibly, part of the ambiguity comes from heterogeneous treatment effects, where the impact of various inputs depends on the local circumstances, demands, and capacities.

Turning to table 2.16, there is also meager evidence at best for what can be done to increase students' time in school and attainment.[20] Focusing on the 43 high-quality studies, only two findings receive fairly clear support: building more schools increases students' time in school, and in-service teacher training reduces student time in school. The latter result is unexpected and admittedly is based on only two studies, but it may reflect that in-service teacher training takes teachers out of the classroom, so that the primary effect is similar to that of teacher absence. The randomized trials to date again provide insufficient evidence for clear policy directions, although if many more were conducted it is possible that clearer policy conclusions could be drawn.

Taken as a whole, these studies are consistent with much of the current policy discussion that the focus should shift from basic school and

Table 2.16 Overall summary of estimated school attainment and time impacts from tables 2.12–2.14

Teacher/school variable	All 79 studies	43 high-quality studies	RCTs
School Infrastructure			
Textbooks/workbooks	Positive?/Ambiguous (3)[a]	Positive?/Ambiguous (3)	Positive (1)
Library	Positive (2)	—	—
Roof/wall/floor	Positive?/Ambiguous (2)	Positive?/Ambiguous (2)	—
Building new schools	Positive (3)	Positive (3)	Positive?/Ambiguous (2)
School quality index	Positive (2)	—	
Teacher Characteristics			
Education level	Positive?/Ambiguous (4)	Positive?/Ambiguous (4)	—
Experience	Positive?/Ambiguous (5)	Positive?/Ambiguous (4)	—
Training (in service)	Mostly negative (2)	Mostly negative (2)	—
School Organization			
Pupil-teacher ratio	Inconclusive (3)	Inconclusive (3)	—
School provides meals	—	—	Inconclusive (1)
Cost of attending	Negative?/Ambiguous (4)	Negative?/Ambiguous (4)	—
Merit-based scholarship	Inconclusive (2)	Inconclusive (2)	Inconclusive (1)

[a] Number of studies in parentheses

teacher characteristics to changing incentives in schools and permitting more local decisionmaking; if the effects are generally small or if they depend on, say, local capacity, it is then difficult to set overall resource policies at the national or international level. Indeed, the variation in results may reflect that some interventions work well in some contexts but have no effect, or even negative effects, in other contexts. This evidence would be consistent with cross-country evidence that generally indicates positive effects from more local autonomy in decisionmaking (at least when there is also an accountability system in place) (see Hanushek and Woessmann 2011).

This state of affairs raises the question about the value of research on the effect of basic school and teacher characteristics on student learning and time in school. The various research efforts have led to many ambiguous results—either because there are few consistent results or because the methodological problems are too large. A deeper appreciation for the methodological issues in obtaining causal estimates has emerged in the past two decades. Both the inconsistent results from past work and the distinct possibility of rather deep methodological problems suggest that a continued quest for identifying the specific inputs of teachers and schools from cross-sectional analyses of samples of convenience is unlikely to provide strong policy guidance.

But a complementary conclusion is that conducting research into policy relevant aspects of schooling often requires early researcher involvement in the design and data collection before programs or policies are introduced. For several classes of policy issues—largely ones involving well-identified programs and specific resources—obtaining randomized or quasi-randomized observations is key to instilling confidence in research results. Randomized control trials provide the easiest to understand research design, and it is probably the case that researchers who focus on education have historically underinvested in their use. At the same time, actually implementing these can be time-consuming, difficult, and expensive—leading to a limited number of such analyses to date, although a larger number are either currently underway or will soon be started.

Two other kinds of approaches offer promise. First, the availability of panel data provides the possibility of addressing a wider range of issues while still being sensitive to the threats to statistical analysis. For example, much of the recent analysis of large panels of administrative data in the United States has shown how panel data techniques can reduce analytical problems while opening up a much wider range of analyses.

Second, with the cooperation of government policymakers, randomization in the implementation of education programs across villages or over time can provide the kinds of variation that are needed to evaluate the impacts of these programs. This approach is distinct from researcher-driven RCTs because the programs being evaluated are chosen by the government. Further, given sufficient training, governments can evaluate these interventions with no need to bring in expatriate academic researchers. More specifically, this approach builds on local ideas for programs that local policymakers believe are likely to lead to improvements, and it also capitalizes on the fact that funding for many programs is frequently insufficient to introduce a new program across all possible locations. By staggering the introduction of a given program over time, it is possible to develop a built-in control group to assess the impact of that program. But here is where early involvement (by either higher-level decisionmakers or outside researchers) is essential, because, for example, giving the program first to the most politically powerful locales or to the most needy locales (as opposed to a random selection of locales) reduces, if not eliminates, the analytical possibilities.

Part of future success in designing and implementing effective education policies is introducing an evaluation mindset. The absence of interest in learning about the efficacy of new programs or policies is not restricted to developing countries, but is indeed present in developed countries. But the evidence to date reviewed in this chapter underscores the importance of this perspective. This review of existing evidence suggests little in the form of "best practices" that can readily be introduced through central provision or through regulatory approaches. This realization implies that progress is likely to proceed with local experimentation built on local knowledge and capacities. Yet local experimentation is unlikely to be successful unless there is a process of evaluation that works to continue the policies and programs that rigorous evaluations demonstrate are successful and to discontinue those that such evaluations indicate are unsuccessful.

One other aspect of this review deserves mention. Nothing has been said along the way about the costs of any programs. Clearly, effective policy needs to consider both the benefit side and the cost side, particularly in developing countries where resource constraints are binding at low levels. However, very few of the existing evaluations have provided solid information about costs of programs and policies. This topic is further addressed by Dhaliwal, Duflo, Glennerster, and Tulloch in chapter 8.

At the beginning of this chapter we noted that education, and especially the skills developed through high-quality education, can have an enormous positive impact on individuals' lives and on countries' economic growth. Yet education is a complicated process, and in both developed and developing countries policymakers and researchers are trying to understand which policies are most likely to improve education outcomes. In this review we have found that, despite a large and increasingly sophisticated literature, remarkably little is known about the impact of education policies on student outcomes in developing countries. There are two likely reasons for this. The first is that what works best may vary considerably across countries and even within countries, which implies that future research should attempt to understand which policies work best in which settings. The second is that much of the literature has focused on basic school and teacher characteristics, when in fact the ways that schools are organized may matter most. Such a conclusion implies that future research should focus on how schools are organized and the incentives faced by teachers, administrators, parents, and students. Indeed, some research on these topics has already been done, and that research is summarized in chapters 5, 6 and 7 of this book. Yet before turning to that research, the next two chapters focus on programs that can help prepare students even before they start primary school: early childhood development programs (chapter 3) and child health programs (chapter 4).

Appendix 2A. Search Terms

The methodology used to search for papers is described in detail in section 2.3 above. This appendix reports the specific search terms used. The search terms used to search EconLit from 1990 to 2010 are as follows. The code "KW" refers to a key word.

> KW=education and KW=("class size" OR "school size" OR "Student teacher ratio" OR "Pupil teacher ratio" OR "School expenditure*" OR "expenditure per pupil" OR "texbook*" OR "instructional material*" OR "Workbook*" OR "exercise book*" OR "computer*" OR "laptop*" OR "internet" OR "school infrastructure" OR "Facilities" OR "Building condition*" OR "Laborator*" OR "lab" OR "labs" OR "Librar*" OR "Desk*" OR "Teaching tools" OR "teaching guide*" OR "blackboard*" OR "chalk*" OR "electricity" OR "table*" OR "bench*" OR "chair*" OR "roof*" OR "wall*" OR "floor*" OR "window*" OR "bathroom*" OR "plumbing" OR "teacher quality" OR "teacher efficacy" OR "teacher knowledge" OR "teacher salar*" OR "teacher training" OR "teacher experience" OR "teacher education" OR "teacher absenteeism" OR "teacher gender" OR "class preparation" OR "lesson planning" OR "homework" OR "evaluation" OR "follow-up" OR "monitoring of pupil performance" OR "testing" OR "remedial program*" OR "teaching practices" OR "instructional time" OR "length of instructional program" OR "hours" OR "school day" OR "curriculum" OR "principal quality" OR "principal training" OR "principal education" OR "prin-

cipal experience" OR "staff assessment*" OR "teacher assessment" OR "school inspection*" OR "parent* involvement" OR "production function" OR "school resources" OR "school inputs" OR "School quality" OR "Pedagogical inputs" OR "pedagogical resources")

These search terms yielded over half a million results in ERIC. To narrow the results to a reasonable number, results in ERIC were further limited to articles that included the name of at least one developing country or related term in the abstract. The search terms used to limit results accordingly are as follows. The code AB refers to abstract.

AB=("developing countr*" OR "Least-Developed Countries" OR "Afghanistan" OR "Albania" OR "Algeria" OR "Angola" OR "Antigua and Barbuda" OR "Argentina" OR "Armenia" OR "Azerbaijan" OR "Bahamas" OR "Bahrain" OR "Bangladesh" OR "Barbados" OR "Belarus" OR "Belize" OR "Benin" OR "Bhutan" OR "Bolivia" OR "Bosnia and Herzegovina" OR "Botswana" OR "Brazil" OR "Brunei Darussalam" OR "Bulgaria" OR "Burkina Faso" OR "Burundi" OR "Cambodia" OR "Cameroon" OR "Cape Verde" OR "Central African Republic" OR "Chad" OR "Chile" OR "China" OR "Colombia" OR "Comoros" OR "Congo" OR "Costa Rica" OR "Côte d'Ivoire" OR "Croatia" OR "Djibouti" OR "Dominica" OR "Dominican Republic" OR "Ecuador*" OR "Egypt*" OR "El Salvador" OR "Salvadoran" OR "Equatorial Guinea" OR "Eritrea" OR "Estonia*" OR "Ethiopia*" OR "Fiji*" OR "Gabon*" OR "Gambia*" OR "Georgia*" OR "Ghana*" OR "Grenada*" OR "Guatemala*" OR "Guinea" OR "Guinea-Bissau" OR "Guyana" OR "Haiti" OR "Honduras" OR "Hungary" OR "India" OR "Indonesia" OR "Iran" OR "Iraq" OR "Jamaica" OR "Jordan" OR "Kazakhstan" OR "Kenya" OR "Kiribati" OR "Kosovo" OR "Kuwait" OR "Kyrgyz Republic" OR "Lao People's Democratic Republic" OR "Latvia" OR "Lebanon" OR "Lesotho" OR "Liberia" OR "Libya" OR "Lithuania" OR "Macedonia" OR "Madagascar" OR "Malawi" OR "Malaysia" OR "Maldives" OR "Mali" OR "Mauritania" OR "Mauritius" OR "Mexico" OR "Moldova" OR "Mongolia" OR "Montenegro" OR "Morocco" OR "Mozambique" OR "Myanmar" OR "Namibia" OR "Nepal" OR Nicaragua" OR "Niger" OR "Nigeria" OR "Yugoslav" OR "Oman" OR "Pakistan" OR "Panama" OR "Papua New Guinea" OR "Paraguay" OR "Peru" OR "Philippines" OR "Poland" OR "Qatar" OR "Romania" OR "Russia" OR "Rwanda" OR "Samoa" OR "São Tomé and Príncipe" OR "Saudi Arabia" OR "Senegal" OR "Serbia" OR "Seychelles" OR "Sierra Leone" OR "Solomon Islands" OR "South Africa" OR "Sri Lanka" OR "St. Kitts and Nevis" OR "St. Lucia" OR "St. Vincent and the Grenadines" OR "Sudan" OR "Suriname" OR "Swaziland" OR "Syrian Arab Republic" OR "Tajikistan" OR "Tanzania" OR "Thailand" OR "Timor-Leste" OR "Togo" OR "Tonga" OR "Trinidad and Tobago" OR "Tunisia" OR "Turkey" OR "Turkmenistan" OR "Uganda" OR "Ukraine" OR "United Arab Emirates" OR "Uruguay" OR "Uzbekistan" OR "Vanuatu" OR "Venezuela" OR "Vietnam" OR "Yemen" OR "Zambia" OR "Zimbabwe" OR "North Korea" OR "Cuba") and not AB=("U.S." OR "U.K." OR "Europe" OR "US" OR "UK" OR "Japan" OR "Canada" OR "Australia")

Appendix 2B. Studies Examined in This Paper

The following 79 papers passed the phase 3 quality review, described in section 2.3. The 43 preceded by an asterisk (*) passed the phase 4 screening and were considered to be "high quality." Two asterisks indicate that the paper is also one of the 13 randomized control trials (RCT).

**Alderman, Harold, Jooseop Kim, and Peter F. Orazem. 2003. "Design, Evaluation, and Sustainability of Private Schools for the Poor: The Pakistan Urban and Rural Fellowship School Experiments." *Economics of Education Review* 22 (3): 265–74.

Anderson, Joan B. 2000. "Factors Affecting Learning of Mexican Primary School Children." *Estudios Economicos* 15 (1): 117–52.

———. 2008. "Principals' Role and Public Primary Schools' Effectiveness in Four Latin American Cities." *Elementary School Journal* 109 (1): 36–60.

*Angrist, Joshua D., and Victor Lavy. 1999. "Using Maimonides' Rule to Estimate the Effect of Class Size on Scholastic Achievement." *Quarterly Journal of Economics* 114 (2): 533–75.

*———. 2001. "Does Teacher Training Affect Pupil Learning? Evidence from Matched Comparisons in Jerusalem Public Schools." *Journal of Labor Economics* 19 (2): 343–69.

*———. 2002. "New Evidence on Classroom Computers and Pupil Learning." *Economic Journal* 112 (482): 735–65.

Arif, G. M., and Najam us Saqib. 2003. "Production of Cognitive and Life Skills in Public, Private, and NGO Schools in Pakistan." *Pakistan Development Review* 42 (1): 1–28.

*Asadullah, M. Niaz. 2005. "The Effect of Class Size on Student Achievement: Evidence from Bangladesh." *Applied Economics Letters* 12 (4): 217–21.

Aslam, Monazza. 2003. "The Determinants of Student Achievement in Government and Private Schools in Pakistan." *Pakistan Development Review* 42 (4): 841–75.

Bacolod, Marigee P., and Justin L. Tobias. 2006. "Schools, School Quality and Achievement Growth: Evidence from the Philippines." *Economics of Education Review* 25 (6): 619–32.

**Banerjee, Abhijit V., Shawn Cole, Esther Duflo, and Leigh Linden. 2007. "Remedying Education: Evidence from Two Randomized Experiments in India." *Quarterly Journal of Economics* 122 (3): 1235–64.

**Barrera-Osorio, Felipe, and Leigh L. Linden. 2009. "The Use and Misuse of Computers in Education: Evidence from a Randomized Experiment in Colombia." Policy Research Working Paper Series. Washington, DC: World Bank.

*Bedi, Arjun S., and Jeffrey H. Marshall. 1999. "School Attendance and Student Achievement: Evidence from Rural Honduras." *Economic Development and Cultural Change* 47 (3): 657–82.

*———. 2002. "Primary School Attendance in Honduras." *Journal of Development Economics* 69 (1): 129–53.

*Behrman, Jere R., et al. 1997. "School Quality and Cognitive Achievement Production: A Case Study for Rural Pakistan." *Economics of Education Review* 16 (2): 127–42.

*Bellei, Cristian. 2009. "Does Lengthening the School Day Increase Students' Academic Achievement? Results from a Natural Experiment in Chile." *Economics of Education Review* 28 (5): 629–40.

*Brown, Philip H., and Albert Park. 2002. "Education and Poverty in Rural China." *Economics of Education Review* 21 (6): 523–41.

*Chen, Xinxin, Chengfang Liu, Linxiu Zhang, Yaojiang Shi, and Scott Rozelle. 2010. "Does Taking One Step Back Get You Two Steps Forward? Grade Retention and School Performance in Poor Areas in Rural China." *International Journal of Educational Development* 30 (6): 544–59.

*Chin, Aimee. 2005. "Can Redistributing Teachers across Schools Raise Educational Attainment? Evidence from Operation Blackboard in India." *Journal of Development Economics* 78 (2): 384–405.

Chudgar, Amita, and Vyjayanthi Sankar. 2008. "The Relationship between Teacher Gender and Student Achievement: Evidence from Five Indian States." *Compare: A Journal of Comparative Education* 38 (5): 627–42.

Du, Yuhong, and Yongmei Hu. 2008. "Student Academic Performance and the Allocation of School Resources: Results from a Survey of Junior Secondary Schools." *Chinese Education and Society* 41 (5): 8–20.

Engin-Demir, Cennet. 2009. "Factors Influencing the Academic Achievement of the Turkish Urban Poor." *International Journal of Educational Development* 29 (1): 17–29.

Fehrler, Sebastian, Katharina Michaelowa, and Annika Wechtler. 2009. "The Effectiveness of Inputs in Primary Education: Insights from Recent Student Surveys for Sub-Saharan Africa." *Journal of Development Studies* 45 (9): 1545–78.

Fuller, Bruce, Lucia Dellagnelo, Annelie Strath, Eni Santana Barretto Bastos, Maurício Holanda Maia, Kelma Socorro Lopes de Matos, Adélia Luiza Portela, and Sofia Lerche Vieira. 1999. "How to Raise Children's Early Literacy? The Influence of Family, Teacher, and Classroom in Northeast Brazil." *Comparative Education Review* 43 (1): 1–35.

*Glewwe, Paul, Margaret Grosh, Hanan Jacoby, and Marlaine Lockheed. 1995. "An Eclectic Approach to Estimating the Determinants of Achievement in Jamaican Primary Education." *World Bank Economic Review* 9 (2): 231–58.

*Glewwe, Paul, and Hanan Jacoby. 1994. "Student Achievement and Schooling Choice in Low-Income Countries: Evidence from Ghana." *Journal of Human Resources* 29 (3): 843–64.

**Glewwe, Paul, Michael Kremer, and Sylvie Moulin. 2009. "Many Children Left Behind? Textbooks and Test Scores in Kenya." *American Economic Journal: Applied Economics* 1 (1): 112–35.

**Glewwe, Paul, Michael Kremer, Sylvie Moulin, and Eric Zitzewitz. 2004. "Retrospective vs. Prospective Analyses of School Inputs: The Case of Flip Charts in Kenya." *Journal of Development Economics* 74 (1): 251–68.

*Glick, Peter, and David E. Sahn. 2009. "Cognitive Skills among Children in Senegal: Disentangling the Roles of Schooling and Family Background." *Economics of Education Review* 28 (2): 178–88.

Glick, Peter, and David E. Sahn. 2010. "Early Academic Performance, Grade Repetition, and School Attainment in Senegal: A Panel Data Analysis." *World Bank Economic Review* 24 (1): 93–120.

Gomes-Neto, João Batista, and Eric A. Hanushek. 1994. "Causes and Consequences of Grade Repetition: Evidence from Brazil." *Economic Development and Cultural Change* 43 (1): 117–48.

Gustafsson, Martin. 2007. "Using the Hierarchical Linear Model to Understand School Production in South Africa." *South African Journal of Economics* 75 (1): 84–98.

*Handa, Sudhanshu. 2002. "Raising Primary School Enrollment in Developing Countries: The Relative Importance of Supply and Demand." *Journal of Development Economics* 69 (1): 103–28.

Hanushek, Eric A., Victor Lavy, and Kohtaro Hitomi. 2008. "Do Students Care about School Quality? Determinants of Dropout Behavior in Developing Countries." *Journal of Human Capital* 2 (1): 69–105.

Hanushek, Eric A., and Javier A. Luque. 2003. "Efficiency and Equity in Schools around the World." *Economics of Education Review* 22 (5): 481–502.

Hungi, Njora. 2008. "Examining Differences in Mathematics and Reading Achievement among Grade 5 Pupils in Vietnam." *Studies in Educational Evaluation* 34 (3): 155–64.

**Inamdar, Parimala. 2004. "Computer Skills Development by Children Using 'Hole in the Wall' Facilities in Rural India." *Australasian Journal of Educational Technology* 20 (3): 337–50.

*Infantes, Pedro, and Christel Vermeersch. 2007. "More Time Is Better: An Evaluation of the Full-time School Program in Uruguay." Policy Research Working Paper Series. Washington, DC: World Bank.

Kalender, Ilker, and Giray Berberoglu. 2009. "An Assessment of Factors Related to Science Achievement of Turkish Students." *International Journal of Science Education* 31 (10): 1379–94.

*Khan, Shahrukh Rafi, and David Kiefer. 2007. "Educational Production Functions for Rural Pakistan: A Comparative Institutional Analysis." *Education Economics* 15 (3): 327–42.

*Kingdon, Geeta, and Francis Teal. 2010. "Teacher Unions, Teacher Pay and Student Performance in India: A Pupil Fixed Effects Approach." *Journal of Development Economics* 91 (2): 278–88.

**Kremer, Michael, Edward Miguel, and Rebecca Thornton. 2009. "Incentives to Learn." *Review of Economics and Statistics* 91 (3): 437–56.

*Lavy, Victor. 1996. "School Supply Constraints and Children's Educational Outcomes in Rural Ghana." *Journal of Development Economics* 51 (2): 291–314.

Lee, Valerie E., and Marlaine E. Lockheed. 1990. "The Effects of Single-Sex Schooling on Achievement and Attitudes in Nigeria." *Comparative Education Review* 34 (2): 209–31.

Lee, Valerie E., Tia Linda Zuze, and Kenneth N. Ross. 2005. "School Effectiveness in 14 Sub-Saharan African Countries: Links with Sixth-graders' Reading Achievement." *Studies in Educational Evaluation* 31 (2–3): 207–46.

**Linden, Leigh. 2008. "Complement or Substitute? The Effect of Technology on Student Achievement in India." JPAL Working Paper, MIT. http://www.povertyaction lab.org/evaluation/complement-or-substitute-effect-technology-student-achievement -india.

*Lloyd, Cynthia B., Barbara S. Mensch, and Wesley H. Clark. 2000. "The Effects of Primary School Quality on School Dropout among Kenyan Girls and Boys." *Comparative Education Review* 44 (2): 113–47.

*Lloyd, Cynthia B., Cem Mete, and Monica J. Grant. 2009. "The Implications of Changing Educational and Family Circumstances for Children's Grade Progression in Rural Pakistan: 1997–2004." *Economics of Education Review* 28 (1): 152–60.

Lockheed, Marlaine E., and Qinghua Zhao. 1993. "The Empty Opportunity: Local Control and Secondary School Achievement in the Philippines." *International Journal of Educational Development* 13 (1): 45–62.

*Louw, Johann, Johan Muller, and Colin Tredoux. 2008. "Time-on-Task, Technology and Mathematics Achievement." *Evaluation and Program Planning* 31 (1): 41–50.

Luschei, Thomas F., and Martin Carnoy. 2010. "Educational Production and the Distribution of Teachers in Uruguay." *International Journal of Educational Development* 30 (2): 169–81.

*Marshall, Jeffery H. 2009. "School Quality and Learning Gains in Rural Guatemala." *Economics of Education Review* 28 (2): 207–16.

Marshall, Jeffrey H., Ung Chinna, Puth Nessay, Ung Ngo Hok, Va Savoeun, Soeur Tinon, and Meung Veasna. 2009. "Student Achievement and Education Policy in a Period of Rapid Expansion: Assessment Data Evidence from Cambodia." *International Review of Education* 55 (4): 393–413.

*Marshall, Jeffery H., Marco Tulio Mejia R., and Claudia R. Aguilar. 2008. "Quality and Efficiency in a Complementary Middle School Program: The 'Educatodos' Experience in Honduras." *Comparative Education Review* 52 (2): 147–73.

McEwan, Patrick J. 1998. "The Effectiveness of Multigrade Schools in Colombia." *International Journal of Educational Development* 18 (6): 435–52.

*Menezes-Filho, Naercio, and Elaine Pazello. 2007. "Do Teachers' Wages Matter for Proficiency? Evidence from a Funding Reform in Brazil." *Economics of Education Review* 26 (6): 660–72.

*Metzler, Johannes, and Ludger Woessmann. 2010. "The Impact of Teacher Subject Knowledge on Student Achievement: Evidence from Within-Teacher Within-Student Variation." Institute for the Study of Labor. IZA Discussion Paper. http://www.iza .org/en/webcontent/publications/papers.

Michaelowa, Katharina. 2001. "Primary Education Quality in Francophone Sub-Saharan Africa: Determinants of Learning Achievement and Efficiency Considerations." *World Development* 29 (10): 1699–716.

Mullens, John E., et al. 1996. "The Contribution of Training and Subject Matter Knowledge to Teaching Effectiveness: A Multilevel Analysis of Longitudinal Evidence from Belize." *Comparative Education Review* 40 (2): 139–57.

**Muralidharan, Karthik, and Venkatesh Sundararaman. 2011. "Contract Teachers: Experimental Evidence from India." *Journal of Political Economy* 119 (1): 39–77.

Nannyonjo, Harriet. 2007. "Education Inputs in Uganda: An Analysis of Factors Influencing Learning Achievement in Grade Six." World Bank Working Paper 98, Africa Human Development Series. Washington, DC: World Bank.

*Naseer, Muhammad Farooq, Manasa Patnam, and Reehana R. Raza. 2010. "Transforming Public Schools: Impact of the CRI Program on Child Learning in Pakistan." *Economics of Education Review* 29 (4): 669–83.

**Newman, John, et al. 2002. "An Impact Evaluation of Education, Health, and Water Supply Investments by the Bolivian Social Investment Fund." *World Bank Economic Review* 16 (2): 241–74.

Nonoyama-Tarumi, Yuko, and Kurt Bredenberg. 2009. "Impact of School Readiness Program Interventions on Children's Learning in Cambodia." *International Journal of Educational Development* 29 (1): 39–45.

**Pandey, Priyanka, Sangeeta Goyal, and Venkatesh Sundararaman. 2009. "Community Participation in Public Schools: Impact of Information Campaigns in Three Indian States." *Education Economics* 17 (3): 355–75.

Psacharopoulos, George, et al. 1993. "Achievement Evaluation of Colombia's Escuela Nueva: Is Multigrade the Answer?" *Comparative Education Review* 37 (3): 263–76.

Raudenbush, Stephen W., Suwanna Eamsukkawat, Ikechuku Di-Ibor, Mohamed Kamali, and Wimol Taoklam. 1993. "On-the-Job Improvements in Teacher Competence: Policy Options and Their Effects on Teaching and Learning in Thailand." *Educational Evaluation and Policy Analysis* 15 (3): 279–297.

**Rosas, R., M. Nussbaum, P. Cumsille, V. Marianov, M. Correa, and P. Flores, et al. 2003. "Beyond Nintendo: Design and Assessment of Educational Video Games for First- and Second-Grade Students." *Computers and Education* 40:71–94.

*Suryadarma, Daniel, Asep Suryahadi, Sudarno Sumarto, and F. Halsey Rogers. 2006. "Improving Student Performance in Public Primary Schools in Developing Countries: Evidence from Indonesia." *Education Economics* 14 (4): 401–29.

**Tan, Jee-Peng, Julia Lane, and Gerard Lassibille. 1999. "Student Outcomes in Philippine Elementary Schools: An Evaluation of Four Experiments." *World Bank Economic Review* 13 (3): 493–508.

*Urquiola, Miguel. 2006. "Identifying Class Size Effects in Developing Countries: Evidence from Rural Bolivia." *Review of Economics and Statistics* 88 (1): 171–77.

Van der Berg, Servaas. 2008. "How Effective Are Poor Schools? Poverty and Educational Outcomes in South Africa." *Studies in Educational Evaluation* 34 (3): 145–54.

Van der Werf, Greetje, Bert Creemers, Rob De Jong, and Elizabeth Klaver. 2000. "Evaluation of School Improvement through an Educational Effectiveness Model: The Case of Indonesia's PEQIP Project." *Comparative Education Review* 44 (3): 329–55.

Van der Werf, Greetje, Bert Creemers, and Henk Guldemond. 2001. "Improving Parental Involvement in Primary Education in Indonesia: Implementation, Effects, and Costs." *School Effectiveness and School Improvement* 12 (4): 447–66.

Warwick, Donald P., and Haroona Jatoi. 1994. "Teacher Gender and Student Achievement in Pakistan." *Comparative Education Review* 38 (3): 377–99.

*Wossmann, Ludger. 2005. "Educational Production in East Asia: The Impact of Family Background and Schooling Policies on Student Performance." *German Economic Review* 6 (3): 331–53.

Yu, Guoxing, and Sally M. Thomas. 2008. "Exploring School Effects across Southern and Eastern African School Systems and in Tanzania." *Assessment in Education: Principles, Policy and Practice* 15 (3): 283–305.

Zhang, Yu, and David Post. 2000. "Mathematics Achievement in Yunnan Province: The Effects of Family, Region, and Teacher Quality." *Education Journal* 28 (1): 47–63.

Zhao, Meng, and Paul Glewwe. 2010. "What Determines Basic School Attainment in Developing Countries? Evidence from Rural China." *Economics of Education Review* 29 (3): 451–60.

Notes

1. The majority of this work, following the seminal studies of Jacob Mincer (1970, 1974), has focused on how school attainment relates to individual earnings, and there are now estimates of the return to schooling for a majority of

countries in the world (Psacharopoulos and Patrinos 2004). More recent work has added measures of achievement to this (e.g., Mulligan 1999; Murnane, Willett, Duhaldeborde, and Tyler 2000; and Lazear 2003), although little of this relates to developing countries (see, however, Hanushek and Zhang 2009).

2. Gross enrollment rates compare numbers of schoolchildren to the size of a specific age cohort so that grade repetition, delayed enrollment, and the like can lead to gross enrollment rates over 100%.

3. Hanushek, Lavy, and Hitomi (2008) find that school dropout decisions are very responsive to the quality of the school (in terms of value-added to achievement).

4. See the World Bank's World Development Indicators. Note that Brazil's gross (net) secondary school enrollment rate increased from 99 (66) in 1999 to 106 (79) in 2005, Educational expenditures (in terms of real US $ per secondary student) increased from, on average, about 1,340 (350) from 1998 to 2000 to about 1,510 (500) from 2004 to 2006 in Argentina (Brazil).

5. The only demand-side program that increased achievement was a Kenyan scholarship program that directly related incentives to achievement (Kremer, Miguel, and Thornton 2009).

6. These conclusions have been controversial, and much has been written about the interpretation of the evidence. For a review of the inconsistencies of effects, see Hanushek 2003. For the range of opinions, see, for example, Burtless 1996; Mishel and Rothstein 2002; and Ehrenberg, Brewer, Gamoran, and Willms 2001.

7. For an early development of this idea, see Kim 2001.

8. A common first assumption made in much of the existing literature is that equation (1) can be approximated by a linear function; this assumption is not particularly restrictive. The estimation generally relies on the model being linear in the parameters, and a variety of specifications that are nonlinear in the variables can be accommodated by this specification, say by adding squared or interaction terms to the variables in (1).

9. This type of problem has also been prominent in many discussions of the estimation of teacher effects in the US literature. If school principals assign teachers to classrooms based on unobserved characteristics of the teachers, the ability to estimate the impact of teachers may be affected; see Rothstein 2010 and Rivkin 2008.

10. Of the 79 papers eventually examined (see below for details), only one examined grade repetition, which is an indirect measure of student learning. Yet repetition can also depend on school policies and other factors (such as crowding in particular grades) and so it is a noisy measure of student learning. Because of this problem, and the lack of studies that examined repetition, we exclude studies of repetition from our analysis of the determinants of student learning. (The sole paper that examined repetition also has regressions with test scores as the dependent variable, so it remains one of the 79 studies.)

11. In the economics literature, most papers that included education as a keyword were studies of the impacts of education on some other social phenomenon, as opposed to studies that investigated the impacts of other factors on education outcomes.

12. A significantly negative effect is not necessarily an error; it could be that some textbooks or workbooks were not well written, or not well matched to the students, and that this caused problems. More generally, one should expect some heterogeneity in the impacts. Given our 10% significance level standard, if a certain school variable had zero impact in all schools one should find that 90% of estimates are not significantly different from zero, while 5% are significantly negative and 5% are significantly positive. As will be seen, there are some cases where more than 5% are significantly positive and more than 5% are significantly negative; such a result suggests heterogeneity in the impacts due to differences across countries and across schools within the same country.

13. While electricity could simply be a general indicator of the physical condition of the school, most of the six studies that examined the impact of electricity included other measures of the physical condition of the school. We tend to interpret electricity literally, although it may be just one of the most important, and most accurately measured, dimensions of the quality of school facilities.

14. In almost all of the school infrastructure studies, the index counts whether schools have some or all of the following: library, cafeteria, science labs, playground, and computer labs. As mentioned previously, electricity could also be part of a general infrastructure measure.

15. Note that both of these findings about teacher characteristics are very much at odds with the US evidence. In the United States, where all teachers have bachelor's degrees and the focus is on advanced degrees, there is virtually no evidence that more education for the teachers helps. Similarly, experience past the first few years of teaching has no effect. See Hanushek 2003.

16. There is currently a debate about the effectiveness of single-sex schools and, implicitly, that female teachers may have a larger impact on girls than boys (see Billger 2009; Kaufman and Yin 2009; Park and Behrman 2010). However, in all but one of the studies examined here estimates are not given separately for male and female students, and the sole exception found no difference.

17. The 14 estimates of teacher quality come from two studies, which define teacher quality in terms of an index of teacher experience, level of education, and scores on math and reading tests.

18. In the United States, pupil-teacher ratios and class sizes can diverge noticeably because teachers have fewer class meetings than students have courses, because teachers perform a variety of nonteaching duties, and so forth. This divergence is likely to be less important for schools in developing countries.

19. For a detailed review and analysis of recent research on contract teachers, see chapter 6 by Galiani and Perez-Truglia.

20. One exception to this lack of evidence is the finding that conditional cash transfer programs induce greater school attendance. This is discussed in detail by Behrman, Parker, and Todd in chapter 5.

References

Banerjee, Abhijit V., Shawn Cole, Esther Duflo, and Leigh Linden. 2007. "Remedying Education: Evidence from Two Randomized Experiments in India." *Quarterly Journal of Economics* 122 (3): 1235–64.

Barrera-Osorio, Felipe, and Leigh Linden. 2009. "The Use and Misuse of Computers in Education: Evidence from a Randomized Experiment in Colombia." World Bank Working Paper 4836. Washington, DC: World Bank.

Billger, Sherrilyn M. 2009. "On Reconstructing School Segregation: The Efficacy and Equity of Single-Sex Schooling." *Economics of Education Review* 28 (3): 393–402.

Blundell, Richard, and Monica Dias. 2009. "Alternative Approaches to Evaluation in Empirical Microeconomics." *Journal of Human Resources* 44 (3): 565–640.

Burtless, Gary, ed. 1996. *Does Money Matter? The Effect of School Resources on Student Achievement and Adult Success.* Washington, DC: Brookings.

Dang, Hai-Anh, and F. Halsey Rogers. 2008. "The Growing Phenomenon of Private Tutoring: Does It Deepen Human Capital, Widen Inequalities, or Waste Resources?" *World Bank Research Observer* 23 (2): 161–200.

Du, Yuhong, and Yongmei Hu. 2008. "Student Academic Performance and the Allocation of School Resources." *Chinese Education and Society* 41 (5): 8–20.

Ehrenberg, Ronald G., Dominic J. Brewer, Adam Gamoran, and J. Douglas Willms. 2001. "Class Size and Student Achievement." *Psychological Science in the Public Interest* 2 (1): 1–30.

Fuller, Bruce, and Prema Clarke. 1994. "Raising School Effects While Ignoring Culture? Local Conditions and the Influence of Classroom Tools, Rules, and Pedagogy." *Review of Educational Research* 64 (1): 119–57.

Glewwe, Paul. 2002. "Schools and Skills in Developing Countries: Education Policies and Socioeconomic Outcomes." *Journal of Economic Literature* 40 (2): 436–482.

Glewwe, Paul, and Michael Kremer. 2006. "Schools, Teachers, and Educational Outcomes in Developing Countries." In *Handbook of the Economics of Education*, ed. Eric A. Hanushek and Finis Welch, 943–1017. Amsterdam: North Holland.

Glewwe, Paul, Michael Kremer, and Sylvie Moulin. 2009. "Many Children Left Behind? Textbooks and Test Scores in Kenya." *American Economic Journal: Applied Economics* 1 (1): 112–35.

Glewwe, Paul, Michael Kremer, Sylvie Moulin, and Eric Zitzewitz. 2004. "Retrospective vs. Prospective Analyses of School Inputs: The Case of Flip Charts in Kenya." *Journal of Development Economics* 74 (1): 251–68.

Hanushek, Eric A. 1995. "Interpreting Recent Research on Schooling in Developing Countries." *World Bank Research Observer* 10 (2): 227–46.

———. 2003. "The Failure of Input-based Schooling Policies." *Economic Journal* 113 (485): F64–F98.

———. 2008. "Incentives for Efficiency and Equity in the School System." *Perspektiven der Wirtschaftspolitik* 9 (Special Issue): 5–27.

Hanushek, Eric A., Victor Lavy, and Kohtaro Hitomi. 2008. "Do Students Care about School Quality? Determinants of Dropout Behavior in Developing Countries." *Journal of Human Capital* 1 (2): 69–105.

Hanushek, Eric A., and Ludger Woessmann. 2008. "The Role of Cognitive Skills in Economic Development." *Journal of Economic Literature* 46 (3): 607–68.

———. 2011. "The Economics of International Differences in Educational Achievement." In *Handbook of the Economics of Education,* vol. 3, ed. Eric A. Hanushek, Stephen Machin, and Ludger Woessmann, 89–200. Amsterdam: North Holland.

Hanushek, Eric A., and Lei Zhang. 2009. "Quality-Consistent Estimates of International Schooling and Skill Gradients." *Journal of Human Capital* 3 (2): 107–43.

Harbison, Ralph W., and Eric A. Hanushek. 1992. *Educational Performance of the Poor: Lessons from Rural Northeast Brazil.* New York: Oxford University Press.

Hedges, Larry V., and Ingram Olkin. 1985. *Statistical Methods for Meta-analysis.* San Diego, CA: Academic Press.

Imbens, Guido W., and Jeffrey M. Wooldridge. 2009. "Recent Developments in the Econometrics of Program Evaluation." *Journal of Economic Literature* 47 (1): 5–86.

Inamdar, Parimala. 2004. "Computer Skills Development by Children Using 'Hole in the Wall' Facilities in Rural India " *Australasian Journal of Educational Technology* 20 (3): 337-350.

Kaufman, Julia, and Liqun Yin. 2009. "What Matters for Chinese Girls' Behavior and Performance in School: An Investigation of Coeducational and Single-Sex Schooling for Girls in Urban China." *International Perspectives on Education and Society*, edited by David P. Baker, Alexander W. Wiseman, 10:185–216.

Kim, Hong-Kyun. 2001. "Is There a Crowding-Out Effect between School Expenditure and Mother's Child Care Time?" *Economics of Education Review* 20 (1): 71–80.

Kremer, Michael. 2003. "Randomized Evaluations of Educational Programs in Developing Countries: Some Lessons." *American Economic Review* 93 (2): 102–4.

Kremer, Michael, Edward Miguel, and Rebecca Thornton. 2009. "Incentives to Learn." *Review of Economics and Statistics* 91 (3): 437–56.

Lazear, Edward P. 2003. "Teacher Incentives." *Swedish Economic Policy Review* 10 (3): 179–214.

Linden, Leigh. 2008. "Complement or Substitute? The Effect of Technology on Student Achievement in India." JPAL Working Paper, MIT. http://www.povertyactionlab.org/evaluation/complement-or-substitute-effect-technology-student-achievement-india.

Lochner, Lance. 2011. "Non-Production Benefits of Education: Crime, Health, and Good Citizenship." In *Handbook of the Economics of Education,* ed. Eric A. Hanushek, Stephen Machin, and Ludger Woessmann, 183–282. Amsterdam: North Holland.

Mincer, Jacob. 1970. "The Distribution of Labor Incomes: A Survey with Special Reference to the Human Capital Approach." *Journal of Economic Literature* 8 (1): 1–26.

———. 1974. *Schooling, Experience, and Earnings.* New York: NBER.

Mishel, Lawrence, and Richard Rothstein, eds. 2002. *The Class Size Debate.* Washington, DC: Economic Policy Institute.

Mulligan, Casey B. 1999. "Galton versus the Human Capital Approach to Inheritance." *Journal of Political Economy* 107 (6): S184–S224.

Muralidharan, Karthik, and Venkatesh Sundararaman. 2008. "Contract Teachers: Experimental Evidence from India." JPAL Working Paper, MIT. http://www.povertyactionlab.org/evaluation/extra-contract-teachers-andhra-pradesh-india.

Murnane, Richard J., John B. Willett, Yves Duhaldeborde, and John H. Tyler. 2000. "How Important Are the Cognitive Skills of Teenagers in Predicting Subsequent Earnings?" *Journal of Policy Analysis and Management* 19 (4): 547–68.

Nannyonjo, Harriet. 2007. "Education Inputs in Uganda: An Analysis of Factors Influencing Learning Achievement in Grade Six." World Bank Policy Research Paper 98. Washington, DC: World Bank.

OECD. "International Development Statistics." http://www.oecd.org/dac/stats/idsonline.

OECD. 2000. "Knowledge and Skills for Life: First Results from PISA 2000." OECD.org. http://www.oecd.org/edu/school/programmeforinternationalstudentassessmentpisa/knowledgeandskillsforlifefirstresultsfrompisa2000-publications2000.htm

———. 2003. "Learning for Tomorrow's World: First Results from PISA 2003." OECD.org. http://www.oecd.org/pisa/pisaproducts/pisa2003/learningfortomorrowsworldfirstresultsfrompisa2003.htm.

———. 2006. "PISA 2006: Science Competencies for Tomorrow's World." OECD.org. http://www.oecd.org/pisa/pisaproducts/pisa2006/pisa2006results.htm#Vol_1_and_2.

———. 2009. "PISA 2009 Results: What Students Know and Can Do." OECD.org. http://www.oecd.org/pisa/pisaproducts/pisa2009/pisa2009keyfindings.htm.

Pandey, Priyanka, Sangeeta Goyal, and Venkatesh Sundararaman. 2009. "Community Participation in Public Schools: Impact of Information Campaigns in Three Indian States." *Education Economics* 17 (3): 355–75.

Park, Hyunjoon, and Jere R. Behrman. 2010. "Causal Effects of Single-Sex Schools on College Attendance: Random Assignment in Korean High Schools." Working Paper. Population Studies Center, University of Pennsylvania, Philadelphia.

Pitt, Mark M., Mark R. Rosenzweig, and Donna M. Gibbons. 1993. "The Determinants and Consequences of the Placement of Government Programs in Indonesia." *World Bank Economic Review* 7 (3): 319–48.

Psacharopoulos, George, and Harry A. Patrinos. 2004. "Returns to Investment in Education: A Further Update." *Education Economics* 12 (2): 111–34.

Rivkin, Steven G. 2008. "Value Added Analysis and Education Policy." Calder Briefs. Center for Analysis of Longitudinal Data in Education Research, Washington, DC. http://www.caldercenter.org/UploadedPDF/411577_value-added_analysis.pdf.

Rosas, Ricardo, Miguel Nussbaum, Patricio Cumsille, Vladimir Marianov, Mónica Correa, Patricia Flores, Valeska Grau, Francisca Lagos, Ximena López, Verónica López, Patricio Rodriguez, and Marcela Salinas. 2003.

"Beyond Nintendo: Design and Assessment of Educational Video Games for First- and Second-Grade Students." *Computers and Education* 40 (1): 71–94.

Rothstein, Jesse. 2010. "Teacher Quality in Educational Production: Tracking, Decay, and Student Achievement." *Quarterly Journal of Economics* 125 (1): 175–214.

Tan, Jee-Peng, Julia Lane, and Gerard Lassibille. 1999. "Student Outcomes in Philippine Elementary Schools: An Evaluation of Four Experiments." *World Bank Economic Review* 13 (3): 493–508.

World Bank. 1998. "World Bank Development Indicators 1998." Washington, DC: World Bank.

———. 1999. "World Bank Development Indicators 1999." Washington, DC: World Bank.

———. 2001. "World Bank Development Report 2000/2001: Attacking Poverty." Washington, DC: World Bank.

———. 2002. "World Bank Development Indicators 2002." Washington, DC: World Bank.

———. 2008. "World Bank Development Indicators 2008." Washington, DC: World Bank.

———. 2012. "World Bank Development Indicators 2012." Washington, DC: World Bank.

3

Preschool Programs in Developing Countries

Jere R. Behrman (University of Pennsylvania)
Patrice Engle (California Polytechnic State University)
Lia Fernald (University of California at Berkeley)

3.1. Introduction

Many studies conclude that early childhood development (ECD) investments have high returns over the life cycle in developing as well as developed countries. ECD investments include the promotion of good health and nutrition, the provision of opportunities for learning, protection from risks such as violence or abandonment, and parenting support and early learning experiences provided by families, media, preschools, or community groups. These investments are often directly made by families, but other institutions such as preschool programs frequently have major roles. For many children in developing countries, however, ECD investments are less extensive than what many observers think that they should be. An estimated 200 million children under 5 years of age in developing countries do not reach their developmental potential (Grantham-McGregor et al. 2007). These children are substantially less able to take advantage of educational opportunities later in life and are less healthy, less productive, and poorer as adults.

Development in preschool-age children includes domains such as cognition, language, and behavior. Delays in children's development occur cumulatively and start as early as conception. These delays may be very costly or almost impossible to reverse during school years and adulthood. Thus Heckman (2006), Doyle et al. (2010), and others have argued that policies to improve human development are most cost-effective if they are high quality, begin as early as possible, and are targeted to the most disadvantaged groups. They also have argued that ECD investments are "win-win" in that antipoverty and productivity goals can be pursued together rather than face productivity-poverty alleviation tradeoffs found in many other policies. Because the impacts are greatest when targeted to the most disadvantaged groups rather than when targeted toward middle- and upper-income groups, reducing poverty and increasing productivity go hand-in-hand.

In this chapter we review what is known and what is not known about one type of ECD investment program, preschool programs for children 3–5 years. The category "preschool programs" refers to any kind of organized early learning group that meets regularly—at least two hours per week according to UNESCO (2011). Preschool programs generally also have a trained group leader or teacher, and can be considered "formal" or "informal," depending on the degree of training of the teacher, the physical site and materials, and the curriculum. Normally these programs are for children from age 3 until they enter first grade (usually when children are 6–8 years old), although in some countries preschool begins earlier. Other terms used for these programs include "kindergarten," "prekindergarten," "preprimary," or "ISCED-0," according to the International Standard Classification of Education (ISCED), revised in 1997 (UNESCO 2011). These preschool programs generally use an activity-based methodology, reflecting the different learning strategies of young children.

We note that these are only one of a number of types of ECD programs. Others include, for example, parenting programs focusing on children less than 3 years of age. We focus on preschool programs because they probably are most related among ECD investments to the formal educational programs that are the subject of the rest of this book and because more systematic studies evaluating preschool programs are available than for most other forms of ECD investments.

Enrollments in preschool programs have increased substantially in developing countries over the past several decades. Figure 3.1 shows the trend from 1970 through 2003, suggesting that over the long term preschool enrollment rates for children have increased monotonically in all

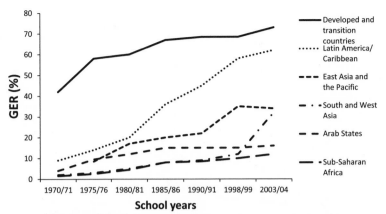

FIGURE 3.1 Regional trends in preprimary enrollment gross enrollment ratios, showing a strong increase in Latin America and the Caribbean.
Note: Figure is adapted from Global Marketing Report (UNESCO 2007, fig. 6.2). Data for East Asia and the Pacific are for developing countries only. Australia, Japan, and New Zealand are included as developed countries. In the original figure there is a broken line between 1990/91 and 1998/99 signifying a break in the data series due to a new classification.
Sources: 1970/71, 1975/76, 1980/81: UNESCO 1991; 1985/86: UNESCO 1998; 1990/91: UNESCO 2000; 1998/99, 2003/4: UIS database.

of the included world regions, though there is a fair amount of variance across regions in both the levels and the trends. By the end of the period covered, Latin America and the Caribbean and Central and Eastern Europe had enrollment rates of about 65%, and over the previous 30 years had increased enrollment more rapidly than North America and Western Europe. None of the other developing regions included, however, had enrollment rates over 45%, and enrollment rates for the Arab states and Sub-Saharan Africa were still less than 12% in 2003/4.

This monotonic trend is less clear in recent data. Figure 3.2 gives more detailed and recent preschool gross enrollment rates for children 3–5 years for selected years starting in 1990 through 2008 for major world regions. As figure 3.2 illustrates, there has been a slow increase in preschool attendance since 1990 in most regions, although in both Central and Eastern Europe, and Central Asia, the ending of the government-funded childcare system of the USSR resulted in rapid declines in the percent of children enrolled, which subsequently has begun to increase. Attendance rates have increased most rapidly in Latin America and the Caribbean and South and West Asia. Levels of enrollment are still low in Sub-Saharan Africa and the Arab states, although rising in Sub-Saharan Africa.

The averages do not reflect the considerable variance by familial socioeconomic status. As figure 3.3 shows with data from selected

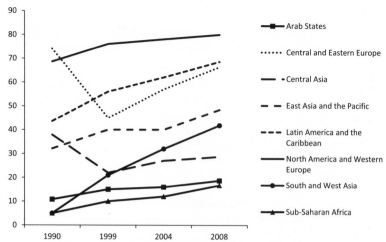

FIGURE 3.2 Weighted mean gross enrollment ratios of preschool and preprimary enrollment by year and by region.
Note: Child age is defined by country; ranges from 3 to 6.
Sources: UNESCO 2006, 2011.

countries, there are dramatic differences within countries in preschool attendance by income level. These differences appear to have increased in some countries over time. For eight countries, data are available on preschool attendance and income quintile for both the nationally representative 2000 UNICEF Multiple Indicator Cluster Surveys (MICS) samples and the 2005 MICS samples. Figure 3.3 shows the ratio of preschool attendance in the wealthiest and poorest quintile, and rates of preschool attendance overall. For example, in Laos, in 2000 a child in the highest quintile was 10 times as likely to attend preschool as a child in the lowest income quintile. By 2005 a child in the highest quintile was over 25 times more likely to attend preschool than a child in the lowest-income quintile.

Disparities of preschool attendance by family socioeconomic status differ over time among these eight countries. Disparities increased in Bosnia and Herzegovina, Cameroon, Cote d'Ivoire, and Laos, whereas they did not increase in Albania, Vietnam, or Sierra Leone. The countries with increasing disparities had low rates of preschool attendance initially and little change in rates of attendance over the period from 2000 to 2005. Rates of attendance increased considerably in both Albania and Vietnam. These increases must have occurred in both the wealthiest and the poorest quintiles since the disparity ratios were fairly consistent over time. On the other hand, in the countries showing the greatest increase in disparities, preschool attendance rates did not change and were low. It is likely that in these countries the increase in preschool attendance was greater among the wealthy and urban population, resulting in increasing disparities. Unless the government can introduce some pro-poor mechanisms and policies, it is likely that the wealthiest children will benefit more from interventions such as preschool, and the result will be a further increase in disparities in educational achievement.

Although there has been fairly extensive documentation of benefit/cost ratios for ECD programs in the United States, relatively little is

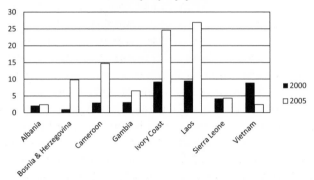

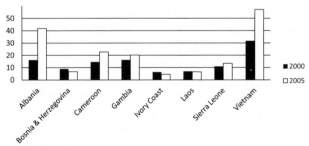

FIGURE 3.3 Distribution of preschool attendance by income levels and changes in preschool attendance rates for 3- and 4-year-olds from 2000 to 2005.
Note: Ratio of attendance in the highest within-country wealth quintile to attendance in the lowest-income quintile.
Source: UNICEF Multiple Indicator Cluster Surveys (MICS) 2 and 3 data; analyses by authors.

known with confidence about the economic justification for preschool or other ECD programs in developing countries. The economic justification must depend on the comparison of benefits and costs or the internal rates of return of each ECD program. Recent surveys in *Lancet*, including Engle et al. (2007, 2011), indicate that there are benefits of ECD programs for child development in developing countries, but the information is limited. Conclusions are based on relatively few studies usually with small samples in a relatively limited number of different policy and market contexts, primarily using cognitive or language outcome indicators and indicators focused on the early life-cycle stages (end of the preschool life-cycle stage, early in the primary school life-cycle stage) rather than longer-run effects over the life cycle or across generations. Analyses are limited by limited program quality information, small scale of operation, and little information on the first three years of life; few studies examine multiple impacts on overall benefits and even fewer studies use sufficiently rigorous designs to assess causality. Evidence on resource costs is scarce for developing countries, with most studies using data referring not to the total resource costs of interest but only to governmental expenditures that do not include private resource costs and may include transfers that should not be confused with resource costs.

This chapter is organized as follows. Section 3.2 considers possible benefits of preschool programs, first by presenting a life-cycle framework for understanding the estimation issues and then summarizing what is known about preschool program impacts from our review of recent studies; we focus on examining what is known about one of the most important predictors of outcomes, the quality of preschool program services. Section 3.3 discusses resource costs related to such programs. Section 3.4 summarizes the gaps in our knowledge and how we should move forward with regard to integrated data collection and analysis in order to better evaluate what works best regarding preschool program investments in developing countries.

The results of this survey of evidence on preschool programs reinforce at least four of the general themes discussed by Glewwe, Hanushek, Humpage, and Ravina in chapter 2. First, education probably increases economic growth and can help reduce inequalities; the twist in the emphasis of our chapter is that education includes preschool education, not just K-12 that is emphasized in the rest of this volume. Second, as for K-12, the *quality* of preschool programs in terms of infrastructure, staff, and curriculum is likely to be important but the empirical results are far from unambiguous. Third, research to date on the quality of preschools, as for K-12, is focused on basic school and teacher characteristics; the way schools are organized and the nature of incentives, however, may matter more, suggesting that future research should focus on these questions. Fourth, local conditions and contexts are likely to be important, with the implications that systematic assessments of programs in particular contexts are likely to have high rates of return even if similar programs have been evaluated in other contexts. Thus, it is likely to be very challenging to provide guidance about "best practices" that can be applied in many contexts without the need for careful consideration of the context and monitoring and assessment of new applications (see Dhaliwal, Duflo, Glennerster, and Tulloch in chapter 8).

3.2. Benefits of Preschool Programs and Other ECD Investments

3.2.1. Framework for Considering Economic Benefits of Preschool Programs and Other ECD Investments. To examine the economic benefits from investments in ECD, including preschool programs, we consider a life-cycle framework, with six life-cycle stages (s): prenatal $(s = 0)$, early childhood (1), late childhood (2), adolescence (3), adulthood (4), and old age (5). ECD investments focus on early childhood, typically considered to be from conception to about 5–6 years, and preschool programs, the focus for this chapter, are primarily for children from 3–5 years of age. We conceptualize children as starting early childhood with a vector of genetic and environmental endowments or "inputs" (I).[1] Conditional on these endowments, ECD is directly affected by investments in children related to factors such as the healthcare system, childcare options, preschool and school systems, markets, and the familial environment. Some of these factors are affected by public policy decisions (P), such as the accessibility and quality of preschool programs. Others reflect familial decisions (F), such as the nature and extent of stimulation and nutrition in the home environment and to what extent the child is exposed to the healthcare system and preschool programs, which in turn reflects responses by caregivers (often parents) to policies (P) and markets (M), given family resources (R), parameters for parental preferences and bargaining rules within the family and among kin (W), parameters for the technological and biological production functions (T) that determine the outcomes of the early childhood life-cycle stage (Y) conditional on the inputs at the start of the stage and the investments in the child during the stage, and a stochastic term related to shocks (U), such as variations in the disease environment in which the family lives.

Economic modeling suggests that parents (or other caregivers) will make these investment decisions in part based on the resources that they have, the prices and policies that they face, and the motives that they have for investing in their children (including altruism and expected possible future benefits, such as old-age support from the children). Because these motives are likely to be forward-looking, the expected impacts of these decisions on outcomes over the child's life and the expected future school, work, and other conditions that may affect the value of these impacts all enter into the parental decisions about investment in ECD. Of course the parents make many decisions that affect many dimensions of ECD, but for simplicity we aggregate these dimensions of interest into three outcomes at the end of the early childhood life-cycle stage (**Y**): (1) cognitive and language skills, (2) socioemotional skills, and (3) health and nutritional status. And, at least for some purposes, we assume that these three composite outcomes are sufficient statistics for all impacts of early childhood over all stages of later life. In such a case the inputs into the next life-cycle stage are these three outcomes at the end of the early childhood life-cycle stage. (If these three outcomes do not incorporate all the outcomes at the end of the early childhood life-cycle stage, other factors such as the genetic and environmental endowments also may be inputs into later stages.)

While some studies attempt to estimate the production technologies that produce outcomes at the end of the early childhood life-cycle stage, most studies estimate some variant of dynamic decision rules for the outcomes of early childhood life-cycle stage, so we focus on these relations:

(1) $$\mathbf{Y}_s = f(\mathbf{P}_s, \mathbf{M}_s, \mathbf{R}_s, \mathbf{W}_s, \mathbf{T}_s, \mathbf{I}_s, \mathbf{U}_s),$$

where all the variables are the vectors defined above for the sth life-cycle stage (here, the early childhood life-cycle stage with $s = 1$), most of the right-side vectors include not only values for the sth stage but also expected values for all future life-cycle stages if parents are forward-looking, and $\mathbf{I}_s$ is the vector of inputs at the start of this life-cycle stage that for the early childhood life-cycle stage includes genetic and environmental endowments.

Relation (1) with $s = 2$, indicating the late-childhood life-cycle stage, also can represent the outcomes of this next life-cycle stage that come from the dynamic decision rules for the late-childhood life-cycle stage, with the inputs for the late-childhood life-cycle stage the outcomes from the early childhood life-cycle stage.[2] The late-childhood life-cycle stage, therefore, starts with the "inputs" of (1) cognitive skills, (2) socioemotional skills, and (3) health and nutritional status at the end of the early childhood life cycle. As during early childhood, there are a number of policy-related, market, and familial factors that, conditional on these inputs, affect the "outcomes" of this stage. These factors may interact with the "inputs" of this stage (the "outcomes" of the previous stage with $I_s = Y_{s-1}$) so that there are dynamic complementarities of the types emphasized, for example, by Cunha et al. (2006) and Cunha and Heckman (2007, 2008). The outcomes of this stage, in turn are the inputs into the next stage, and so on through the life course (and possibly across generations). The outcomes of various stages may include not only the three noted above, but also outcomes such as labor-force participation, wage earnings, marriage-market outcomes involvement in crime and violence, and parenting of the next generation.

It is possible to substitute into the relations for the outcomes of each later life-cycle stage all the links back to the early childhood life-cycle stage that are transmitted across stages by the inputs into any particular stage being the outcomes of the previous stage (since $I_s = Y_{s-1}$). Such substitution permits explicit expression of how the outcomes in each later life-cycle stage relate to factors such as policies, market, and family resources that determined the outcomes in the early childhood life-cycle stage. The vector variables on the right side of these relations also include the expectations held in each stage for future stages and the realizations in each intervening life-cycle stage, so * is used to reflect that the right-side variables include all these expectations and realizations:

(2) $$Y_s = h(P_1, M_1, R_1, W_1, T_1, U_1, P_s^{\star}, M_s^{\star}, R_s^{\star}, W_s^{\star}, T_s^{\star}, U_s^{\star})$$

The partial derivative of relation (2) with respect to the component of P_1 that refers to whether a child attended a preschool program (or the quality of the program), for example, gives the impact of that program on outcomes in the sth subsequent life-cycle stage. To assess the total benefits of interventions or other decisions that affect ECD, a weighted average of all these possible relevant impacts over the life course across all the subsequent life-cycle stages and across generations should be considered. The benefits should include all the private effects on the child being considered and, from a social perspective, any broader "spillover" external effects.

This framework suggests that it is quite challenging to access the benefits of ECD or of interventions to enhance ECD such as preschool programs for a number of reasons that are elucidated in the following points.

3.2.1.1. Econometric Issues. There are a set of econometric issues that make estimation of program impacts difficult.

1. Decisions to invest in preschool programs or other dimensions of ECD are behavioral decisions that parents or other caregivers make in

response to a number of factors, some important ones, which are likely not to be observed by analysts, such as innate abilities, innate health, and current or expected prices that directly or indirectly affect child development. If these unobserved factors have direct effects on outcomes later in the life cycle in addition to any impact through the observed outcomes at the end of the early childhood life-cycle stage (a possibility that is assumed away for simplicity for the discussion above), it may be difficult to identify confidently the impacts of the investments in components of ECD versus the impacts of these unobserved factors.

2. To obtain estimates of the benefits of an intervention in the early childhood life-cycle stage (such as being sent to a preschool program) on outcomes, there must be control for endogenous program placement (Rosenzweig and Wolpin 1986). As is well known, endogenous program placement may bias estimates of program impact in either direction depending on the motive for the program placement and the correlation between program placement and unobserved (to the analyst) characteristics that influence program placement. The bias may be downward, for example, if the placement of public programs is pro-poor in ways that are not observed in the data and those unobserved characteristics in themselves mean that poor children will perform less well than comparison children with regard to outcomes such as cognitive or language skills, socioemotional skills, and health and nutritional status. On the other hand, if program placement favors those who are better off in unobserved ways, for example, because they have more political influence, the bias in estimated program effects that do not control for endogenous program placement is likely to be upwards.

3. To obtain unbiased estimates of the benefits of an intervention in the early childhood life-cycle stage on longer-run outcomes, in addition to controlling for unobserved endowments that might have direct impacts on outcomes later in the life cycle and for unobserved factors that may affect program placement, it is necessary to control for all the elements in the variables on the right side of (2). For example, if an observed investment in children in their early childhood life-cycle stage is more likely, whether because of household decisions or public policies, to occur in contexts in which unobserved expected labor market returns to the investments (in the vector M^*) are higher and there are complementary unobserved investments (e.g., more time spent in parental-home stimulation in the evenings for children who are enrolled in preschool programs, perhaps in response to the same expectations about future labor-market returns), then standard estimates of the impacts of the investment will be biased upwards because they will capture

the effects of the unobserved complementary investment induced by the unobserved expected labor market returns in addition to the direct effects of the intervention. This bias could also be downward, for example, if the unobserved investments are substitutes rather than complements for the observed investment.

4. The effects of investments in the early childhood life-cycle stage may be heterogeneous depending on characteristics of market, cultural and policy contexts, individual children or their families (e.g., Carneiro, Hansen, and Heckman 2003). That is, there may be interactions between investments and such contextual characteristics in relations (1) and (2), possibly because of interactions in the underlying production functions or perhaps because of heterogeneous impacts of markets and policies because families vary in their access to market and policies. Possible heterogeneous impacts depending on market, cultural, and policy contexts mean that estimates from one context, even if very good estimates for that context, should not be blithely assumed to hold for other contexts. Markets may differ importantly with regard to expected labor market outcomes, access to capital and insurance for human resource investments, and information. Policies may differ importantly with regard to general social support or particular provision and subsidization of goods and services particularly germane to preschool programs or other forms of investment in ECD. And within a particular context, impacts may vary considerably depending on individual and family backgrounds, which typically vary substantially even among poor households.

3.2.1.2. Multiple Impacts over the Life Cycle. The multiplicity of the impacts and the long-run nature of many of the relevant impacts pose a set of problems.

1. To evaluate the total benefits, decisions have to be made regarding what are the relevant outcomes of interest and what are intermediate or mediating channels. For example, to what extent are cognitive skills at the end of the early childhood stage an outcome of interest in itself versus a channel through which ECD investments such as preschool programs affect schooling success and adult productivities in labor markets and home activities? To the extent that these cognitive skills at the end of the early childhood stage are mediating channels, it would be double-counting to include among the benefits of ECD the benefits of both the impact on cognitive skills at the end of the early life stage *and* changes in adult productivities.

2. The outcomes of interest vary considerably in kind, from labor-market outcomes to less crime and violent behaviors to better health and

reduced mortality. They also vary with regard to whom is directly affected. For example, the discussion to this point focuses on the impacts on the children in whom preschool or other ECD investments are made. But there may be important effects on others, such as the mothers or other caregivers who may be able to divert time from child care to other uses including economic production and leisure. Or there may be gains to training the preschool staff. But to estimate the overall benefits or to be able to compare benefits with costs requires some weights or "prices" to combine the various impacts. For some possible impacts, such as increased wages in labor markets, valuing the impacts in monetary terms is relatively easy. But for other impacts, such as averting mortality and improving social relations, such valuations are difficult and controversial. For instance, the value of averted mortality at times is empirically measured by the cheapest alternative means of averting mortality and at times by what income-mortality risks adults accept in their occupational choices. The resulting range in the values of averted mortality is enormous.[3]

3. As is reflected in relation (2), to obtain direct estimates of the benefits of an intervention in the early childhood life-cycle stage on outcomes in later life-cycle stages requires data over long stretches of the life cycle (ideally, all of it). Prospective data over long stretches of the life cycle beginning in the early childhood life-cycle stage are rare, though some such data sets exist (e.g., the five Consortium of Health Oriented Research in Transitioning Societies [COHORTS] countries –Brazil, Guatemala, India, Philippines, South Africa have coverage for fairly long periods of time related to early life nutrition, though not much information on stimulation) and in some other cases recall data may help fill in some of the gaps though with the usual limitations of recall data. But even if data do exist for, say, five or six decades of individuals' lives and causal estimates of impacts can be made, there is somewhat of a problem in interpreting inferences made from these data for designing policies today. This is the case because of possible interactions with, say, a preschool program of interest and the market and policy context in which investments in individuals now in their forties were when they were in the early life-cycle stage and since the time they were in the early life-cycle stage (the time series analogue to the cross-sectional discussion in the fourth point). The changes in contexts means that even if longitudinal data are available in some cases with which to make inferences about long-term impacts of such early life investments, the implications for the different contexts of the twenty-first century need to be made with careful efforts to adjust for the changing contexts. Analyses in studies such as Hoddinott et

al. (2008), Behrman et al. (2009), and Maluccio et al. (2009) three to four decades later of the Guatemalan INCAP data based on nutritional supplementation in 1969–77, for example, provide evidence of long-run effects of that supplementation in the contexts in which children passed from the early childhood life-cycle stage to the adult life-cycle stage. But care must be taken in making inferences from such studies about interventions for current children in the early childhood life-cycle stage in the second decade of the twenty-first century because contexts now and in the future are likely different in important respects from those experienced three to four decades ago by the children in these studies.

The primary alternative to using the limited longitudinal data over long segments of individuals' life cycles to estimate the longer-run benefits of investments in the early childhood life-cycle stage is to estimate impacts of early childhood investments on some intermediate outcomes such as cognitive and language skills, socioemotional skills, and health and nutritional status at the end of the early childhood life-cycle stage and then to link those outcomes with other estimates of the relations between such intermediate outcomes and longer-run outcomes from other data sources. For this strategy to be effective, however, some strong assumptions are necessary for these linkages, including that the observed input variables for a given stage include all the relevant variables from previous stages. Moreover, assumptions still have to be made that relations for later life-cycle stages based on past data will hold in the future when the children grow into those stages despite changing contexts in the future.

4. Impacts of ECD investments such as preschool programs are posited to occur over many years in subsequent life-cycle stages in relations such as (2). If there is a return to using resources for investments other than investing in children during their early childhood life-cycle stage, then 1,000 rupees received now is more valuable than 1,000 rupees received, say, in 40 years when the child becomes a prime-age adult because in the intervening decades the rupees received earlier can be reinvested. Therefore it is desirable to calculate the present discounted value (PDV) of investment impacts that occur with some lags into the future. This may affect the value of these investments considerably. For instance, the PDV of receiving 1,000 rupees in 40 years is 307 rupees today if the discount rate is 3%, 97 rupees if it is 6%, and only 22 rupees if it is 10%. However, there is some variance in what are assumed to be the appropriate discount rates, which is unfortunate because for the outcomes later in the life cycle the choice of discount rates is likely to affect substantially the PDV of the benefits.

5. Yet another factor is that obtaining these returns depends on survival, adjusting for which further reduces their PDVs. For example, based on the United Nations Population Division for India, about 91% of children survive to age 10, 83% to age 40, and 66% to age 60. Both discounting and survival are relevant, of course, not only for developments over one's own life cycle, but also for parenting the next generation.

3.2.1.3. Efficiency as Well as Distributional Motives for Policy Guidance.

The ECD literature focuses for the most part on the distributional motive for policy in the form in particular of how ECD-related investments can reduce poverty (or, perhaps, inequality) in the next generation of adults. But for the purpose of guiding policies, it would be desirable to have estimates of the social benefits of ECD investments that include, for example, the spillover effects (whether negative or positive) on others (Knowles and Behrman 2005). This is the case because one major motive for policy interventions, the "efficiency motive," comes into play if there is a differential between the private and the social rates of return, a difference that may arise because of differences between the private and the social benefits.[4] This is a major motive for policy because if differentials exist between the private and the social rates of return to an action, it would be possible to make everyone better off with the same resources and the same technology by reallocations. Or, to make the same point in a different way, if the private incentives are identical to the social incentives, there is no efficiency motive for changing policies to try to change private behaviors (though there may be distributional motives such as reducing poverty).

Because of the econometric issues noted in 3.2.1.1 above, the disturbance term in relation (2) is likely to contain unobserved components that are correlated with investments in the early childhood life-cycle stages, which is likely to cause biases in the estimates of the impact of such investments if this correlation is not broken. Random controlled trials (RCTs) provide one method, often considered to be the "gold standard," of breaking such correlations. Under stronger assumptions econometric methods can be used to break such correlations and therefore to identify causal impacts of investments in the early childhood life-cycle stage on outcomes during that stage or later. These methods include difference-in-difference estimates that compare the changes in children exposed to a "treatment" (investment) with those not exposed, instrumental variable estimates that purge the observed ECD indicators of the components that are correlated with the unobserved variables, propensity score–matching estimators that compare children who received a treatment with children who did not receive the treatment but who in terms of the probability of receiving the treatment based on observed characteristics are comparable, and regression-discontinuity estimators that compare children right below with those right above some eligibility threshold for treatment. Even under the assumptions necessary for these various methods to obtain unbiased estimates of the impact of these investments, such approaches (including RCTs) often only provide "black-box" estimates of the impacts of the investment (or program) actually undertaken. To investigate what happens with different investments or programs with such methods requires obtaining data when the alternatives investments or programs are undertaken. Structural models of the underlying behaviors, in contrast, under the stronger assumptions that may be required to estimate them, permit the investigation of counterfactual policies (Todd and Wolpin [2006] provide an example for schooling in a developing country context). RCTs may help efforts to look inside the black box through structural estimates by providing instruments to help identify the impact of one endogenous variable (e.g., enrollment in a preschool program) on another (e.g., development of cognitive skills or self-regulation).

The available empirical estimates of the impacts of investments in ECD, even if they do deal with the econometric issues, generally do not deal well with the multiplicity of impacts over the life cycle and with the efficiency motive for policy. Instead they tend to focus on one or a few impacts usually for some relatively small age duration, generally early in the life cycle. Nevertheless, these estimates may be informative about some possibly key building blocks for obtaining estimates of the overall benefits of investing in ECD.

Finally, it should be noted that the points discussed here in assessing the benefits for investments in the early childhood life-cycle stage are generally parallel to those for investing in education (or other human resources such as health and nutrition) in later life-cycle stages, though for investments in later life-cycle stages there may be additional complications because of the endogenous inputs from the earlier stages, including the early childhood life-cycle stage. In practice, in assessing the impacts of education in subsequent life-cycle stages such as in the form of schooling, often the effects of investments in the early childhood life-cycle stage are not incorporated into the analysis. If, as seems plausible within life-cycle frameworks such as those discussed in this section, investments in the early childhood life-cycle stage are correlated with subsequent investments, this practice may lead to misleading attribution to later investments, such as in schooling, some of the effects of the preschool investments. A study from Guatemala of an adult cognitive-skills production function, for example, reports that ignoring the preschool investments and the endogeneity of schooling choices together results in estimates of schooling impacts that are twice as high or more than would be obtained with treatment of investments in all life-cycle stages as endogenous and including preschool as well as school-age investments (Behrman et al. 2008).

3.2.2. Recent Evidence on ECD Impacts.

Engle et al. (2007, 2011) provide two recent reviews of ECD program impacts in developing countries. The studies included in these reviews had to (1) relate to programs that promote child development through components of psychosocial support such as stimulation, responsive interaction, early education, or other social investments, often in combination with health, nutritional, social safety net, or educational interventions;[5] (2) exist since 1990; (3) include what Engle et al. (2007, 2011) rated has adequate comparison groups to permit causal inferences; and (4) focus on children 0–6 years old and to report cognitive, language, social-emotional, or mental health outcomes (though analyses examining related outcomes, such as parent caregiving or preschool attendance, were also included). Engle et al. (2007) identify 20 studies that met these criteria and Engle et al. (2011) identify 42 additional studies that met these criteria on a variety of ECD programs, not just preschool. Most of these studies are of programs that are directed considerably or even exclusively to children from disadvantaged backgrounds, particularly with regard to poverty, so in a gross sense they deal with the fourth point in section 3.2.1.1, "Econometric Issues" (above), of heterogeneous impacts by focusing on children from poor backgrounds.

Despite the thorough search underlying these reviews, fairly few studies permit even relatively crude comparisons among studies because of the range of interventions considered and varying approaches to estimation (e.g., what assumptions are necessary for the estimation approach used, what controls are included). If all the studies using different measures for cognitive skills are considered together, there are 8 studies for parenting/family strengthening programs (often part of primary health care or other programs) and 14 studies for organized early childhood learning centers (e.g., preschools) for which effect sizes (calculated using standard techniques) are presented.[6] Table 3.1 gives the medians and the ranges for the effect sizes on cognitive skills from these studies. For both parenting and center programs, the ranges of estimated effect sizes

Table 3.1 Impacts of ECD programs in developing countries

	Cognitive skills effect sizes		
	Median	Range	Number of Studies
Center-based preschool and day care	0.33	0.06 to 1.15	14
Parent and parent-child interactions	0.28	−0.05 to 0.80	8

Sources: Compiled from Engle et al. 2007, 2011.

are fairly large, but for both type of programs the median estimates are about 0.30, which is a considerable effect size.[7]

These estimates are promising but—within the framework above—have a number of limitations. *First*, these estimates refer to but one of the major aggregate outcomes of the early childhood stage (cognitive development) discussed in section 3.2.1, though perhaps the most predictive of the three aggregate outcomes considered. *Second*, they are mostly for outcomes for children still in the early childhood life-cycle stage or not far beyond that stage. Therefore they provide very little direct information about the effects on longer-run subsequent outcomes of interest—for example, schooling success, labor market outcomes, adult social behaviors—in the subsequent life-cycle stages. *Third*, though they are focused on disadvantaged children, the summaries in the *Lancet* articles do not report possible heterogeneous impacts among these families. *Fourth*, the estimates are conditional on the relatively few particular resource, market, and policy contexts considered, and may not generalize to other contexts with different markets, policies, resources, cultures, and institutions. The impacts for a context in which most women are active in labor markets, for example, may be much different than for a context in which almost no women participate in the labor market. *Fifth*, the estimates as summarized in these two *Lancet* articles generally do not provide much information about the dependence of the program impacts on the ages when children enroll, the duration of exposure, or interactions between program characteristics and family background, though a few studies that are included find these to be important factors (e.g., Armecin et al. 2006; Behrman, Cheng, and Todd 2004; Ghuman et al. 2005; Noboa-Hidalgo and Urzúa 2012; Urzúa and Veramendi 2010).

Table 3.2 summarizes conclusions on program effectiveness from the *Lancet* reviews according to the strength of the evidence as perceived by the *Lancet* articles' authors: moderately high, moderate, or low. The two moderately high conclusions were that preschool programs can be effective, and that higher-quality programs, as defined in each study, are

Table 3.2 Conclusions on levels of knowledge regarding preschool programs for developing countries

Level of knowledge	Intervention (preschool) type or characteristics	Findings
Moderately high	Preschool programs, both formal and nonformal	Exposure to preschool programs can result in improved child development, and can have long-term effects on child development and school performance.
	Quality improvement in curriculum, training of staff, and program delivery in preschool programs	Higher quality results in improved outcomes for children.
Moderate	Formal vs. informal preschool	Generally formal has stronger results but some informal programs are also found to have impacts.
	Programs targeted at most disadvantaged	Some evidence for greater effects on poorest children; other studies show effects for all children.
	Cost of preschool compared to benefits	Ratio appears to be positive but relatively few studies and evidence from small-scale studies.
	Long-term effects of preschool on early adulthood outcomes	Data from only very few studies.
Low	Number of years of preschool	Possible more effects in first year; depends on quality, degree to which program changes with child age.
	Number of hours per week of exposure by child age (can be too much)	No data from developing countries.
	Age at which child begins to attend preschool (3, 4, or preprimary)	Some evidence for greater impact for longer duration or earlier initiation for ECD programs but little evidence for younger children for daycare.
	Importance of having a culturally relevant curriculum	Often stated but little experimental evidence.
	How to integrate preschool with health and nutrition programs	Some correlation but little causal data.
	How to scale up programs and maintain quality	Unclear—appears to depend on each situation.
	Value of preschool for children with disabilities or special needs (e.g., HIV, malnutrition)	Almost no studies identified.

Sources: Engle et al. 2007, 2011

associated with better outcomes for children, primarily cognitive but also socioemotional. The reviews of studies in these *Lancet* articles also suggest at a "moderate" level of confidence that effects are larger for children who are poorer, and for programs that are formal rather than community-based. Also of "moderate" confidence is that benefits are greater than costs; there are several studies showing benefit-to-cost ratios that are within the 4-to-1 range. The number of questions with no clear answers, and therefore "low" evidence, ranges from how many years of preschool continue to be effective, at what age children should enter preschool, and how to integrate preschool programs with health and nutrition interventions.

We now consider in more depth the evidence about preschool program characteristics or program "quality." Table 3.3, at the end of this chapter, provides considerable additional detail on a subset of the studies covered in the *Lancet* reviews for which there is some information on the impact of program characteristics and on an additional set of studies that are not covered in those reviews. In the text below, we do not review studies that compare children who attend with those who do not attend preschool. Here, we are focusing on the population of children attending preschool, and examining what elements of preschool quality are associated with child development. As described below, there are three types of studies examining quality: (1) observational studies correlating variables relating to quality with child- or classroom-level outcomes; (2) intervention studies with a more comprehensive approach to educational improvement (e.g., facilities, curriculum, training); (3) intervention studies, usually focusing on improving one specific component of educational quality.

3.2.2.1. Observational Studies Examining Preschool Quality. The largest observational study addressing preschool quality included data from 10 developed and developing countries (Finland, Greece, Hong Kong, Indonesia, Ireland, Italy, Poland, Spain, Thailand, and the United States), and looked at several process and structural variables relating to preschool quality and how those variables related to child outcomes at age 7 (Montie et al. 2006). The authors found that in all countries, better language and cognitive performance at school age were associated with having had a greater number of free-choice activities during preschool (in contrast with activities mandated by the teacher), having had a better educated teacher, having had less time in whole group activities and more time in smaller groups, and having had a greater number and variety of materials for the children to use in the classroom. One other smaller study in Bangladesh also correlated preschool qualities with child outcomes and found that preschool quality measures were significantly associated with verbal and nonverbal reasoning and school readiness (Aboud 2006). A large, cluster-randomized study conducted in Chile found that improving quality in teachers and teachers' aides—through intensive training in instructional strategies and continuous coaching—resulted in significant improvements in classroom-level

outcomes (Yoshikawa et al., under review); direct measures of child development outcomes were not included in the analysis. The domains that improved in the intervention classrooms included emotional and instructional support and classroom organization.

3.2.2.2. Interventions with a Comprehensive Approach to Educational Improvement.

Some quality interventions have attempted to change several aspects of preschool quality known to be associated with improvements in child outcomes, including facility quality, teacher training and/or background and experience, curriculum and/or program used in the classroom, teaching style, materials such as books, and access to media such as radio or television. With all the studies testing integrated programs with many components, it is impossible to determine which part of the program was responsible for the beneficial effects.

For example, a series of papers examining preschool quality in Bangladesh describe a multifaceted intervention (the "Succeed" program), which included improving teacher-led and child-initiated activities, improving materials such as reading books and exercise books for the children, training for teachers to engage children in conversations during play, adding increased sophistication and structure in the mathematics curriculum, emphasizing open discussion after story reading rather than rote learning, and exposing children to Sisimpur (*Sesame Street*) in the preschools (Aboud et al. 2008; Aboud and Hossain 2011). Findings were that the quality of the preschool math program in particular had the greatest effect on child development outcomes, whereas the quality of the language and literacy programs did not affect the outcomes that were measured (when controlling for mother's education). In a related preschool quality improvement intervention in Bangladesh, which focused more explicitly on promoting language and literacy, intervention children performed better on nonverbal reasoning and school readiness, but not on vocabulary (Moore et al. 2008).

In several countries—Kenya, Zanzibar, Uganda—the Madrasa preschools have been used as a model for high-quality preschools. In the Madrasa model, the curriculum focuses on active child learning and uses materials and content combining religious with secular education. The materials used are low-cost and widely, locally available. Findings from a study comparing children in the Madrasa preschools with preschools offering standard care (teacher-directed and didactic) found higher scores in the Madrasa programs, with a suggestion that the first year and a half in Madrasa preschools result in larger changes than the second or third years (Malmberg et al. 2011). An earlier study of the same preschools found that the children in the Madrasa preschools performed better on four cognitive subtests of the British Ability Scales and on the African Child Intelligence Test (Mwaura et al. 2008) than children in the standard preschools.

Studies comparing higher and lower quality of preschools in China (Rao et al. 2012a) found that children in higher-quality preschools performed better on tests of school readiness and achievement than comparison children. In Peru children in schools with formally educated, paid teachers and higher-quality materials and sites were compared with children of volunteer, untrained teachers who worked in community settings with less-adequate materials. Children who had the higher-quality teachers performed better on math and language scales (Cueto and Diaz 1999) and were more likely to attend school in the correct age for their grade in a longer-term follow-up (Diaz 2006). Similarly, another study in Cambodia explicitly tested children in "formal" (community-based) compared with "informal" (home-based) settings, and found that children in formal preschools performed better in terms of tests of child assessment (Rao et al. 2012b).

Many studies described above report only on a one- or two-year follow-up period. Two studies, however, have reported much longer follow-up periods. One analysis of an integrated two-year preschool program took place in Mauritius, where an enrichment program contained elements relating to nutrition, education, and physical exercise (Raine et al. 2003). In a 17-year follow-up of the program, participants were less likely to have personality disorders (specifically schizotypal) or antisocial behavior. The second example is for the Turkish Early Enrichment Project (TEEP) that has been followed up for two decades (Kagitcibasi et al. 2001, 2009). In the higher-quality preschool model tested in Turkey, the program had better child/teacher ratios, a clear program of daily activities, and higher-quality materials available. In the lower-quality centers, there was no emphasis on play or creative activities, and it was considered to be more focused on "custodial" care. As a consequence of the TEEP program, a higher percentage of children attended college.

Most of the integrated preschool programs varied greatly in terms of length of intervention, but without a strong evident correlation between length of a child's participation in the program and the child's outcomes. For example, in Cambodia, the SRP program (School Readiness Program) was a very intensive two-month program that included a 14-day teacher training program, teacher support, infrastructure support, and curriculum support (Nonoyama-Tarumi and Bredenberg 2009). In spite of the short length of the program, children enrolled in the intervention performed better on tests of school readiness and school achievement in the one-year follow-up assessment.

3.2.2.3. Quality Interventions in One Specific Educational Domain.

The programs described in this next section differ from the earlier group in that a single component of educational quality was changed rather than changing several components simultaneously. A novel intervention in Jamaica used the "Incredible Years" Teacher Training program, for example, which involved seven full-day teacher workshops (once per month) in which teachers were trained with skills for classroom engagement, effective classroom management, and strategies to promote socioemotional development (Baker-Henningham et al. 2009). This program was then supplemented by an additional 14 child lessons and a set of materials, including hand puppets and visual aids. In comparison with children in the two comparison preschools that received no intervention, children in the three intervention preschools had better behavior and were rated as having higher "interest" and "enthusiasm." Behavior in teachers also improved: there was an increase in the amount of time promoting social and emotional skills.

An intensive four-week reading program was tested with preschoolers in Bangladesh. Teachers in the intervention group were taught to use open-ended questions and to introduce new words to attempt to teach preschoolers to express themselves better. The intervention group showed a larger expressive vocabulary as a consequence of the program (Opel et al. 2009). Similarly, low-income children in Costa Rica who were exposed to a literacy intervention performed better at follow-up than children who had not been exposed to the program (Rolla San Francisco et al. 2006). The groups who performed best had either tutoring or three interventions combined: tutoring, classroom activities, and work with families. Improved materials alone had no impact.

The use of media has also been tested as a specific quality-improvement measure. For example, in Zanzibar, an interactive radio intervention (RISE) was used in conjunction with an existing preschool curriculum, and provided children with 30-minute broadcasts of formal curriculum with songs, games, stories, and other embedded activities (Morris et al. 2009). Exposure to the radio program had a significant effect on topic area knowledge in the language Kiswahili (Swahili) but not in the other two areas that were measured.

In sum, both comprehensive educational approaches and component-specific approaches to educational improvement have been shown to have an effect on child outcomes, particularly in cognitive development. The value of involving families in improving preschool outcomes is not yet clear and has not been explicitly tested. The most successful interventions in preschools used more child-centered methods adapted to the learning styles of young children, included teacher training and clearly defined interventions. None of these studies, however, included an assessment of the cost of the quality improvement. More work needs to be done to determine the most cost-effective methods for improving preschool quality and the benefit-to-cost ratios of these improvements.

3.3. Costs of ECD Investments and Benefit-Cost Ratios

Estimates of impacts alone, or even the weighted average of impacts to obtain "benefits" in the sense that the term is used in section 3.2 (and how it is used in benefit-cost analysis), do not provide enough information to judge whether programs are desirable or not, given that resources always have alternative uses. Quite aside from the challenges noted in estimating benefits in section 3.2.1, there is the separate challenge of measuring the resource costs of the programs or other investments.

To evaluate fully ECD interventions, such as preschool programs, and to compare them with alternative uses of public resources, it is necessary to also have estimates of resource costs in order to be able to calculate benefit/cost ratios or internal rates of return. We emphasize that the correct cost concept refers to the real resources that society uses for an intervention, whether public or private resources or distortions introduced by taxes and other means of financing public expenditures. The public real-resource costs include the time of public employees and goods and services that have alternative uses, but *not* pure transfers that only redistribute purchasing power among members of society. For this reason the public budgetary costs do *not* necessarily represent the public real-resource costs (to say nothing of the total real-resource costs) because transfers may be important components of public expenditures—with many conditional cash-transfer programs providing important examples. In addition to the public-resource costs, the private-resource costs may be considerable if, for example, mothers have to spend considerable time to assure that their children attend centers or to participate in such programs. The distortion costs reflect the impacts of changed incentives due, for example, to taxes on labor efforts and may be considerable—for example, some estimates suggest a quarter of public sector expenditures or more (Harberger 1997). For all of these reasons, studies that compare governmental budgetary costs across interventions are not comparing real resource costs and may be fundamentally misleading about the relative real resource costs across interventions.

We also note that, within the framework presented in section 3.2.1, most of the real resource costs of ECD interventions occur in early childhood, not with lags of many years as for many of the impacts of interest for such interventions. Therefore the importance of discounting and adjusting for child survival are likely to be much less on the cost side than on the benefit side for ECD interventions. But they are not likely to be entirely absent. If ECD interventions result in subsequent increased schooling or training, for example, there are likely to be associated increased real resource costs in adolescence or adulthood for those activities. And, again, these are likely to include public-sector (in the form of teacher time and other school inputs), private (in the form of the opportunity costs of delayed labor force entry due to more schooling), and distortion costs (to raise the public funds for the additional public schooling expenditures).

Given that to calculate benefit-cost ratios or internal rates of return the real resource costs are equally important as the benefits, it might seem that there would be more-or-less equal efforts to assemble information on real resource costs for ECD interventions throughout the developing world as for ECD impacts. But that is not the case. In sharp contrast to the reviews of impacts in Engle et al. (2007, 2011) and elsewhere, we are unaware of any such surveys of real resource costs of individual ECD interventions in developing countries. Engle et al. (2011), however, provide some suggestive estimates based on aggregate data of the potential gains to be obtained based on earning-schooling relations from partially closing the gap between preschool participation rates for children from families in the top quintile of the income distribution and other children in each of 73 developing countries. Subject to caveats that they discuss, these imply benefit-to-cost ratios generally well above one, in the range of 14.3–17.6 for a 3% discount rate and in the range of 6.4–7.8 for a 6% discount rate. These are suggestive of significant potentially large gains, but are fairly far removed from the estimates for specific ECD interventions or even preschool intervention in particular in specific contexts in developing countries that would be valuable for better policy guidance.

3.4. What Do We Need to Know?

In this chapter we have tried to present an economic perspective on one type of ECD programs in developing countries, preschool for children 3–5, discuss the challenges in evaluating benefits and costs from these programs, and summarize the limited empirical evidence that currently is available to inform their benefits and costs and what preschool policies should be followed in various contexts. There is some systematic evidence that preschool programs in developing countries may have substantial positive effects in some contexts, reinforced by aggregate estimates that are suggestive of possibly high benefit-to-cost ratios. But there are large gaps in the literature regarding the benefits of preschool programs in developing countries with respect to incorporating the full range of possible impacts over the life cycle, variations in the quality of preschool services, the importance of timing and of family background, the roles of different types of providers, the total resource costs of such programs, and the responsiveness of families and different types of providers to various incentive schemes as opposed to direct provisions of services. With regard to the last point, for example, there is little or no evidence regarding the responsiveness to provision of vouchers or subsidies for preschool programs even though there is other recent evidence that the impact of vouchers and performance-based incentives can be considerable for learning in school (Behrman et al. 2012; Bravo, Mukhopadhyay, and Todd 2010). There also are large gaps in measuring real resource costs and in understanding alternative financing and management possibilities and related appropriate policies.

Given the suggestions of substantial impacts in developing countries, there is a high priority for collecting more information and undertaking much more systematic analyses of a number of (not just preschool) ECD interventions in developing countries. These are critical issues that must be considered when designing, implementing, and developing ECD policies. To advance substantially, certain dimensions of data are critical: longitudinal information on those treated and comparable controls regarding both what is happening in program centers and what is happening at home to be able to trace costs and impacts over time, including possible complementarities over the life cycle; household-based sampling strategies to avoid the selectivity that comes from ECD center-based information if enrollments are not near universal; information on heterogeneous backgrounds of the disadvantaged children targeted that captures any relevant heterogeneity among the poor; integrated information on various characteristics of ECD service providers that might affect various dimensions of child development and the responsiveness of these providers to various incentives and the costs of ECD service provision; information on various approaches to ECD programming including child age (0–3 years vs. 3–5 years), modality (e.g., parent-based, center-based, media, or transfers); information that will permit exploration of efficiency motives for policies including imperfections in key markets (e.g., financing of ECD and other human-resource investments, insurance, information) and possible externalities of ECD interventions; experimental evidence through more RCTs that will illuminate the effectiveness of various policy strategies including providing incentives and not just trying to change inputs directly. With such data more systematic methods could be used to estimate impacts and costs with less risk of biases due to behavioral responses, measurement error, and unobserved variables—and structural models could be developed to investigate counterfactual policies and longer-run impacts of such policies. The potential of what can be learned through better data and better analyses is substantial.

We also note that the argument for investing more in early life is based in part on limited estimates that the marginal rates of returns or benefit-to-cost ratios to investing in early life versus the alternative of investing in later life-cycle stages are relatively high *given the current levels of investment at various life-cycle stages*. If there are diminishing marginal products to investing at any life-cycle stage, then if more and more resources were shifted from later-life to early life investments presumably the marginal rates of return to early life investments would decline and those to later-life investments increase until the two are equated—at which point any further shifts in investments from later-life to early life investments would not be warranted from a productivity point of view. This observation raises a number of important questions. Why are current investments relatively low in early life compared to later life so that existing estimates suggest much higher marginal rates of return to the former than to the latter? What are the private and public incentives that lead to what appears to be a misallocation of resources among life-cycle stages? How can these incentives be changed to have a better allocation of resources among life-cycle stages? To what extent is the explanation for the apparent misallocation due to information problems? Should there in fact be reallocations among life-cycle stages or from investments other than in human capital to early life investments? What expansion in early life investments would be needed to reduce the marginal rates of return to the levels for later life-cycle stages, particularly since prevention is more effective than treatment?

In summary, the economic analysis of preschool programs, and of ECD more generally, in developing countries is suggestive, though limited to date—but already shows some substantial possible benefits from the expansion of ECD programs. It has considerable potential for informing questions regarding what types of ECD programs and other

Table 3.3 Analysis of program evaluations that have examined quality interventions, comparing "improved" and "standard" preschools

Study authors, year, design	Quality intervention	Findings and measures	Conclusions relating to assessment of quality
Aboud and Hossain 2011 Bangladesh: Follow-up comparison of children in enriched preschools with those in nonenriched preschools during first and second grades. Intervention group, sample at follow-up: $n = 178$ 1st grade (2006), $n = 180$ 1st grade (2007), $n = 179$ 1st grade (2008), $n = 127$ 2nd grade (2008). Control group, sample at follow-up: $n = 92$ in government schools (2005), $n = 85$ in nongovernmental schools (2008), $n = 131$ in 1st grade (2008),	The quality intervention included: 1. Teacher-led and child-initiated activities: teachers read a story, taught literacy through letter recognition and writing, conducted structured games, and arranged for free play. 2. Exercise books for literacy were provided to children to write letters. 3. More thought-provoking storybooks were used, and more varied learning materials were rotated monthly for play. 4. Teachers were taught how to engage children in individual conversations during play. 5. Sisimpur, Sesame Street Bangladesh episodes began to be shown monthly in preschools, and their outreach books and games appeared. 6. Children received a more sophisticated and structured mathematics program, and were engaged in open discussion about stories in order to minimize group responses and rote learning.	Math quality (measured by ECERS) significantly contributed to the prediction of math achievement in first but not second grade. The combined mean of the Language and Literacy qualities (measured by ECERS) did not predict writing or reading beyond mother's education.	Certain preschool qualities (e.g., quality of preschool math program) had a greater impact than others on children's later achievement. Teachers had no systematic program to implement and few materials other than those in play corners, so activities depended on their own inclination and aptitude.
Aboud, Hossain, and O'Gara (2008) Bangladesh: Follow-up comparison of children in enriched preschools with those in nonenriched preschools during first grade.	"Succeed program" teachers are trained to employ student-centered methods and developmentally and locally appropriate learning materials. Parents manage the schools and have access to storybooks through the Reading for Children program. Community reading and study points are being set up to support school entrants. Parents attend monthly meetings to learn and talk about their children's development.	The mean scores of children who attended each preschool were correlated with the overall average on the six subscales along with the two curricular subscales literacy and math. The six-subscale preschool quality score correlated significantly with two of the six competencies; however, the math quality score correlated with all six competencies.	Quality of preschool math program had significant effect on child outcomes at first-grade follow-up. Overall preschool quality did not have similar effect.

Table 3.3 *(continued)*

Study authors, year, design	Quality intervention	Findings and measures	Conclusions relating to assessment of quality
Aboud (2006) Bangladesh: $n = 400$ children (4.5–6.5 years old). Correlations between preschool quality measures and child development outcomes were calculated.	No explicit quality intervention, but measurement of preschool quality and correlation with child outcomes.	ECERS is significantly correlated with verbal and nonverbal reasoning and school readiness. Material use was correlated with nonverbal reasoning and school readiness.	Preschool quality correlates with child outcomes, particularly relating to nonverbal reasoning and school readiness.
Baker-Henningham et al. (2009) Jamaica: Cluster randomized intervention Five preschools participated—three assigned to intervention group and two assigned to control group. Preschool-aged children. No specific age listed.	Intervention involved seven full-day teacher workshops (once per month) using the Incredible Years Teacher Training program and individual in-class consultations. The program was supplemented by 14 child lessons in each class. Each school was provided with a set of materials to conduct child lessons including a hand puppet and visual aids. The same resources were provided to control schools but teachers received only two days training using the Teacher Training program.	Significant intervention benefits for teacher behavior (measured using structured observation) (Cueto and Diaz 1999) and increase in the extent to which teachers promoted children's social and emotional skills. Significant benefits of child behavior (measured with a rating scale) with increase in children's appropriate behavior and in children's interest and enthusiasm	Study concludes training teachers in effective classroom management and strategies to promote socio-emotional competencies is a promising approach to improve emotional climate and child behaviors and participation.
Cueto and Diaz (1999) Peru: Compared two types of preschool programs: higher quality (Centro de Educacion Inidial [CEI]) and lower quality (Programas No Escolorizadoes de Educacion Inicial [PRONOEI]) $n = 300$ second-grade children from nine state schools in Lima in districts where state schools had poor dropout and repetition rates. Retrospective questions about preschool attendance.	Higher-quality preschools (CEI) are run in facilities provided by the Ministry of Education and offer formal preschool education with the Ministry's curriculum. In CEI schools, preschool teachers are professionals with teaching degrees in preschool education. The lower-quality preschools (PRONOEI) are run in communities where there is no formal preschool education, usually rural areas or shanty towns, and provide caregiving services and cognitive and socio-emotional development. The PRONOEIs have a volunteer caregiver, usually a woman volunteer from the community, chosen and appointed by a community organization.	Children who went to a CEI performed better during the first year of primary education, having higher marks in both math and language compared with children who did not attend preschool, while those who went to a PRONOEI showed no statistically significant difference from those without preschool education.	Children in more formal preschools with paid, professional teachers outperformed those in less-formal preschools, with volunteer teachers.

Diaz (2006) Peru: Compared two types of preschool program: higher quality (Centro de Educacion Inidial [CEI]) and lower quality (Programas No Escolorizados de Educacion Inicial [PRONOEI]) Children (7.5–8.5 years old) drawn from the YLS-Peru, $n = 356$ (boys) and $n = 306$ (girls). Retrospective questions about preschool attendance.	Higher-quality preschools (CEI) are run in facilities provided by the Ministry of Education and offer formal preschool education with the Ministry's curriculum. In CEI schools, preschool teachers are professionals with teaching degrees in preschool education. The lower-quality preschools (PRONOEI) are run in communities where there is no formal preschool education, usually rural areas or shanty towns, and provide caregiving services and cognitive and socio-emotional development. The PRONOEIs have a volunteer caregiver, usually a woman volunteer from the community, chosen and appointed by a community organization.	CEI attendance had a statistically significant and positive association with on-age school attendance and achievement in writing and math. Children who attended a CEI were 12% more likely to attend school in the correct grade for their age, 15% more likely to write the sentence "Bread is tasty" correctly, and 19% more likely to give the correct answer to the maths calculation "2 × 2" than children who did not. There were no significant effects of attendance at PRONOEI schools.	Children in more formal preschools with paid, professional teachers outperformed those in less formal preschools, with volunteer teachers.
Kagitcibasi, Sunar, and Bekman (2001) Turkey: Medium-term follow-up (4 and 7 years) of children in the Turkish Early Enrichment Project (TEEP): higher v. lower quality preschool. Intervention group: $n = 35$ Control group: $n = 52$	The "higher-quality model" provided a program that met stringent criteria for providing a high-quality educational environment as determined by objective assessments of child/caretaker ratios, daily program of activities, equipment available, and attitudes of the staff, using rating scales by trained observers and interviews with the staff. The "lower-quality model" comparison group was custodial centers, which neither provided nor encouraged play or any creative activities, and did not offer materials or activities that could promote learning. These centers merely kept the children quiet and obedient during the day.	The parent-focused intervention had numerous sustained effects in terms of school attainment, higher primary school grades and vocabulary scores, better attitudes toward school, and better family and social adjustment, while most effects of center-based intervention had dissipated (with the exception of negative effects of custodial, as opposed to educational, daycare).	Home-based child enrichment through the mother was a highly effective strategy in this case, and had many positive effects on child development.

Table 3.3 (continued)

Study authors, year, design	Quality intervention	Findings and measures	Conclusions relating to assessment of quality
Kagitcibasi, Sunar, Bekman, Baydar, and Cemalcilar (2009) Turkey: Long term follow-up (19 and 23 years) of children in the Turkish Early Enrichment Project (TEEP): higher v. lower quality preschool. Intervention group: $n = 34$ Control group: $n = 49$	The higher-quality "enrichment" model provided a program that met stringent criteria for providing a high-quality educational environment as determined by objective assessments of child/caretaker ratios, daily program of activities, equipment available, and attitudes of the staff, using rating scales by trained observers and interviews with the staff. The lower-quality model comparison group was custodial centers, which neither provided nor encouraged play or any creative activities, and did not offer materials or activities that could promote learning. These centers merely kept the children quiet and obedient during the day.	A significantly higher percentage of participants experiencing enrichment attended college. There was a trend indicating that the participants who experienced enrichment had higher educational attainment than the participants who did not experience enrichment.	The majority of the children who received early enrichment had better trajectories of development into young adulthood in the cognitive/ achievement and social developmental domains than children who did not receive enrichment.
Malmberg, Mwaura, and Sylva (2011) Kenya, Zanzibar, Uganda: Matched non-Madrasa Resource Center (MRC) preschools (comparison group) to MRC in each geographical area. 10–12 children were randomly selected (with stratification to ensure gender balance) from each preschool class and invited to participate. 321 children from preschools: 153 from comparison preschools and 168 from the intervention preschools. All from disadvantaged Muslim communities in three countries in East Africa.	Madrasa Resource Center (MRC): Curriculum focuses on active child learning, combined secular and religious education, and classroom materials that are low-cost and available in the community. This model contrasts with the more teacher-directed and didactic methods of the comparison preschools (state and NGO). In the MRC, children are mixed across age groups and continue classes with the same teacher over several years, whereas others are single age and change each year.	Used multilevel modeling of time within child within schools at three levels. No difference by group at time 1, but a significant difference in favor of MRC at time 2. Intervention group had significantly higher cognitive scores at time 2 (.40 SD higher) and time 3. A quadratic effects suggested that the first 1–1.5 years in MRC resulted in a significantly larger change than in the third year, but this was not seen in the non-MRC preschools. Quality of preschool (ECERS) affected both, but the effect was stronger in the MRC preschools; only seen at time 3 for the comparison preschools.	The effect of preschool quality was stronger in the intervention group.

Study	Method	Findings	Conclusions
Montie, Xiang, and Schweinhart (2006) Finland, Greece, Hong Kong, Indonesia, Ireland, Italy, Poland, Spain, Thailand, United States	IEA Preprimary Project is a longitudinal, cross-national study of preprimary care and education designed to identify how process and structural characteristics of the settings children attended at age 4 are related to their age 7 cognitive and language performance. Investigators collaborated to develop common instruments to measure family background, teachers' characteristics, setting structural characteristics, experiences of children in settings, and children's developmental status. Data from 10 countries are included in the analysis.	Four consistent findings across countries: 1. Children who were in preprimary settings in which free choice activities predominated had significantly better language performance at age 7 than those in settings in which personal/social activities predominated. 2. As level of teacher education increased, children's age-7 language performance improved. 3. The less time children spent in whole group activities, the better was their age-7 cognitive performance. 4. As the number and variety of materials in settings increased, children's age-7 cognitive performance improved.	Language at age 7 improves as teachers' number of years of full-time schooling increases and the predominant type of activity teachers propose in settings is free choice rather than personal/social. Age-7 cognitive performance improves as children spend less time in whole group activities and the variety of equipment and materials available increases.
Moore, Akhter, and Aboud (2008) Bangladesh: Pre-/post- intervention-matched comparison design. 138 children—67 from regular preschools and 71 from intervention preschools.	Intervention preschools revised their curriculum to give more prominence on language and literacy. Nonverbal reasoning was also increased in the classrooms by giving children a math bag with materials. Free rather than assigned time also took place daily for 40 mins. and teachers were taught how to use individualized talk to encourage children to expand their repertoire and verbalize ideas and actions. More play materials were also provided. Formal learning was altered to include more working in small groups. Technical officers providing training to preschool teachers were given additional training on child-centered learning.	Intervention preschool children made greater gains compared to regular preschoolers on nonverbal reasoning skills (measured using the WPPSI-III) and school readiness but not vocabulary. Intervention children also show better school readiness results as compared to control children. No significant differences in terms of social play (measured using the Play Observation Scale). Preschool quality was assessed using the Activities and Program Structure subscales of the ECERS.	Comprehensive intervention for preschool quality improvement—included curriculum revisions, individualization of curriculum, focus on play materials—resulted in improvements in nonverbal reasoning and school readiness but not vocabulary.

Table 3.3 *(continued)*

Study authors, year, design	Quality intervention	Findings and measures	Conclusions relating to assessment of quality
Morris, Philip, Othman, and Mitchell (2009) Zanzibar: Quasi experimental design, comparing $n = 269$ from the nonformal model, $n = 515$ from the formal model, and $n = 193$ from the combination model. Pre-/post-comparison of each group; representative samples of three treatments (formal, nonformal, or combination preschool setting + RISE) and controls (formal or nonformal preschool only).	RISE: Interactive radio instruction for child-friendly ECD pedagogy. Teacher instructions embedded in programs for children. 30-minute broadcasts of formal Zanzibar curriculum with games, songs, stories, and activities that encourage problem solving and self-directed exploration. Four subject areas: Kiswahili language, math, English, and basic life skills.	Treatment outperformed control students by 7.5 points out of 75 total points (or 10%), overall. The greatest gains in Kiswahili. Gains greater for girls than for boys. Nonformal and formal groups increased their test scores relative to the control group by approximately 9 (12%) and 11 (14.6%) points, combination groups improved less.	Radio instruction is a promising quality add-on for preschool programs.
Mwaura, Sylva, and Malmberg (2008) Kenya, Uganda, Zanzibar: $n = 423$ pretest and 18 months later from 47 preschools Pre-/post-test quasi-experimental evaluation with an intervention group (children from Madrasa preschools) and two comparison groups (children from non-Madrasa preschools).	Madrasa community-based preschool model in three countries; active learning model with community participation compared to standard teacher-directed preschools and no school attendance.	Children attending the Madrasa Resource Center preschools achieved significantly higher scores overall and on four cognitive subtests (subscales of the British Ability Scales and the African Child Intelligence Test).	Children with both types of preschool experience performed better than the home (comparison) group; however, children attending Madrasa Resource Center preschools achieved significantly higher scores overall.

Nonoyama-Tarumi and Bredenberg (2009)			
Cambodia: Intervention group: $n = 473$ students from 10 schools. Control group: $n = 458$ students from 10 schools Pre-/post-comparison of experimental group (received School Readiness Program) and students who did not receive the program. Intervention occurred in first two months of grade 1 and follow-up occurred one year later.	SRP implementation included various components, from the development of special curricular documentation, a 14-day teacher training program to orient new teachers to the program, a regular monitoring regimen to support teachers in their implementation, physical upgrading of classrooms, to formalized student assessment for monitoring and reporting purposes. Before the beginning of the school year, teachers received intensive training in using the bridging curriculum as well as the need for certain desired changes in classroom practice. Teachers acquired a repertoire of numerous activities involving songs, role plays, drawing, games, and other activities for teaching designated lessons. It was believed that providing instruction in this way would prove to be more engaging for children, build their confidence, and provide positive reinforcement for being in a school environment over a four-hour period each day.	Children who received the SRP intervention performed significantly higher than children who did not receive the intervention in both school readiness skills and achievement of formal curriculum when tested one year later.	High-quality two-month training program immediately before grade 1 has positive effects on child outcomes one year later. Many areas of quality were addressed, including teacher support and training, classroom upgrades, activities, lesson planning, etc.
Opel, Ameer, and Aboud (2009)			
Bangladesh: 78 children from the control group. 75 children from the intervention group. Children were sampled from five control preschools and five intervention preschools. Mean age in months 66.15 (SD = 10.8) Cluster randomized field trial comparing children in preschools with intervention to those without intervention.	Four-week dialogic reading intervention with preschoolers to increase their expressive vocabulary, using eight children's books. Books contained sufficient number of new words appropriate for 5-year-olds, story plot was interesting, and illustrations were attractive for preschoolers and helpful to teachers to explain the story. Each book was covered in three days by teachers with 30–40 mins/day spent on the story. Both intervention and control teachers received the books, but intervention teachers were trained to use open-ended questions and picture cards of the new words.	Intervention group showed significant improvements in expressive vocabulary with a large effect size. Children in the intervention group rose from 26% to 54% whereas control children did not improve.	Authors reported concern whether teachers (often with paraprofessional status) could overcome the large gap between their current reading style and the demands of dialogic reading.

Table 3.3 (*continued*)

Study authors, year, design	Quality intervention	Findings and measures	Conclusions relating to assessment of quality
Raine et al. (2003b) Mauritius: Longitudinal study of a randomly selected intervention group with a matched control group on all variables. 83 children were assigned to an experimental enrichment program from 3–5 years of age at time of recruitment. 335 children in control group.	Enrichment program started at age 3 and lasted two years. Consisted of three key elements: nutrition, education (stimulation, art, drama, music, etc.) and physical exercise. Teacher: pupil ratio of 1:5. Also included walking, field trips, instruction in basic hygiene, and medical inspections every two months. Education activities focused on verbal skills, visual spatial coordination, conceptual skills, and memory and perception. Children in the control group attended petite ecoles with a traditional grade-school curriculum and teacher:pupil ratio of 1:30.	Children who participated in the enrichment program at ages 3–5 years had lower scores for schizotypal personality and antisocial behavior at age 17 years and for criminal behavior at age 23 years, compared with the control subjects. The beneficial effects of the intervention were greater for children who showed signs of malnutrition at age 3 years, particularly with respect to outcomes for schizotype at ages 17 and 23 and for antisocial behavior at age 17.	Inability to determine which components of the intervention (education, nutrition, or physical exercise) accounted for the most beneficial effects.
Rao, Sun Zhou, and Zhang (2012) China: Pre-/post-test control group design with controls for confounding variables Compared performance of children in three kinds of preschools with control group on achievement in grade 1 (study I *n* = 203); Study II *n* = 207).	Four groups: two "appropriate"—kindergarten, separate preprimary class, and two "not appropriate"—"sitting in" a grade 1 class, or no preschool experience.	Children with appropriate preschool experiences (kindergartens or separate preprimary classes) had higher school-readiness scores and achievement scores at the end of grade 1 than other two groups. Kindergarten was associated with improved first-grade final math and literacy. There was a bigger effect at the end of the year on achievement tests of literacy. School Readiness Composite of the Bracken Basic Concept Scale–Revised (BBCS-R); first-grade math and literacy achievement (end of first grade). Quality of preschool with Early Childhood Environment Rating Scale–Revised Version (ECERS-R), Early Childhood Environment Rating Scale Extension (ECERSE), and Early Childhood Classroom Observation Measure (ECCOM).	Teachers in the age-appropriate kindergarten group provided a more child-friendly classroom climate, had better management skills, and showed higher instructional quality than teachers in the other programs. Both kindergarten and separate pre-primary class teachers provided more activities relevant to children's experiences than the grade 1 teachers, and there were noticeable differences in classroom climate between separate pre-primary and grade 1 classes.

| Rao, Pearson, Sun, Pearson, and Constas (2012)

Cambodia: 1312 children at pretest, 1184 at post-test in state preschool (548), community-based preschool (292), home-based preschool (352), and no preschool (120) from six provinces. Used LHM cluster randomized controls; pre-/post-test control group design. | Three kinds of preschools and nonattendees: state preschool (formal), community-based preschool (meets two hours in the morning), home-based preschool, and no preschool. | Children in formal preschool better than other three groups; home-based and community preschool children both outperformed controls even after controlling for all potential confounding variables on locally developed tests.

Assessment test based on locally developed standards—total and subscale. Controls for group matching were pretest scores one year earlier, SES differences, province, and history of preschool. | Controls for group matching were pretest scores one year earlier, SES differences, province and history of preschool. |
| Rolla San Francisco, Arias, Villers, and Snow (2006)

Costa Rica: 210 low-income Costa Rican kindergarteners aged 5 randomly assigned to one of 6 groups. About 30 per group. Pre-/post-test control group design. | Examined differential impact of three early literacy interventions—tutoring with materials, classroom activities with materials, all, and work with families with materials, all, and control with materials only. | Similar on pretest, on post-test the tutoring and combination of all had print composite scores two points higher (1SD higher) than the other intervention groups and one point (.5 SD) higher than the control group (control plus materials alone).

High-quality materials to teachers without training had no impact. Language composite and print composite tests to measure emergent literacy skills. | Tutoring or a combination of all three interventions were the most effective. Study did not include an explicit measure of classroom quality. |
| Yoshikawa et al. (under review)

Chile: 32 schools assigned to "Full UBC condition" and 32 assigned to "Comparison" condition. Cluster randomized sample. | "Full UBC condition" included: 18 sessions for teachers and teacher aides. Training included two primary domains (oral language and early literacy development and coordination of early childhood education with health services) and two secondary domains (socio-emotional development and family involvement). | Classroom Assessment Scoring System (CLASS), which focuses on interactions between students and teachers. Subscales include Emotional Climate, Instructional Support, and Classroom Organization. No individual child-level outcomes were measured. | Multidimensional measurement of classroom quality and teacher/student interaction significantly improved with intervention. |

Note: Entries are listed alphabetically by author. Some of the material in the table is also presented in Engle et al. 2007 and 2011 papers.

interventions are most promising in various developing country con-texts. But it is also limited in various respects so further data collection and analyses are likely to have high payoffs, including careful monitor-ing and analyses of programs in new contexts even if they are based on the apparent best practice in other contexts, attention to costs as well as impacts, and exploration of various incentives systems and not only the direct public provision of programs or program inputs.[8]

Notes

1. Such endowments have been found to be important determinants of adult outcomes in developing and developed economies (e.g., Alderman and Behrman 2006; Behrman and Rosenzweig 1999, 2002, 2004; Behrman, Rosenzweig, and Taubman 1994; Heckman, Stixrud, and Urzúa 2006; Urzúa 2008).

2. Most of the rest of this book focuses on what we call here the "late-childhood life-cycle stage," the years for K-12 schooling, though not always with attention to the endogenous outcomes at the end of the early childhood life-cycle stage (Y): (1) cognitive and language skills; (2) socioemotional skills; and (3) health and nutritional status. Alderman and Bleakley (chapter 4) is an excep-tion that explicitly addresses the relation between the third of these outcomes at the end of the early childhood life-cycle stage on subsequent schooling success.

3. Some illustrations are given for estimating the benefits from improved early life nutrition in Alderman and Behrman (2006) and Behrman, Alderman, and Hoddinott (2004). Summers (1992) uses the cheapest alternative way to avert mortality for estimates for Pakistan (vaccinations), which translates into $1,250 (2005 US$). Perhaps at the other extreme is the "revealed-preference" model based on labor-market choices and mortality risk-wage choices, probably the leading approach for estimates of the value of averting mortality in the United States. This approach has been developed and promoted most visibly by Viscusi (1993, 2008) and has been adopted for use by various U.S. governmental agen-cies (Viscusi and Aldy 2003; Robinson 2007). This approach as applied by Bar-tick and Reinhold (2010), for example, values the cost of a death of an infant in the United States at $10.56 million (2007 dollars), which with the expected life at birth in 2007 of 77.7 years in the United States and with a 3% annual rate of return would yield a constant annuity stream of $342,000 per year or 7.9 times the mean real U.S. gross domestic product (GDP) per capita in 2007.

4. Private benefits are what individuals actually receive as the result of their actions. It does not include the benefits of the actions that might spill over to the other members of the community. These external benefits (also known as exter-nalities) are captured in the social benefits.

5. Thus, programs that have significant impacts on children in developing countries, such as salt iodization, but do not have a psychosocial program com-ponent are not included. Estimates of the impacts of some early life nutritional interventions without psychosocial program components find that the impacts are considerable (e.g., Behrman, Alderman, and Hoddinott 2004; Victora et al. 2008) and in some cases there is evidence of long-run effects three to four de-

cades later in adulthood or on the next generation (e.g., Behrman et al. 2009; Hoddinott et al. 2008; Maluccio et al. 2009).

6. For no other outcome measure are there as many as five studies with effect sizes. The estimates for comprehensive programs in Engle et al. (2007) are included with the early childhood learning centers in this summary.

7. For the other measures used, some of the median effect sizes are of the same general magnitude as for cognitive skills (e.g., for parenting 0.28 for motor skills in one study and 0.35 for socioemotional skills for three studies) but not all of them (e.g., for parenting 0.17 for the HOME measure for three studies).

8. See Behrman, Parker, and Todd (chapter 5), Galiani and Perez-Truglia (chapter 6), and MacLeod and Urquiola (chapter 7) for consideration, respectively, of incentives for students and parents, school management systems, and competition and educational productivity at the K-12 level.

References

Aboud, F. E. 2006. "Evaluation of an Early Childhood Preschool Program in Rural Bangladesh." *Early Childhood Research Quarterly* 21 (1): 46–60.

Aboud, F. E., and K. Hossain. 2011. "The Impact of Preprimary School on Primary School Achievement in Bangladesh." *Early Childhood Research Quarterly* 26 (2): 237–46.

Aboud, F. E., et al. 2008. "The Succeed Project: Challenging Early School Failure in Bangladesh." *Research in Comparative and International Education* 3 (3): 295–307.

Alderman, Harold, and Jere R. Behrman. 2006. "Reducing the Incidence of Low Birth Weight in Low-Income Countries Has Substantial Economic Benefits." *World Bank Research Observer* 21 (1): 25–48.

Armecin, G., J. R. Behrman, P. Duazo, S. Ghuman, S. Gultiano, E. M. King, and N. Lee. 2006. Office of Population Studies, University of San Carlos ECD Team. "Early Childhood Development through Integrated Programs: Evidence from the Philippines." Cebu City, New York, Philadelphia and Washington: Universities of Pennsylvania and San Carlos (Office of Population Studies), Population Council and World Bank.

Baker-Henningham, H., et al. 2005. "The Effect of Early Stimulation on Maternal Depression: A Cluster Randomised Controlled Trial." *Archives of Disease in Childhood* 90 (12): 1230–34.

———. 2009. "A Pilot Study of the Incredible Years Teacher Training Programme and a Curriculum Unit on Social and Emotional Skills in Community Pre-schools in Jamaica." *Child: Care, Health and Development* 35 (5): 624–31.

Bartick, Melissa, and Arnold Reinhold. 2010. "The Burden of Suboptimal Breastfeeding in the United States: A Pediatric Cost Analysis." *Pediatrics* 125 (5): 1048–58.

Behrman, J., Y. Cheng, and P. Todd. 2004. "Evaluating Preschool Programs When Length of Exposure to the Program Varies: A Nonparametric Approach." *Review of Economics and Statistics* 86 (1): 108–32.

Behrman, Jere R., Harold Alderman, and John Hoddinott. 2004. "Hunger and

Malnutrition." In *Global Crises, Global Solutions*, ed. Bjørn Lomborg, 363–420. Cambridge: Cambridge University Press.

Behrman, Jere R., John Hoddinott, John A. Maluccio, Erica Soler-Hampejsek, Emily L. Behrman, Reynaldo Martorell, Manuel Ramirez and Aryeh D. Stein. 2008. "What Determines Adult Cognitive Skills? Impacts of Pre-School, School-Years and Post-School Experiences in Guatemala." IFPRI Discussion Paper no. 826. International Food Policy Research Institute, Washington, DC.

Behrman, Jere R., Susan W. Parker, Petra E. Todd, and Kenneth I. Wolpin. 2012. "Aligning Learning Incentives of Students and Teachers: Results from a Social Experiment in Mexican High Schools." University of Pennsylvania, Philadelphia: PIER Working Paper No. 13-004. Available at SSRN: http://ssrn.com/abstract=2206883 or http://dx.doi.org/10.2139/ssrn.2206883.

Behrman, Jere R., and Mark R. Rosenzweig. 1999. "'Ability' Biases in Schooling Returns and Twins: A Test and New Estimates." *Economics of Education Review* 18:159–67.

———. 2002. "Does Increasing Women's Schooling Raise the Schooling of the Next Generation?" *American Economic Review* 92 (1): 323–34.

———. 2004. "Returns to Birthweight." *Review of Economics and Statistics* 86 (2): 586–601.

Behrman, Jere R., Mark R. Rosenzweig, and Paul Taubman. 1994. "Endowments and the Allocation of Schooling in the Family and in the Marriage Market: The Twins Experiment." *Journal of Political Economy* 102 (6): 1131–74.

Behrman, Jere R., et al. 2009. "Nutritional Supplementation of Girls Influences the Growth of Their Children: Prospective Study in Guatemala." *American Journal of Clinical Nutrition* 90 (5): 1372–79.

Bravo, David, Sankar Mukhopadhyay, and Petra E. Todd. 2010. "Effects of a Universal School Voucher System on Educational and Labor Market Outcomes: Evidence from Chile." *Quantitative Economics* 1 (1): 47–95.

Carneiro, P., K. Hansen, and J. J. Heckman. 2003. "Estimating Distributions of Treatment Effects with an Application to the Returns to Schooling and Measurement of the Effects of Uncertainty on College Choice." *International Economic Review* 44 (2): 361–422.

Cueto, S., and J. J. Diaz. 1999. "Impacto de la educación inicial en el rendimiento en primer grado de primaria en escuelas públicas urbana de Lima." *Revista de Psicología* 17:74–90.

Cunha, F., and J. J. Heckman. 2007. "The Technology of Skill Formation." *American Economic Review* 97 (2): 31–47.

———. 2008. "Formulating, Identifying and Estimating the Technology of Cognitive and Noncognitive Skill Formation." *Journal of Human Resources* 43 (4): 738–82.

Cunha, F., J. J. Heckman, L. J. Lochner, and D. V. Masterov. 2006. "Interpreting the Evidence on Life Cycle Skill Formation." In *Handbook of the Economics of Education*, ed. E. Hanushek and F. Welch, 597–812. Amsterdam: North Holland.

Diaz, J. J. 2006. *Preschool Education and Schooling Outcomes in Peru*. Lima, Peru: Children of the Millennium Publications.

Doyle, O., C. P. Harmon, J. J. Heckman, and R. E. Tremblay. 2010. "The Timing of Early Childhood Intervention: How Early Is Early?" UCD Geary Institute and UCD School of Public Health and Population Science, University College Dublin. http://www.ucd.ie/geary/static/publications/workingpapers/GearyWp200705.pdf.

Engle, P. L., et al. 2007. "Strategies to Avoid the Loss of Developmental Potential in More than 200 Million Children in the Developing World." *Lancet* 369 (9557): 229–42.

———. 2011. "Strategies for Reducing Inequalities and Improving Developmental Outcomes for Young Children in Low-Income and Middle-Income Countries." *Lancet* 378 (9799): 1339–53.

Ghuman, S., J. R. Behrman, J. B. Borja, S. Gultiano, and E. M. King. 2005. "Family Background, Service Providers, and Early Childhood Development in the Philippines: Proxies and Interactions." *Economic Development and Cultural Change* 54 (1): 129–64.

Grantham-McGregor, S., Y. B. Cheung, S. Cueto, P. Glewwe, L. Richter, and B. Strupp. 2007. "Child Development in Developing Countries 1: Developmental Potential in the First 5 Years for Children in Developing Countries." *Lancet* 369:60–70.

Harberger, Arnold C. 1997. "New Frontiers in Project Evaluation: A Comment on Devarajan, Squire and Suthiwart-Narueput." *World Bank Research Observer* 12 (1): 73–82.

Heckman, J. J. 2006. "Skill Formation and the Economics of Investing in Disadvantaged Children." *Science* 312:1900–1902.

Heckman J. J., J. Stixrud, and S. Urzúa. 2006. "The Effect of Cognitive and Noncognitive Abilities on Labor Market Outcomes and Social Behavior." *Journal of Labor Economics* 24 (3): 411–82.

Hoddinott, John, et al. 2008. "The Impact of Nutrition during Early Childhood on Income, Hours Worked, and Wages of Guatemala Adults." *Lancet* 371:411–16.

Kagitcibasi, C., et al. 2001. "Long-Term Effects of Early Intervention: Turkish Low-Income Mothers and Children." *Applied Developmental Psychology* 22:333–61.

———. 2009. "Continuing Effects of Early Enrichment in Adult Life: The Turkish Early Enrichment Project 22 Years Later." *Journal of Applied Developmental Psychology* 30 (6): 764–79.

Knowles, James C., and Jere R. Behrman. 2005. "Economic Returns to Investing in Youth." In *The Transition to Adulthood in Developing Countries: Selected Studies*, ed. Jere R. Behrman, Barney Cohen, Cynthia Lloyd, and Nelly Stromquist, 424–90. Washington, DC: National Academy of Science–National Research Council.

Malmberg, L.-E., et al. 2011. "Effects of a Preschool Intervention on Cognitive Development among East African Preschool Children: A Flexibly Time-Coded Growth Model." *Early Childhood Research Quarterly* 26:124–33.

Maluccio, John, et al. 2009. "The Impact of Improving Nutrition During Early Childhood on Education Among Guatemalan Adults." *Economic Journal* 119 (537): 734–63.

Montie, J. E., et al. 2006. "Preschool Experience in 10 Countries: Cognitive and Language Performance at Age 7." *Early Childhood Research Quarterly* 21:313–31.

Moore, A. C., et al. 2008. "Evaluating an Improved Quality Preschool Program in Rural Bangladesh." *International Journal of Educational Development* 28 (2): 118–31.

Morris, E., et al. 2009. "Radio Instruction to Strengthen Education (RISE) in Zanzibar: Impact Study." Boston: Educational Development Center and USAID.

Mwaura, P. A. M., et al. 2008. "Evaluating the Madrasa Preschool Programme in East Africa: A Quasi-Experimental Study." *International Journal of Early Years Education* 16 (3): 237–55.

Noboa-Hidalgo, Grace E. and Sergio S. Urzúa. 2012. "The Effects of Participation in Public Child Care Centers: Evidence from Chile." *Journal of Human Capital* 6 (1): 1–34.

Nonoyama-Tarumi, Y., and K. Bredenberg. 2009. "Impact of School Readiness Program Interventions on Children's Learning in Cambodia." *International Journal of Educational Development* 29 (1): 39–45.

Opel, A., et al. 2009. "The Effect of Preschool Dialogic Reading on Vocabulary among Rural Bangladeshi Children." *International Journal of Educational Research* 48 (1): 12–20.

Raine, A., et al. 2003. "Effects of Environmental Enrichment at Ages 3–5 Years on Schizotypal Personality and Antisocial Behavior at Ages 17 and 23 Years." *American Journal of Psychiatry* 160 (9): 1627–35.

Rao, N., et al. 2012a. "Early Achievement in Rural China: The Role of Preschool Experience." *Early Childhood Research Quarterly* 27 (1): 66–76.

Rao, N., et al. 2012b. "Is Something Better than Nothing? An Evaluation of Early Childhood Programs in Cambodia." *Child Development* 83 (3): 864–76.

Robinson, Lisa A. 2007. "Policy Monitor: How US Government Agencies Value Mortality Risk Reductions." *Review of Environmental Economics and Policy* 1:283–99. doi:10.1093/reep/rem018.

Rolla San Francisco, A., et al. 2006. "Evaluating the Impact of Different Early Literacy Interventions on Low-Income Costa Rican Kindergarteners." *International Journal of Educational Research* 45 (3): 188–201.

Rosenzweig, Mark R., and Kenneth J. Wolpin. 1986. "Evaluating the Effects of Optimally Distributed Public Programs." *American Economic Review* 76 (3): 470–87.

Summers, Lawrence H. 1992. "Investing in All the People," *Pakistan Development Review* 31 (4): 367–406.

Todd, Petra, and Kenneth I. Wolpin. 2006. "Using a Social Experiment to Validate a Dynamic Behavioral Model of Child Schooling and Fertility: Assessing the Impact of a School Subsidy Program in Mexico." *American Economics Review* 96 (5): 1384–1417.

UNESCO. 2006. "EFA Global Monitoring Report 2007: Strong Foundations: Early Childhood Care and Education." UNESCO, Paris.

———. 2010. Institute for Statistics. Paris: UNESCO.

———. 2011. "Global Monitoring Report 2011." UNESCO, Paris.

Urzúa, Sergio. 2008. "Racial Labor Market Gaps: The Role of Abilities and Schooling Choices." *Journal of Human Resources* 43 (4): 919–71.

Urzúa, Sergio, and Gregory Veramendi, in collaboration with Centro de Microdatos. 2010. "The Impact of Out-of-Home Childcare Centers on Early Childhood Development." Northwestern University, for IDB Research Network on Early Childhood Development, Evanston, IL.

Victora, C. G., L. Adair, C. Fall, P. C. Hallal, R. Martorell, L. Richter, and H. S. Sachdev. 2008. "Maternal and Child Undernutrition: Consequences for Adult Health and Human Capital." *Lancet* 371 (9609): 340–57.

Viscusi, W. Kip. 1993. "The Value of Risks to Life and Health." *Journal of Economic Literature* 31:1912–46.

———. 2008. "How to Value a Life." *Journal of Economics and Finance* 32:311–23.

———. 2010. "The Heterogeneity of the Value of Statistical Life: Introduction and Overview." *Journal of Risk and Uncertainty* 40 (1): 1–13.

Viscusi, W. Kip, and Joseph E. Aldy. 2003. "The Value of a Statistical Life: A Critical Review of Market Estimates Throughout the World." *Journal of Risk and Uncertainty* 27 (1): 5–76.

Yoshikawa, H., D. Lyva, C. E. Snow, E. Treviño, A. Rolla, M. C. Barata, C. Weiland, and M. C. Arbour. (Under review). "Interim Impacts on Classroom Quality of an Initiative to Improve the Quality of Preschool Education in Chile: A Cluster-Randomized Trial."

4

Child Health and Educational Outcomes

Harold Alderman (International Food Policy Research
Institute and World Bank)
Hoyt Bleakley (University of Chicago)

4.1. Introduction

The good news: in recent years many countries have made
significant progress in reducing childhood mortality. The
bad news: malnutrition and childhood infections still impact the future of millions of children. As a child grows
beyond the first few years of life, the risk of mortality re-
cedes but the risk of illness remains a major determinant
of his or her future because health will have a significant
impact on how the child fares in school. Even if a person is
perfectly healthy as an adult, the damage from childhood
disease and malnutrition can be hard to undo. Most of a
person's development happens early in life. Childhood is
therefore a key period for building human capital, and
the benefits of health and nutrition early on could have
effects that persist throughout the life course. Beyond the
general importance of childhood as the basis of human-
capital formation, there are also shorter "critical periods"
during childhood during which subsequent development
might be hampered if certain inputs are missing during a
particular, biologically determined age window.

Consider two distinct pathways by which health influences learning. First, there is the immediate one: children who are sick often miss school and those who are malnourished when they are in school might not learn at the same rate as well-nourished children. Second, there is the lagged effect. Much of the success of a child in school depends on what happens before that child reaches school; children whose mental and physical growth have been suppressed by disease and malnutrition in the past might come to school today less able to learn. Further, these two pathways interact: children who learned more yesterday (perhaps because of better health at the time) come to school better prepared to learn today. In section 4.2, we present a simple model of schooling that incorporates these dynamic interactions, and use it to illustrate some of the issues in interpretation and estimation.

We then turn to some of the evidence that links childhood health to human capital. This literature stresses the importance of certain nutritional inputs in the first few years of life, including the time in the womb. We present evidence particularly on two categories of health risks: malnutrition and parasitical infections. There is little doubt that these are major public-health concerns. We offer them as a (partial) alternative to prioritization based on the global burden of disease (Jamison et al. 2006) and the ranking of disability adjusted life years (DALYs). We have chosen not to use the DALY approach for two main reasons. First, DALY prioritizations currently do not yet take into consideration a full spectrum of outcomes. While the contribution of the DALY approach is that it provides a metric to assess loss of life and physical disabilities, it does not gauge the consequences of impaired cognitive capacity or noncognitive abilities. Second, the DALY calculations focus on proximate causes of mortality rather than underlying risks. Although malnutrition is often not a direct cause of mortality, it is a primary risk factor for many diseases ranked high on the global burden of disease, including respiratory disease and measles.[1] Thus, the discussion of nutrition addresses a root cause of many of the diseases that affect childhood. Similarly, the DALY approach understates subclinical morbidity and thus could underestimate the impact of parasites.

Thus, section 4.3 discusses findings relating early life nutrition to school performance and adult income. Section 4.4, in turn, reviews evidence on how childhood disease, in particular tropical parasites, impacts schooling and income. In addition, tables 4.1 and 4.2 provide summaries of selected studies discussed in sections 4.3 and 4.4, respectively. In section 4.5, we discuss some implications both for policy and for future research.

As a point of departure, we note that developing countries have perhaps made more progress in increasing quantity rather than quality of the education received by their citizens. This suggests that policymakers might now lean toward interventions that improve the quality of learning in school, and that better child health might help along this dimension. There are compelling reasons to believe that important inputs to child health are underprovided: diseases are canonical examples of externalities, and parents might underinvest in the early life nutrition of the children because of imperfect altruism, credit constraints, or simply ignorance. We then note how interventions that improve childhood health disproportionately benefit the poor, and therefore make societies more equitable. Indeed, investments in public health represent one of those few opportunities to improve both equity and efficiency simultaneously.

4.2. A Simple Model of Childhood Health and Human Capital

This section lays out some of the key features of a simple life-cycle model of schooling in which endogenous human capital in period 1 (preschool) influences the production of additional human capital in period 2 (classroom).[2] The human capital acquired in the preschool and schooling periods leads to adult outcomes in a third period. Human capital can be considered rather broadly and can include noncognitive and cognitive skills as well as health. The noncognitive skills include a range of socio-emotional behavioral factors such as conduct, motivation, persistence, teamwork, and attitudes toward risk. Increasingly, these are seen as being as—or more—important to labor-market outcomes as well as other aspects of adult living (Heckman, Stixrud, and Urzúa 2005). While these noncognitive skills are recognized as important in such studies, the majority of empirical estimates of the impact of human capital on earnings use schooling or learning or a combination as proxies for the broader range of human capital.

An important feature of the life-cycle model is the testable assumption that learning at school (L_2) is influenced by initial period human capital (H_1). If $\partial L_2 / \partial H_1 > 0$, that is, if learning in school increases with higher levels of initial human capital, then skill gaps widen over time. Moderately sized shocks to a child's health then would lead to major differences in school outcomes over the years of primary and secondary education and would be in keeping with what Cunha and Heckman (2007) call "self-productivity."

Another feature of a life-cycle model to consider is whether the impact of an investment in school (I_2) is higher for more able students. If the $\partial^2 L_2 / \partial I_2 \partial H_1 > 0$, then investments in a later period have a larger return for students that entered school with more human capital relative to those with lower ability or poorer health. Cunha and Heckman (2007) refer to this as "dynamic complementarity." Whether dynamic complementarity will magnify inequality in earlier investments in health is an empirical question. Conceptually, there may also be inputs in schooling that substitute for early child investments and thus compensate for limited amounts of inputs earlier.

Therefore, timing matters for many, if not most, investments in health and other aspects of human capital. Cunha and Heckman (2009) call a period critical if, after that period, an input has no measurable impact. A sensitive period occurs if that period has the highest response to an input, even if at a later date some increase of the skill is nevertheless also possible. The timing has obvious implications for the design of cost-effective programs and for the benefits (or absence of benefits) of any "second-chance" investments for those individuals who had limited human-capital investments in an earlier period. Similarly, self-productivity and dynamic complementarity affect whether there is a necessary trade-off between efficiency and equity in investments in school. Because economic efficiency implies larger investments where the returns are highest, in the presence of complementarity more resources would be allocated to the higher-performing students who are often those from households who were able to invest more in health prior to the child reaching school age. However, if investments prior to school are such that there is no income gradient in H_1 or if there is no complementarity in school-level investments, then efficient investments can also promote equity.

We can rank the expected magnitude of these two channels, at least to a first approximation. "Self-productivity" is the direct effect of human capital in one period on subsequent human capital production. "Dynamic complementarity" is an indirect effect that arises because the government or an individual makes additional investments in response to improved early life health and other human capital. But a change in the level of investments that is induced by improved health will not be of first-order importance; indeed, this is almost by definition since the complementarity is based on the second derivative of a learning production function. The direct effect is of first-order importance, in contrast. One way to think of this direct effect is in terms of health improving the productivity of all of the inframarginal investments. The indirect effect instead works through what was a marginal investment to begin with.

We illustrate some of these ideas in figure 4.1, which relates lifetime income to various hypothetical ages at which the child might leave school and enter the labor market. Consider first the solid lines, which refer to a baseline case in which the burden of disease and malnutrition in childhood is high. The solid curve labeled "MB" represents the marginal benefit of staying in school. Its downward slope reflects diminishing marginal benefits of education, which is the standard assumption. The solid curve labeled "MC" represents increasing marginal costs of staying in school. MC includes both the direct costs of going to school (such as tuition, uniforms, and transportation) and the opportunity cost of time (such as foregone earnings or home production). The MC curve slopes upward in concert with the higher earnings potential that comes both with age and from having learned something in school. The optimal choice of schooling is when marginal benefit equals marginal cost, at the point labeled e.

Next consider what happens if this child were healthier, which we represent with the dashed curves. If health makes it easier for the child to learn in school, it would shift the marginal benefits upwards to some new curve like the one labeled "MB'." But the MC curve would also shift up to MC', because improved health also increases the opportunity cost of school. This could happen for two distinct reasons: first, because healthier children are better unskilled workers; and, second, because healthier children learn more from the schooling that they have already received. This last channel means that the shift in MB and MC are inextricably linked: children who learn better also learn faster, and so the opportunity cost of staying in school rises more quickly.

The relative importance of direct versus indirect effects is seen in figure 4.1. Here, childhood health and education are complements: the reduction in disease and malnutrition shift the optimal choice to e', which is greater than e. The indirect effect, that is, the effect on income via complementary investments that were induced from the improvement in health, is seen in the figure as the areas A plus B. Nevertheless, the healthier child would have earned higher income even absent any change in time in school, which is what we refer to as the direct effect. The direct effect is seen in the figure as the areas C plus D. It is evident from the graph that the indirect effect is larger than the direct effect.[3]

The contribution of various sorts of early life human capital to laterlife outcomes can, in principle, be measured. Nevertheless, it is a challenge to determine what causes a shortfall in a child's potential and to assess whether this can be prevented or reversed in a cost-effective

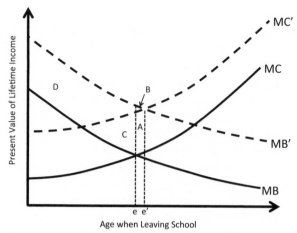

FIGURE 4.1 How improving child health affects schooling and income in the standard model.

manner. One clear challenge is the scarcity of data on individuals over time; analyses of preschool-aged populations are often unable to examine schooling outcomes. Even with such longitudinal data, it is necessary to find some factors that influence outcomes in period 1 yet are sufficiently transitory *not* to affect subsequent schooling decisions directly. It is clearly difficult to separate causes of ill health from other causes of poor schooling that will also affect lifetime productivity; preschooler health and subsequent educational attainments *both* reflect household decisions regarding investments in children. Generally, to control for such behavioral determinants it is necessary that the data from earlier periods of heightened health and nutritional vulnerability contain information on programs that are not correlated with household decisions yet affect health. Alternatively, or additionally, economic or weather-related shocks in one period may help identify the impact of health that these shocks affect, providing the direct impact on other household assets and income can be isolated.

Moreover, even when data are adequate to distinguish the impact of severe deprivation, it is not clear that the outcome attributed to one cause has the same economic consequences as a similar outcome that is primarily due to a different cause. For example, does low birth weight (LBW) reflecting maternal malaria have the same consequences on cognitive development as would LBW primarily due to untreated sexually transmitted infections of the mother or caused by iron and folate deficiency anemia? To some degree there are biological models that provide structure to help address such questions and reinforce the external validity of individual studies. However, the vast majority of the evidence available comes from developed countries (see, e.g., Almond and Currie 2010). While physiology may vary little across borders, health and education technology does and the elasticity of substitution of inputs between periods and their costs will differ. Thus, we argue below that it is important to look at the range and consistency of results on health and learning to support generalizations beyond individual studies.

This issue of heterogeneity is also relevant to a curious pattern such as that reported in chapter 2 of this book. While the authors of the review in that chapter rightfully highlight the inconsistency of the results on inputs into schooling, with positive and significant results partially offset by negative effects, the distribution is not one that might be expected with the true value centered on zero. For example, 14 of the 46 coefficients on pupil-teacher ratios in the studies deemed with the best estimation strategies are significantly negative while three are significantly positive. However, with a two-tailed test and a 10% significance level one would expect two significant coefficients of each sign. This—and similar mixed results in the study—are thus less evidence of small effects than an indication of heterogeneity of impact. Quite plausibly the heterogeneity reflects local capacity and school organization as the authors conclude. But—without refuting this hypothesis—the range of impacts can also reflect the heterogeneity of students' backgrounds and capacity for learning, including health. For example, Glewwe, Kremer, and Moulin (2009) observe that the provision of textbook in rural Kenya did not raise scores on average although this intervention did have a favorable impact for those students with the highest initial test scores. This, then, is consistent with dynamic complementarity, which exacerbates initial inequality of skills. There are, however, few studies that assess the heterogeneity of returns to inputs with regards to the health history of students.

4.3. Nutrition and Maternal Health

This section reviews a few key studies that document the impact of a shock in the first few years of a child's life on his or her subsequent schooling. Indeed, a shock that influences schooling may occur while the child is still in utero. The "grandmother" of this area of research is the Dutch famine study. Toward the end of World War II, food rations were in very short supply in the Netherlands. The resulting "hunger winter" of 1945 ended abruptly with the Allied liberation of that country. Follow-up studies found negative impacts of being in the womb during

Table 4.1 Selected studies of relationship between childhood nutrition and human capital

	Explanatory variable	Description	Place	Age at treatment (or exposure)
Alderman et al. 2001	Longitudinal data on nutrition	Nutrition at a very young age can impact schooling. Malnourished girls were less likely to enter school than girls with better nutrition.	Pakistan	Children at age 5
Alderman, Hoddinott, and Kinsey 2006	Malnourishment in early life	Malnourished children entered school later, completed fewer years, and were shorter than the median child in a developed country.	Zimbabwe	Ages 1–3
Alderman, Hoogeveen, and Rossi 2009	Malnourishment in early life	Nutrition at a very young age can impact schooling. Malnourished children entered school later, completed fewer years of school, and were shorter than the median child in a developed country.	Tanzania	Children under 5
Almond and Mazumder 2011	In the womb during Ramadan (fasting)	Learning disabilities more prevalent among those in the first trimester in utero during fasting period.	Uganda, Iraq	In utero
Behrman et al. 2010	Nutritional supplements (INCAP trial)	Early life nutrition affects schooling and wages via cognition more so than via stature.	Guatemala	Age 0–3
Behrman, Alderman, and Hoddinott 2004	Iodine supplementation	High rates of return to prenatal iodine supplements.	Global	Schoolchildren
Christian et al. 2010	Iron and zinc supplements	Micronutrients affect cognitive abilities, even *in utero.* Treated children had better cognitive abilities and motor skills.	Nepal	In utero
Field, Robles, and Torero 2009	Rollout of iodization campaign	Micronutrients affect cognitive abilities and education, even in utero. Children whose mothers received supplements had more years of schooling than those whose mothers did not.	Tanzania	In utero
Glewwe, King, and Jacoby 2001	Malnourishment in early life	Nutrition at a very young age can impact schooling. Better-nourished children perform better in school due to earlier enrollment and higher productivity.	Philippines	Age 0–2

Study	Intervention/Variable	Description	Country	Population
Gordan et al. 2009	Iodine supplementation	Even though there is a sensitive period for iodine supplementation in utero, nevertheless later intervention can have benefits, albeit smaller ones.	New Zealand	Schoolchildren
Grantham-McGregor, Chang, and Walker 1998	In-school feeding program	There is insufficient evidence to determine whether education outcomes can be improved by providing nutrition through daily breakfast.	Jamaica	Schoolchildren
Hoddinott et al. 2008	Nutritional supplements (INCAP trial)	Nutrition has long-run impacts on education. Children who received supplements attained higher schooling.	Guatemala	Age 0–3
Lozoff et al. 2006	Iron supplementation	Micronutrient deficiencies can result in impaired cognitive development. The difference between anemic and non-anemic children's test scores increase with age.	Costa Rica	Age 1–2
Lukowski et al. 2010	Iron deficiency	Micronutrients have long run effects on cognitive abilities. Individuals who lacked iron had impaired cognitive functions as young adults.	Costa Rica	Infancy
Maccini and Yang 2009	Rainfall in year of birth	Nutrition immediately after birth can affect education. Low rainfall led to temporary reductions of nutrition to girls born in these years. This led to less schooling and shorter heights compared to girls born in years with normal rainfall.	Indonesia	Main result is rainfall in 1st year of life
Maluccio et al. 2009	Nutritional supplements (INCAP trial)	Nutrition has long-run impacts on education. Children who received supplements scored higher on cognitive tests 20–40 years later.	Guatemala	Age 0–3
Stein et al. 1975	Exposure to famine (Dutch hunger winter)	Those in utero during a famine had worse health later in life.	Netherlands	In utero
Walker et al. 2007	Iron supplementation	Micronutrient deficiencies can result in impaired cognitive and motor skills if not treated.	Global	Infants
Yamauchi 2008	Longitudinal data on nutrition (height proxy)	Nutrition at a very young age can impact schooling. Children with worse nutrition fared worse in school than those with better nutrition.	South Africa	Children under 6
Zimmermann et al. 2006	Iodine supplementation	See Gordan et al. (2009).	Albania	Schoolchildren

the famine on childhood growth, and (small) effects on IQ in adulthood, for example. (See Stein et al. 1975.) Beyond just these specific results, the Dutch famine study also provides a guide to identifying in-utero effects. Namely, if a shock is large and sharply timed, then only a narrow band of cohorts would be exposed to it while in the womb. One can assess retrospectively whether the time in utero is particularly sensitive to the shock by analyzing outcomes across cohorts. The most affected cohorts should be visible as a "blip" when graphing the sensitive outcome. Indeed, the nature of the Dutch famine is such that researchers are able to identify different long-term risk by the trimester in which the child's mother was most affected by food shortages.

In recent years, other scholars have followed this model and found further evidence that the time in the womb is a sensitive period. For example, Almond (2006) shows that children from a cohort whose mothers were pregnant during the 1918 influenza epidemic in the United States received less schooling. Most noteworthy is that this cohort had lower rates of graduation from high school and also reported lower earnings in the censuses of 1960, 1970, and 1980. But, as with many studies in this literature, the details of the mechanism that led to the measured outcomes is not fully elucidated. Similarly, a study by Almond and Mazumder (2011) of fasting during Ramadan shows that women who fast during the first trimester of pregnancy increase the risk of disabilities later for their children in the womb.

To elaborate, the study by Almond, as well as others, confirms that a disadvantage in preschool can lead to cognitive and motor impairment—that is, a health shock can lead to a reduced human capital stock that, in turn, influences the expected returns to schooling. However, in many studies in this literature it is not clear whether this result is directly due to changes in physical and mental capacity or indirectly due to loss of stimulation and of reduced interaction with the child's environment in the wake of illness. In the former case, preventing the shock is critical for a child's life's trajectory in Cunha and Heckman's sense of the term (2009). In the latter case, prevention is likely still the most efficient strategy, but a wider range of compensatory policies may also be practical.

Bharadwaj and Neilson (2011) have found evidence that the immediate attention to very low birth weight can prevent some loss of cognitive capacity. Using a regression discontinuity design to study Chile's policy of extra medical care provided to children born smaller than 1,500 grams, they note that by the time these children attended between the fourth and eighth grades of school they scored significantly higher on math tests than children who weighed slightly more than the cutoff for extra medical care at birth.

In the absence of such apparently successful preventive measures, reduced capacity can have an immediate effect on schooling through demand as well as influence the learning achieved per year of schooling. For example, Akresh et al. (2012) show that families in Burkina Faso allocate more schooling to the children within the household who have higher abilities compared to siblings. Similarly, Rosenzweig and Zhang (2009) find that in China the twin with the lower birth weight receives less education.

The link between demand for education and health begins early; children who are malnourished often start school late, either because parents feel the child is not ready or because the schools themselves discriminate on the basis of health and nutrition. Delayed entry does not necessarily lead to less completed education.[4] However, under a prevailing model of the returns to education this would be an expected consequence of delayed enrollment if the opportunity cost of a year of schooling increases with age. Moreover, even with no change in total years of schooling, late enrollment leads to lower expected lifetime earnings; in order to maintain total years of schooling with delayed entry, an individual would have to enter the workforce later. As Glewwe and Jacoby (1995) illustrate, for each year of delay in entry to primary school in Ghana a child in their study loses 3% of lifetime wealth.

A further—and probably predominant—means by which health prior to school influences subsequent educational outcomes is through self-productivity; conditional on years of schooling, ability itself strongly determines learning in school, which, according to the evidence presented by Hanushek and Woessmann (2008), is the real determinant of subsequent earning opportunities, not enrollment. Raising the productivity of a student's time in school enhances learning, which in turn fosters more demand for schooling.

Evidence on the impact of nutrition in the vulnerable period of a child's first two years on subsequent schooling (as well as the impact of the sensitive prenatal period) comes from a wide range of studies. For example, by taking advantage of differences in nutritional status between siblings in the Philippines, Glewwe, Jacoby and King (2001) were able to show that better-nourished children performed significantly better in school, partly because they enter school earlier and thus have more time to learn but mostly because of greater learning productivity per year of schooling.

As illustrated with the Glewwe, Jacoby, and King (2001) paper, panel data is at the core of studies addressing this question. Alderman, Hoddinott, and Kinsey (2006), for example, tracked a cohort of Zimbabweans over two decades and found both delayed school initiations and fewer grades completed for those who were malnourished as children. This study extrapolates beyond the drought shocks and civil unrest used for identification to project what the median preschool child in the sample would have achieved if he had reached the stature of a median child in a developed country by adolescence. The scenario indicates that with improved nutrition the child would be 3.4 centimeters taller, have had completed an additional 0.85 grades of schooling, as well as have started school six months earlier. Similar results have been reported from the nutritional consequences of droughts in Tanzania (Alderman, Hoogeveen, and Rossi 2009) and from changes in health policy in South Africa (Yamauchi 2008). Temporal variation in prices provide yet another means to identify the impact of nutrition on subsequent schooling; Alderman et al. (2001) used this approach to show that malnourished girls—but not boys—in Pakistan were less likely to enter school.

Maccini and Yang (2009) look at the long-term implication of rainfall shocks in Indonesia and find that, although the deviations in rainfall linked to the household data studied are not of a magnitude likely to be termed droughts, girls born in years of low rainfall have less schooling than those born in years with normal rainfall. They also achieved smaller adult heights. The impact of a shortfall of rain in a year immediately prior to birth does not have a measureable impact. Maccini and Yang interpret this as implying the shocks have an effect during the critical period of weaning rather than the prenatal period. The limited period of vulnerability is consistent with extensive epidemiological evidence (Shrimpton et al. 2001) and also renders unlikely an interpretation that the loss of household assets was of a sufficient magnitude and duration to directly affect schooling demand when the child reached the appropriate age. As neither the schooling of boys nor their adult heights were affected by these rainfall deviations, Maccini and Yang hypothesize that gender discrimination accounts for the pattern.[5]

The range of instruments used for local identification of the impact of nutrition on schooling provides some reassurance that the overall impact of malnutrition is robust over different proximate causes of the malnutrition and, thus, generalizable. Additional evidence in the impact of nutrition on long-term outcomes comes from a unique tracking of cohorts of children in Guatemala for a quarter of a century following a randomized nutritional intervention. The studies from the Guatemala panel verify that the indirect inferences of the impact of nutrition on schooling. This project followed children who received nutritional supplements as children and also followed a randomized control group. When these individuals were between 25 and 42 years old, both men and women who had received the supplements prior to the age of 3 years had higher scores on cognitive tests (Maluccio et al. 2009). Another study using this sample (Hoddinott et al. 2008) found that schooling attainment increased for both men and women.[6]

Many studies of nutrition and learning use height as an endogenous indicator of nutritional status and then include this variable in a second-stage estimate of schooling demand or of learning or, occasionally, wages. However, it is unlikely that height per se accounts for the majority of the improvement in schooling and earnings. More plausibly, height is an indicator of overall health and cognitive ability. Indeed, further analysis of the data used in the two Guatemala studies cited above—both of which report outcomes of a nutritional intervention but do not use height as an intermediary variable—indicate that the cognitive effects of the supplementary feeding rather than its impact on physical size drive the outcomes for adults (Behrman et al. 2010).

Most micronutrient deficiencies have only a small impact on stature—and thus do not show up in standard anthropometric measurements—yet micronutrients have a major impact on cognitive abilities. In particular, iodine deficiency is a well-known cause of reduced mental capacity beginning in the prenatal period. Meta-analyses using different samples have been consistent in their findings that iodine deficiency can affect brain development, with individuals with an iodine deficiency having, on average, 13.5 points lower IQs than comparison groups (Zimmermann 2009). Consistent with this evidence, Field, Robles, and Torero (2009) show that a decade and a half after mothers in Tanzania received iodine supplementation their children had on average 0.35–0.56 years of additional schooling, with the impact greater for girls. While this study was not a randomized experiment, the authors constructed a counterfactual by comparing sibling and age cohorts in the context of a rollout of a discrete program. As such, this study illustrates the underlying model in which an input in the first early childhood period increases school investments and presumably (though not measured in the cited paper) learning.

The case of iodine again raises the issue of sensitive versus critical periods for inputs. Most evidence indicates that if iodine deficiency is not prevented in utero, subsequent programs will not be able to offset the consequent developmental delays. Hence, there is a fairly narrow critical period to prevent iodine deficiency. More recent research, however, shows that iodine supplementation for schoolchildren with *mild or moderate* iodine deficiencies can, in fact, increase performance on cognitive tests (Gordon et al. 2009; Zimmermann et al. 2006). Thus while salt fortification with iodine is widely acknowledged as one of most cost-effective nutrition interventions known (Behrman, Alderman, and Hoddinott 2004), there is, nevertheless, some economic benefits to later programs for children with moderate deficiencies. As the earlier intervention remains the more effective, fortification or supplementation of women of child-bearing age addresses a sensitive period for subsequent schooling.

Iron-deficiency anemia is another micronutrient deficiency with clear implications for a child's cognitive and motor development. A review of early child development in the *Lancet* claims that, while the evidence of impairment is conclusive, "the short-term improvements seen in iron supplemented infants suggest that adverse effects can be prevented, reversed, or both, with iron earlier in development or before iron deficiency becomes severe or chronic" (Walker et al. 2007, 148). The review, however, also notes that there is less evidence that later supplementation will fully mitigate the consequences of early deficiency.[7] Among these consequences are increased grade repetition and lower IQ measures persisting into school-age years.

Lozoff, Jimenez, and Smith (2006) provide a notable longitudinal study of iron supplementation in children ages 1 and 2, tracking the same individuals 18 years later in Costa Rica, which illustrates the difficulty in reversing early deficiencies. In the original intervention, anemia was corrected with iron supplements in the treatment group but not in the control. Results are reported for children without anemia at the end of the intervention as compared to those with anemia (hence this compares children in the treatment group and nonanemic children in the control group, with anemic children in the control group). Children received cognitive tests at five different points up to age 19.

The results suggest that in the middle SES group, those with adequate iron status scored 8–9 points above those who remained anemic in early childhood, a difference that was maintained up to age 19. The gains for children in the lower SES group were similar in early childhood; those with adequate iron status scored 10 points higher in early childhood. The gain for this group, however, increased to 25 points at age 19. This implies that individuals in the chronic iron-deficiency group not only tested lower in infancy but also showed a more marked decline, and hence, an increasing gap, in subsequent cognitive test performance.

Good iron status before and/or after iron therapy in infancy appeared to attenuate the decline.[8]

Another experiment that has been tracked longitudinally provided iron, as well as zinc, to Nepali mothers during pregnancy (Christian et al. 2010). When these children were 7–9 years old they had improved performance on both cognitive and noncognitive measures. In particular, the treated children had higher scores on tests of working memory, inhibitory control, and fine motor functioning. Such longitudinal evidence on noncognitive functioning is relatively rare. Yet, it is in keeping with another study of 19-year-old individuals who were deficient in iron as infants in Costa Rica (Lukowski et al. 2010). This study found that individuals who had experienced chronic severe deficiencies had impaired executive function and recognition memory as young adults.

Another less-objective dimension of nutrition of interest for its interaction with schooling is hunger. This may limit a child's ability to concentrate in school and thus affect the amount of learning per day of schooling. A few studies have attempted to investigate this avenue of increased receptivity to instructions by looking at the tie between hunger and classroom performance using an experimental design. Available results, however, are not conclusive regarding long-term consequences, perhaps in part because controlled studies are hampered by difficulties in running experiments for an appreciable duration as well as the difficulty of encouraging parents to conform to the protocols of research design and the inability to use a placebo. Moreover, as shown in Grantham-McGregor, Chang, and Walker (1998), while feeding children may improve attention, its impact on learning depends on the classroom organization. This provides another perspective on the complementarity of teaching inputs and health.

The improvement in learning shown in this experiment, and similar studies, gives impetus to the provision of meals for students. While such programs may serve as a means to transfer resources to low-income students and are regularly observed to increase enrollment or attendance, their contribution to nutrition or to learning is less often observed.[9] For the former, the concern is that school-aged children are less vulnerable to undernutrition than to obesity. Also at issue for direct learning impacts is the timing of meals; meals at midday are more common than meals at the start of the class period but are less likely to foster concentration on classroom activities. School feeding programs can also contribute directly to nutrition if they are fortified, particularly with iron. While not all school feeding programs are fortified, the range of appropriate technology was widened with recent advances in extruder fortified rice.

This is done by adding a small amount of fortified processed kernels manufactured from rice flour to rice grains. The technique has proven acceptable to consumers and adds less than 5% to the cost of this staple. The potential for fortification has some conflict with the increased focus on local sourcing of foods since these foods are less likely to be centrally processed and, thus, less likely to be fortified in scale.

A final consideration for this section is the long-term impact of diarrheal disease; the short-term impact of lost activity is readily apparent, but the evidence of the importance of diarrheal disease for the intellectual development of any child who does not succumb to the attendant risk of fatal dehydration is less clear. We consider this risk here since malnutrition and diarrhea are strongly linked in young children. (Conversely, diarrhea is not generally a symptom of parasite infections.) To the degree that the diarrhea/nutrition link is a vicious circle, the long-term consequences of diarrhea would be similar to the measured consequences of malnutrition. This is consistent with longitudinal evidence such as a study tracking young children in *favelas* of Brazil which found an association of diarrhea incidence with subsequent schooling (Lorntz et al. 2006). This and similar studies, however, have small samples and are not able to determine any direct impact of diarrhea on future capacity for learning from the indirect impact though malnutrition. It is not, however, important to unpack this pathway to be able to ascertain that oral rehydration or zinc therapy for children with diarrhea will be cost effective (Horton, Alderman, and Rivera Dommarco 2009).

4.4. Parasite Burdens

As with nutritional deficiencies, parasite burdens may lead to impairment of a child's cognitive ability. For example, Eppig, Fincher, and Thornhill (2010) note that the global distribution of IQ is strongly associated with the disease burden of a country even when average temperature, education levels, and GDP are included in a multivariable regression. They hypothesize that diarrheal disease and parasites account for this relationship. However, as the DALY measure used in this regression is endogenous, other studies are needed to bolster this hypothesis.

While a young child is particularly vulnerable to malnutrition and to infections, a school-aged child is not immune from similar health shocks that entail medium- to long-run loss of cognitive ability. Worm infection rates, for example, peak in primary school–aged children. Similarly, early bouts of malaria do not provide full immunity to reoccurrence. To a fair degree, the impact of disease on schooling works though the same mechanisms as during the earlier period. One substantial difference in this period, however, comes from studies that show an impact on schooling via noncognitive factors such as the loss of time in school attributed to morbidity. It is, however, often difficult to separate this effect from direct impairment of ability.

The importance of deworming is indicated in a well-known study by Miguel and Kremer (2004). The study reports results of an experiment that provided deworming medicine to primary schoolchildren in Kenya. Following World Health Organization recommendations, schools with helminth prevalence over 50% were mass-treated with a broad-spectrum deworming medicine, albendazole, every six months, and schools with schistosomiasis prevalence over 30% were mass-treated with praziquantel annually. The treatment led to a 25% reduction in absenteeism. While no improvement in learning was recorded, this may reflect the fact that learning is cumulative and that there was only a modest time between rounds, perhaps insufficient to make a noticeable change to stock of knowledge (rather than the flow of attendance).[10] Indeed, a follow-up to the original intervention (Baird et al. 2011) shows higher earnings among the treated. The authors found the deworming experiment to be cost effective at increasing participation relative to supply-side interventions such as the provision of textbooks.

This finding is reinforced in several other recent experimental studies with preschool children. Bobonis, Miguel, and Sharma (2006) describe a study in which preschool children were provided iron supplementation and deworming medicine in a randomized trial. Children in the treatment group had less absenteeism. In particular, children who were initially anemic at baseline had a larger response to the intervention. The experiment, however, did not assess cognitive capacity nor were they able to track the children into the primary school years to measure subsequent performance. Ozier (2011) examined the impact on preschool children of the intervention in Miguel and Kremer's study and found substantial decreases in wormloads and increases in cognitive outcomes much later in childhood. This study highlights the importance of positive spillovers outside the target population, as well as the need to follow up on outcomes well after the intervention, by which time the stock of cognitive skills will have had a chance to grow.

The benefits of childhood deworming carry on into adulthood, according to a study by Bleakley (2007), who measured the impact of a hookworm-eradication campaign in the southern United States, ca. 1910, where children had infection rates of 30–40%. Children growing up in areas that benefited from the antihookworm campaign saw

Table 4.2 Selected studies of relationship between childhood disease burden and human capital

	Explanatory variable	Description	Place	Age at treatment (or exposure)
Baird et al. 2011	Deworming treatment	Follow up on post-school outcomes of school-based deworming finds higher consumption and wages among treated.	Kenya	Schoolchildren
Barreca 2010	Malaria fluctuations induced by interannual weather variations	Exposure to malaria reduces years of schooling.	US South, ca. 1920	In utero, infancy
Bleakley 2007	Childhood exposure to deworming campaign	Long run benefits to deworming such as increased literacy, attendance, and income if childhood infection is reduced.	US South, ca. 1912	Childhood
Bleakley 2010b	Malaria control (exposure to eradication campaigns)	Individuals born after malaria eradication had higher income and literacy than those born before eradication, relative to nonmalarious areas.	US, Brazil, Colombia, Mexico	Childhood
Bobonis, Miguel, and Sharma 2006	Iron supplements and deworming medicine	Treatment led to improved attendance.	India	Pre-school children
Clarke et al. 2008	Malaria treatment	Treatment led to improved cognition (attention) but not to higher educational achievement.	Kenya	Schoolchildren
Cutler et al. 2010	Malaria control (exposure to eradication campaigns)	Household consumption was higher for those born after malaria-eradication campaign, relative to low-malaria areas. Mixed effects for time in school.	India	Early childhood
Epping, Fincher, and Thornhill 2010	Parasite prevalence in country	The global distribution of IQ is associated with prevalence of parasitic disease across countries.	Global	n/a

Study	Data/Treatment	Findings	Location	Age group
Fernando et al. 2003	Longitudinal data on malaria	Malaria exposure related to lower cognitive performance later on.	Sri Lanka	Childhood
Fernando et al. 2006	Malaria treatment	Higher test scores and school attendance.	Sri Lanka	Schoolchildren
Horton, Alderman, and Rivera 2009	Diarrhea treatment (oral rehydration, zinc therapy)	High rates of return.	Global	Early childhood
Jukes et al. 2006	Malaria treatment	Long-term follow-up; treated children had half a grade more of schooling 14 years later.	Gambia	Early childhood
Lorntz et al. 2006	Longitudinal data on diarrhea	Early life diarrhea predicts educational outcomes.	Brazil	Early childhood
Lucas 2010	Malaria control (exposure to eradication campaigns)	Women born after malaria eradication had higher levels of education and literacy than those born before eradication.	Sri Lanka, Paraguay	Early childhood
Miguel and Kremer 2004	Deworming treatment	Treatment led to improved attendance, but not in test scores, possibly because there was not enough time between treatment and testing for results to show.	Kenya	Schoolchildren
Ozier 2011	Spillovers from deworming treatment	Deworming effects may take time to accumulate. Children treated for parasites exhibited increases in cognitive outcomes later on.	Kenya	Pre-school children
Thuilliez 2010	Longitudinal data on malaria	Treatment is important, especially in developing countries. High prevalence of malaria is linked to higher primary repetition rates.	Mali	Childhood
Thuilliez et al. 2010	Longitudinal data on malaria	Malaria exposure related to lower cognitive performance later on.	Mali	Childhood

large increases in literacy, school attendance, and income, relative both to earlier cohorts and uninfected areas. The changes in these outcomes coincide with childhood exposure to the eradication efforts, which further suggests that we are measuring the effect of deworming rather than some regional trend. According to those estimates, childhood exposure to hookworm depressed adult income significantly in the US South. Instrumental-variables estimates of the effect of hookworm on income can be interpreted as follows: If someone's point-in-time probability of hookworm infection in childhood goes from zero to one, it reduces his adult income by 43%. (This refers to persistent infection, not to having ever been infected.)

Deworming is a promising approach in part because of the low cost of the interventions (Hall, Horton, and de Silva 2009) as well as the externalities that are expected from reducing the transmission of a disease vector. Moreover, it is a public-health priority because parasites are prevalent in much of the developing world. The latter point could as easily be stated for malaria. This motivates research into the impact of malaria on schooling. One indication of this impact comes from cross-sectional regression analysis using Demographic Health Survey data from Mali aggregated at the cluster level suggests that a higher prevalence of malaria in a community is linked to higher primary repetition rates (Thuilliez 2010).

A follow-up longitudinal study in one village in Mali provides supportive evidence (Thuilliez et al. 2010). This study used child fixed effects to assess the impact of a bout of malaria on four measures of cognitive ability: vocabulary (crystallized intelligence), writing, visual memory as an indicator of selective attention, and inductive reasoning (fluid intelligence). Both clinical episodes and asymptomatic malaria (as indicated by parasite counts) led to lower test scores although the effect of the latter was lower. Using lagged variables, the study ascertained that the effects of the presence of the parasite persist for at least one month but decrease with time.

The longitudinal results from Mali are in keeping with results from Sri Lanka, a country with a less serious burden of malaria than most tropical Africa countries (Fernando et al. 2003). This study looked at the relation of the number of clinical cases of malaria (confirmed by microscopy) a child had over a six-year period and performance on grade-specific tests of language and mathematics. The multivariate regression results showed the more bouts of malaria, the lower both test scores.

Experimental evidence supports these results. For example, the longitudinal results from Sri Lanka are supported by a double-blind trial that provided chloroquine to children in grades 1–5. Absenteeism was reduced by 62% over a nine-month period and scores in tests of both mathematics and language improved by about 25% (Fernando et al. 2006). Similarly, Clarke et al. (2008) provided intermittent preventive treatment (IPT) for malaria to schoolchildren in Kenya using a randomized, double-blind placebo-controlled design. IPT has been found to be safe for preventative programs, although there is concern that the evolution of drug resistance needs to be carefully monitored. Three treatments were provided at four-month intervals with improvements in tests of classroom attention as well as in anemia rates. However, no improvement in education achievement was noted. As mentioned in a different context above, this may reflect the time span of the study.[11]

A somewhat different perspective on malaria prophylaxis for school-aged children was reported in a study that followed children 14 years after a trial designed to assess alternative treatments to prevent malaria morbidity in young children in the Gambia (Jukes et al. 2006). The conclusions of this study are necessarily muted since roughly half the sample was lost to the follow-up and also due to the post- (initial) trial provision of prophylaxis medicine to the control group. There were no clear differences in cognitive development scores covering memory, reasoning, and knowledge, although these scores were higher the longer a child was in the treatment. However, the treatment group had achieved half a grade more of schooling. The researchers concluded that the effect was likely due to the prevention of cerebral malaria in a few children as well as the reduction of anemia in a larger cohort.

Yet another approach to this question comes from the retrospective analysis of various malaria-eradication campaigns (many using DDT spraying) in the twentieth century. Bleakley (2010b) analyzes the effect of one's childhood exposure to malaria on income later in adulthood in a retrospective follow-up of malaria-control campaigns in the United States (ca. 1920) and in Brazil, Colombia, and Mexico (ca. 1955). The design is essentially a difference in differences, with earlier cohorts and cohorts in nonmalarious regions serving as comparison groups. The basic finding is that cohorts born after eradication had higher income and literacy as adults than the preceding generation, relative to cohorts from nonmalarious areas, with a pattern coincident with childhood exposure to the campaigns. The magnitude of the change in income associated with childhood malaria is substantial: when comparing the least malarious with the most malarious areas within a country, in the range of 12% (in the United States) to 40% (in Latin America). Although one can never rule out that the intervention had effects through channels besides estimated malaria infection, the results suggest that persistent childhood malaria infection reduces adult income by 50%. (The normalized effects are similar across the four countries.) Two other retrospective papers also find that childhood exposure to malaria-control campaigns had impacts on human capital.[12]

4.5. Policy Implications and Conclusions

As countries progress toward the goal of universal basic education, this initial success places greater emphasis on increasing the quality of learning within the classroom. Without diminishing the importance of school inputs, teacher quality, and classroom organization, it should be readily apparent that optimizing school performance also requires additional investments in the health of the child. Which investments and, given a lifetime model, when they need to be made remain problematic and the scope of a range of studies. Even the maxim promoting the relative value of prevention compared to cure—while true more often than not—does not necessarily rule out two effective curative interventions discussed in this review, treatment for intestinal parasites and intermittent treatment for malaria, as potential key public health programs to be integrated into educational systems.

A shift in emphasis from school quantity to learning quality suggests a more refined notion of complementarity when measuring the impact of health on time in school, whose price varies with the opportunity cost of time. If better childhood health makes a child a better worker and/or allows the child to learn more quickly, this raises the opportunity cost of time. So, while improving child health might raise the marginal benefit of education, it also raises the marginal cost, leaving the overall effect of child health on time in school ambiguous (Bleakley 2010a; Yamauchi 2008). This ambiguity implies that it is difficult to interpret studies that use the age of leaving school as the central outcome. Instead, this analysis indicates that we should focus on measures of school productivity such as test scores or, even better, adult income.

The evidence in this chapter, as well as studies presented in other reviews (such as Behrman, Alderman, and Hoddinott 2004), indicate high rates of economic return from investments in preschool health, mostly due to the increased productivity that comes from improved cognitive and noncognitive skills. But such returns reveal relatively little about the public rationale for the investments.

In the case of infectious disease, the externalities of, say, deworming are readily apparent. Reducing the transmission of disease, therefore, is a public good. Furthermore, evaluating policies without paying attention to such spillovers can lead to substantial bias in which programs are judged successful and which are not (Bundy et al. 2009; Philipson 2000). This stands in curious contrast with many policy-evaluation studies, which seem to proceed from the assumption that the best interventions are the ones that cause the largest increase in program takeup or input use. This might be correct if all inputs generate the same externality on net, but surely this is a heroic assumption. And, indeed, in the case in which the externalities are small, selecting programs based on which has the highest elasticity biases things toward interventions that generate the least consumer surplus (because the demand curve is flat). This suggests that future evaluations should seek to measure spillovers rather than demand elasticities, if the goal of the public sector is to reduce market failures.

Other common rationales for increased public investment in private health include (1) imperfect credit markets;[13] (2) imperfect parental altruism; and (3) information gaps that lead to private underinvestment. In the interest of space, this chapter has not presented evidence in support of these underlying rationales for public investments. However, implicitly, the evidence presented does bolster the theme of public-health measures as a form of a "second-best" argument. This is because virtually all governments invest a large share of their public spending on education. Whatever reasons they may have to motivate such public investments in what is largely the private good of individual learning and earning capacity, any investment that increases the efficiency of these expenditures improves the allocation of public resources. Thus, since improving private health raises the rate of return to subsequent schooling investment, it makes these committed (i.e., inframarginal) public investments more effective.

The analysis above also helps us understand what is being tested in some of the empirical work in this literature. As we argued above, the direct effect of childhood health on other human capital is likely to be larger than the degree to which the returns to other investments later in childhood respond to health shocks early in childhood. That is, self-productivity should be a key area of focus rather than the indirect effect though dynamic complementarity. Still, a search for substitutes for early health may be important since these may provide a second chance later in life. If we cannot prevent malnutrition or low birth weight despite current efforts, we need to find substitutes in human-capital formation.

Finally, an additional argument for such public investments comes from the (unmeasured, but easily assumed) preference for equity that most governments exhibit. As argued by Heckman and others, early investments in human capital can increase equity. Societies, at least in their public rhetoric, generally place an equity weight on an increase in income that accrues to the poor, such that a dollar transferred to a poor household or earned by a poor household has a higher value in assessing national priorities than a similar dollar amount for the average household. To an even greater degree, societies value equity of opportunity. Thus, to the degree that investments in education assist low-income households to participate in overall economic growth, an additional justification exists for the core argument promoting public heath investments. While many programs to increase equity are targeted with direct means tests, public health programs in school generally are not. Nevertheless, because the burden of disease is often greater the poorer the household, public health measures in school provide particular focus on the needs of the poor.

Demand-side programs to encourage schooling by lowering the price—indeed, by sometimes creating a negative marginal price—may also assist in addressing equity. However, by increasing the gap between resource costs and the price the household faces, this is achieved at some economic inefficiency. In contrast, an increase of schooling that is a result of higher returns due to better health—that is, via increased efficiency in learning—does not distort prices at the schooling level. This implies that the changes in schooling are reached not by moving along the demand curve but by shifting the curve outward. Thus, by improving equity (addressing problems that disproportionately afflict the poor) *and* improving efficiency (e.g., reducing disease spillovers, enhancing the productivity of public spending on schooling), improving childhood health can be a rare "double play" that avoids the usual equity/efficiency tradeoff.

Acknowledgments

The authors wish to thank Karthik Muralidharan and Paul Glewwe for helpful comments, and Lucy Shen for excellent research assistance.

Notes

1. See, for example, the website for Disease Control Priorities Project at http://www.dcp2.org/pubs/GBD/4/Table/4.7.
2. More detailed models with similar objectives can be found in chapter 3 of this volume as well as in Almond and Currie 2010, Behrman, Glewwe, and Miguel 2007, and Cunha and Heckman 2007. For an application of this

approach to early child development in low-income settings see Alderman and Vegas 2011.

3. This is not a quirk of the graph, but rather a general result from optimization theory, specifically the Envelope Theorem. See Bleakley 2010a for more on this point. This idea is also related to Harberger's well-known analysis of triangles versus rectangles in considering shifts of demand curves.

4. It is possible, for example, that the lost opportunity for learning from a delay in starting school may be partially offset by improved school readiness (Glewwe, King, and Jacoby 2001).

5. However, almost all evidence of discrimination against girls in nutritional outcomes—either due to shocks or to more regular patterns of investments in human capital—comes from South Asia and, even then, the evidence is largely limited to northwestern India. With some exceptions, the absence of differences in nutritional outcomes by gender is less likely to result in a journal article than its presence.

6. Additionally this study reports that men earned on average 44% higher wages. This is on the higher end of the range derived indirectly or from studies that compare twins with different birth weights. There was not a significant increase of wages for women in this cohort—perhaps due to limited wage opportunities in the communities.

7. An analysis published after Walker et al. however, notes that supplements for children older than 7 do improve intelligence (Sachdev, Gera and Nestel 2005). Moreover, Luo et al. 2102 presents an example of a successful school-based program of iron supplementation.

8. Lozoff et al. (2006) references Matthew 25:29: "For everyone who has will be given more, and he will have an abundance. Whoever does not have, even what he has will be taken from him." This appears to be a statement of self-productivity, albeit from a rather different discipline than Cunha and Heckman (2007).

9. School feeding is covered in greater depth in Behrman, Parker and Todd (chapter 5 of this volume) as well as Adelman, Gilligan, and Lehrer 2008 and Alderman and Bundy (2012).

10. King and Behrman (2009) point out that the time frame for an impact evaluation is often its Achilles heel.

11. This trial is being followed up with a larger trial in Kenya (Brooker et al. 2010).

12. Lucas (2010) shows that women born after malaria eradication in Sri Lanka and Paraguay completed more years of schooling and were more literate. Her estimates for literacy are similar in magnitude to those by Bleakley (2010a). Cutler et al. (2010) analyze the malaria-eradication campaign in India and find malaria exposure in the first few years of life had little effect on education, but lowered consumption later in life. Their headline number for consumption is lower than what we reported above for income, but estimates are similar once adjusted for their focus on just the first years of life (instead of all of childhood) and for their sample being 20–25 years old, ages at which the returns to skill are lower. Barreca (2010) focuses instead on short-run variation in early life malaria

induced by weather fluctuations, and finds that infection from malaria in utero reduces ultimate educational attainment.

13. In theory, a simpler fix for a capital-market imperfection lies in somehow increasing the provision of credit via subsidies or transfers. Nevertheless, governments might be worried that such transfers might promote rent seeking in a way that in-kind assistance does not.

References

Adelman, Sarah, Daniel O. Gilligan, and Kim Lehrer. 2008. "How Effective Are Food for Education Programs? A Critical Assessment of the Evidence from Developing Countries." *IFPRI Food Policy Review No. 9*. Washington, DC: International Food Policy Research Institute.

Akresh, Richard, Emilie Bagby, Damien de Walque, and Harounan Kazianga. 2012. "Child Ability and Household Human Capital Investment Decisions in Burkina Faso." *Economic Development and Cultural Change* 61 (1): 157–86.

Alderman, Harold, Jere Behrman, Victor Lavy, and Rekha Menon. 2001. "Child Health and School Enrollment: A Longitudinal Analysis." *Journal of Human Resources* 36 (1): 185–205.

Alderman, Harold, and Donald Bundy. 2012. "School Feeding Programs and Development: Are We Framing the Question Correctly?" *World Bank Research Observer* 27 (2): 204–21.

Alderman, Harold, John Hoddinott, and William Kinsey. 2006. "Long-Term Consequences of Early Childhood Malnutrition." *Oxford Economic Papers* 58 (3): 450–74.

Alderman, Harold, Hans Hoogeveen, and Mariacristina Rossi. 2009. "Preschool Nutrition and Subsequent Schooling Attainment: Longitudinal Evidence from Tanzania." *Economic Development and Cultural Change* 57 (2): 239–60.

Alderman, Harold, and Emiliana Vegas. 2011. "The Convergence of Equity and Efficiency in ECD Programs." In *No Small Matter: The Interaction of Poverty, Shocks, and Human Capital Investments in Early Childhood Development*, ed. Harold Alderman, 155–83. Washington, DC: World Bank.

Almond, Douglas. 2006. "Is the 1918 Influenza Pandemic Over? Long-Term Effects of *In Utero* Influenza Exposure in the Post-1940 U.S. Population." *Journal of Political Economy* 114 (4): 672–712.

Almond, Douglas, and Janet Currie. 2010. "Human Capital Development before Age Five." NBER Working Paper 15827. http://www.nber.org/papers /w15827.

Almond, Douglas, and Bhashkar Mazumder. 2011. "Health Capital and the Prenatal Environment: The Effect of Ramadan Observance during Pregnancy." *American Economic Journal: Applied Economics* 3 (4): 56–85.

Baird, S., J. H. Hicks, M. Kremer, and E. Miguel. 2011. "Worms at Work: Long-Run Impacts of Child Health Gains." Working Paper, Poverty Action Lab, October. http://www.povertyactionlab.org/publication/worms-work-long-run -impacts-child-health-gains.

Barreca, Alan. 2010. "The Long-Term Economic Impact of In Utero and Postnatal Exposure to Malaria." *Journal of Human Resources* 45 (4): 865–92.

Behrman, Jere, Harold Alderman, and John Hoddinott. 2004. "Hunger and Malnutrition." In *Global Crises, Global Solutions,* ed. Bjorn Lomborg, 363–420. Cambridge: Cambridge University Press.

Behrman, Jere, Paul Glewwe, and Edward Miguel. 2007. "Methodologies to Evaluate Early Childhood Development Programs." Doing Impact Evaluation Paper #9. Washington, DC: World Bank.

Behrman, Jere, John Hoddinott, John Maluccio, and Reynaldo Martorell. 2010. "Brains versus Brawn: Labor Market Returns to Intellectual and Physical Health Human Capital in a Developing Country." University of Pennsylvania. Unpublished manuscript.

Bharadwaj, Prashant, and Christopher Neilson. 2011. "Early Life Health Interventions and Academic Achievement." UCSD. Unpublished manuscript.

Bleakley, Hoyt. 2007. "Disease and Development: Evidence from Hookworm Eradication in the American South." *Quarterly Journal of Economics* 122 (1): 73–117.

———. 2010a. "Health, Human Capital, and Development." *Annual Review of Economics* 2 (September): 283–310.

———. 2010b. "Malaria in the Americas: A Retrospective Analysis of Childhood Exposure." *American Economic Journal: Applied Economics* 2 (2): 1–45.

Bobonis, Gustavo J., Edward Miguel, and Charu Puri Sharma. 2006. "Anemia and School Participation." *Journal of Human Resources* 41 (4): 692–721.

Brooker, Simon, George Okello, Kiambo Njagi, Margaret M Dubeck, Katherine E Halliday, Hellen Inyega, and Matthew C. H. Jukes. 2010. "Improving Educational Achievement and Anaemia of School Children: Design of a Cluster Randomised Trial of School-Based Malaria Prevention and Enhanced Literacy Instruction in Kenya." *Trials* 11:93.

Bundy, Donald A. P., Michael Kremer, Hoyt Bleakley, Matthew C. H. Jukes, and Edward Miguel. 2009. "Deworming and Development: Asking the Right Questions, Asking the Questions Right." *PLOS/NTD* 3 (1): e362. http://www.plosntds.org/article/info:doi/10.1371/journal.pntd.0000362

Christian, P., L. E. Murray-Kolb, S. K. Khatry, J. Katz, B. A. Schaefer, P. M. Cole, S. C. Leclerq, and J. M. Tielsch. 2010. "Prenatal Micronutrient Supplementation and Intellectual and Motor Function in Early School-Aged Children in Nepal." *JAMA* 304 (24): 2716–23.

Clarke, Siân E., Matthew C. H. Jukes, J. Kiambo Njagi, Lincoln Khasakhala, Bonnie Cundill, Julius Otido, Christopher Crudder, Benson B. A, Estambale, and Simon Brooker. 2008. "Effect of Intermittent Preventive Treatment of Malaria on Health and Education in Schoolchildren: A Cluster-Randomised, Double-Blind, Placebo-Controlled Trial." *Lancet* 372 (9633): 127–38.

Cunha, Flavio, and James Heckman. 2007. "The Technology of Skills Formation." *American Economic Review* 97 (2): 31–47.

———. 2009. "The Economics and Psychology of Inequality and Human Development." *Journal of the European Economic Association* 7 (2–3): 320–64.

Cutler, David, Winnie Fung, Michael Kremer, Monica Singhal, and Tom Vogl. 2010. "Early-Life Malaria Exposure and Adult Outcomes: Evidence from

Malaria Eradication in India." *American Economic Journal: Applied Economics* 2 (2): 72–94.

Eppig, Christopher, Corey Fincher, and Randy Thornhill. 2010. "Parasite Prevalence and the Worldwide Distribution of Cognitive Ability." *Proceedings of Royal Society B* 277:3745–53.

Fernando, D., D. de Silva, R. Carter, K. N. Mendis, and R. Wickremasinghe. 2006. "A Randomized, Double-Blind, Placebo-Controlled, Clinical Trial of the Impact of Malaria Prevention on the Educational Attainment of School Children." *American Journal of Tropical Medicine and Hygiene* 74 (3): 386–93.

Fernando, S. D., D. M. Gunawardena, M. R. S. S. Bandara, D. De Silva, R. Carter, K. N. Mendis, and A. R. Wickremasinghe. 2003. "The Impact of Repeated Malaria Attacks on the School Performance of Children." *American Journal of Tropical Medicine and Hygiene* 69 (6): 582–88.

Field, Erica, Omar Robles, and Maximo Torero. 2009. "Iodine Deficiency and Schooling Attainment in Tanzania." *American Economic Journal: Applied Economics* 1 (4): 140–69.

Glewwe, Paul, and Hanan Jacoby. 1995. "An Economic Analysis of Delayed Primary School Enrollment and Childhood Malnutrition in a Low Income Country." *Review of Economics and Statistics* 77 (1): 156–69.

Glewwe, Paul, Hanan Jacoby, and Elizabeth King. 2001. "Early Childhood Nutrition and Academic Achievement: A Longitudinal Analysis." *Journal of Public Economics* 81 (3): 345–68.

Glewwe, Paul, Michael Kremer, and Sylvie Moulin. 2009. "Many Children Left Behind? Textbooks and Test Scores in Kenya." *American Economic Journal: Applied Economics* 1 (1): 112–35.

Gordon, Rosie C., Meredith C. Rose, Sheila A. Skeaff, Andrew R. Gray, Kirstie M. D. Morgan, and Ted Ruffman. 2009. "Iodine Supplementation Improves Cognition in Mildly Iodine-Deficient Children." *American Journal of Clinical Nutrition* 90:1264–71.

Grantham-McGregor, S. M., S. Chang, and S. P. Walker. 1998. "Evaluation of School Feeding Programs: Some Jamaican Examples." *American Journal of Clinical Nutrition* 67 (4): 785S–789S.

Hall, Andrew, Susan Horton, and Nilanthi de Silva. 2009. "The Costs and Cost-Effectiveness of Mass Treatment for Intestinal Nematode Worm Infections Using Different Treatment Thresholds." *PLoS Neglected Tropical Diseases* 3 (3): e402.

Hanushek, Eric, and Ludger Woessmann. 2008. "The Role of Cognitive Skills in Economic Development." *Journal of Economic Literature* 46 (3): 607–68.

Heckman, James, Jora Stixrud, and Sergio Urzúa. 2005. "The Effects of Cognitive and Non-cognitive Abilities on Labor Market Outcomes and Social Behavior." *Journal of Labor Economics* 24 (3): 411–82.

Hoddinott, John, John Maluccio, Jere Behrman, Rafel Flores, and Reynaldo Martorell. 2008. "Effect of a Nutrition Intervention during Early Childhood on Economic Productivity in Guatemalan Adults." *Lancet* 371:411–16.

Horton, Susan, Harold Alderman, and Juan Rivera Dommarco. 2009. "Hunger and Malnutrition." In *Global Crises, Global Solutions: Costs and Benefits,* ed. Bjorn Lomborg, 305–54. Cambridge: Cambridge University Press.

Jamison, D. T., J. G. Breman, A. R. Measham, G. Alleyne, M. Claeson, D. B. Evans, P. Jha, A. Mills, and P. Musgrove 2006. *Disease Control Priorities in Developing Countries*. 2nd ed. Washington, DC, and New York: World Bank and Oxford University Press.

Jukes, M. C. H., M. Pinder, E. L. Grigorenko, H. B. Smith, G. Walraven, E. M. Bariau, R. J. Sternberg, L. J. Drake, P. Milligan, Y. B. Cheung, B. M. Greenwood, and D. A. P. Bundy. 2006. "Long-Term Impact of Malaria Chemoprophylaxis on Cognitive Abilities and Educational Attainment: Follow-Up of a Controlled Trial." *PLoS Clinical Trials* 1 (4): e19.

King, Elizabeth, and Jere Behrman. 2009. "Timing and Duration of Exposure in Evaluations of Social Programs." *World Bank Research Observer* 24 (1): 55–82.

Lorntz, B., A. M. Soares, S. R. Moore, R. Pinkerton, B. Gansneder, V. E. Bovbjerg, H. Guyatt, A. M. Lima, and R. L. Guerrant. 2006. "Early Childhood Diarrhea Predicts Impaired School Performance." *Pediatric Infectious Disease Journal* 25 (6): 513–20.

Lozoff, Betsy, Elias Jimenez, and Julia Smith. 2006. "Double Burden of Iron Deficiency in Infancy and Low Socioeconomic Status: A Longitudinal Analysis of Cognitive Test Scores to 19 Years." *Archives of Pediatric and Adolescent Medicine* 160 (11): 1108–13.

Lucas, Adrienne M. 2010. "Malaria Eradication and Educational Attainment: Evidence from Paraguay and Sri Lanka." *American Economic Journal: Applied Economics* 2 (2): 46–71.

Lukowski, Angela, Marlere Koss, Mathew Burden, John Jonides, Charles Nelson, Niko Kaciroti, Elias Jimenez, and Betsy Lozoff. 2010. "Iron Deficiency in Infancy and Neurocognitive Functioning at 19 Years: Evidence of Long-Term Deficits in Executive Function and Recognition Memory." *Nutritional Neuroscience* 13 (2): 54–70.

Luo, Renfu, et al. 2012. "Nutrition and Educational Performance in Rural China's Elementary Schools: Results of a Randomized Control Trial in Shaanxi Province." *Economic Development and Cultural Change* 60 (4): 735–72

Maccini, Sharon, and Dean Yang. 2009. "Under the Weather: Health, Schooling, and Economic Consequences of Early-Life Rainfall." *American Economic Review* 99 (3): 1006–26.

Maluccio, John, John Hoddinott, Jere Behrman, Reynaldo Martorell, Agnes Quisumbing, and Aryeh Stein. 2009. "The Impact of Improving Nutrition during Early Childhood on Education among Guatemalan Adults." *Economic Journal* 119 (537): 734–63.

Miguel, Edward, and Michael Kremer. 2004. "Worms: Identifying Impacts on Education and Health in the Presence of Treatment Externalities." *Econometrica* 72 (1): 159–217.

Ozier, Owen. 2011. "Exploiting Externalities to Estimate the Long-Term Effects of Early Childhood Deworming." Unpublished manuscript. Department of Economics, University of California, Berkeley.

Philipson, Tomas J. 2000. "External Treatment Effects and Program Implementation Bias." Working Paper T0250. National Bureau of Economic Research, Cambridge, MA. http://www.nber.org/papers/t0250.pdf.

Rosenzweig, Mark, and Junsen Zhang. 2009. "Do Population Control Policies Induce More Human Capital Investment? Twins, Birth Weight and China's 'One-Child' Policy." *Review of Economic Studies* 76 (3): 1149–74.

Sachdev, H., T. Gera, and P. Nestel. 2005. "Effect of Iron Supplementation on Mental And Motor Development in Children: Systematic Review of Randomised Controlled Trials." *Public Health Nutrition* 8 (2): 117–32.

Shrimpton, R., C. Victora, M. de Onis, R. Costa Lima, M. Blössner, and G. Clugston. 2001. "Worldwide Timing of Growth Faltering: Implications for Nutritional Interventions." *Pediatrics* 107:75–81.

Stein, Zena, Mervyn Susser, Gerhart Saenger, and Francis Marolla. 1975. *Famine and Human Development: The Dutch Hunger Winter of 1944–1945.* London: Oxford University Press.

Thuilliez, Josselin. 2010. "Fever, Malaria and Primary Repetition Rates amongst School Children in Mali: Combining Demographic and Health Surveys (DHS) with Spatial Malariological Measures." *Social Science and Medicine* 71 (2): 314–23.

Thuilliez, Josselin, Mahamadou S. Sissoko, Ousmane B. Toure, Paul Kamate, Jean-Claude Berthélemy, and Ogobara K. Doumbo. 2010. "Malaria and Primary Education in Mali: A Longitudinal Study in the Village of Donéguébougou." *Social Science and Medicine* 71 (2): 324–34.

Walker, Susan, Theodore Wachs, Julie Meeks Gardner, Betsy Lozoff, Gail Wasserman, Ernesto Pollitt, Julie Carter and the International Child Development Steering Group. 2007. "Child Development: Risk Factors for Adverse Outcomes in Developing Countries." *Lancet* 369 (9556): 145–57.

Yamauchi, F. 2008. "Early Childhood Nutrition, Schooling and Sibling Inequality in a Dynamic Context: Evidence from South Africa." *Economic Development and Cultural Change* 56:657–82.

Zimmermann, Michael. 2009. "Iodine Deficiency in Pregnancy and the Effects of Maternal Iodine Supplementation on the Offspring: A Review." *American Journal of Clinical Nutrition* 89 (2): 668S–672S.

Zimmermann, M. B., K. J. Connolly, M. Bozo, J. Bridson, F. Rohner, and L. Grimci. 2006. "Iodine Supplementation Improves Cognition in Iodine-Deficient Schoolchildren in Albania: A Randomized, Controlled, Double-Blind Study." *American Journal of Clinical Nutrition* 83 (1): 108–14.

5

Incentives for Students and Parents

Jere R. Behrman (University of Pennsylvania)
Susan W. Parker (Centro de Investigación y Docencia
Económicas, Mexico)
Petra E. Todd (University of Pennsylvania)

5.1. Introduction

How individuals respond to incentives is central to economics. Whether such responses are large or small or quick or slow influences the effectiveness of incentive-based policy interventions. Over the past half century, the perceived importance of responses to incentives in development economics has increased substantially, questioning once-conventional wisdom regarding nonresponsive peasant farmers and the low costs of policy distortions directed toward squeezing savings out of agriculture and favoring infant industries. In recent decades, there has also been increasing concern in the development literature and among policymakers about how incentives affect education, health, nutrition, and other so-called social sectors.

Incentive programs for students and parents for primary and secondary school education have spread rapidly in developing countries in recent decades.[1] This chapter provides an overview of what is known about the effectiveness of various kinds of incentive programs aimed at improving educational outcomes.

The educational outcomes of primary interest, presumably, are those that increase productivity, such as cognitive skills and possibly noncognitive skills related, for example, to executive function (or self-regulation or "cognitive control"—related to staying on task, resisting temptations, and selective attention). Most of the literature on incentives for students and parents analyzes incentives tied to inputs in the production of skills—such as school enrollment, school attendance, grade repetition, and completed years of schooling—rather than direct measures of skills.

Whether such incentives are effective or not does not depend solely on the form of the skill production function. It also depends on decisions regarding the choices of inputs that are made by a number of entities—children, parents, teachers, and school administrators—subject to the information that they have, the incentives they face, and the resources they have. The effectiveness of incentives for students and parents is likely to depend on the production function technology and on inputs into that production function provided by students and parents, as well as by other entities. If the production function technology is characterized by strong complementarities between student effort and teacher effort, for example, then the responsiveness of student learning to a given level of student incentives is likely to vary considerably depending on the extent of teacher effort. That the relevant decisions regarding inputs into the knowledge production function are made by many entities, each with his or her own objectives, also means that there are likely to be spillovers on other behaviors of all these entities, which may include some unintended and perhaps undesired consequences. For example, parents could conceivably respond to improvements in school quality, such as a decrease in the pupil-teacher ratio, by spending less time learning with children at home.

Estimating the impacts of educational incentives for students/parents is challenging, because the impacts may depend on the behavioral responses of multiple entities and because there are potentially important, unobserved factors, such as student, teacher, and parental abilities and preferences. This chapter does not provide an extended discussion of the estimation challenges, but it is useful to briefly note the major evaluation approaches that are used in the studies summarized below.[2] Before-and-after comparisons (double-difference [DD]) between treatment and control students/parents with random assignment of treatment (randomized controlled trials [RCTs]) is an approach with strong advocates, but not without difficulties regarding, for example, selective attrition, little insight into counterfactual treatments, and often high costs of maintaining experiments for sufficiently long periods to capture the effects throughout multiple school years and thereafter on adult productivity. Before-and-after comparisons between treatment and control students/parents without random assignment have the same difficulties and in addition require strong assumptions about similar distributions of time-varying unobserved factors between treatment and control groups. Econometric techniques such as propensity score matching (PSM), regression discontinuity (RD), and instrumental variables (IV) also tend to require stronger assumptions than do RCTs regarding, for instance, whether there are important time-varying unobserved factors (PSM) or to what extent estimates can be generalized from the neighborhood for which RD estimates or IV instruments have empirical relevance, or the strength of tests for violations of the underlying assumptions (e.g., overidentification tests for IV estimates). Finally, an alternative approach that is attractive for exploring the effects of counterfactual policies, at the cost of stronger assumptions required for obtaining the model parameters, is the use of structural models.[3]

In the rest of this chapter we survey recent programs that provide educational incentives for students/parents for grades K-12 schooling in developing countries.[4] We divide this survey into the following components: the schooling component of conditional cash-transfer (CCT) programs (section 5.2), incentives conditional on test performance (section 5.3), school vouchers (section 5.4), and food-for-education (FFE) programs (section 5.5). Section 5.6 concludes.

The results of this survey of evidence on incentives for students and parents reinforce at least three of the general themes discussed by Glewwe, Hanushek, Humpage, and Ravina in chapter 2. First, spending does not necessarily translate directly into learning. Second, it is critical to look at incentive systems and to understand what behaviors are incentivized to produce better educational systems. Third, local conditions and contexts are likely to be important, with the implication that systematic assessments of programs in particular contexts are likely to have high rates of return even if similar programs have been evaluated in other contexts and that it is likely to be very challenging to provide guidance about "best practices" that can be applied in many contexts without the need for careful consideration of the context and monitoring and assessment of new applications (see Dhaliwal, Duflo, Glennerster, and Tullochin in chapter 8 below).

5.2. Schooling Component of Conditional Cash-Transfer Programs

Conditional cash-transfer (CCT) programs have spread rapidly in the past decade and a half since they were initiated in Brazil and Mexico in the mid-1990s. Many CCTs have as one component transfers conditional on primary or secondary school enrollment and attendance. Typically CCTs have other objectives, however, than just increasing schooling. These other objects are related to health and nutrition and short-run poverty alleviation. The multiplicity of objectives and bundled program components make evaluation of just the schooling component challenging.[5] Because CCTs have been reviewed extensively in a number of venues recently, we focus on recent studies that are not covered in what is probably the most visible of these reviews, the Fiszbein and Schady (2009) World Bank Research Policy Report (hereafter "WB report"). We begin by providing a brief history of CCTs. We then turn to a summary of the evidence from the WB report and finally spend the remainder of this section on studies carried out since its publication.

5.2.1. Brief History and Extent of Existing CCT Programs. CCTs provide cash to poor families in exchange for family investments in human capital, principally sending children to school and family members attending regular health clinic visits. CCTs aim to both alleviate current poverty conditions by providing monetary assistance to poor families and to reduce the probability of poverty in the next generation by increasing human capital investment of children today. Benefits are generally provided to the mother/female head of the household, motivated by previous economic studies that suggested that resources controlled by females have larger impacts on child well-being than those controlled by males.[6]

The Mexican (PROGRESA/Oportunidades) and Brazilian (Bolsa Escola) programs began at about the same time in the mid-1990s and remain the largest and most extensive CCT programs, covering over a quarter of the population in their respective countries. Results of the Mexican program became well known relatively early in large part because of the randomized evaluation undertaken when the program began, which resulted in a significant number of early studies and publications showing generally positive results on such indicators as household expenditures on food, school enrollment, and health clinic visits. These positive results arguably contributed to the adoption of CCT programs by a number of other Latin American countries in the following years. By 2010 CCTs had spread to over 30 countries on five continents including some efforts in developed countries, such as the Opportunities NYC conditional cash program in New York. The widespread adoption of CCT programs likely reflects their perceived attractiveness to governments and in particular the idea of conditioning transfers. While conditioning has costs (compliance and monitoring costs for instance), the conditioning also likely makes CCT programs more palatable politically by avoiding the appearance of a "handout."

CCTs, by subsidizing schooling, are unambiguously expected to increase schooling of child and youth beneficiaries. Broadly speaking, it is useful to think of investment in schooling as being determined by equating the marginal cost in terms of foregone earnings from work and foregone leisure to the marginal benefit of spending additional time in school, in particular, higher earnings as an adult. School subsidies affect the marginal costs of schooling in the same way as would a decrease in the child wage rate: the subsidy reduces the shadow wage (or relative value) of children's time in activities other than school and thus leads to reallocation of resources toward schooling.

5.2.2. Summary of World Bank 2009 Research Policy Report and Comments.
The World Bank Policy Research Report (2009), "Conditional Cash Transfers: Reducing Present and Future Poverty," provides an excellent description of the results of CCT programs from around the world. Here we provide only a brief summary of their reported results on educational variables from chapter 5 of the WB report.

In general, the summary based on six Latin American countries (Chile, Colombia, Ecuador, Honduras, Mexico, and Nicaragua) and four outside that region (Bangladesh, Cambodia, Pakistan, and Turkey) shows that all programs studied have significant impacts on school enrollment in the initial years of program operation. Magnitudes of program effects range for the Latin American countries from 2 to 13 percentage points and for countries outside the region, from 11.1 to 31.3 percentage points, although for Turkey impacts are statistically insignificant.

The WB report also provides some evidence on the heterogeneity of CCT impacts. A general finding is that impacts at schooling levels where enrollments are lower tend to be greater (note this can reflect both variation between countries or variations within a country by schooling level at which transfers are provided). This finding is partly mechanical; for instance, in Mexico and Colombia primary school enrollments were quite high prior to the introduction of CCTs so there was little room for large impacts to be found on primary school enrollments.

In other dimensions, the WB report considers heterogeneity in impacts by size of the monetary transfer, age/grade of child, and socioeconomic background. The country level results do not show strong evidence of countries with higher transfers as a percentage of per capita expenditure obtaining larger impacts. With respect to age/grade effects, there is some evidence, principally from PROGRESA/Oportunidades, of larger impacts at transition grades, for example, between primary and secondary school. Finally, studies from Nicaragua, Cambodia, Honduras, and Mexico demonstrate that the impacts of CCTs on school enrollments tend to be larger for poorer than for less poor families.

In the last section of chapter 5, the WB report consider the impacts on what they term "final" outcomes in education, focusing on accumulated grades of schooling (one study) and impacts on achievement tests (four studies). The report emphasizes that none of these studies shows significant impacts of CCTs on achievement tests. With respect to final outcomes on schooling, the authors cite one study based on comparing two beneficiary groups of adolescents participating in PROGRESA/Oportunidades, one with 18 months more time receiving benefits than the other. This study shows that this 18-month difference in receiving benefits leads to an increase of about 0.2 years of schooling for those aged 9–15 years preprogram.

The conclusion of the WB report is that these first studies of the impacts of CCTs on final educational outcomes are somewhat disappointing. Note that of the four studies of impacts on achievement tests, two are based on achievement tests applied to students in school. Since CCTs affect enrollment, and thus the composition of who takes the achievement tests on which impacts are calculated, such studies likely underestimate the impacts on achievement as those students most likely to enroll in response to the CCTs are likely more marginal students. The findings of these two studies then should perhaps be deemphasized. The other two studies the WB report cites (Behrman, Parker, and Todd 2009a; Filmer and Schady 2011) analyze achievement tests applied in the household, thus avoiding the problem of conditioning on current school attendance. Both studies show that significant impacts on schooling enrollment and grades completed from CCTs do not seem to have led to increases in scores on standardized achievement tests.

5.2.3. New Evidence on Impacts. In this section, we present a number of new studies carried out after the WB report as well as several others not mentioned. First, we turn to studies that analyze the evidence on which design features are most important for explaining how CCTs affect educational indicators, in particular the importance of conditioning

Table 5.1 Selected recent evaluations of CCTs since the WB study: Short- and long-run impacts

Country, program (study)	Method: data and estimation techniques	Significant impacts		
		1. Enrollment	2. Attendance	3. Performance in school; grades of schooling/test scores
Brazil, Bolsa Escola (Glewwe and Kassouf 2012)	School level panel data combined with differences in year in which Bolsa Escola begins, school and time fixed effects added.	Grades 1–4, increased enrollment by 5.5% grades 5–8 by 6.5%		Reduces dropout by 0.5 percentage points grades 1–4, 0.4 for grades 5–8. Increases grade promotion: 0.9 percentage points for grades 1–4, 0.3 for grades 5–8
Colombia, Bogota CCT (Barrera-Osorio et al. 2011)	Oversubscription model, randomly assigned to 3 groups: (a) basic CCT; (b) basic CCT with portion delayed to beginning of next school year (savings); and (c) basic CCT with some benefits conditioned to graduation/enrollment in vocational school.	Savings and tertiary variants increases reenrollment next year by 4 percentage points versus 1.6 percentage points of basic CCT.	All three variants increase school attendance by 3–5 percentage points.	
Colombia, Familias en Accion (Baez and Camacho 2011)	Matching and regression discontinuity analysis.			4–8 percentage increase in probability of graduating from high school, no effect on achievement tests.
Malawi (Baird, McIntosh, and Ozler 2011)	Random assignment of 176 Census enumeration areas (EA) between treatment and control, and random assignment of 88 treatment EAs to conditional and unconditional benefits, girls 13–22.		Increase of 9.2 percentage points on fraction of time attended under conditional benefits, insignificant for unconditional benefits.	Significant improvement of .14 SD on English test score, 0.12 SD on TIMMS mathematics test score, and 0.17 SD on cognitive test for conditioned group; no significant effects for unconditioned group.

Table 5.1 (*continued*)

Country, program (study)	Method: data and estimation techniques	Significant impacts		
		1. Enrollment	2. Attendance	3. Performance in school; grades of schooling/test scores
Mexico, PROGRESA/ Oportunidades (Angelucci et al. 2010)	Random assignment of 506 communities to treatment and control. Eligibility determined through means-tested household survey and poverty regression. Papers compares impacts for those with other family members residing in the villages (connected) to those with no other family members in the village (isolated). Double difference regressions.	Increase of 8.3 percentage points on enrollment in secondary school for youth in connected households, insignificant results for isolated households		
Mexico, PROGRESA/ Oportunidades (Behrman, Parker, and Todd 2009b)	Difference in difference estimators using experimental and nonexperimental design. Initial random assignment of 506 communities to treatment and control, controls incorporated 18 months later. New comparison communities added to the evaluation sample. Eligibility determined through means-tested household survey and poverty regression. Children 0–8 preprogram.			Increases of 0.5 grades of schooling after six years of the program for both boys and girls aged 6–8 preprogram.
Mexico, PROGRESA/Oportunidades (Bobonis and Finan 2009)	Random assignment of 506 communities to treatment and control. Eligibility determined through means-tested household survey and poverty regression. Compares eligible and ineligible households in treatment and control communities.	Increases enrollment of eligible children with 6–7 grades of schooling by 8.5 percentage points and ineligible children in grades 6–7 by 5.6 percentage points.		

Study	Methodology	Results	
Mexico, PROGRESA/Oportunidades (de Brauw and Hoddinott 2010)	Nearest neighbor matching comparing beneficiaries with completed grades 3–8 who receive enrollment forms with those who did not.	Those not receiving enrollment form show impacts lower by 4.5 percentage points than for the group who receives the form.	
Mexico, PROGRESA/Oportunidades (Lalive and Cattaneo 2009)	With 506 communities from experimental design, uses IV regressions to estimate peer effects, the instrument is eligible children in the same school grade in the community.	10 percentage point increase in peer group school attendance leads to a 5 percentage point increase in individual school attendance.	
Mexico, Urban PROGRESA/Oportunidades (Behrman, Parker, and Todd 2012)	Difference in difference matching, before and after estimators after two years of program operation.	Significant impacts on girls 6–20 of 2.5 percentage points after 2 years of benefits.	Significant impacts on boys aged 6–20 of 0.1 additional grades, 0.12 additional grades for girls.
Nicaragua, Red de Protección Social (Dammert 2010)	Random assignment of 42 communities into treatment and control. All households eligible to participate. Regression estimates and quantile treatment effects.	Increase of 18 percentage points in enrollment for boys and 12 percentage points for girls. Effects concentrated on lowest quintile by per capita expenditures.	
United States, Opportunities NYC (Riccio et al. 2010)	Random assignment of eligible households in six high-poverty communities in NYC.	No significant impacts on primary and secondary students. Increased by 5 percentage points ninth graders with at least 95% attendance.	Reduced proportion repeating ninth grade in 5.8 percentage points for upper half of distribution of ninth graders. No significant impacts for primary and secondary school students. Increased proportion passing Regents exam in 5.9 percentage points for ninth graders in upper half of distribution.

transfers. Second, we present new studies on short-term indicators that have taken place since the WB report and also review existing studies on differential impacts by gender. Finally, we discuss several new studies on the impacts of CCTs on final or longer term educational indicators. Table 5.1 summarizes the impact studies detailed in this section.

5.2.3.1. Why CCTs Affect Schooling. Martinelli and Parker (2008) provide a framework for modeling the effects of CCTs. In particular, with regard to human capital investment, they focus on three effects of the program: (1) an income effect that increases investment in human capital due to the increase in family income; (2) a substitution effect that increases investment in schooling through the conditionality of transfers to school enrollment/attendance; and (3) the practice of giving money to the mother/female head of the family that might increase schooling investment if resources controlled by females are invested to a greater extent in child human capital. Several recent empirical studies attempt to study the relative importance of these components, with particular emphasis on whether similar outcomes might be achieved under unconditional rather than conditional transfer programs. Conditioning transfers is costly both for the program (because compliance must be monitored) and for individuals (who incur costs associated with complying with program conditionality requirements).

Conditionality. Baird, McIntosh, and Ozler (2011) present experimental evidence on the importance of conditionality, based on evidence from Malawi where never-married girls between the ages of 13 and 22 who were enrolled in school prior to the program in 176 enumeration areas were sampled. The 176 enumeration areas were randomly assigned to treatment and control. The 88 treatment areas were further divided into two groups, one where benefits were conditional and one where benefits were identical but unconditional.[7,8]

The results demonstrate that school attendance and enrollment were significantly higher in the conditioned group when data based on teacher-reported attendance and enrollment (rather than student/family reports) were used. In fact, impacts on attendance and enrollment are always significant for the conditioned group and rarely significant for the unconditioned group. Consistent with these findings, the conditioned group shows higher scores on math and English achievement tests and a cognitive (Raven's) test, whereas the unconditioned group shows no significant impacts as compared with the control group.[9]

De Brauw and Hoddinott (2010) study the importance of conditionality in the Mexican PROGRESA/Oportunidades program. They take advantage of the fact that there are a number of beneficiary households who report not receiving enrollment forms at the beginning of the program, arguing that for these households benefits are effectively unconditional as the program cannot monitor students for whom they have no information on whether they are enrolled. The authors compare program impacts for those who report receiving the enrollment forms and those who do not, using a variety of controls to try to ensure that differences between these two groups in the absence of the program are not responsible for the differences in observed enrollment. The authors report that for those households not receiving the enrollment forms, impacts of the program are between 5 and 10 percentage points smaller than for those groups receiving the forms.[10]

Size of Transfer. An issue related to the importance of conditionality relative to the income effect of CCT programs is the importance of the size of the transfer, in particular, if similar effects as to those obtained might be obtained at a lower transfer level or if larger effects might be obtained with a higher transfer amount. Since most CCT programs do not vary the amounts of the transfer provided, this question has been difficult to study empirically and has been studied only through cross-country comparisons or in structural evaluations of social programs. A couple of recent studies, however, have implemented variations in the amounts of transfer received for a given child and thus allow an initial examination of the issue.

In particular, Filmer and Schady (2011) study the effect of a Cambodian transfer program using a regression discontinuity design. The program constructs a poverty index based on variables related to the probability of dropout, which include socio and demographic characteristics of the household in which the child lives, including parental presence and schooling, siblings, and durable goods in the household. Children with a high probability of dropping out are assigned to receive a $60 transfer, those with a medium probability of dropping out are assigned a $45 transfer, and those with a low probability of dropping out do not receive a grant. This program design creates a discontinuity in eligibility effectively creating a cutoff between receiving an offer of $60 versus $45 and between $45 and no transfer. Their results show that both the $60 and $45 scholarship have large effects on improving school enrollment by about 25 percentage points. There are no significant differences between the $60 and $45 scholarship. Filmer and Schady also emphasize that the scholarship amounts are quite low compared to other CCT programs; the $45 scholarships represents only about 2% of a beneficiary family's consumption expenditures, so the large impacts are all the more striking.

Baird, McIntosh, and Ozler (2011) in the transfer program in Malawi described above also randomly vary the amounts received under the conditional and unconditional branches of the program by the household and the female beneficiary. Their results show little sensitivity of enrollment impacts to the size of benefits under the conditional groups. Nevertheless, the results do show significant responsiveness to transfer amounts for the unconditional transfer group with each additional dollar provided leading to an increase in enrollment of 0.08.

Parental Gender Roles. Gitter and Barham (2008) analyze the Nicaraguan CCT program to test whether impacts on school enrollment are higher in households where women hold more power (measured as women's level of education divided by men's level of education). Their results suggest that impacts of CCTs are higher when the woman holds more power in the household.

5.2.3.2. New Studies on Short-Run Educational Indicators and the Heterogeneity of Impacts.

New Studies of Short-Run Impacts. Brazil's Bolsa Escola program, beginning about the same time as the Mexican PROGRESA/Oportunidades, is the largest, in terms of number of beneficiaries, conditional cash-transfer program in the world. Nevertheless, little is known about its potential impacts. A recent study, however (Glewwe and Kassouf 2012), takes advantage of school records and variation in the time of implementation of Bolsa Escola to estimate the impact of Bolsa Escola on enrollment, dropout, and grade promotion for primary and secondary school enrollment. Using yearly school-level data from 1998 to 2005 (before and after program implementation), as well as data on which schools have Bolsa Escola recipients, the authors estimate that the program increased enrollment by about 5.5% in grades 1–4 (6.5% in grades 5–8); lowered dropout rates by 0.5 percentage points in grades 1–4 (0.4 percentage points in grades 5–8); and raised grade promotion rates (probability of advancing to the next grade) by 0.9 percentage points in grades 1–4 (0.3 in grades 5–8). Because only about a third of all school children receive Bolsa Escola, the authors argue that the actual impacts on those receiving the program are about three times larger.

There is little evidence about the impacts of CCTs in urban areas, as most programs have been carried out in rural settings. An exception is a recent experiment in Bogota, Colombia, where a conditional transfer program for youth in grades 6–11 was implemented with three different variants (Barrera-Osorio et al. 2011): a CCT based on school attendance ("basic" treatment), a variant that distributes two-thirds of the funds based on school attendance and the remaining third into a savings account to be given to the family later in the year when the funds might be useful for expenditures associated with reenrollment ("savings"), and a final variant with payments for school attendance identical to the "savings" variant are provided and a significant incentive is conditional on graduation from secondary school and enrollment in the next level of school ("tertiary").

The overall findings show a number of significant impacts of the basic CCT variant with significant effects on attending school (about 3 percentage points), and reenrolling in the following year (1.6 percentage points). Nevertheless, both alternative variants (savings and tertiary) have similar or larger impacts on attendance as the basic CCT and significantly larger impacts on reenrollment in the following year (about 4 percentage points for savings and tertiary versus less than 2 for basic). Based on this evidence, the authors argue that reallocating funds so that at least some transfers are conditional on completion or reenrollment could provide greater overall impacts of conditional cash-transfer programs. A potential caveat, however, is that Barrera-Osorio et al. find that participation in the program (pooling all three treatments because of sample-size issues) has negative impacts on *untreated* children in the same family who were registered but not selected for treatment by the lottery. These negative effects are large enough (for instance, reducing in 10 percentage points the probability for girls of reenrolling in school relative to households with no treated children) that the authors conclude that "parents with a treated child appear to take educational opportunities from untreated siblings." In fact, the negative effects on an untreated sibling appear to be even larger than the size of the positive impacts on siblings, which tempers to some extent the overall positive results of the evaluation. These sibling results, however, are based only on the treatment sample of households with two children who registered for the program where only one was randomly selected, a minority of all treated households.

Another urban study is based on the extension of the rural Mexican PROGRESA/Oportunidades program to urban areas (Behrman et al. 2012). In the Mexican case the urban program was identical in terms of the cash and in-kind benefits offered in rural areas, although differing in terms of the targeting mechanism. Estimates for the first two years of operation show significant impacts on enrollment and grades of completed schooling. Overall for children aged 6–20, enrollment increases by about 3 percentage points in the first year with higher impacts for younger children and grades of schooling increasing by 0.1 grades in the first year.[11]

Impacts by Gender of Children. An important dimension where impacts of CCTs might differ is by gender of the children. Both costs and benefits of participating in CCTs might vary, for example, the opportunity costs of school might be different between boys and girls and the benefits in terms of increases in lifetime earnings due to additional education might also differ by gender. Note that boys in many poor countries where CCTs operate tend to have higher participation in paid work whereas girls have higher participation in domestic work.

Generally, existing CCT programs, when they provide transfers for both boys and girls, provide identical transfers. Only in the PROGRESA/Oportunidades program, transfers are about 15% higher at the secondary (grades 7–9) and high school levels (grades 10–12) for girls than boys. This feature was originally motivated by the higher dropout rates of girls than boys after primary school in rural areas of Mexico, although in fact overall grades of completed schooling were similar for boys and girls at the time of program implementation. This design feature would be expected to increase program impacts of girls relative to boys, relative to other programs.

Table 5.2 presents impacts of CCTs on enrollment and attendance by gender for programs where both boys and girls are eligible and for those studies that carry out impacts by gender. Note we include studies previously cited in the WB report because the WB report does not report how impacts of CCTs differ by gender. Surprisingly perhaps, only about half of available studies of the educational impacts of CCTs actually report results by gender. Of those reporting results by gender, the PROGRESA/Oportunidades program is the only program where impacts (for enrollment) are significantly higher for girls than boys.[12] However, there are several instances where impacts are significantly higher for boys than girls, although the majority show no significant differences in impacts by gender. Enrollment impacts are higher in Colombia (Familias en Accion) at the secondary level for boys and in Nicaragua (Red de Proteccion Social) for boys aged 7–13. While higher impacts for girls in the PROGRESA/Oportunidades program might not be surprising given the higher transfer amounts for girls, in fact longer-term studies of

Table 5.2 Impact of CCTs on schooling, by gender

Country (authors)	Program	Age/grade/zones	Indicator	Impacts Boys	Impacts Girls
Colombia (Attanasio, Fitzsimmons, and Gomez 2005)	Familias en Accion	Age 8–13, semirural	Enrollment	0.021*	0.005
		Age 14–17, semirural	Enrollment	0.069**	0.034*
		Age 8–13, rural	Enrollment	0.031*	0.027*
		Age 14–17, rural	Enrollment	0.071**	0.042
Colombia (Barrera-Osorio et al. 2011)	Pilot: Basic CCT	Grades 6–11	Enrollment	0.016	0.014
	Pilot: CCT with some payments delayed (savings)	Grades 6–11	Enrollment	0.048*	0.048*
Jamaica (Levy and Ohls 2007)	Program of Advancement through Health and Education	Age 7–17	Days attended (a)	0.42	0.44
Mexico (Behrman et al. 2012)	Urban PROGRESA/Oportunidades program	Age 6–20	Enrollment	0.015	0.025*
Mexico (Behrman, Parker, and Todd 2011)	PROGRESA/Oportunidades	Age 6–20	Grades of schooling	0.010*	0.012*
		9–10 preprogram	Grades of schooling (after 6 years of benefits)	1***	0.7***
		11–12	Grades of schooling (after 6 years of benefits)	0.93***	0.75***
		13–15	Grades of schooling (after 6 years of benefits)	0.55***	0.03
Mexico (Behrman, Sengupta, and Todd 2005)	PROGRESA/Oportunidades	Age 6–14 (simulates participation for 8 years from 6–14)	Grades of schooling	0.92	0.68
Mexico (Schultz 2004)	PROGRESA/Oportunidades	Primary	Enrollment	0.008**	0.009**
		Secondary	Enrollment	0.06***	0.09***
Nicaragua (Dammert 2009)	Red de Proteccion Social	Age 7–13	Enrollment	0.18*	0.12*
Nicaragua (Maluccio and Flores 2005)	Red de Proteccion Social	Age 7–13	Enrollment	0.17*	0.18*

PROGRESA/Oportunidades are suggestive of final impacts slightly favoring boys (table 5.2).

In summary, most studies show similar impacts of CCTs for girls and boys, with a couple of contexts where CCTs appear to improve educational outcomes for boys more than for girls. This evidence thus suggests that CCTs do not act to reduce gender inequalities in education favoring boys. Note, however, that Grant and Behrman (2010) have shown that gender gaps in education favoring boys have greatly fallen across the developing world. In fact, in terms of grades attained, girls once enrolled do as well or better on average than boys at all ages in most developing countries.

Other Heterogeneities in CCT Impact Studies. Dammert (2009) studies the heterogeneity of impacts of the CCT program Red de Proteccion Social in Nicaragua, focusing on impacts by age and poverty and also carrying out quantile treatment effect regressions.[13] She shows that program impacts on school attendance are higher in households where the household head has a lower schooling level. Using quantile regressions, she shows that impacts on schooling are higher in poorer households as measured by the level of household expenditures. These results showing higher impacts for poorer households are generally consistent with the WB report's observation that at an aggregate level CCTs tend to have higher impacts in poorer countries.

Angelucci et al. (2010) use the PROGRESA/Oportunidades evaluation sample to test whether impacts of the program on secondary school enrollment differ by whether extended family members are present in the village. The paper constructs extended families in the village using the fact that Mexicans have two last names (their mother's first last name and their father's first last name), which do not change, even with marriage. The data contain information on both last names so that, for instance, brothers and sisters living in separate households inside the village can be identified because they will have the same two last names. The analysis shows that impacts on school enrollment are significant only for families with extended families in the villages. The authors hypothesize that these intriguing results reflect that extended families share resources in a way that encourages or allows impacts in secondary schooling for credit-constrained households.

Spillovers. Behrman, Sengupta, and Todd (2005) report that they could find no evidence of spillover effects on noneligible children in their evaluation of the PROGRESA/Oportunidades rural program in which small communities have both beneficiary and nonbeneficiary families. In their study, they examine program effects through impacts on transition matrices that estimate for each transition between ages, the probability of transition between possible educational states including the outcomes of enrollment, dropout, failure, and repetition between two years. Their methodology estimates the transition matrices for treatment and controls and tests for significant differences between the two. Their results show that for each transition matrix for the ages studied (6–14) there are no significant differences between the transition matrices for noneligible children in the treatment and control groups.

Lalive and Cattaneo (2009) and Bobonis and Finan (2009), in contrast, report that the same PROGRESA/Oportunidades program increased significantly the school enrollment and progression of noneligible children and youth in treatment communities. Bobonis and Finan study only enrollment and progression at the secondary school level where their sample are youth who have completed sixth-grade preprogram, and Lalive and Cattaneo study only enrollment of youth who had completed fourth, fifth, and sixth grade. Behrman, Sengupta, and Todd (2005) focus on children between the ages of 6 and 14 using the transition matrixes described above, so the samples used as well as the methodology are somewhat different, potentially explaining the differences in the results obtained.

5.2.3.3. Impacts of CCTs on Longer-Run Indicators of Education.
CCT programs have two complementary objectives. The first is to reduce current poverty by providing monetary benefits to poor households. The second is to reduce future poverty by providing incentives for increased human capital investment of children in poor households. This second objective thus relates to the long-term impacts of CCTs, where a question of considerable interest is whether the initial short-term impacts observed by CCTs on increasing enrollment and attendance translate into greater completed grades of schooling and whether this final increase in schooling is associated with higher wages when children become adults and enter the labor market.

The WB report on CCTs argues that the few studies available on impacts on final or longer-run indicators of schooling are disappointing. We now review three additional studies that became available after the WB report and that demonstrate perhaps more nuanced results. Behrman, Parker, and Todd (2009b, 2011) study the impact of CCTs in Mexico on grades of schooling after nearly six years of program benefits. Using both experimental and nonexperimental impact estimators,

Behrman, Parker, and Todd (2009b) show that children entering primary school when the program began achieve about half a year of additional schooling. Behrman, Parker, and Todd (2011) show that children aged 9–12 when the program began (close to the transition between primary and secondary school where impacts on enrollment have tended to be the highest [e.g., Schultz 2004]) achieve close to an additional completed grade of schooling. Behrman, Parker, and Todd (2011) also carry out a benefit-cost analysis and demonstrate that the benefits (measured in terms of future simulated earnings) substantially exceed the costs of conditional transfers unless both the returns to schooling are very low and the discount rate is extremely high. Finally, Baez and Camacho (2011), for the case of the Colombian program Familias en Accion, find that the program improves high school graduation rates by 4–8 percentage points for youth participating between one and seven years in the program, using both matching and regression discontinuity analysis. However, they find no significant impact of participation in the program on standardized achievement tests performed at the end of high school. A qualification to this finding is that the standardized achievement tests were applied only to those actually enrolled in school and thus impact estimates here are contaminated with selection in who is in school, likely resulting in an underestimation of the impacts on achievement tests, as discussed in the previous section.

With regard to other studies of the impact of CCTs on achievement, to our knowledge the only study thus far to show significant impacts of CCTs on achievement is the Baird, McIntosh, and Ozler (2010) study mentioned above, which shows significant impacts on achievement tests after two years of operation of the CCT program in Malawi. The magnitudes of the impacts are increases of 0.14 standard deviations on English achievement and 0.12 on math achievement tests (using Trends in International Math and Science Study [TIMSS] questions), although strangely insignificant impacts on math achievement tests based on the Malawi curriculum. The achievement tests were carried out in the home, a critical feature to avoid underestimating impacts due to changes in the composition of students who attend school in the treatment group. Another difference from the previous studies of achievement tests cited from Mexico and Colombia is the evidently much poorer context of Malawi. As noted in the WB review of the impact of CCTs on enrollment and attendance, larger impacts have been noted in poorer contexts and achievement tests may be similar in this regard.

Much further work needs to be done to study the extent to which conditional cash-transfer programs increase achievement. Only a few studies exist and the majority analyze test results from tests conducted in school, which are likely to underestimate impacts on learning through selection effects on who attends school. The fact that there are only a few available studies reflects the lack of available data on standardized achievement tests among most evaluations of CCTs particularly during baseline applications. Measuring the impact of CCTs on learning should be a central goal in the continued analysis of the impacts of CCTs on final educational outcomes and the accumulation of human capital.

Combining conditional cash transfers with improvements on the supply and teacher side might prove more effective at improving achievement by providing incentives for teachers as well as demand-side subsidies, although there is little evidence on combined initiatives of this sort. In section 5.3 we will describe interventions that link student incentives directly to achievement rather than enrollment or attendance.

Finally, note that it is still relatively early to directly observe long-term impacts of CCTs on variables such as salaries and employment. Even with the older CCT programs such as the Mexican PROGRESA/ Oportunidades program, the first generation of child recipients are only now entering early adulthood, presumably when significant impacts on employment might begin to appear. Thus, the full intergenerational effects of CCTs are only now beginning to be possible to study and represent an exciting area for future research.

5.2.4. Summary. What has been learned about CCTs since the WB report? A number of recent papers attempt to look into the "black box" of CCT programs and analyze which features of these programs most affect investment in education. As detailed by Martinelli and Parker (2008), CCTs can be expected to affect human capital investment through a number of mechanisms. And, given the generally bundled nature of most CCTs, it is difficult to isolate the impact of each feature. The research reported in this section is suggestive that conditionality is responsible for an important fraction of schooling impacts and that unconditional transfers would not achieve similar education impacts. Of course a cost-benefit analysis of conditional versus unconditional transfers would have to take into account the presumably lower costs of unconditional transfers, given the costs associated with monitoring and complying with conditionality. Additionally, while this chapter focuses on education, there is evidence that conditional cash-transfer programs have positive impacts on child health. This improved health may also improve educational outcomes (see Alderman and Bleakley, chapter 4, this volume). With respect to who in the family receives the transfers, previous studies and those detailed here support that females tend to invest more in the human capital of their children than males and that impacts of CCTs may be higher when the woman holds more power in the household.

Recent studies continue to reinforce the evidence that CCTs positively affect enrollment and school attendance. Many CCT programs are relatively recent and thus existing evaluations focus heavily on short-run educational indicators. Arguably, the main impacts of interest of CCTs are the long-run impacts on indicators such as grades of completed schooling, achievement tests, and labor-market outcomes. The few new studies of longer-term impacts of CCTs are encouraging in terms of showing significant impacts on the accumulation of grades of schooling. Results from the Malawi CCT are the first to show that a CCT program affects measured achievement, furthermore over a relatively short period of time (two years), although a couple of previous studies in other contexts did not show significant impacts on achievement. Given the large number of CCTs and the diversity of contexts combined with the still few available studies of longer-term impacts, there remains a great need for continued follow-up and study of the longer-run impacts of CCTs. Because longer-term evaluation inevitably involves following the populations under evaluation (which tend to be highly mobile) through longitudinal data collections, both new and existing CCT programs should implement fieldwork strategies in order to be able to follow and minimize attrition of the evaluation samples.

It also seems that further innovation with respect to CCTs programs would be useful. In particular, whereas it has largely been shown that CCTs in a variety of contexts improve enrollment and attendance, there are still a number of design issues that could be addressed in further initiatives. For instance, variations in the timing and the amounts of payments could be considered, to analyze to what extent impacts might vary or be made more efficient. Additionally, given thus far the somewhat-limited impacts on learning and achievement observed, CCTs might consider conditioning benefits on other educational variables besides enrollment and attendance. In the next section, we turn to experiences in linking benefits to educational performance variables.

5.3. Student Performance-Based Incentive Programs

Over the last decade, there has been substantial interest in improving the performance of schools by providing financial incentives for better performance. Even if the production process by which schools transform inputs into educational outcomes cannot be easily discerned, it may be possible to increase the efficiency of the educational process and/or ensure that the process is oriented towards improving student outcomes by providing incentives that are contingent on outcomes (also see Glewwe in chapter 1). However, there is also a risk with incentive programs that they could detract from student performance, for example, if they encourage schools to focus on a certain subset of students to the exclusion of others or if they encourage schools to focus their efforts only on outcomes that are tested. We now review the evidence on the effectiveness of a variety of performance incentive programs aimed at students that provide incentives to increase learning effort. We also describe the results of a few studies that implement both performance incentive programs and input-based programs and compare the effectiveness of these two types of policies.

Angrist and Lavy (2009) study the effects of an Israeli cash-incentive program for students. The program randomized 40 high schools (including both Arab and Jewish religious schools) in or out of a cash-incentive program. The program offered all students within the selected treatment schools incentives for progressing from tenth to eleventh grade, eleventh to twelfth grade, and for passing the Bagrut exam. The program was originally intended to last for three years, but due to adverse publicity lasted only one year. Angrist and Lavy find from the school-based randomized trial that the incentives program increased Bagrut passing rates by 6–8 percentage points.

Kremer, Miguel, and Thornton (2009) evaluate the impacts of a merit scholarship program for girls in Kenya. The scholarships were implemented in two districts with random assignment between treatment and control schools. The scholarships were awarded to the top-scoring 15% of sixth-grade girls on standardized achievement tests and included the paying of school fees and a transfer for school supplies to the girls' parents. On average girls in participating schools raised their achievement by 0.2 standard deviations. Kremer, Miguel, and Thornton also estimate impacts by quartile of achievement in order to analyze where impacts are concentrated in the distribution. The estimated largest impacts on achievement for girls are for those in the second quartile of the distribution, a group that Kremer, Miguel, and Thornton argue would seem to have relatively low probabilities of winning an award. Nevertheless, for girls the results also show that the lowest two quartiles did not show any significant improvement, suggesting that the worst-off students did not improve their achievement significantly in response to the award. The results for boys, who did not receive any incentive for their achievement,

also show significant improvements in achievement and these gains occur both in the second quartile and in the lowest quartile, suggesting
significant spillover effects, although in one of the two main study sites
there is a strange negative effect on achievement for boys in the top quartile. Overall, then, while the incentive program improved achievement
at an aggregate level, the evidence is mixed on the distributional nature
of the improvements. A final observed effect is that both student and
teacher school attendance increased in program schools.

Behrman et al. (2012) evaluate the effects of a three-year Mexican
incentive program to align learning incentives (ALI). The program randomly allocated 88 Mexican high schools (grades 10–12) to three different treatment groups and to a control group. The three treatment groups
receive incentives based on student achievement attained on curriculum-
based tests developed by an outside testing agency (CENEVAL) and administered by the Ministry of Education relative to their performance a
year earlier. The treatment groups differ only in terms of who in each
treatment group receives the incentive payments. In the first treatment
(T1) allocated to 20 schools, only students receive incentive payments.
A second treatment (T2) allocated to another 20 schools provides monetary incentives to teachers based on achievement. A third treatment (T3)
that is also allocated to 20 schools provides monetary incentives to both
students and teachers, where the incentives are based both on individual
performance and on group performance on the same tests. Students receive incentives based on their own test score level and improvement
and on the performance of their class, whereas teachers receive incentives based on the performance of their own class and of the school as a
whole. In this third treatment, incentive payments are also given to non-
math teachers and to principals, again based on student math-test performance. Finally, in addition to the three treatment groups, 28 schools
were allocated to a control group that took the same achievement tests
but otherwise received no intervention.

An evaluation under conservative assumptions about possible cheating finds that the third treatment that provided both individual and
group incentives to both students and teachers produces significant and
very large positive impacts on math test scores by about 0.6 standard deviations in the third program year for the cohort entering high school in
2008–9. The student-only incentive program was also effective in producing better performance for all three grades, although effects were
somewhat smaller than the third treatment, about 0.2 to 0.3 standard
deviations. For both the student-only incentives and the group with stu-

dent, teacher, and director incentives, it is noteworthy that quantile regression analysis showed significant impacts on achievement were observed at all parts of the student distribution. Finally, the teacher-only incentive program seems not to have been effective at improving student achievement. One potential explanation for the lack of results in the teacher-only incentives group is that without increased effort from students, increased teacher effort is not effective at promoting learning, particularly at the advanced level of high school where the ALI program was implemented.

To summarize, while there are only a few studies of student achievement linked to performance incentives in developing countries on which to draw some conclusions,[14] all of these studies show significant effects on variables associated with learning. Given the relative lack of evidence that programs such as CCTs increase achievement test scores in spite of increasing enrollment, this is noteworthy. In particular it is suggestive that to improve learning, conditioning transfers might better be done on variables closely associated with learning, rather than on the more indirect variables of attendance or enrollment.

An important design issue in this regard is how learning should be rewarded, for example, whether absolute levels of learning should be the benchmark or improvements in learning over time or both. The Mexican ALI program is based for tenth- and eleventh-graders on both levels and improvement in learning; for example, those who have the highest scores receive large incentives but, for a given test score, those who improved their learning most receive the largest awards.[15] And it is noteworthy that at all levels of the achievement test distribution, there are significant similar-sized impacts as a percentage of the control group score. Although the Kenya scholarship program only provides incentives to the top 15% of those in the class, there were some significant impacts on learning on those further down in the distribution.

A concern with conditioning on achievement is that incentives rewarding achievement might increase inequality if high-achieving students are more likely to have more privileged family backgrounds. Linking monetary incentives to improvements rather than levels of learning should reduce the possibility that achievement incentives increase inequality. From an operational perspective, basing incentives in part or completely on improvements rather than on absolute levels is perhaps more complicated operationally and requires a baseline measure of learning at the beginning of the year in addition to a test at the end of the year. A benefit of targeting benefits at least partly to improvement is that such targeting provides incentives to all to improve and at least in the ALI program discussed here appears to lead to an improvement in learning for those with low as well as high initial test performance.

We close this section by mentioning a few other issues related to conditioning directly on performance or achievement. If benefits are directly linked to results on tests, then tests may effectively become "high stakes" for treatment groups versus "low stakes" for control groups, so that differences between the groups might reflect differences in effort on the tests rather than more learning on the part of the treatment group. This can be investigated through evaluating impacts on alternative tests on the same material that have similar stakes for all groups or retesting after the program has ended. Further, high-stakes tests may create greater incentives for "teaching to the test" (though this does not seem troublesome if the test is based on the curriculum and the curriculum indeed reflects what society thinks students should learn) and for cheating. Finally, an often-expressed concern that has been studied with respect to linking incentives to achievement is that motivation may be reduced when cash incentives are not available and students may find learning less intrinsically enjoyable. Some researchers report evidence that this has occurred in some contexts (Deci, Koestner, and Ryan 1999). However, Kremer, Miguel, and Thornton (2009) note in their study of Kenya (described earlier) that evidence of test gains continued to be observed a year following the removal of incentives, with no evidence of reduced intrinsic motivation.

5.4. School Voucher Programs

School vouchers are a particular type of incentive program that provides payments to parents and/or students (or directly to the school on the parents'/students' behalf) to cover the cost of school attendance at a private or public school. School vouchers were proposed by Friedman (1955, 1962) as a way of improving school quality, particularly for children from lower-income families. Advocates of voucher programs point to their value in fostering school competition, which is thought to generate quality improvements in both public and private school systems, and to their potential value in promoting equality of educational opportunity (Brighouse 2000; Hoxby 2001, 2003; Rouse 1998). However, critics caution that voucher programs deplete already poorly funded public school systems of revenue and of their best students and teachers, and may increase inequality (e.g., Carnoy 1997; Ladd 2002).

Chile is unusual in having implemented a nationwide school voucher program three decades ago (1981).[16] Vouchers in Chile are publicly funded, with voucher funds following children to public or selected private schools. Governmental and private schooling sectors coexist with free entry into the private sector and some governmental monitoring of the quality of all schools.[17] There are three broad types of schools: municipal schools, private subsidized schools, and private nonsubsidized (fee-paying) schools. Private subsidized schools and municipal schools are financed primarily through the per capita governmental voucher, although in 1994 a change in the law allowed private schools and municipal high schools to charge a small add-on tuition.[18] Private nonsubsidized schools, which have about a 6% market share and include both religious (mainly Catholic) and lay schools, are financed from private tuitions. Parents are free to choose among municipal and both types of private schools. An important difference between public and private schools' admissions policies is that private schools can be selective, whereas public schools can be selective only if there is excess demand. In all types of schools, students take standardized tests in the fourth, eighth, and tenth grades and schools' average test results are published annually.

Bravo, Mukhopadhyay, and Todd (2010) study the effects of Chile's 1981 school voucher reform on educational and labor market outcomes of individuals who were exposed to the reform using a behavioral model approach. Specifically, they develop and estimate a dynamic discrete choice model of school attendance and work decisions using panel data from the 2002 and 2004 waves of the Encuesta Proteccion Social (EPS) survey. The model allows components of future earnings and of the payoff to different types of schooling to be unknown at the time of making schooling and labor-market decisions. It incorporates permanent unobservable heterogeneity, in the form of discrete types, assumed to be known to individuals but unknown to the econometrician (Heckman and Singer 1984). Identification of the effects of the voucher reform comes from differences in the schooling and work choices made and earnings returns received by individuals within the same ten-year birth cohort who were differentially exposed to the reform. The model is estimated for males, mainly to avoid consideration of fertility choices but also because men in Chile have a much stronger labor force attachment than do women.

Model simulations show that the voucher reform significantly increased the demand for private subsidized schools and decreased the demand for both public and nonsubsidized private schools. It increased high school (grades 9–12) graduation rates by 3.6 percentage points and the percentage completing at least two years of college by 2.6 percentage points. Individuals from poor and nonpoor backgrounds on average experienced similar schooling attainment gains. The reform also increased lifetime utility and modestly reduced earnings inequality.

There are a number of other studies of how the Chilean voucher programs affected student test scores (e.g., Contreras 2001; Hsieh and Urquiola 2003, 2006; McEwan 2001; McEwan, Urquiola, and Vegas 2008; Mizala and Romaguera 2000; Sapelli and Vial 2002). Test score data were not systematically gathered until after the reforms were initiated, so the studies are not informative about the changes in school performance from the pre-reform period. They are informative, though, on whether private school attendance in the post–voucher initiation era is associated with higher test scores. Some of the studies also examine whether the voucher program increased sorting and benefited high-ability students at the expense of low-ability students, an outcome predicted by some theoretical models (see, e.g., Epple and Romano 1998).

In analyzing test score differences between public and private schools, one encounters multiple selection problems, because the types of children attending each school are self-selected and, for older children, test scores are usually only available for children attending school. Using fourth-grade school level average achievement test scores, a grade for which attendance is almost universal, Mizala and Romaguera (2000) and Bravo, Contreras, and Sanhueza (1999) find that the gap in test score performance between municipal and subsidized private schools is small after controlling for geographic and socioeconomic characteristics. McEwan and Carnoy (2000) similarly examine the relationship between type of school attended and student achievement of fourth-graders. They find that nonreligious voucher schools are no more effective than public schools in producing achievement but that Catholic voucher schools are more effective.

A few studies explicitly control for school-type selectivity using frameworks that allow for selection on unobservables. Sapelli and Vial (2002) find test score gains for second-graders associated with attendance at private subsidized schools to be largest for children attending those types of schools.[19] McEwan (2001) examines the effects of attendance at public or private voucher schools on eighth-grade test scores using a control function approach to account for school selectivity and finds no significant achievement differences between public and nonreligious voucher schools, but a small test score advantage for Catholic voucher schools.

Auguste and Valenzuela (2003) and Gallego (2002) analyze the relationship between test scores and school competition and find that competition tends to increase test scores. However, Hsieh and Urquiola (2006) find that community average standardized test scores did not increase faster in communities where private-sector enrollment expanded more, interpreted as a measure of competition.[20] Parry (1997a, 1997b) describes many features of the Chilean voucher system and documents the dramatic expansion in the supply of private schooling that followed the introduction of the voucher reforms. There is evidence that some high-quality private schools responded to the voucher program by expanding their capacity and enrollment and opening new schools. There was also substantial new entry into the private school market. The newer subsidized private schools tended to be for-profit as opposed to religious schools, to open in higher population density areas and to attract children from somewhat lower socioeconomic backgrounds than had attended private schools before the reform (Parry, 1997a, 1997b; Hsieh and Urquiola 2006).

Most studies of non-US voucher programs focus on Chile, but a small literature examines programs in other countries. For example, Angrist et al. (2002) evaluate the impact in selected Colombian cities of the Programa de Ampliación de Cobertura de la Educación Secundaria (PACES) voucher program. The vouchers were introduced in 1991 and covered about one-half the cost of private secondary schools for over 125,000 poor children. The voucher subsidies were renewable annually with satisfactory academic performance. One potential drawback of the program is that it gave private schools an incentive to not ask students to repeat grades, as this would result in the loss of the scholarships.

Evaluation of PACES was facilitated by the fact that vouchers were awarded by lottery in some municipalities with excess demand for them. Angrist et. al. (2002) find significant positive impacts of the PACES program on grade progression rates, schooling attainment after three years, and standardized test scores. A longer-term follow-up study by Angrist, Bettinger, and Kremer (2006) uses administrative records to study the effect of the PACES program on secondary school completion rates and on scores on college admission tests. The study finds that secondary school completion rates increased by 15–20%, that a higher proportion of the lottery winners took college admissions tests, and that test scores increased by 0.2 standard deviations, with the largest gains observed for boys in math.

5.5. Food-for-Education (FFE) Programs

In the early twenty-first century an estimated 120 million children were not attending school, in part because of hunger or malnourishment

(USDA 2004).[21] The majority of the children who never enroll in school are girls.[22] FFE programs have been advocated to increase school enrollment, school attendance, and performance in school. FFE programs are fairly extensive in developing countries with both international and national involvement. For example, the World Food Program (WFP) covered 22.6 million children in such programs in 2008, and the Brazilian government alone covered 36 million children age 0–14 years in such programs a few years earlier (WFP 2006, n.d.).

FFE programs typically involve school feeding programs (SFP) and/or take-home rations (THR) for student enrollment and regular attendance (often defined as 85% of the school days in a time interval, such as a month). If a child receives food at school, this is an increase in real income for the child's family, which provides an incentive for child enrollment in and attendance at school. The family can redistribute part or all of that income gain to other household members through reducing the food provided at home to children who receive food at school.[23] The value of that real income to the family presumably equals the value of the food bundle received for school enrollment/attendance in local market prices if they can sell the food, as would seem likely for THR, though it may be of less value for food from SFP that presumably could not be resold. This is a direct incentive for child enrollment/attendance in school. The program may improve performance in school through, for example, increasing learning directly through inducing greater enrollment/attendance if learning increases with more time in school.

Typically FFE programs attempt to target poorer families through means testing or through targeting schools attended primarily by children from poorer families. They also attempt to target areas in which enrollment/attendance rates are significantly less than universal so that they have some potential for impact. Given significant gender differences favoring boys in ever-enrollment rates in the developing world, it would seem that even if the programs intended to be gender neutral, they would have greater impact on school enrollment and attendance for girls than for boys. In addition to the effects of greater school enrollment/attendance on children induced to go to school by FFE programs, learning may be increased for all children who are recipients of FFE if the program increases the quantity or the nutritional quality of the food that the children consume. Both of these could be induced by the increased family real income or by providing more nutritious food in-kind than the family would elect to purchase were they given monetary income of equivalent value to the real income increased through the FFE in-kind transfer.[24] These health/nutritional effects may occur for children who are FFE recipients but who do not increase their time in school, though a priori it would seem that the total learning effects would be greater for children who are induced to spend more time in school in addition to any benefit from improved health and nutrition.

The cost of FFE programs presumably equals the cost of the food at the school where it is distributed, including the costs of transporting and distributing the food, which may be considerable, particularly if the food is imported internationally, as often is the case. There also may be distortion costs if public revenues are raised to finance such programs and if the FFE purchases in the markets of origin of the food or the distribution in the markets in which the FFE food is distributed are large relative to the respective markets. In both origin and destination markets, of course, price changes induced by the programs imply welfare loses (i.e., for consumers in origin markets, for producers in destination markets) that are partially offset by welfare gains (for producers in origin markets, for consumers in destination markets). Finally there are costs, as compared with cash transfers, due to storage costs, spoilage, and loss to pests. From the perspective of the program's aims, there also are costs in the form of leakages to nontargeted individuals.

FFE programs in developing countries have a fairly long history in comparison with the other educational incentives for students and parents discussed in this chapter. The World Food Program (WFP), for example, has operated such programs for over 45 years. The US government, in some cases in partnership with the WFP, also long has been involved in FFE programs.[25] Reviewing 22 studies, Levinger (1986) concluded that SFPs increase enrollment, but the impact on academic performance is mixed and depends on local conditions. The studies that he reviewed, however, are based on experiences of a quarter century ago or more and the quality of the underlying evaluations is not clear, so for both reasons his review may not be very relevant currently. We focus on more recent studies. We first review briefly some of the experience of the United States and WFP programs in the past decade, and then summarize some individual micro-studies of the impacts of FFE programs.

5.5.1. United States Governmental Programs. The Global Food for Education (GFE) program, administered by the US Department of Agriculture (USDA), fed nearly 7 million children through 48 school feeding projects involving about 4,000 schools in 38 countries between September 2001 and December 2003 (USDA 2004). USDA allocated $300 million to establish this pilot program and support education in developing countries, particularly in countries committed to universal schooling for their children. The GFE program also encouraged the involvement of other donors and local networks, including parent-teacher groups, to support feeding programs and assume greater responsibility for local education. Complementary donations from other organizations during the GFE program totaled almost $1 billion, supporting activities such as training in HIV/AIDS prevention, the improvement of school gardens to promote self-reliance, and the construction of classrooms, school kitchens, water systems, and sanitation facilities.

To monitor and evaluate these programs, uniform questionnaires were applied to a purposeful (block-random) sample of participating schools in each country (USDA 2003, appendix 1). The intent was to evaluate changes in enrollment, attendance, and performance.

Table 5.3 summarizes the resulting estimated enrollment impacts for 40 programs, about half administered by the WFP and about half administrated by other private voluntary organizations (PVO). The estimates in this table indicate considerable variation between the WFP- and the PVO-administered programs, among countries, across regions, and between girls and boys. The country-level gender-specific estimates range from −6.5% for males in the PVO Ugandan case to 32.3% for females in the WFP Pakistani case. With the exception of Vietnam, Uganda, and Georgia (for males only), the estimated enrollment effects are positive. The reported overall WFP average is 10.4% and the reported overall PVO average is 6.0%, with the WFP reporting higher percentage changes for girls than for boys (11.7% versus 8.0%) but the PVO reporting the opposite (5.7% versus 6.9%).

USDA (2004, p. 5) states that school attendance was the most difficult GFE indicator to reliably measure and document because of differences in how schools define and record attendance. Although accurate and consistent attendance data were not available, program monitors received feedback through focus-group discussions and reports by teachers, school administrators, parents, and students. All projects repeatedly confirmed that attendance rates increased after the feeding began. School officials and program monitors found this qualitative evidence to be significant and compelling, though clearly more systematic evidence would be desirable.

USDA (2004, p. 5) also states that every organization and program monitor from both the WFP- and the PVO-administered projects reported that students receiving food at school performed better. These conclusions were based on focus-group reports and direct observations that students receiving meals concentrated better, demonstrated improved attitudes toward learning, comprehended subject matter faster,

Table 5.3 Global Food for Education (GFE) program estimated enrollment impacts

	World Food Program (WFP) projects				Private Voluntary Organizations (PVO) projects		
	Males	Females	Total		Males	Females	Total
CENTRAL AND SOUTH AMERICA							
Colombia	17.1%	16.8%	16.9%	Bolivia (two projects)	5.5%	5.1%	5.3%
Dominican Republic	1.1%	1.4%	1.2%	Dominican Republic	4.3%	4.3%	4.3%
El Salvador	1.8%	2.4%	2.1%	Guatemala (two projects)	7.1%	5.3%	6.1%
Honduras	5.5%	4.8%	5.1%	Honduras	11.6%	13.8%	12.6%
Nicaragua	9.8%	8.4%	9.1%	Nicaragua	17.4%	10.2%	13.3%
Peru	0.9%	0.9%	0.9%				
Total for region	6.1%	5.8%	5.9%	Total for region	6.5%	5.5%	5.9%
ASIA							
Bhutan	1.5%	3.6%	2.4%	Bangladesh	27.7%	20.0%	24.0%
Cambodia	6.7%	8.5%	7.5%	Kyrgyzstan	2.6%	2.9%	1.9%
Pakistan	–	32.3%	32.3%	Vietnam	–3.6%	–4.3%	–4.0%
Tajikistan	3.2%	2.9%	3.1%				
Total for region	3.8%	11.8%	10.8%	Total for region	8.3%	5.2%	6.7%
EAST AFRICA AND MIDDLE EAST							
Ethiopia	16.1%	17.7%	16.7%	Eritrea	9.2%	12.1%	10.1%
Kenya	0.0%	0.3%	0.1%	Lebanon	5.2%	2.7%	3.8%
Mozambique	8.5%	7.9%	8.2%	Uganda	–6.5%	–5.4%	–5.9%
Tanzania	26.6%	26.2%	26.4%				
Uganda	9.7%	13.2%	11.2%				
Total for region	12.2%	13.1%	12.5%	Total for region	3.7%	3.1%	3.2%

Table 5.3 *(continued)*

	World Food Program (WFP) projects				Private Voluntary Organizations (PVO) projects		
	Males	Females	Total		Males	Females	Total
WEST AFRICA							
Cote d'Ivoire	9.0%	10.4%	9.6%	Benin	9.5%	10.5%	10.4%
Cameroon	17.0%	27.4%	20.5%	Congo (Brazzaville)	6.8%	8.2%	7.5%
Gambia	9.3%	12.5%	10.8%				
Ghana	6.7%	15.4%	10.4%				
Total for region	10.5%	16.4%	12.8%	Total for region	7.0%	8.3%	7.7%
				EASTERN EUROPE			
				Albania (three projects)	6.4%	4.6%	4.6%
				Bosnia-Herzegovina	15.3%	10.4%	2.5%
				Georgia	−1.3%	3.3%	2.0%
				Moldova	4.8%	9.3%	6.0%
				Total for region	6.1%	6.3%	5.3%
TOTAL FOR WFP SCHOOLS	8.0%	11.7%	10.4%	TOTAL FOR PVO	6.9%	5.7%	6.0%

Note: The above figures include 19 of the 22 WFP projects and 21 of the 26 PVO projects, including the project conducted by the government of the Dominican Republic.

and were more energetic. Teachers, school administrators, and parents immediately noted changes in the children when the feeding projects began. The contrast in attention span and behavior before and after feeding was particularly dramatic in cases where the projects started in the middle of a school year. To quantitatively measure performance indicators, data should be collected over a long period of time. Because of the relatively short duration of the GFE pilot program, long-term measurements are not available. Nevertheless, the qualitative data gathered from school communities and parents who interacted with students on a daily basis, and corroborated by those who visited the schools, supported the conclusion of improved performance associated with school feeding—though, again, more systematic evidence would be desirable.

The USDA (2004, p. 3) claims subsequently to have applied many of the lessons and best practices learned from the pilot GFE program to administer the McGovern-Dole International Food for Education and Child Nutrition Program, which was authorized by the Farm Security and Rural Investment Act of 2002. These lessons are summarized in USDA (2004, pp. 9–10) to pertain to four areas:

1. Strengthening program sustainability
2. Using food creatively to support educational programs
3. Involving parents and local government in support of schools
4. Integrating health, nutrition, and environmental education.

Most of the specific points that are made under these four areas are fairly general or regard complementary interventions such as water disinfection education and deworming programs where needed. But some of them point more directly to the direct incentives effects of FFE programs on students and their families—in particular, to offer take-home rations to offset the potential loss of income to families when their children attend school.

In addition to these four lessons, based on USDA's experience with the pilot GFE program, USDA (2004, pp. 11–12) concludes that six areas merit increased attention or emphasis in FFE programs:

1. Targeting girls, particularly in the upper grades of primary school and secondary school at which grades female dropout rates often tend to increase;
2. Addressing gender equity in cases in which women appear to be doing most of the volunteering in food preparation and management;

3. Improving data collection and baseline planning, which in many cases appears skewed by pressure from local and national administrations to present attendance and enrollment records in such a way as to qualify the schools for certain subsidies or other forms of assistance;

4. Planning commodity use to directly go to beneficiaries so that there are not fewer financial resources than anticipated if local prices are lower than anticipated;

5. Expediting commodity deliveries; and

6. Planning exit strategies.

According to USDA (2010), USDA was scheduled to donate more than 100,000 tons of US agricultural commodities valued at nearly $170 million (including freight costs and technical assistance) in fiscal year 2010 under the McGovern-Dole Program to feed more than 4.8 million children in 18 developing countries in Africa, Asia, Latin America, and the Middle East. Up to the start of 2010, the McGovern-Dole Program had provided meals to more than 22 million children.

United States governmental FFE programs, thus, appear to have provided fairly substantial incentives for school enrollment and attendance over a number of years. The efforts to evaluate these programs broadly, however, appear fairly limited.[26] The most extensive effort appears to have been with the GFE pilot program, the results of which are summarized above. The evaluation had some apparent strengths, including collection of fairly uniform information across many sites and the block-randomization sampling strategy to lessen distortions due to small samples.

But there also seem to be some important limitations. The projects for FFE in the evaluation sample are selected purposively to maximize expected impacts, not randomly from such larger population of interest, so it would seem that the estimates obtained would be upper bounds for effects if the FFE were applied elsewhere. The evaluation depends only on treatment schools in difference estimates, not difference-in-difference estimates using information on what changes occurred with control schools as well. Given a general secular upward trend in school enrollments in many developing countries for other reasons, this also would seem, at least in such cases, to result in estimated upper bounds for program effects. The evaluation considers systematically only enrollment, with only anecdotal information on attendance and performance. The evaluation does not consider systematically real resource costs, but focuses on governmental budgetary expenditures—with particular emphasis on such expenditures for the US government (i.e., the emphasis on sustainability is focused on whether local governments or other entities could keep the program going if the United States terminates its involvement).

5.5.2. World Food Program. As noted, the WFP has operated FFE projects for over 45 years, in a number of cases in collaboration with US governmental projects such as those just summarized. The factsheet on "2008 Figures on WFP School Feeding Programmes" (WFP n.d.) states that there were 22.6 million beneficiaries (49.3% girls) in 68 countries assisted with direct expenditures of US$500 million; 2.7 million girls and 1.6 million boys were provided with take-home rations; 29% of projects also had deworming (12 million children were dewormed); 48% of projects included a health, nutrition, and hygiene education package; 55% of WFP-assisted schools were equipped with potable water and sanitary facilities; and 25% of school equipped with fuel-efficient stoves. The factsheet also gives "outcome statistics" including that, in WFP-assisted schools, net enrollment rates were 76% for girls and 78% for boys, attendance rates were 92.6% for girls and 92.7% for boys, and 97.7% of the teachers stated that children's ability to concentrate and learn in school improved as a result of school feeding (but information is not provided on the changes in enrollment and attendance due to the projects).

The WFP FFE program, thus, has long been a large activity. WFP (2009) indicates that there are at least 134 evaluations of these projects in the WFP archives that go back to at least 1963. This document summarizes the lessons learned from a subset of studies on 33 countries selected due to factors such as the quality of the studies and their recency:

> This comprehensive analysis leads to the new "gold standards," eight quality benchmarks for school feeding: a) sustainability; b) sound alignment with the national policy framework; c) stable funding and budgeting; d) needs-based, cost-effective quality programme design; e) strong institutional arrangements for implementation, monitoring and accountability; f) strategy for local production and sourcing; g) strong partnerships and intersector coordination; h) strong community participation and ownership. (2009, p. 7)

These standards refer primarily to operational dimensions of programs. Standard (e) includes among seven components that "There is a resourced monitoring and evaluation system in place that is functioning, forms part of the structures of the lead institution and is used for the implementation and feedback" (p. 27). But no guidance is provided in this document about how high-quality evaluations should be undertaken. Indeed this document on lessons learned in 45 years provides no summary of what has been learned about the impacts of these decades of experience with FFE projects on school enrollment, assistance, and performance or guidance regarding evaluation of projects.

Though we have been able to find concerns about how to promote systematic evaluations through, for example, promoting independent evaluations (e.g., WFP 2008), we have not been able to find broad systematic evaluations of the overall impacts on enrollment, attendance, and performance beyond those summarized above with regard to the collaborative work with the US governmental programs (table 5.3 above) and a few of the individual studies discussed below (table 5.4 below). Based on what we have been able to locate, there probably is a need for increased systematic evaluation of the impacts and costs of overall WFP FFE activities.

5.5.3. Evaluations of Individual Projects. Adelman, Gilligan, and Lehrer (2008) review the empirical literature on the impacts of FFE projects on school enrollment, attendance, and performance with focus on the studies that they judge to have "the strongest methodology for identifying causal impacts." This literature includes experimental studies, such as randomized controlled trials; experimental field trials; studies using quasi-experimental methods, such as natural or administrative experiments; and nonexperimental studies using careful evaluation designs. They note that "although the literature on the impacts of FFE programs is vast, high-quality studies with evaluation designs that provide causal impact estimates are relatively few."

Table 5.4 summarizes 12 studies that we have been able to find that satisfy such criteria. These studies tend to be concentrated in a few countries: four on Bangladesh, two on Uganda, and one each on Burkina Faso, Chile, Jamaica, Lao PDR, Peru, and the Philippines. The diversity of data sources and of study contexts is even less than the number of studies, with some of the studies differing only in methodological approaches or in outcomes considered but based on the same data. The studies on Bangladesh use difference-in-difference (DD), instrumental variable (IV), or propensity score matching (PSM) estimators with behavioral data. The study on Chile uses regression discontinuity (RD) estimates based

Table 5.4 Selected evaluations of individual School Food Programs (SFP) and Take Home Rations (THR)

Country, SFP or THR (study)	Method: Treatment on Treated (TOT) vs. Intent to Treat (ITT), data and estimation techniques	Significant impacts			
		1. Enrollment	2. Attendance	3. Performance in school	
				3a. Progression indicators	3b. Test scores
Bangladesh SFP (Ahmed 2004)	TOT: Comparison after year of program operation between treatment (mid-morning snack of fortified wheat biscuits) and similar nontreatment communities; regression of whether school-aged child enrolled in primary school (or attendance if enrolled) on dichotomous variable = 1 if child in program community (0 otherwise), child and household characteristics, and location fixed effects.	Up significantly by 14.2 percentage points (number of students per teacher 72 in program schools compared to 65 in control schools).	Up significantly by 1.3 days per month.	Dropout rates down by 7.5 percentage points.	Achievement test scores for 1,648 students in fifth grade up by 15.7%.
Bangladesh THR (Ahmed and del Ninno 2002)	TOT: IV used for primary-school child program participation—whether program available in union of child's residence; control those who did not receive treatment (including those who would not have been treated).	If household received sample mean ration for 5 months, probability of one of their children being enrolled in school up by 7.9–8.4 percentage points.	Attendance based on school registers (and random unannounced visits) in program schools was 70%, compared to 58% nonprogram schools.	From 1999 to 2000, about 6% of beneficiaries dropped out, compared to 15% of nonbeneficiaries in program schools.	Statistically significant negative impact on achievement test scores of fourth-grade students in program schools compared to those in nonprogram schools.
Bangladesh THR (Meng and Ryan 2010)	ITT: Propensity score matching, difference in-differences; control those who did not receive treatment but who would have been eligible if in treatment area; 600 households from 60 villages in 30 Unions and 10 Thanas, 400 households from FFE Unions (209 households with 399 children age 6–13 are program-eligible households, 191 households with 336 children age 6–13 are noneligible) and 200 from non-FFE Unions (200 households with 343 children age 6–13).	15–26 percentage points higher school-participation rates, relative to their counterfactuals who would have been eligible for the program had they lived in the program-eligible areas; 15–18 percentage points for boys and 23–26 percentage points for girls; 6–9 years insignificant and 10–13 years.		Conditional on school participation, participants also stay at school 0.7–1.05 years longer.	

Table 5.4 *(continued)*

Country, SFP or THR (study)	Method: Treatment on Treated (TOT) vs. Intent to Treat (ITT), data and estimation techniques	1. Enrollment	2. Attendance	3a. Progression indicators	3b. Test scores
				Significant impacts	
				3. Performance in school	
Bangladesh THR (Ravallion and Wodon 2000)	TOT: control those who did not receive treatment (including those who would not have been treated).	Every 114 kg of grains received annually (sample average) increases enrollment by 18–19 percentage points.			
Burkino Faso SFP and THR (Kazianga, de Walque, and Alderman 2009)	ITT: prospective random assignment of 45 schools in 2006–7 school year to (1) SFP (15 schools), (2) THR that provide girls with 10 kg of cereal flour each month, conditional on 90% attendance rate (16 schools), or (3) control group (14 schools). Random sample of 48 households around each school with about 4,140 children.	For girls age 6–12, 6.4 percentage points with SFP and 6.5 percentage points for THR; no significant impact on boys of meals.	Absenteeism up a day per month.		Significant reduction of 0.5 points (out of max of 4) for 13–15-year-old boys of SFP; significant reduction of 22 seconds (out of max of 120 seconds) for girls 6–15 years to answer math question for SFP; no significant effects on WISC and Raven's tests and forward and backward digit spans.
Chile SFP (McEwan 2010)	TOT: regression-discontinuity design based on targeting by school vulnerability index applied to administrative data.	No significant effect on school enrollment or on age of first-grade enrollment.		No significant effect on grade repetition.	No significant effect on fourth-grade standardized test scores.
Jamaica SFP (Powell et al. 1998)	TOT: 814 2nd-5th-grade students randomly assigned to daily breakfast (576–703 kcal, 27 g protein) or placebo (orange slice with 18 kcal) for school year (8 months).	Up 1.9 and 3.1 percentage points for adequately nourished children and under-nourished children, respectively.			

Study	Methodology				
Lao PDR SFP and/or THR (Buttenheim, Alderman, and Friedman 2011)	ITT: difference-in-difference estimators with propensity-score weighting for 2006–8 longitudinal survey for about 4,500 households in four districts in Northern Laos.	No significant effect on school enrollment.			
Peru SFP (Jacoby, Cueto, and Pollitt 1996)	TOT: 10 schools randomly assigned to SFP (breakfast) or to control for 30 days for 4th & 5th grade students.		Up 0.58 percentage points in treatment schools and down 2.92 percentage points in control schools (significant difference).		
Philippines SFP (Tan, Lane, and Lassibille 1999)	TOT: randomly assigned to 10 schools (alone in 5 schools; with parent-teacher partnerships in 5) with comparison with 10 randomly selected control schools with double-difference estimates.			Decreased dropout rates but not statistically significant.	Positive for first-grade achievement for English scores and, with parent-teacher partnership, mathematics scores.
Uganda SFP & THR (Adelman et al. 2009; Alderman, Gilligan, and Lehrer 2010)	ITT: compares difference-in-differences outcomes among 3 randomly assigned groups: beneficiaries of WFP's subsidized SFP in 11 learning centers (40,897 children), beneficiaries of an experimental THR giving equivalent food transfers in 10 learning centers (35,534 children), and control group in 10 learning centers (60,939 children); 6–14-year-olds in Internally Displaced People's (IDP) camps in Northern Uganda, 2005–7.	8.9 percentage points for 6–13-year-olds conditional on not being enrolled at baseline; both programs reduced age of entry by about 0.20 years or 2 SDs.	Based on unannounced attendance visits, positive significant impacts of both SFP and THR on morning attendance of children aged 10–17, ranging from 8 to 12 percentage points; for children age 6–17, SFP and THR increase afternoon attendance by 14.6 and 14.1 percentage points; no significant effects on self-reported attendance.	SFP reduced probability of repetition for boys age 6–13 years by about 0.20; SFP significantly more likely to stay in primary school; no significant impact on probability of progressing to secondary school.	THR increases math scores of 11–14-year-olds 16.7 points. Both SFP and THR programs had large significant impacts on math scores of 11–14-year-olds who had delayed school entry. SFP weakly increased literacy test scores of 11–14-year-olds by 6.4 points, but fell for 6–10-year-olds. THR had significant improvements in Primary Leaving Exam scores. Both THR and SFP improve cognitive function in terms of manipulating concepts. Girls in THR demonstrated improvements in short-term memory and (weakly) in reasoning and perceptive ability. THR had weakly larger impacts on reasoning ability (Raven's test) than SFP (significant at 5% for boys).

on discontinuities in quantities of food provided based on cutoffs in a "school vulnerability index." The study on Lao PDR uses DD estimates with PSM to establish counterfactuals. The other studies present DD estimates with random assignment of treatment usually at the school or community level, though in the study for Jamaica at the individual level.

School Enrollment. These studies suggest significantly positive impacts on school enrollments in a number of cases that range from 6.4 to 26 percentage points, though in some cases there are not significant effects (e.g., SFP in Chile and for boys in Burkino Faso, both SFP and/or THR for Lao PDR). The estimated effects in some cases are larger for girls than for boys: 6.4 percentage points versus insignificant for SFP in Burkino Faso (Kaziaga, de Walque, and Alderman 2009) and 15–18 percentage points versus 23–26 percentage points for THR in the PSM estimates for Bangladesh (Meng and Ryan 2010). The estimates at least in some cases appear to be fairly sensitive to the estimation procedure. For example, for the Bangladeshi THR program using the same data Ahmed and del Ninno (2002) report IV estimates of 7.9–8.4 percentage points while Meng and Ryan (2010) report PSM estimates of 23–26 percentage points. Finally, one study (the only study to investigate this question) finds a significant impact of both SFP and THR programs on age of initial enrollment of about −0.2 years in Uganda (Alderman, Gilligan, and Lehrer 2010).

School Attendance. Five of the studies report increases in attendance, ranging from 1.9 to 14.6 percentage points. But several points are worth noting. First, the Jamaican study reports that these increases were higher for undernourished (3.1 percentage points) versus adequately nourished (1.9 percentage points) children. Second, the relatively high percentage point increases are for the Ugandan Internally Displaced People's camps based on unannounced attendance visits. Interestingly, the self-reported data do not indicate any attendance effects in this case. Third, the Ugandan estimates do not differ for SFP versus THR programs, despite what would seem to be incentives more directed at children in the former.[27] Fourth, the Burkina Faso study finds significantly negative effects on attendance. Kazianga, de Walque, and Alderman (2009) attempt to explain the latter result by noting that the household response likely depends on the relative availability of child labor in the household. They report that the school absenteeism increased among households with low child-labor supply and decreased for households with relatively large child-labor supply. Although the results for households with relatively large child-labor supply are reassuring, it still is not clear why households with relatively low labor supply are induced to increase absenteeism rather than, say, reduce it less than households with relatively high labor supply.

Performance in School. The results for progression through school are limited and mixed. The Bangladeshi THR reduced dropout rates by about 9%, and conditional on school participation, students also stayed in school 0.7–1.1 years longer. These are fairly substantial effects. But the Chilean SFP and the Ugandan THR did not significantly affect any indicators of school progression. The Philippines SFP did not significantly affect dropout rates, but the Ugandan SFP reduced the probability of grade repetition for boys age 6–13 years by about 20 percentage points and students were significantly more likely to stay in primary school though there was no significant impact on the probability of progressing to secondary school.

The results for test performance also are mixed. The Philippines SFP program had significantly positive effects for first-grade achievement for English scores and for (but only with parent-teacher partnerships) mathematics scores. The Bangladeshi SFP program increased fifth-grade achievement test scores by 15.7% but the Bangladeshi THR had a statistically significant negative impact on achievement test scores of fourth-grade students. The Ugandan THR increased math scores of 11–14-year-olds by 16.7 points, and both SFP and THR had large significant impacts on math scores of 11–14-year-olds who had delayed school entry. The Ugandan SFP weakly increased literacy test scores of 11–14-year-olds by 6.4 points, but these fell for 6–10-year-olds. The Ugandan THR significantly improved Primary Leaving Exam (PLE) scores. The Ugandan THR and SFP both improved cognitive function in terms of manipulating concepts. Girls in the Ugandan THR program also demonstrated improvements in short-term memory and (weakly) in reasoning and perceptive ability. The Ugandan THR had somewhat larger impacts on reasoning ability (Raven's test) than SFP (significant at 5% for boys). The Burkino Faso SFP significantly reduced math scores for boys age 13–15, but increased the speed (though not the score) of girls on math tests. The Ugandan SFP and THR both had no significant effects on WISC and Raven's tests of cognitive skills or on forward and backward digit span tests. The Chilean SFP had no significant impacts on fourth-grade standardized test scores.

These mixed results do not seem to justify the conclusion that SFP have much greater impact on test scores than THR as might be expected if feeding children during the school day, while they are learning, would improve their learning performance, and possibly their cognitive development. However only the Ugandan and Burkino Faso cases permit a direct comparison, and in the latter it is not clear that the real income value of the SFP and THR are the same.

Spillover Effects. One possible spillover effect is that other members of the household might benefit from the increased real income due to the FFE program. Only the study for Burkino Faso among those that are summarized in table 5.4 addresses this possibility (Adelman et al. 2009). This study finds in villages that received THR, children between 12 and 60 months old experienced a 0.38 standard deviation increase in weight-for-age (significant at the 5% level) and a 0.33 increase in for weight-for-height (significant at the 10% level). Also, there were changes in the time use of the school-age children that might have spillover effects on the time use and other outcomes of household members: THR significantly reduced girls participation in farm and nonfarm labor, SFP reduced girls' participation in tending for younger siblings, and both SFP and THR increased girls' participation in fetching water, THR increased girls' participation in other household chores, and SFP increased boys' participation in fetching wood.

Another possible spillover effect is through schools. If FFE programs increase enrollment, they may increase class size and change the composition of classes toward students with less strong backgrounds who were induced to enroll at the margin by the FFE program. Ahmed and Arends-Kuenning (2006) investigate these possibilities for Bangladesh's FFE program, which, as noted with respect to studies that are summarized in table 5.4, increased school enrollment, which increased class sizes. Their analysis focuses on the impact of FFE on the achievement test scores of students who did not receive FFE benefits. They find evidence for a negative impact of FFE on the test scores of nonbeneficiary students through peer effects related to the larger share of FFE students in the class but no significant class size effects.

5.5.4 Summary of FFE Programs. FEE programs that provide incentives in-kind in terms of food for child enrollment and attendance in schools are widespread in the developing world. A number of studies are interpreted to provide evidence of fairly substantial impacts on enrollments in contexts in which enrollments otherwise would be low and undernourishment is common, though many of the results of these studies must be qualified because of questions about how well the counterfactual is represented by the controls, if any, who are used. Relatively few studies use random assignments of treatment or statistical methods to provide more confident conclusions about the impacts of FEE programs. These studies also seem to indicate significant enrollment effects, as well as significant attendance effects, but more limited and mixed results regarding effects on performance in school and limited evidence on spillover effects. And in most cases (though the Chilean study is an exception), there is no information on a random representation of children in school catchment areas, so even the current understanding of the enrollment effects must be qualified. The estimated effects also seem to vary in a number of cases with the age and gender of the children, with a weak suggestion of larger effects for girls than for boys. The evidence about the relative merits of SFP versus THR is also limited, but does not support the possible advantage of SFP because of positive immediate benefits from being better fed while literally in school. All in all, thus, the evidence about the impacts of FFE programs suggests some positive effects, but many gaps in what we know that call for further research.

But much larger research gaps are with regard to the real resource costs of FFE programs. A potential drawback of FFE or THR programs in comparison with the CCT, incentive performance, and school voucher programs reviewed in sections 5.2–5.4, for example, is the transport and distribution costs associated with getting the food to the intended beneficiary. The logistics of getting food transported, often from overseas, and of arranging for the preparation of meals entail a significant additional program cost. Only a few of the studies on FFE programs that are reviewed in this section pay any attention to even some of the components of the resource costs, and none of them attempts to estimate the full resource costs including, for example, the opportunity costs of the time teachers spend implementing FFE programs and the distortions costs in various markets for such programs. Based on a narrower definition of costs that focuses on material costs (but not administrative costs or distortionary costs), Bundy et al. (2009, p. xviii) estimate that the average per capita cost of THR is US$50 per year and of SFP is US$40 per year, with the latter less easily targeted. They note that for poorer countries such costs are of the same order of magnitude as overall per-student primary school costs. If, as seems likely, total resource costs are of a similar or greater magnitude, then the internal rates of return to real resources used for FFE may not be very high—though there may be some important distributional benefits in terms of increasing resources for very poor households. In any case, perhaps the most important research gap for FFE programs pertain to information on their real resource costs.

5.6. Conclusions

The time and efforts of students and parents are clearly important inputs into education. Incentives for students and parents might therefore have potentially significant impacts on education, although such impacts would seem a priori to depend also on the other inputs into educational production functions, such as those of schools and teachers.

The currently available estimates suggest some fairly broad responses in terms of students' behaviors to various types of incentives in developing countries. Most incentive programs that have been tried are tied to enrollment and attendance, rather than test performance or other measures of knowledge or skills acquisition. There is strong evidence that incentives of this kind increase enrollment and attendance, but there is not much evidence that they lead to increased knowledge, mainly because of the lack of studies documenting the effects of such programs on test score outcomes. One challenge in estimating the effect of enrollment/attendance incentive programs on test-score outcomes is that the tests are usually administered at schools and school attendance decisions are affected by the program. If the program brings into school children who would otherwise not attend, then test-score comparisons between treatment and comparison groups that are not corrected for selection would tend to find lower test scores among program participants. One tentative conclusion of this review is that incentives for students often seem to be effective in terms of the targets to which the incentives are tied in the contexts studied, but we do not yet have much evidence on whether they are effective in terms of other objectives, such as achievement and possible noncognitive outcomes related to executive function.

There would seem to be potential for gains in student achievement from tying the incentives directly to achievement and possibly other outcomes of interest. If the incentives are tied to achievement levels and, as is likely, students from better-off families have more access to complementary home and school inputs into the production of achievement than do students from poorer families, the incentives are potentially disequalizing and regressive. To avoid such distributional results, it may be desirable to design incentive structures so that they reward increases in achievement, perhaps with greater rewards for children starting from lower levels, as in the Mexican incentive program to align learning incentives (ALI) discussed above and in more detail in Behrman et al. 2012. Of course if targeting of incentives to achievement levels or gains or to other outcomes is to work well, it is desirable that there be good measures of the outcomes toward which the incentives are targeted. This may mean that the returns to investing, for example, in developing better tests of curricular material are high, assuming of course that the curriculum reflects what society thinks it is desirable for students to learn. The existing studies on incentive programs that link incentives to performance and learning tend to show significant positive impacts on standardized tests. Although further studies are needed, it would seem a promising avenue for educational interventions to improve achievement would be linking benefits directly to achievement variables and to other indicators that are thought to have longer-run impacts on productivity.

It must be noted, however, that the available estimates are but a limited guide to making generalizations about desired incentive policies. First, the available estimates are for particular contexts and do not necessarily carry over to different contexts with different markets, policies, and other conditions. The estimates for FFE programs, for example, are generally (though with the exception of Chile) for very poor contexts with significant numbers of school-age children not enrolled in school and with low levels of nutrition because such programs have been targeted to such areas. Although this targeting seems sensible, it means that we do not know much about what impacts FFE programs would have in other contexts in which, for example, the impact on learning would be primarily through students being better nourished rather than being induced to enroll in school. The dependence on context, of course, poses a challenge for efforts to ascertain "best practices" with broad external validity (see Dhaliwal, Duflo, Glennerster, and Tulloch in chapter 8 below). Second, there has been little exploration about the extent to which the effects of student and parent incentives depend on the other inputs into the educational production process though, as noted, this is likely to be critical in that there are complementarities and substitution with other inputs into learning, both contemporaneously and over the life cycle (e.g., as with the dynamic complementarities emphasized by Cunha and Heckman 2007). Third, the exploration to date of student and parent incentives has paid very little attention to "noncognitive skills," including socio-emotional skills and self-discipline, even though recent research has increasingly emphasized the importance of these skills in adult socio-economic success. Fourth, most of the available research is focused on fairly short time periods, but what is likely to be of greater interest is the longer-run impacts of the incentives being studied. Even if there are not persistent gains in terms of cognitive skills, for example, there may be important private and societal gains in other dimensions, such as reduced adult criminal activity (e.g., Heckman 2006). Fifth, to make policy decisions it would be desirable to have benefit-cost or internal rates of return to the real resources used for the alternative incentives, which requires estimates of both impacts and resource costs, but the longer-run impacts have hardly been explored and the real resource costs of various student and parental incentive programs hardly considered. Such benefit-cost ratios or internal rates of return would illuminate the nature of distribution-efficiency tradeoffs or complementarities in policies being considered. Sixth, the types of incentives considered have been limited with, for example, little attention to different incentive structures, such as tournaments.

Thus, current knowledge about the effectiveness of student and parental incentives is quite limited. Many of the studies reviewed here indicated that incentive-based policies are potentially effective as a means for increasing educational outcomes, but there is substantial scope for further implementation, systematic data collection, and study of these kinds of programs.

Acknowledgments

We thank Eric Hanushek, Harry Patrinos, Paul Glewwe and other conference participants and two reviewers for the University of Chicago Press for useful comments.

Notes

1. See Galiani and Perez-Truglia in chapter 6 in this volume for discussion of incentives for teachers.
2. For recent discussions of these approaches and their strengths and limitations, see, for example, Banerjee and Duflo 2009, Deaton 2010, and Stock 2010.
3. Counterfactual policies are policies of interest that have not been implemented yet or that differ in some ways from the policies actually implemented.
4. With the help of Nykia Perez, director of Information Services at the Population Studies Center at the University of Pennsylvania, to identify studies relevant for this chapter, we searched the following databases and selected out subsets of results: EconLit, ERIC, IBSS: International Bibliography of the Social Sciences, PAIS International, Social Services Abstracts, Sociological Abstracts, and Worldwide Political Science Abstracts. Searches included two or more of these bulleted elements in combination, so that results would include element 1 AND element 2, with the exception of the last on the list (i.e., AND NOT is meant to exclude results with those terms). KW means keyword search within

these databases and it simultaneously searches The Title, Abstract and Subject descriptors assigned to the citation:

(KW= education)

(KW= (cash transfers) or (incentives) or (educational finance) or (transfer programs) or (conditional cash transfers) or (conditional cash transfer) or (education production function) or (scholarships) or (grants) or (loans) or (food) or (lunch) or (breakfast))

(KW= (social inclusion) or (poverty alleviation) or (dispari*) or (inequality) or (antipoverty) or (equal*) or (poverty))

(KW= impac* or outcom* or consequ* or effects or effect)

AND NOT (KW= (higher education) or (universit*) or (colleg*) or (post-secondary))

5. Some studies suggest that these programs would be inefficient were increasing schooling their only objective because they do not increase schooling as much as possible for a given budgetary constraint (e.g., de Janvry and Sadoulet 2006; Todd and Wolpin 2006), but such a critique does not hold if the CCT has other goals such as alleviating current poverty as, for example, in the Mexican PROGRESA/Oportunidades program.

6. These studies depended on strong identifying assumptions to attempt to identify causal effects from behavioral data. Most CCTs have not tested this assumption. However a two-year pilot project underway in Morocco is using an experimental design to evaluate the impact on "student attendance, dropout rates, test scores and household welfare" inter alia of which parent transfers are given by having half of the transfers go to mothers and the other half to fathers. But according to the website as of April 2011, results from this study were not yet available (http://www.povertyactionlab.org/evaluation/conditional-cash-transfers-education-morocco).

7. In the conditional group, the benefits included a transfer for attending school plus payment for school fees. The unconditional group received the transfer payment unconditionally plus the average amount of school fees paid in the conditional group.

8. The Moroccan program described in note 6 also randomly assigned conditional and nonconditional transfers, but results are not currently available.

9. Surprisingly, those in the conditioned group showed significantly higher incidences of marriage and early childbearing than those in the unconditioned group. Compared with the control group, the conditioned group showed no impacts on the probability of marriage or childbearing during the program, but those in the unconditioned group showed reductions in both variables on the order of 7–8 percentage points. This difference is likely attributable to the fact all girls in the unconditional group receive transfers, while a significant proportion of girls in the conditioned group who do not comply with the conditionality requirements do not receive any transfers.

10. It is unclear in the paper the extent to which these households did receive grants even though enrollment and attendance were not being verified and whether/when the program realized that for these households requirements to pay the grant were not being complied with.

11. Whereas nearly all CCT programs to date have been implemented in developing country contexts, there are several pilot CCT programs that have been undertaken in the United States. Riccio et al. (2010) present initial results for the most well-known of these, New York City's CCT pilot program "Opportunities." This program has a different approach to most other CCTs that provide specific monetary amounts linked only to enrollment and attendance. In particular, the program consisted of 11 different behaviors that were rewarded, ranging from enrollment and regular attendance to parental participation in parent conferences to graduating from high school to scoring at a proficient level on achievement tests. The initial results were relatively disappointing, showing no overall significant effects on any schooling indicator after two years of program benefits and the pilot was not continued.

12. Behrman, Sengupta, and Todd (2005) estimate impacts of PROGRESA/Oportunidades on enrollment, grade progression, and failure which in some cases show higher impacts of the program for boys. In simulated results based on these initial impacts, they conclude the net effect of impacts is to increase grades of schooling for boys by 0.92 and of girls by 0.68; see table 2.2.

13. Djebbari and Smith (2008) study heterogeneity of impacts in the PROGRESA/Oportunidades program but focus mostly on impacts on per capita household expenditures.

14. There are a few studies that have evaluated effects of student incentive programs in the United States. Jackson (2009) uses nonexperimental data to examine a program implemented in Texas schools that served underprivileged adolescents, which pays both students and teachers for passing grades on Advanced Placement (AP) exams. The results show that the program led to increases in AP course and exam-taking, increases in the number of students with high SAT/ACT scores, and increases in college matriculation. Fryer (2010) reports results from four different field experiments that implemented student incentive programs of various kinds in low performing urban schools in Chicago, Dallas, New York City, and Washington, DC. In New York City, payments were given to fourth- and seventh-grade students conditional on their performance on 10 standardized tests. In Chicago, incentives were paid to ninth-graders every five weeks for grades in five courses. The Dallas program gave second-graders $2 per book read, with an additional requirement of passing a short quiz on the subject of the book. Last, in DC, incentives were given to sixth-, seventh-, and eighth-graders on a composite index intended to capture their school attendance, behavior, and three measures of inputs in educational production. Fryer finds that incentives are effective in promoting student achievement when incentives are tied to inputs in educational production but are not effective if they are tied to outcomes.

15. In the twelfth grade, monetary awards are only given to those achieving adequate or high levels of test performance independent of their change in test performance because the goal of high school is to attain adequate achievement levels and the twelfth-grade test is at the end of the high school career.

16. The voucher program was introduced along with decentralization reforms by Augusto Pinochet's military government in 1981. Prior to 1981, governmental subsidies were provided to private schools. However, the voucher re-

form instituted a more direct relationship between funding levels and children's school attendance decisions.

17. For example, schools are required to have licensed teachers. They also do not receive additional voucher payments for class sizes that exceed 45 students (McEwan and Urquiola 2005).

18. Municipal schools sometimes receive some additional funding in the form of governmental transfers when the voucher amounts are not sufficient to cover schools' operating expenses.

19. Sapelli and Vial (2002) also find that the relative performance of private and municipal schools depends on whether municipal schools receive additional governmental subsidies. In areas where the municipal schools do not receive extra subsidies and expenditure on students is comparable to that in private subsidized schools, there is a significant test-score gain from attending private subsidized schools.

20. Rather, they find that average repetition and grade-for-age worsened in such areas relative to other communities. A potential limitation of the analysis is that it examines differences in test scores over time, though the tests were not comparable over time prior to 1998, when test equating was introduced. Also, the study analyzes school test scores for children age 10–15, and children who dropped out are not included in the testing. If areas with increasing private school enrollment had children at high risk for dropping out staying in school longer, then one might expect to see higher repetition rates and a lower grade-for-age.

21. This source also states that research suggests that school meals bring more children into school, keep them coming back each day, and make it easier for them to learn, with reference to Ahmed and Billah 1994, Del Rosso and Marek 1996, Levinger 1986, "and many more" (p. 4, n. 1).

In addition to the literature search described in n. 2 above, for section 5.5 we searched International Food Policy Research Institute (IFPRI) sources separately because IFPRI has been an important source of studies in this literature but is not covered in the data bases that were searched. Our search yielded six of the studies covered in Adelman, Gilligan, and Lehrer (2008) (see section 5.5.3) plus some additional more recent studies. We do not include the Vermeersch and Kremer (2004) randomized SFP evaluation in western Kenyan preschools that Adelman, Gilligan, and Lehrer do include because the present chapter is limited to K-12 schooling. See chapter 3 by Behrman, Engle, and Fernald for a survey on preschool programs in developing countries and see chapter 6 by Alderman and Bleakley for a survey on child health and schooling that is related to the topic of this section.

22. See Grant and Behrman 2010. The same study reports that, conditional on entering school, generally throughout the developing world, in the early twenty-first century girls average at least as high schooling attainment as do boys.

23. Jacoby (2002) finds virtually no intrahousehold reallocation of calories on average in response to a school feeding program in the Philippines, but reallocation was more pronounced in poorer households. Jacoby explains his finding by arguing that either the specific feeding program (snacks at school) is not

substitutable with household food, or it is the reflection of a "labeling effect" as argued by Kooreman (2000) using Dutch data.

24. Calorie elasticities with respect to income for such populations probably are significantly positive, but much less than 1.0 so the real income increases due to FEE programs induce some additional calorie consumption (though there is an old controversy about the magnitudes of these elasticities, e.g., Behrman and Deolalikar 1987, Bouis and Haddad 1992, Lipton 1988, Subramanian and Deaton 1996). There are many fewer estimates of other (other than caloric) nutrient elasticities, and the existing estimates range considerably.

25. The US government distributes food overseas through several programs, some administered by USDA and some by the US Agency for International Development (AID). These programs fall under the Agricultural Trade Development and Assistance Act of 1954 (also known as Public Law 480 or the Food for Peace program), the Food for Progress Act of 1985, and Section 416(b) of the Agricultural Act of 1949 (Frisman 2002).

26. Though there have been more extensive efforts to evaluate a small subset of these programs in some of the studies that are summarized in table 5.4.

27. Alderman, Gilligan, and Lehrer (2010) find that school enrollments respond more to school quality indicators for THR households than for SFP households and interpret this to mean that the locus of decisionmaking reflecting whom is directly impacted by the program (i.e., children in SFP, parents for THR) matters. But the differential responses to additive school quality indicators (not ones that are interactive with SFP and THR) between the SFP and THR households seems to suggest that there was not randomization between the two groups of households, not that THR induces greater responses to school quality than does SFP because parents are more directly impacted.

References

Adelman, Sarah W., Harold Alderman, Daniel O. Gilligan, and Kim Lehrer. 2009. "The Impact of School Feeding Programs on Cognitive Development and Learning: Experimental Evidence on the Role of Nutrition and Schooling from Northern Uganda." International Food Policy Research Institute, Washington, DC.

Adelman, Sarah W., Daniel O. Gilligan, and Kim Lehrer. 2008. "How Effective Are Food for Education Programs? A Critical Assessment of the Evidence from Developing Countries." International Food Policy Research Institute, Washington, DC.

Ahmed, Akhter U. 2004. "Impact of Feeding Children in School: Evidence from Bangladesh." International Food Policy Research Institute, Washington, DC.

Ahmed, Akhter U., and Mary Arends-Kuenning. 2006. "Do Crowded Classrooms Crowd Out Learning? Evidence from the Food for Education Program in Bangladesh." World Development 34:665–84.

Ahmed, Akhter U., and K. Billah 1994. "Food for Education Program in Bangladesh: An Early Assessment." Bangladesh Food Policy Project, International Food Policy Research Institute, Washington, DC.

Ahmed, Akhter U., and Carlo del Ninno. 2002. "The Food for Education Program in Bangladesh: An Evaluation of its Impact on Educational Attainment and Food Security." FCND Discussion Paper 138. International Food Policy Research Institute, Washington, DC.

Alderman, Harold, Daniel O. Gilligan, and Kim Lehrer. 2010. "The Impact of Food for Education Programs on School Participation in Northern Uganda." International Food Policy Research Institute, Washington, DC.

Angelucci, Manuela, Giacomo de Giorgi, Marcos A. Rangel, and Imran Rasul. 2010. "Family Networks and School Enrollment: Evidence from a Randomized Social Experiment." *Journal of Public Economics* 94:3–4, 197–221.

Angrist, Joshua D., Eric Bettinger, Erik Bloom, Elizabeth King and Michael Kremer. 2002. "Vouchers for Private Schooling in Colombia: Evidence from a Randomized Natural Experiment." *American Economic Review* 92 (5): 1535–59.

Angrist, Joshua D., Eric Bettinger, and Michael Kremer. 2006. "Long-Term Consequences of Secondary School Vouchers: Evidence from Administrative Records in Colombia." *American Economic Review* 96 (3): 847–62.

Angrist, Joshua, and Victor Lavy. 2009. "The Effects of High Stakes High School Achievement Awards: Evidence from a Randomized Trial." *American Economic Review* 99 (4): 1384–1414.

Attanasio, Orazio, Emla Fitzsimons, and Ana Gomez. 2005. "The Impact of a Conditional Educational Subsidy on School Enrollment in Colombia." Institute for Fiscal Studies, London.

Auguste, Sebastian, and Juan Pablo Valenzuela. 2003. "Do Students Benefit from School Competition? Evidence from Chile." University of Michigan, Ann Arbor.

Baez, Javier, and Adriana Camacho. 2011. "Assessing the Long Term Effects of Conditional Cash Transfers on Human Capital: Evidence from Colombia." World Bank Policy Research Working Paper no. 5681. Washington, DC: World Bank. Available at SSRN: http://ssrn.com/abstract=1865119.

Baird, Sarah, Craig McIntosh, and Berk Ozler. 2011. "Cash or Condition? Evidence from a Cash Transfer Experiment." *Quarterly Journal of Economics* 126 (4): 1709–53.

Banerjee, Abhijit V., and Esther Duflo. 2009. "The Experimental Approach to Development Economics." *Annual Review of Economics* 1:151–78.

Barrera-Osorio, Felipe, Marianne Bertrand, Leigh Linden, and Francisco Perez. 2011. "Improving the Design of Conditional Transfer Programs: Evidence from a Randomized Education Experiment in Colombia." *American Economic Journal: Applied Economics* 3 (April): 167–95.

Behrman, Jere R., and Anil B. Deolalikar. 1987. "Will Developing Country Nutrition Improve with Income? A Case Study for Rural South India." *Journal of Political Economy* 95 (3): 108–38.

Behrman, Jere R., Jorge Gallardo-Garc ia, Susan W. Parker, Petra E. Todd, and Viviana Velez-Grajales. 2012. "How Conditional Cash Transfers Impact Children and Adolescent Youth in Urban Mexico." *Education Economics* 20 (3): 233–59. Special Issue: International Workshop on the Applied Economics of Education, 2011.

Behrman, Jere R., Susan W. Parker, and Petra E. Todd. 2009a. "Medium-Term Impacts of the *Oportunidades* Conditional Cash Transfer Program on Rural Youth in Mexico." In *Poverty, Inequality, and Policy in Latin America*, ed. Stephan Klasen and Felicitas Nowak-Lehmann, 219–70. Cambridge, MA: MIT Press.

———. 2009b. "Schooling Impacts of Conditional Cash Transfers on Young Children: Evidence from Mexico." *Economic Development and Cultural Change* 57 (3): 439–77.

———. 2011. "Do Conditional Cash Transfers for Schooling Generate Lasting Benefits? A Five-Year Follow-Up of *Oportunidades* Participants." *Journal of Human Resources* 46 (1): 93–122.

Behrman, Jere R., Susan W. Parker, Petra E. Todd, and Kenneth I. Wolpin. 2012. "Aligning Learning Incentives of Students and Teachers: Results from a Social Experiment in Mexican High Schools." PIER Working Paper no. 13-004, University of Pennsylvania, Philadelphia. Available at SSRN: http://ssrn.com /abstract=2206883 or http://dx.doi.org/10.2139/ssrn.2206883.

Behrman, Jere R., Piyali Sengupta, and Petra Todd. 2005. "Progressing through PROGRESA: An Impact Assessment of a School Subsidy Experiment in Rural Mexico." *Economic Development and Cultural Change* 54:237–75.

Bobonis, Gustavo, and Frederico Finan. 2009. "Neighborhood Peer Effects in Secondary School Enrollment Decisions." *Review of Economics and Statistics* 91 (4): 695–716.

Bouis, Howarth E., and Lawrence J. Haddad. 1992. "Are Estimates of Calorie-Income Elasticities Too High? A Recalibration of the Plausible Range." *Journal of Development Economics* 39 (2): 333–64.

Bravo, David, Dante Contreras, and Claudia Sanhueza. 1999. "Rendimiento Educacional, Desigualdad, y Brecha de Desempeño Privado/Público: Chile 1982–1997." Working paper.

Bravo, David, Sankar Mukhopadhyay, and Petra Todd. 2010. "Effects of School Reform on Education and Labor Market Performance: Evidence from Chile's Universal Voucher System." *Quantitative Economics* 1:47–95.

Brighouse, Harry. 2000. *School Choice and Social Justice*. Oxford: Oxford University Press.

Bundy, D., C. Burbano, M. Grosh, A. Gelli, M. Jukes, and L. Drakes. 2009. *Rethinking School Feeding: Social Safety Nets, Child Development, and the Education Sector*. Washington, DC: World Bank.

Buttenheim, Alison, Harold Alderman, and Jed Friedman. 2011. "Impact Evaluation of School Feeding Programs in Lao PDR." World Bank Policy Research Working Paper 5518. Washington, DC: World Bank. Available at http:// elibrary.worldbank.org/content/workingpaper/10.1596/1813-9450-5518.

Carnoy, Martin. 1997. "Is Privatization through Education Vouchers Really the Answer? A Comment on West." *World Bank Research Observer* 12 (1): 105–6.

Contreras, Dante. 2001. "Evaluating a Voucher System in Chile: Individual, Family and School Characteristics." Universidad de Chile, Santiago.

Cunha, Flavio, and James J. Heckman. 2007. "The Technology of Skill Formation." *American Economic Review* 97 (2): 31–47.

Dammert, Ana. 2009. "Heterogeneous Impacts of Conditional Cash Transfers: Evidence from Nicaragua." *Economic Development and Cultural Change* 58 (1): 53–83.

de Brauw, Alan, and John Hoddinott. 2010. "Must Conditional Cash Transfer Programs Be Conditioned to Be Effective? The Impact of Conditioning Transfers on School Enrollment in Mexico." *Journal of Development Economics* 96 (2): 359–70. doi:10.1016/j.jdeveco.2010.08.014.

de Janvry, Alain, and Elisabeth Sadoulet. 2006. "Making Conditional Cash Transfer Programs More Efficient: Designing for Maximum Effect of the Conditionality." *World Bank Economic Review* 20 (1): 1–29.

Deaton, Angus. 2010. "Instruments, Randomization and Learning about Development." *Journal of Economic Literature* 48:424–55.

Deci, E. L., R. Koestner, and R. M. Ryan. 1999. "A Meta-Analytic Review of Experiments Examining the Effects of Extrinsic Rewards on Intrinsic Motivation." *Psychological Bulletin* 125:627–68.

Del Rosso, Joy Miller, and Tonia Marek. 1996. "Class Action, Improving School Performance in the Developing World through Better Health and Nutrition." Washington, DC: World Bank. http://documents.worldbank.org/curated /en/1996/10/696196/class-action-improving-school-performance-developing -world-through-better-health-nutrition.

Djebbari, Habiba, and Jeffrey Smith. 2008. "Heterogeneous Program Impacts in PROGRESA." *Journal of Econometrics* 145 (1–2): 64–80.

Epple, Dennis, and Richard E. Romano. 1998. "Competition between Private and Public Schools, Vouchers, and Peer-Group Effects." *American Economic Review* 88:33–62.

Filmer, Deon, and Norbert Schady. 2011. "Does More Cash in Conditional Cash Transfer Programs Always Lead to Larger Impacts on School Attendance?" *Journal of Development Economics* 96:150–57.

Fiszbein, Ariel, and Norbert Schady, with Francisco H. G. Ferreira, Margaret Grosh, Nial Kelleher, Pedro Olinto, and Emmanuel Skoufias. 2009. *Conditional Cash Transfers: Reducing Current and Future Poverty*. Washington, DC: World Bank.

Friedman, Milton. 1955. "The Role of Government in Education." In *Economics and the Public Interest*, ed. R. A. Colo, 123–44. New Brunswick, NJ: Rutgers University Press.

———. 1962. *Capitalism and Freedom*. Chicago: University of Chicago Press.

Frisman, Paul. 2002. "USDA Use of Surplus Food for Foreign Aid," Report 2002-R-0596. US Department of Agriculture Report, Washington, DC. http:// www.cga.ct.gov/2002/olrdata/env/rpt/2002-R-0596.htm.

Fryer, Roland. 2010. "Financial Incentives and Student Achievement: Evidence from Randomized Trials." Working paper. Harvard University, Cambridge, MA.

Gallego, Francisco. 2002. "Competencia y Resultados Educativos: Teoria y Evidencia Para Chile," *Cuadernos de Economia* 39 (118): 309–52.

Gitter, Seth R., and Bradford L. Barham. 2008. "Women's Power, Conditional Cash Transfers and Schooling in Nicaragua." *World Bank Economic Review* 22 (2): 271–90. doi:10.1093/wber/lhn006.

Glewwe, Paul, and Ana Lucia Kassouf. 2012. "The Impact of the Bolsa Escola/ Familia Conditional Cash Transfer Program on Enrollment, Drop Out Rates and Grade Promotion in Brazil." *Journal of Development Economics* 97:505–17.

Grant, Monica J., and Jere R. Behrman. 2010. "Gender Gaps in Educational Attainment in Less Developed Countries." *Population and Development Review* 36 (1): 71–89.

Heckman, James J. 2006. "Skill Formation and the Economics of Investing in Disadvantaged Children," *Science* 312 (June 30): 1900–1902.

Heckman, James J., and Burton Singer. 1984. "A Method for Minimizing the Impact of Distributional Assumptions in Econometric Models for Duration Data." *Econometrica* 52:271–320.

Hoxby, Caroline. 2001. "Would School Choice Change the Teaching Profession." *Journal of Human Resources* 37 (4): 846–91.

———. 2003. "School Choice and School Productivity: Could School Choice Be a Tide that Lifts All Boats?" In *The Economics of School Choice*, ed. Caroline M. Hoxby, 287–342. Chicago: University of Chicago Press.

Hsieh, Chang-Tai, and Miguel Urquiola. 2003. "When Schools Compete, How Do They Compete? An Assessment of Chile's Nationwide School Voucher Program." NBER Working Paper no. W10008. National Bureau of Economic Research, Cambridge, MA.

———. 2006. "The Effects of Generalized School Choice on Achievement and Stratification: Evidence from Chile's Voucher Program." *Journal of Public Economics* 90 (8–9): 1477.

Jackson, Clement. 2009. "A Little Now for a Lot Later: A Look at a Texas Advanced Placement Incentive Program." Working paper. Cornell University Institute for Labor Relations (ILR), Ithaca, NY.

Jacoby, E., S. Cueto, and E. Pollitt. 1996. "Benefits of a School Breakfast Programme among Andean Children in Huaraz, Peru." *Food and Nutrition Bulletin* 17 (1): 54–64.

Jacoby, Hanan G. 2002. "Is There an Intrahousehold 'Flypaper Effect'? Evidence from a School Feeding Programme." *Economic Journal* 112: 196–221.

Kazianga, Harounan, Damien de Walque and Harold Alderman. 2009. "School Feeding Programs and the Nutrition of Siblings." World Bank Policy Research Working Paper no. 4976. Washington, DC: World Bank.

Kooreman, P. 2000. "The Labeling Effect of a Child Benefit System." *American Economic Review* 90 (3): 571–83.

Kremer, Michael, Edward Miguel, and Rebecca Thornton. 2009. "Incentives to Learn." *Review of Economics and Statistics* 91 (3): 437–56.

Ladd, Helen. 2002. "School Vouchers: A Critical View." *Journal of Economic Perspectives* 16 (4): 3–24.

Lalive, Rafael, and M. Alejandra Cattaneo. 2009. "Social Interactions and Schooling Decisions." *Review of Economics and Statistics* 91:457–77.

Levinger, Beryl. 1986. "School Feeding Programs in Developing Countries: An Analysis of Actual and Potential Impact." US Agency for International Development Evaluation Special Study no. 30.

Levy, Dan, and James Ohls. 2007. "Evaluation of Jamaica's PATH Program: Final Report." Mathematica Policy Research, Washington, DC. *www .mathematica-mpr.net/.../JamaicaPATH.pdf.*

Lipton, Michael. 1988. *Attacking Undernutrition and Poverty: Some Issues of Adaptation and Sustainability.* Ithaca, NY: Pew/Cornell Lecture Series on Food and Nutrition Policy.

Maluccio, John A., and Rafael Flores. 2005. *Impact Evaluation of a Conditional Cash Transfer Program: The Nicaraguan Red de Proteccion Social.* International Food Policy Research Institute. http://ideas.repec.org/p/fpr/resrep/141 .html.

Martinelli, Cesar, and Susan W. Parker. 2008. "Do School Subsidies Promote Human Capital Investment among the Poor?" *Scandinavian Journal of Economics* 110:261–76.

McEwan, Patrick J. 2001. "The Effectiveness of Public, Catholic, and Non-Religious Private Schools in Chile's Voucher System." *Education Economics* 9 (2): 103–28.

———. 2010. "The Impact of School Meals on Education Outcomes: Discontinuity Evidence from Chile." Wellesley College, Wellesley, MA.

McEwan, Patrick J., and Martin Carnoy. 2000. "The Effectiveness and Efficacy of Private Schools in Chile's Voucher System." *Educational Evaluation and Policy Analysis* 22 (3): 213–39.

McEwan, Patrick J., and Miguel Urquiola. 2005. "Economic Behavior and the Regression-Discontinuity Design: Evidence from Class Size Reduction." Columbia University, New York.

McEwan, Patrick J., Miguel Urquiola, and Emiliana Vegas. 2008. "School Choice, Stratification and Information on School Performance: Lessons from Chile." *Economia* 8 (1): 1–42.

Meng, Xin, and Jim Ryan. 2010. "Does a Food for Education Program Affect School Outcomes? The Bangladesh Case." *Journal of Population Economics* 23:415–47.

Mizala, Alejandra, and Pilar Romaguera. 2000. "School Performance and Choice: The Chilean Experience." *Journal of Human Resources* 35 (2): 392–417.

Parry, Taryn Rounds. 1997a. "Decentralization and Privatization: Education Policy in Chile." *Journal of Public Policy* 17 (1): 107–33.

———. 1997b. "Theory Meets Reality in the Education Voucher Debate: Some Evidence from Chile." *Education Economics* 5 (3): 307.

Powell, C. A., S. P. Walker, S. M. Chang, and S. M. Grantham-McGregor. 1998. "Nutrition and Education: A Randomized Trial of the Effects of Breakfast in Rural Primary School Children." *American Journal of Clinical Nutrition* 68:873–79.

Ravallion, M., and Q. Wodon. 2000. "Does Child Labour Displace Schooling? Evidence on Behavioural Responses to an Enrollment Subsidy." *Economic Journal* 110:C158–C175.

Riccio, James, Nadine Dechausay, David Greenberg, Cynthia Miller, Zawadi Rucks, and Nandita Verma. 2010. "Toward Reduced Poverty across Generations: Early Findings from New York City's Conditional Cash Transfer Program." MDRC. Mimeo.

Rouse, Cecilia. 1998. "Private School Vouchers and Student Achievement: The Effect of the Milwaukee Parental Choice Program." *Quarterly Journal of Economics* 113:553–602.

Sapelli, Claudio, and Bernadita Vial. 2002. "The Performance of Private and Public Schools in the Chilean Voucher System." *Cuadernos de Economia* 39 (118): 423–54.

Schultz, T. Paul. 2004. "School Subsidies for the Poor: Evaluating the Mexican PROGRESA Poverty Program." *Journal of Development Economics* 74:199–250.

Stock, James H. 2010. "The Other Transformation in Econometric Practice: Robust Tools for Inference." *Journal of Economic Perspectives* 24 (2): 83–94.

Subramanian, Shankar, and Angus Deaton. 1996. "The Demand for Food and Calories." *Journal of Political Economy* 104 (1): 133–62.

Tan, Jee-Peng, Julia Lane, and Gerard Lassibille. 1999. "Student Outcomes in Philippine Elementary Schools: An Evaluation of Four Experiments." *World Bank Economic Review* 13 (3): 493–508.

Todd, Petra E., and Kenneth I. Wolpin. 2006. "Using a Social Experiment to Validate a Dynamic Behavioral Model of Child Schooling and Fertility: Assessing the Impact of a School Subsidy Program in Mexico." *American Economics Review* 96 (5): 1384–1417.

USDA (U.S. Department of Agriculture—Foreign Agricultural Service with Food and Nutrition Service National Agricultural Statistics Service). 2003. "The Global Food for Education Pilot Program: A Review of Project Implementation and Impact." US Department of Agriculture—Foreign Agricultural Service, Washington, DC. Available at www.fas.usda.gov/excredits/gfe/congress2003/index.html

———. 2004. "The Global Food for Education Pilot Program: Final Report." US Department of Agriculture—Foreign Agricultural Service, Washington, DC.

USDA (U.S. Department of Agriculture—Foreign Agricultural Service FAS). 2010. "USDA'S McGovern-Dole International Food for Education Program Expected to Feed 5 Million Children This Year." February 26. Available at http://www.fas.usda.gov/scriptsw/PressRelease/pressrel_dout.asp?Entry.

Vermeersch, C., and M. Kremer. 2004. "School Meals, Educational Achievement and School Competition: Evidence from a Randomized Evaluation." Working Paper. Washington, DC: World Bank.

WFP (World Food Programme). 2006. "Reviewing the Evidence: Food for Education Experts Seminar." Rome: WFP.

———. 2008. "WFP Evaluation Policy." Rome: WFP.

———. 2009. "Learning from Experience: Good Practices from 45 Years of School Feeding." Rome: WFP.

———. n.d. "2008 Figures WFP School Feeding Programmes." Rome: WFP.

6

School Management in Developing Countries

Sebastian Galiani (University of Maryland)
Ricardo Perez-Truglia (Harvard University and
Universidad de San Andres)

6.1. Introduction

The developing world has implemented many different policies to catch up with the educational outcomes observed in the more advanced countries. In the past, policies were usually based on the premise that increasing the spending on education inputs would improve educational attainment. However, the link between spending on school inputs and student performance does not seem strong enough to account for the gap between the developing world and OECD countries. Therefore, in recent years considerable attention has been given to school management. Thus, this chapter explores the literature on interventions that focus on the *way* in which resources are managed, instead of focusing on the amount of resources used.

We define "School Management" as the system through which schools are organized to manage their resources. It includes three main branches: the school market (whether schools are public or private, and the regulation of competition in the schooling system), the administration of schools (whether the system is centralized or there is a school-based management of power, knowledge, and budget), and the school organization (involving the curriculum, class size, tracking of students, incentives, and contracts to teachers, among others).

In this chapter we review the empirical literature on three different aspects of School Management. First, we address the effect of school decentralization on educational outcomes (section 6.3). Second, we analyze topics related to the tracking of students within schools (section 6.4), and third, we explore the effect of different teacher-incentive schemes, including pay for performance and contract teachers (section 6.5). The topics studied are timely given the recently adopted reforms in these areas. Recent experience with these reforms provides a body of evidence that can be used to reach some conclusions regarding their effectiveness. By no means is our list exhaustive. In fact, in this volume there are interesting analyses of other relevant issues that fall under our broad definition of School Management, such as school competition (see chapter 7) and topics related to incentives for parents and students (see sections 5.3 and 5.4 in chapter 5). Last, we do not cover other important issues, such as curriculum design, for which the evidence is still limited.

The aim of this chapter is to introduce the big questions regarding school decentralization, tracking of students, and teacher incentives, as well as to explore the main tradeoffs implied in the policies targeted at those aspects of School Management. There is controversy about the efficacy of these policies and the way they should be applied under different contexts. For example, economists and some policymakers seem to be sympathetic to decentralization measures, but there is no consensus about the potential benefits of tracking and contract teachers. Furthermore, while reforms involving school decentralization and teacher incentives have been relatively widespread during the last decade in the developing world, tracking has lacked similar popularity.

Regarding the methodological approach adopted in this chapter, we focus especially on the empirical evidence in each topic. First, we provide a simple theoretical framework to illustrate the main potential gains and sources of tradeoffs. With the framework in mind, we construct a large—though nonexhaustive—review of empirical papers that study the topic at hand. The ultimate goal of the chapter is to understand the causal effect of these types of interventions on educational performance. Therefore, identification issues are of first-order importance. In the review we mainly include papers that exploit experimental or quasi-experimental identification strategies. Those methods have proven to be the most accurate in reconstructing the counterfactual needed to study the fundamental problem of causal inference. Nevertheless, we also include important cross-sectional studies of correlations between variables of interest, but we always make clear the potential sources and direction of possible bias in the nonexperimental estimates.

Another methodological concern that is important for understanding the message we want to transmit concerns the comparison across results that comes from different types of studies. For example, in the tracking section we report observational or quasi-experimental studies that find no (or even a negative) effect of this intervention on students' performance, while we also review randomized experiments showing a positive impact of tracking. The way in which we should reconcile the results is to understand the heterogeneity of both the settings and the methods exploited. Unfortunately, for the time being, different settings are studied with different methodologies, so it is not obvious whether the differences in findings across studies are due only to differences in methodology or also to differences in the true parameters across the different settings. Nevertheless, a priori, we rely more on the results reported in experimental studies due to their higher credibility in identifying the causal effects of the interventions.

The last methodological issue we want to emphasize is closely related to the previous one. Even though experimental studies are internally valid, they do not necessarily have external validity (an issue obviously not exclusive to experimental studies, though). Therefore, the results cannot be generalized without further assumptions. Furthermore, external validity issues are somewhat more pressing when the effects of the interventions are heterogeneous across populations. For example, we show that in the case of tracking the effects of this intervention are highly dependent on the distribution of students' performance. Essentially, it is important to know whether the distribution is bimodal or unimodal. Assumptions regarding this distribution will be needed to extend the experimental results from one setting to other settings: for example, the distribution of students is probably very different in the United States and Kenya.[1] This fact, of course, does not diminish at all the importance of a study conducted under particular conditions. What it is more, we are often specifically interested in understanding how a policy or intervention works in a specific context.

Our main findings regarding the three School Management interventions studied in this chapter are the following. Decentralization programs seem to be successful in increasing the average performance of students. However, the better-off communities or schools tend to profit more from this intervention; thus future studies should attempt to understand how school autonomy affects poor and wealthy communities differently. Regarding tracking, the experimental evidence is still scarce, but it seems, at least in the context of a poor country where student performance is highly heterogeneous, that tracking increases the performance of all students. Finally, the results of teacher-incentive interventions are generally positive, though the precise design of the compensation scheme is key for producing long-lasting improvements in learning. Also, in very poor countries, contract teachers have positive results in reducing absenteeism of teachers and improving the performance of students. However, understanding whether these results can be attributed to incentives, decentralization of hiring decisions, or other mechanisms is essential to improving contract design for tenured civil-service teachers and to better benefit from the combination of the two types of teachers.

Finally, we would like to point out that in most of the studies reviewed—as in the majority of impact evaluation papers—the focus is on the average treatment effect on the treated population, which can be interpreted as the effect of the interventions on a random treated unit. The final assessment of these effects, however, would depend on the "welfare function" implicitly used by society to judge the results of the different policies and programs adopted. Nevertheless, as mentioned above, some programs may generate a gain on average but at the same time an increase in inequality. In those cases, the fact that there is a positive effect on average is genuinely valuable, yet it might be worth looking for complementary policy instruments to compensate for the increase in inequality, especially in cases when the cost of redistribution is high. The type and cost of the complementary interventions would depend on the context. We discuss these interventions in section 6.6.

Section 6.7 concludes and suggests some challenges for future research. Appendix 6A summarizes the main findings and methodologies of the reviewed papers.

6.2. Improving Educational Outcomes: School Inputs and School Management

Improving educational outcomes is one of the top priorities in most countries, especially in the developing world, which lags behind high-income countries in many indicators. This concern is partially driven by the idea that the formation of human capital through education is one of the main drivers of economic growth.

For many years, the goal of education policies in developing countries was to increase spending on school inputs, such as the quantity and quality of teachers, school infrastructure, and so on. However, the available evidence suggests that the correlation between per-student spending and student performance is not very robust. And more important, even if one considers the studies with credible identification strategies that find positive impacts of school inputs on educational attainment, the effects seem to be relatively modest and thus insufficient to help the developing world catch up with developed countries.

For example, thorough cross-country studies (such as Fuchs and Woessmann 2007 and Hanushek and Kimko 2000) find a weak relationship between per-student spending and test scores; a similar pattern has been found by Hanushek and Luque (2003), who evaluate the effect of class size, teacher experience, and education on test scores.[2] Furthermore, they find no evidence supporting the conventional view that school resources are relatively more important in poor countries.[3] In contrast, Barro and Lee (2001), using panel data with fixed effects, find positive and significant results of increasing school resources.[4]

The microevidence is in line with the macroevidence. Several papers have employed experiments or quasi-experiments to study the effect of input-based policy interventions on educational outcomes, and they also find modest results. One typical example of these interventions is reducing class size. For example, Angrist and Lavy (1999) employ a regression discontinuity design to exploit a rule that determines the division into classes in public schools in Israel (the Maimonides rule). These authors find that reducing class size induces a significant increase in reading and math scores for fifth-graders and a smaller increase in reading scores for fourth-graders, while no effect is found for third-graders. Krueger (1999) studies Tennessee's STAR Project, which randomized kindergarten students to small or regular-sized classes, and followed them for four years. The effects of a small class on student performance on standardized tests are positive on average, but modest. Chapter 2 in this volume provides a detailed review of school resources programs in developing countries and concludes that such programs have modest effects on student outcomes.

In summary, there does not seem to be a strong relationship between school inputs and educational outcomes. Given the large differences across countries in educational attainment, we might wonder which other interventions might help reduce these disparities.[5] More specifically, we are interested in factors that could be affected by public policies. In fact, since the late 1990s the literature has been shifting toward the study of School Management reforms. The first contributions compared performance across countries with different school systems, but recently some studies exploited quasi-experimental and experimental identification strategies. The topics analyzed include school autonomy, external/exit exams, and other accountability measures.[6] Other institutional features that have been analyzed include the level of competition from private schools and characteristics of the preprimary education.[7]

We consider that School Management might be one direction in which we could find an answer for how to improve educational outcomes, in light of the weak contribution of school resources. Finally, we would like to emphasize that an important advantage of some School Management interventions is that if they improve educational outcomes, they would likely be cost-effective as, in general, no extra resources are needed; only the existing ones should be managed in a different way. This is especially encouraging for developing countries, which typically face very tight budget constraints.

6.3. School Decentralization

Decentralization is the delegation of the management of resources to lower levels of the public administration, which leads to local provision of decentralized services. Decentralization of public services is a major institutional innovation throughout the world (Bird and Vaillancourt 1998) and there is an ongoing wave of decentralization in the developing world.[8] In particular, school decentralization has been advocated by public officers and international organizations worldwide.[9]

The main argument in support of decentralization in general, and school decentralization in particular, is that it brings decisions closer to the people, thereby alleviating information asymmetries, improving accountability, and targeting the needs of the communities. However, decentralization can also degrade service provision in poor communities that lack the ability to voice and defend their preferences, or where local authorities have weak technical capabilities to manage resources (Galiani, Gertler, and Schargrodsky 2008).

6.3.1. Theoretical Framework. In order to discuss the tradeoffs implied in decentralization, we provide a simple theoretical framework based on Galiani, Gertler, and Schargrodsky (2008). For the sake of simplicity, in the model we introduce decentralization as a binary choice. Assume there are $i=1,2,...,I$ provinces, and within each one of them there are different communities $j=1,2,...,J$. Each community ij has a representative school. In order to produce education, e_{ij}, the government makes an effort b_{ij} in each community. This effort is determined by the spending on two educational inputs, $b_{ij}^a \geq 0$ and $b_{ij}^b \geq 0$ (for instance, the government can invest in teachers and nonteacher educational inputs):

$$b_{ij} = \gamma_{ij} b_{ij}^a + (1 - \gamma_{ij}) b_{ij}^b$$

This linear functional form has extreme implications: if γ_{ij} were observable and $\gamma_{ij} > \frac{1}{2} \, (\gamma_{ij} < \frac{1}{2})$ then the government would only invest in $b_{ij}^a (b_{ij}^b)$, while if $\gamma_{ij} = \frac{1}{2}$ the government would be indifferent between any combination of b_{ij}^a and b_{ij}^b. We choose this extreme functional form to keep the algebra simple.

In a decentralized government the decisionmakers are more aware of the needs of the local communities: the decentralized governments can observe their own γ_{ij} directly. On the other hand, we assume that the central government only knows the statistical distribution of γ_{ij} across communities, but it does not know the γ_{ij} of any particular community. Each community also invests its own managerial effort, a_{ij}, in the production of education (for example through voicing local preferences and demands). The production technology for education is given by:

$$e_{ij} = \left(\left(\kappa_{ij} a_{ij} \right)^{\alpha} + (b_{ij})^{\alpha} \right)^{\frac{1}{\alpha}}$$

The parameter $0 < \alpha < 1$ captures the degree of complementarity between the efforts of the community and the government. The parameter $0 \leq \kappa_{ij} < 1$ represents the efficiency of community ij's effort. Since the authorities are closer to the people, a decentralized government can better complement and exploit the efforts of its members. We will represent this fact by assuming that $\kappa_{ij} = 0 \, \forall i \, \forall j$ when education is provided centrally and κ_{ij} can be positive if the system is decentralized.

In the centralized case, the problem of the government is very simple: since this case implies $\kappa_{ij} = 0 \, \forall i \, \forall j$, every community will always choose $a_{ij}^c = 0$ (no managerial effort at the community level). The only source of (unobserved) heterogeneity across communities is given by the parameter γ_{ij}. For the sake of simplicity, we assume that the distribution of γ_{ij} has mean ½ and is symmetric around ½. Under regularity conditions, that would imply that the government will split a given investment b_{ij} in equal parts among b_{ij}^a and b_{ij}^b. Finally, assume that the central government's opportunity cost from spending b_{ij} on education is $\left(\sum_{ij} b_{ij}^{\frac{2}{\phi}} \right)^{\phi}$. The quadratic

functional form ensures that the opportunity cost is convex. The parameter $0 < \phi \leq 1$ represents the economies of scale from providing the public good centrally, where a lower ϕ suggests stronger economies of scale.
Under a decentralized government the cost is given by $\sum b_{ij}^2$. Finally,
denote $N=I*J$ to the total number of representative schools.

The problem of the centralized government becomes: $\underset{\{b_{ij}\}}{Max}\, N \cdot b_{ij} - \left(N \cdot b_{ij}^{\phi}\right)^{\frac{2}{\phi}}$

And the solution is: $b_{ij}^c = e_{ij}^c = \dfrac{N^{1-\phi}}{2}\ \forall i\,\forall j$.

Now we can turn to the case of decentralization. The benevolent government maximizes the utility of each community, but using weights
$\theta_{ij} > 0$—where a higher value of θ_{ij} indicates that the government has
a stronger preference for educational outcomes in community ij. This
captures the fact that local preferences between spending on education
and other spending can be different in local communities than for the
central government. We assume that under centralization $\theta_{ij} = 1 \forall (i, j)$.
Under decentralization it could be the case that the local governments
may be influenced by local elites who might bias the provision of public
services against the poor, so $\theta_{ij} < 1$ in poorer communities (Bardhan and
Mookherjee 2005).

The timing of the model is as follows. The government first decides
its managerial effort b_{ij} in each community. Communities then observe
the government contribution and choose their own managerial effort a_{ij}.
Remember that the local government observes γ_{ij}. To keep the algebra
simple, we denote: $\hat{\gamma}_{ij} = max\{\gamma_{ij}, 1-\gamma_{ij}\}$. Therefore, $\hat{\gamma}_{ij} - \dfrac{1}{2}$ is a measure of how
"special" the needs of community ij are, relative to the average needs.

The equilibrium under decentralization is derived in appendix 6A—
the derivation is similar to that of the centralized case. The educational
outcome under decentralization is:

$$e_{ij}^d = \frac{\theta_{ij}\ \hat{\gamma}_{ij}^2}{2}\left(1 - \kappa_{ij}^{\frac{\alpha}{1-\alpha}}\right)^{\frac{\alpha-2}{\alpha}} = \frac{\theta_{ij}\ \hat{\gamma}_{ij}^2}{2}\ \lambda(\kappa_{ij}, \alpha)$$

where it can be shown that $\partial\lambda(\kappa_{ij}, \alpha)/\partial\kappa_{ij} > 0$ and $\partial\lambda(\kappa_{ij}, \alpha)/\partial\alpha > 0$. We can
compare how education in community ij does under decentralization rel-
ative to centralization by analyzing the tradeoffs implied through comparative statics in the following expression:

$$e_{ij}^d - e_{ij}^c = \frac{1}{2}\left[\theta_{ij}\hat{\gamma}_{ij}^2\lambda(\kappa_{ij},\alpha) - N^{1-\phi}\right],$$

where a positive number would mean that decentralization produces a better outcome. First of all, notice that all communities share the parameters (ϕ, N, α), while the parameters ($\kappa_{ij}, \theta_{ij}, \hat{\gamma}_{ij}$) are specific to each community ij, thereby generating heterogeneous effects.

A lower ϕ or a higher N represents the economies of scale from providing education centrally. Both parameters increase the relative attractiveness of the centralized system, represented by the term $N^{1-\phi}$, whose effect is homogeneous across communities.

Decentralization brings decisions closer to the people, thereby alleviating information asymmetries (e.g., Oates 1972). The benefits from decentralization are increasing in $\hat{\gamma}_{ij}$, which measures how "special" the needs of community ij are. Through this channel, we would expect both the poorest and richest communities to benefit the most from decentralization given their largest distance from the median community in the country. Thus, this channel has an ambiguous effect on educational inequality across communities.

By bringing decisions closer to the people, decentralization also improves accountability and empowers participation of the local community, which is represented by a greater κ_{ij} (since $\partial\lambda(\kappa_{ij}, \alpha)/\partial\kappa_{ij} > 0$). Furthermore, this effect will be augmented by the degree of complementarity between government and community effort, which is represented by a higher α (since $\partial\lambda(\kappa_{ij},\alpha)/\partial\alpha > 0$). The effect of κ_{ij} is highly heterogeneous across communities: it is likely that communities with higher physical and human capital will have a higher κ_{ij}, which will then magnify the effects of education. Indeed, the policymakers can explicitly target these aspects of school autonomy (e.g., Pradhan et al. 2011).

There is only one parameter left to analyze: $\theta_{ij} > 0$, which represents how local preferences for spending in education differ relative to the preferences of the central government. Remember we assumed $\theta_{ij} = 1 \forall(i, j)$ under centralization. In the case of decentralization it could be one (as in centralization), or different than one. If $\theta_{ij} > 1$, the local government gives relatively more importance to education than the central government. The interesting case is when under decentralization $\theta_{ij} < 1$, which could have two possible interpretations.

On one hand, it could be that local governments have different preferences—for example, they consider spending on health to be more important than on education. In this case, $\theta_{ij} < 1$ would decrease the production of education under decentralization, but it would still increase social welfare as local governments are choosing a mix of spending closer to local needs (Faguet and Sanchez 2006). Regarding inequality, all communities should experience an increase in welfare (and a decrease in education spending), relative to the centralized case; as a community's parameter gets further from 1, the greater are the community's gains.

On the other hand, $\theta_{ij} < 1$ may indicate that local governments are more prone to be dominated by the local elite (Bardhan and Mookherjee 2005, 2006). In particular, this effect is more likely to appear in poor areas, where the institutions are weaker. As a consequence, this effect of decentralization is likely to exacerbate inequality in educational outcomes across communities. Indeed, there is some empirical evidence about how local governments can hurt local minorities (see Alesina, Baqir, and Hoxby 2004).[10]

In summary, the theoretical model raises the possibility of an equity-efficiency tradeoff from decentralization: even if decentralization had a large positive effect on the average community, it could be very prejudicial for poor communities or for communities with bad governance. Thus, in the empirical literature review that follows we will focus both on the average effect of decentralization and on the distribution of these effects across communities.

6.3.2. Review of the Empirical Literature. There are several strands in the empirical literature on decentralization. First, there are cross-country studies that look at the regression of educational attainment on measures of school decentralization (and other control variables); they find positive correlation between student performance and decentralization (e.g., OECD 2010; Woessmann 2003).[11] Second, other papers report positive results from decentralization using a before-and-after-reforms analysis. For example, Faguet and Sanchez (2006) show that in Bolivia the priorities of local governments changed after decentralization, redirecting more investment toward education, and in Colombia decentralization of education finance improved enrollment rates in public schools. In addition to this, other studies have compared schools that changed autonomy levels with schools that did not. Jimenez and Sawada (1999, 2003) study the impact of EDUCO program (Education with Community Participation) in El Salvador, which was designed to expand education to isolated rural areas by decentralizing education through the direct involvement and participation of parents and community groups. They find that the program did not have a significant effect on math and language tests, but did have a positive effect on students' attendance and probability of continuing in school.[12]

Many authors have studied the decentralization process in Brazil. Madeira (2007) exploits longitudinal data on primary schools to evaluate the effects of the decentralization reform in Sao Paulo. He finds that decentralization increased dropout rates and failure rates across all primary school grades but improved several school resources, like the number of VCRs and TVs per hundred students, and increased enrollment.[13] The author notes that the results are partially driven by the democratization of school access. Paes de Barros and Mendoça (1998) distinguish between three processes in Brazilian's decentralization during the 1980s: direct transfer of funds to schools, election of principals, and the creation of local school councils. They find positive but modest results of decentralization and an increase in inequality, since committees in low-income areas were less prone to be involved in School Management.

However, the identification strategy of the above-mentioned papers does not allow one to rigorously assess the causal impact of decentralization on educational outcomes. This is mainly due to a potential selection bias when the decentralization/program assignment rule is not exogenous or because there are other, unobservable changes that are contemporaneous with the decentralization process, which may confound estimates of the effects of decentralization. Indeed, there seems to be evidence of the presence of differences in unobservable characteristics related to decentralization across groups: Gunnarsson et al. (2009) report that school autonomy and parental participation vary more within countries than between countries, which suggests that the decision of local communities to exercise their autonomy is probably endogenous.

To overcome these potential problems, Galiani, Gertler, and Schargrodsky (2008) rely on a quasi-experimental design to exploit exogenous variability in school decentralization. That can provide a plausibly credible identification of the causal effect of decentralization on educational attainment. They take advantage of a decentralization reform in Argentina, where two systems of secondary schools—one administered by the provinces and the other by the central government—existed side by side in the same communities for over a century. Between 1992 and 1994, the central government transferred all its secondary schools to provincial control.[14] The authors use the exogenous variation in the jurisdiction of administration of secondary schools generated by this policy intervention to identify the causal effect of school decentralization on educational outcomes. They employ a dataset containing information for the period 1994–1999 on 3,456 public schools, accounting for 99% of all public secondary schools: 2,360 were always provincial and 1,096 were transferred from the national to the provincial government between 1992 and 1994. Specifically, they compare changes in student outcomes at different lengths of exposure to decentralization to changes in outcomes of students in schools that were always under provincial control.

Galiani, Gertler, and Schargrodsky (2008) find that decentralization had an overall positive effect on student test scores: math test scores increased by 3.5% and Spanish test scores rose by 5.4%, on average after five years of decentralized administration. However, the gains were exclusively in schools located in nonpoor municipalities. In fact, in their most robust results—including province-year fixed effects—they report that decentralization did not improve average test scores in schools located in poor municipalities.

Finally, to date there is scarce experimental evidence of decentralization reforms. To the best of our knowledge, the available experimental evidence is based on programs that employed a different notion of decentralization than the one implied in the reported nonexperimental and quasi-experimental settings reviewed previously. For example, Benveniste and Marshall (2004) randomized locally managed grants for schools in Cambodia with positive average results.[15] And Lassibile et al. (2010) study workflow-enhancing interventions in Madagascar, showing positive average impacts of these interventions.[16]

In summary, most of the studies with a credible identification strategy suggest that there are positive average effects from different types of decentralization reforms (see table 6.1). However, we should note that the effects of decentralization reforms depend on many country-specific features such as the political regime, power of local governments, and commitment of the central administration to transfer funds, among others. Consequently the generalization of these results is problematic without understanding the underlying structural mechanisms at work.

As far as the distributional effects are concerned, those papers that study impacts across groups tend to find that poor communities fail to gain from decentralization reform, which in turn increases inequality. There is also evidence in the developed world that richer regions benefit relatively more from decentralization, though the poorer also experience net gains.[17]

We consider that it is of first-order importance to disentangle the channels through which decentralization reform affects communities in order to help those who do not benefit from it. Following the stylized

Table 6.1 School decentralization

Name	Methodology	Place/date	Population	Dependant variable	Independent variable/reform/ treatment	Results
Galiani, Gertler and Schargrodsky 2008	Panel of schools; Differences-in-differences (DiD)	Argentina, 1994–99	Fifth-year secondary students	Standardized Math and Spanish test scores	Central government transferred all its secondary schools to provincial control.	Decentralization had an overall positive effect on student test scores: math test scores increased 3.5%** and Spanish tests rose 5.4%** on average after five years of decentralized administration. However, decentralization had no significant impact on poor municipalities.
Madeira 2007	Panel of schools; DiD	Brazil, 1996–2003	All public primary school students in the state of São Paulo	Dropout, failure, enrollment rates and school resources	Sao Paulo State Education Reform	On average, one year of decentralization increases dropouts by 0.6s.d.**, failure rates by 1 s.d.** and increased VCRs and TVs per hundred students by 0.1 s.d.**. One year of decentralization increased enrollment by 0.2 s.d. on average. The results are partially driven by the democratization of the school access. Effects where more perverse in rural and poor areas, widening the gap between good and bad schools.
Salinas Pena and Solé-Ollé 2009	Panel of provinces; DiD	Spain, 1987–2005	16-year-old students, passing from compulsory to noncompulsory education	Survival rate as a measure of educational attainment	Spanish decentralization period. Dummy variable for decentralized provinces	Decentralization had a positive effect on enrollment in nonvocational training programs at the expenses of vocational training programs, which might reflect a better match between population preferences and educational policies. The effect on survival rate is more than 1.6%** percent on average, but it appears to be positively correlated with per capita income of the region
Paes de Barros and Mendoca 1998	Panel of states; DiD	Brazil, 1981–93	Primary school students	Repetition and dropout rates, standardized test scores	Dummies for intervention, using the different timing of the interventions across states	Decrease on repetition rate (−2.4*** points); no impact on test scores
Jimenez and Sawada 1999	Cross section of students; IV for EDUCO school	El Salvador, 1996	Third-grade students	Standardized math and language test scores and student absenteeism	EDUCO program	Decentralization improved students' language skills (0.43 s.d.†) and diminished student absences (by around 3.5*)

Table 6.1 (*continued*)

Name	Place/date	Methodology	Population	Dependant variable	Independent variable/reform/treatment	Results
Jimenez and Sawada 2003	El Salvador 1996–2003	School-level panel data; Heckman correction model	Third-grade students in rural schools	Retention and repetition rates	EDUCO program	Students in EDUCO schools are 0.36** more likely to continue in school after 2 years.
King and Özler 2005	Nicaragua, 1995–97	Matching schools that participated and did not participate in the reform; IV for de facto autonomy	Both primary and secondary school students	School enrollment rates, levels of student grade repetition and dropouts, math and language test	A governmental program transferred key management tasks from central authorities to school councils.	Autonomy *de jure* does not affect student's performance. Higher *de facto* autonomy in some administrative decisions, especially in the ability to hire and fire school personnel, is correlated with a better student achievement. A one standard deviation increase in the number of decisions made by school council at the primary level is associated with an increase of 6.73%** in math test score, or 4.05%** in for Spanish test score in secondary schools.
Faguet and Sanchez 2008	Bolivia, 1991–96, Colombia, 1993–2004	Panel of states; Before-after estimator	Primary and secondary school students. All Bolivian municipalities and 85% of Colombian municipalities	Expenditure and investment by sectors.	Dummy for the years after the reform has taken place	In Colombia: increase in student enrollment in public schools (by 0.1***) In Bolivia: change in investment patterns of local governments, making them more responsive to local needs
Benveniste and Marshall 2004	Cambodia, 1999–2003	Randomization by district	Primary school students	Dropout and pass rates, standardized test scores	Treated schools received a grant that was invested in priorities determined by local stakeholders, as well as technical advisors to help planning and implementation activities	Increase pass rates (4.2%*** and 4.3%*** after two and three years of the program), lowered dropout (1.1%*** and 1.2%*** after two and three years of the program, respectively), improved achievement (0.13* standard deviations)

*, **, and *** are significance at 10%, 5% and 1% level, respectively; † not significant at 10% level

model, there could be different explanations such as the presence of powerful local elites who may impose their own needs, or parents who may not know how to collaborate in the production of education. If we can identify the specific reasons for the failure of decentralization reform in poor communities, then we will be able to design complementary interventions to make the most out of decentralization.

6.4. Tracking

The concept of tracking refers to a way in which students of the same cohort are allocated into classes, that is, by tracking students by prior achievement and assigning the best half to one class and the weaker half to another class. Tracking is a controversial policy: on the one hand, by grouping students in more homogeneous groups teachers find it easier to target their teaching to the students, which improves educational outcomes; but on the other hand, if students benefit from better peers, tracking could impose serious disadvantages on low-achieving students by pooling them with worse students. Therefore, tracking—like decentralization—implies a tradeoff between equity and efficiency. Also, teachers can also react by changing the way they teach because of tracking, such as targeting to the best or to median students.

6.4.1. A Model of Tracking. Before stepping into the empirical literature, in the spirit of Duflo, Dupas, and Kremer (2011), we first present a stylized model to illustrate this tradeoff. Denote θ_{ij} to be the unidimensional skill level for student i in class j, which is a continuous variable with support $\left[\underline{\theta}, \bar{\theta}\right]$. The teacher can "target" a single ability level: for example, he or she can focus on teaching the least-gifted students, the median student, or the most-gifted students. Let $T_{ij} \in \left[\underline{\theta}, \bar{\theta}\right]$ denote the ability level chosen by the teacher as a target. The cost for student i in class j from being in the class is greater the more distant the student's θ_{ij} is from T_{ij}. Because the teacher wants to maximize the educational outcomes, his problem is conceptually equivalent to the Hotelling problem of horizontal differentiation with a Social Planner.

The selection of T_{ij} depends on the distribution of skills in the class. Figures 6.1a and b show two different distributions of skills within a class. In figure 6.1a the distribution of skills is unimodal, so the teacher will likely choose T_{ij} equal to the mode of the distribution. In figure 6.1b the distribution of skills is bimodal, so the choice of T_{ij} is likely to be either at one of the modes or in the middle of the two modes, depending on the convexity of the cost function of the students and on how much

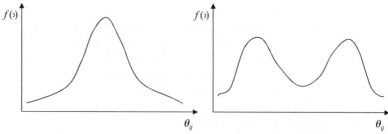

FIGURE 6.1A Unimodal distribution.   **FIGURE 6.1B** Bimodal distribution.

the teacher values equity versus efficiency. The benefits from tracking will be higher if skills are distributed like in figure 6.1b rather than in figure 6.1a.

However, tracking may lead to greater inequality if there are peer effects in the classroom. Indeed, there is empirical evidence about the importance of intraclass peer effects (see, e.g., Burke and Sass 2013; Ding and Lehrer 2007; Jackson 2010; Zimmerman 2003).

We have to take into account that peer effects can substantially change the distribution of tracking effects. Let N_j be class j's size. Students choose study effort, e_{ij}. The educational outcome, y_{ij}, is not only a function of own effort and type, but also a function of the efforts and types of the other students inside the classroom, η_{ij}. One possible functional form could be:

$$y_{ij} = \theta_{ij}e_{ij}g(\eta_{ij}) \text{ with } \eta_{ij} = \frac{1}{N_j - 1}\sum_{k \neq i}\theta_{kj}e_{kj},$$

where $g(\cdot)$ is an increasing function that takes positive values, which represents the complementarity between own effective effort (and type) and peers' effort (and type). Peer effects work through two channels. First, tracking has direct peer effects because it changes the composition of skills in the classroom, so every student faces peers with a different composition of skills. Second, tracking has indirect peer effects, because the students adapt to each other's effort.[18]

To clarify the effects of tracking, imagine that we take two identical groups of students and we do the following experiment: we take the least-skilled student from group 1 and swap it with the most-skilled student from group 2. Both groups now have more homogenous skills, so on average the teacher can better target the teaching style: that is, T_{ij} will go up (down) in group 1 (2).

We can see what will happen with students in both groups. Most students in group 1 will be closer to the teacher's target, and therefore they will increase their effort, e_{ij}. They will also benefit directly from having better peers, and from the reinforced effort through the peer effects, $g(\eta_{ij})$. Thus, the welfare of most students in this group is expected to rise. Nevertheless, the least-skilled students in group 1 might actually become slightly further away from the teaching target. Even in this case, they will benefit in net terms because they gain from having better peers and from their peers' higher effort (through the reinforced learning, $g(\eta_{ij})$). In group 2 everyone will face a negative direct effect because of having less-skilled peers, through $g(\eta_{ij})$. Since the group is more homogeneous, most students get closer to the teacher's target, which is beneficial (although the most skilled students in the group can become further away from the target). Thus, the net effect on the welfare of the members of group 2 will depend upon the importance of the magnitude of the peer effects, $g(\cdot)$, relative to the potential gains from better teacher targeting.

The tracking intervention consists of repeating the above intervention until we reach two nonoverlapping groups of students. If there are no peer effects, then the net effect from tracking will be positive for everyone except for the students who were originally near the median skill (who became actually further away from the teaching target). The effect on inequality would be ambiguous, depending on whether the top individuals in the higher class benefit more than the bottom individuals in the lower class.

But if peer effects are significant, then anything can happen. If peer effects mean mainly that students' efforts are very complementary, then every student may benefit in net terms, as the students that benefited from better targeting will exert a higher effort and thus benefit the students who face negative direct effects (i.e., those with worse targeting and/or worse peers). However, if the direct benefits from better targeting are small relative to the direct negative effect of having worse peers, then most students in the lower class will be worse off with tracking while most students in the higher class will be better off with tracking. As a consequence, sizeable peer effects can induce an efficiency-equity tradeoff.

6.4.2. Review of the Empirical Literature. Table 6.2 summarizes the main findings of the studies that have analyzed tracking interventions. The most elementary empirical strategy to assess the effects from tracking consists of comparing students in tracking and nontracking schools. The earlier empirical estimations seemed to suggest that although tracking was beneficial for the high-skilled students, it ended up hurting the low-skilled students, thus augmenting inequality (see, e.g., Argys, Rees, and

Table 6.2 Tracking

Name	Methodology	Place/date	Population	Dependant variable	Independent variable/ reform/treatment	Results
Duflo, Dupas, and Kremer 2011	Randomized Trial	Kenya, 2005–7	Grade 1 students	Standardized math and language test scores	121 primary schools received funds to hire an extra contract teacher and split the class into two sections. In 60 randomly selected schools, students were randomly assign to each class, while in the other 61 they were ranked by prior achievement.	Tracking had positive effects on all students. Students in tracking schools have on average 0.14* s.d. higher test scores than those in nontracking schools (0.16** one year after the experiment finished).
Betts and Shkolnik 2000	Panel of students; using test scores before some schools began to track	USA, 1987–92	Students at grades 7–12	Standardized math tests	Dummy for tracking schools.	High ability students benefited from tracking while low ability students did not benefit.
Hanushek and Woessmann (2006)	Panel of countries; difference in difference	18–26 countries, 1995–2003	Fourth- to eighth-grade students	Standardized international tests in reading, mathematics and science	Dummy if the student attends to a school in a system that tracks in that grade.	Early tracking increases educational inequality: it can account for one quarter of the difference in inequality between the most equitable and the most inequitable country. There is also some evidence that early tracking reduces mean performance.
Burke and Sass 2008	Panel of students; student and teacher fixed effects	Florida, USA, 1999–2004	Students at grades 3–10	Standardized reading and math test scores	Average fixed effects of classroom peers.	Teacher and peer quality is correlated, resulting in possible bias on previous studies that omitted teacher variables. Low achieving students experience a 0.82 point boost to their math score from 1 point increase in the mean peer's score, whereas high ability students will receive 0.1** point increase under de same treatment. Strong positive effect for the lower achieving students from having peers from the higher quartile of the distribution, but the opposite happens for high achieving students with poor quality peers.

Study	Methodology	Country, year	Sample	Outcome variable	Instrument / variables	Results
Figlio and Page 2002	Panel of students in Tracking and Nontracking schools; Difference in Difference, IV for tracking status	USA, 1987–94	Eighth- to tenth-grade students	Change from eighth to tenth grade in student's IRT math score	Instrument tracking status of the school and track of the student (reported by the principal of the school) with the number of courses required for state graduation, the number of schools in the county, and the fraction of voters in the county who voted for President Reagan.	No evidence that tracking hurts low-ability children.
Hoffer 1992	Cross section of schools; propensity score matching	USA, 1987–89	Seventh graders and tenth graders	Math and science standardized test scores	Dummy variables indicating if a student is placed in an heterogeneous group, or in a high-, middle-, or low-ability group.	There is evidence of a positive effect of tracking for high ability students (0.08** and 0.24 standard deviations in science and mathematics, respectively) and a negative effect for low ability students (around 0.3** and 0.34** standard deviations), summing up to a negative average effect.
Argys, Rees, and Brewer 1996	Cross section of students, OLS with a selectivity correction term	USA, 1988	10th-grade students in public schools	Standardized math test scores	Dummy variables indicating if a student is placed in an heterogeneous group, or in a high-, middle-, or low-ability group.	Differential effect of tracking, helping students in high ability tracks and students in average ability tracks (5%** and 2%** gain in math test score, respectively) on the expenses of students in low ability tracks (5%** loss). They find a small positive net effect, suggesting an overall efficiency gain.

*, ** and *** are significance at 10%, 5% and 1% level, respectively; † = not significant at 10% level

Brewer 1996; Hoffer 1992; Kerckhoff 1986). In particular, the PISA 2009 Assessment Framework (OECD 2010) was very critical of tracking programs because of the possibility that they increase the differences across students while not improving overall performance.[19] Exploiting a more elaborated strategy, Hanushek and Woessmann (2006) also look at country-level differences, but using students of different cohorts to get a difference-in-difference estimate. They still find that early tracking substantially increases educational inequality and they also argue that early tracking reduces mean performance.

Betts and Shkolnik (2000) provide a good summary of the nonexperimental literature, and argue that the existing consensus against tracking was largely based on invalid comparisons. Intuitively, most of the papers they review compare the top students or the bottom students in tracking schools to the average students in nontracking schools.[20] Indeed, Betts and Shkolnik show that when students of similar ability levels in tracking and nontracking high schools are compared, the findings are strikingly different: high-ability students benefit from tracking, low-ability students neither benefit nor get hurt, although there is some evidence that middle scoring students may be hurt (see also Figlio and Page 2002).[21]

However, the decisions to work/enroll in tracking/nontracking schools by teachers and parents/students might be endogenous. Ideally we would like to have experimental or quasi-experimental evidence on tracking programs to avoid this potential problem. Fortunately, there is one paper with experimental evidence that provides a credible identification strategy for the effect of tracking on students' performance.

Duflo, Dupas, and Kremer (2011) performed a randomized controlled trial to study the effects of tracking in Kenya. In 121 schools that used to have a single first-grade class, that grade was split into two sections. In 60 schools, randomly selected out of the 121, students were assigned to sections based on prior achievement as measured by first term grades, assigning the top and bottom halves to different sections. In the remaining 61 schools, students were randomly assigned to one of the two sections. The findings are very encouraging for supporters of tracking: students in tracking schools scored on average 0.14 standard deviations higher than students in non-tracking schools at the end of the program (18 months later); students at all levels of the distribution benefited from tracking, and this effect persisted one year after the program ended.

Regarding the direct and indirect peer effects discussed above, the authors find that while the direct effect of high-achieving peers is positive, tracking benefited lower-achieving pupils indirectly by allowing teachers to teach at their level. Together, these results show that peers affect students both directly and indirectly by influencing teacher behavior, in particular by influencing the teacher's effort and choice of target teaching level (closer to the median student).[22] Therefore, these findings suggest that there is a substantial chance that tracking could be a beneficial policy.

Tracking is particularly attractive because the intervention is standardized; the only need for its implementation is to change the rule by which students are grouped into classes. In contrast, the details of school decentralization usually depend on many characteristics of the country (the size of the country, the power of local elites, and so on).

Nevertheless, there are some concerns regarding the external validity of this experiment that should be taken into account. For instance, as Duflo, Dupas, and Kremer (2011) point out, the behavior of teachers is crucial for the results: if the policy is generalized, teachers may sort to the higher- or lower-level sections of the classes (see also Pop-Eleches and Urquiola 2011). They also emphasize that in the experiment many key factors that could affect the results were left unchanged, such as the resources for the classes and the class size. It could be the case, however, that in a scaling-up process the resources would not be split evenly between classes. For example, resources may be allocated to help the worse-achievers to catch up.

Furthermore, it might be that the degree of peer effects may change if the experiment is performed in higher grades (instead of first and second), because the effects may be stronger in older children (e.g., they compete for status, they collaborate in homework). Also, there are some cultural and socioeconomic factors that may change the results in other countries, because they may affect the initial distribution of students. For instance, in very poor communities there are many students with special needs (e.g., suffering from domestic violence, malnutrition), so the problem of the teacher may look more like figure 6.1b, with the low mode of students being those with special needs. On the contrary, in not-so-poor communities the students' needs may be substantially more homogenous, thereby reducing the potential targeting-benefits from tracking. Duflo, Dupas, and Kremer (2011) make a similar point, arguing that their results are more likely to be found in Sub-Saharan Africa and South Asian countries, rather than in the United States. Hopefully, further experimental evidence will contribute to our understanding of the key assumptions to ensure the external validity of these findings.

6.5. Teacher Incentives

The role of compensation policy in influencing worker performance has been extensively analyzed in the theoretical and empirical literature. In this section we analyze different compensation and incentive-based policies. Of particular interest in the recent empirical literature are the effects that compensation policies have on worker productivity, often referred to as "incentive effects." More specifically, we are interested in whether paying teachers on the basis of their students' performance induces them to improve the overall quality of teaching and hence increases student learning.

Mostly, teachers are paid according to observable characteristics, like educational background, experience or tenure. However, those measures are usually poor predictors of better student outcomes (see, among others, Rivkin, Hanushek, and Kain 2005). The idea behind paying teachers on the basis of direct measures of their students' performance is that this provides them an incentive to improve the quality of their teaching and thereby increase their students' learning.

6.5.1. Theoretical Framework. In this section we discuss interventions that introduce pay-for-performance incentives. We adapt the model in Franceschelli, Galiani, and Gulmez (2008) on compensation in firms to a school setting in order to formalize two probable consequences from the introduction of pay-for-performance interventions: (a) it might increase the effort (outcomes) of both high- and low-productivity teachers; (b) it might also increase the turnover among low-productivity teachers.

Teachers' utility depends positively on income, T, and negatively on effort, X: $u(T,X)$, with $u'_T(\ ) > 0$ and $u'_X(\ ) < 0$. A teacher's output is given by the performance of the students, q, which depends on the teacher's level of ability, A, and his or her effort, X: $q = f(X,A)$ with $\partial f(\ )/\partial X > 0$ and $\partial f(\ )/\partial A > 0$. If a teacher is fired, he or she will receive a compensation equal to Z, and if the teacher is not fired, he or she will receive a wage $W = Y + b(q) > Z$ (note that the wage may depend upon the teacher's performance).

The probability of a teacher being fired is given by: 1 if $q < q_0$; $\delta(q) = \dfrac{q_1 - q}{q_1 - q_0}$ if $q_0 \leq q < q_1$ and 0 if $q_1 \leq q$. That is, the teacher will be fired with probability 1 if her students do not achieve an average score of at least q_0; if q is between q_0 and q_1 then the probability that a teacher will be fired is linearly decreasing on the level of performance of her students; and if the average performance of the students surpasses the threshold

q_1 then the probability of being fired is zero. Recall that the teacher's wage, if she is not fired, is given by $W = Y + b(q)$. There are two possible wage schedules. Under the flat-wage scheme, $b(q) = 0$ for every q (i.e., an hourly wage). Under the pay-per-performance scheme $b(q) = 0$ if $q \leq q_1$ and $b(q) = b^*(q - q_1)$ if $q > q_1$. In sum, the employer (schools) sets three key parameters: $\Omega = \{q_0, q_1, b\}$.

We define $q^*(A)$ as the Nash equilibrium solution to this problem. It can be shown that, under the hourly wage system, $q^*(A)$ is an increasing function of A under the basic-wage scheme (proposition 1 in Franceschelli, Galiani, and Gulmez 2008). Intuitively, higher-ability teachers will display a better performance because by doing so they can reduce their chances of being fired. However, note that if the probability of being fired is negligible or even null as a function of the students' performance—as it is often the case for school teachers in developing countries—then teachers will exert very low, if any effort.

It can also be shown that under the pay-for-performance scheme there will be a cutoff level A^* such that if $A > A^*$, then the teacher will decide to produce in the piece-rate segment and if $A < A^*$, the teacher will decide to produce in the basic wage segment when offered the option (proposition 2 in Franceschelli, Galiani, and Gulmez 2008). We will refer to "low-ability" teachers as those with $A < A^*$ and to "high-ability" teachers as those with $A > A^*$.

Proposition 3 in Franceschelli, Galiani, and Gulmez (2008) analyzes the dynamics when the system changes from a flat-wage regime to a pay-for-performance scheme. They show that both low- and high-ability teachers will raise their output levels, but for different reasons: low-ability teachers will raise their output because of the stricter endogenous dismissal policy and high-ability teachers will increase their output in response to the introduction of the piece-rate component in the wage scheme. Thus, the channel of the incentive effect is different for those workers seeking the basic wage and those workers seeking the piece-rate component of the wage. Finally, Franceschelli, Galiani, and Gulmez show that—at least under certain parametric assumptions—a rise in the turnover rate for low-ability teachers is expected after the implementation of the piece-rate with a basic wage.

Franceschelli, Galiani, and Gulmez (2010) test the predictions of this model in a quasi-experimental setting when a textile firm decided to shift one of its plants to a piece-rate plus basic wage scheme while the other plant continued to be paid on an hourly basis. Using longitudinal data on worker productivity in the two plants before and after the first plant changed its payment scheme, they find that the implementation of the pay-per-performance system had a strong positive effect on productivity (28%, on average) and that many workers continued to receive the basic wage after the changeover to the new incentive scheme. The effect of treatment was a 29% increase in the average productivity of workers aiming at the basic wage and a 26% increase for workers seeking the piece-rate component of the wage. Thus, the evidence presented in the paper suggests that the change in the incentive scheme made, endogenously, the dismissal policy of the firm stricter, inducing even low-ability workers to increase their productivity.

6.5.2. Review of the Empirical Literature. The main obstacle in assessing incentive effects empirically is the endogeneity of contractual arrangements. Some recent papers, however, analyze the effect of different compensation schemes for teachers using experiments to induce exogenous changes in the compensation schemes (see table 6.3 for a summary). Nevertheless, they find mixed results.

Muralidharan and Sundararaman (2011) provide evidence from a large-scale randomized evaluation of a teacher performance-pay program implemented in 300 public schools in the Indian state of Andhra Pradesh. They study the effect of a teacher performance pay (a bonus calibrated to be around 3% of a typical teacher's annual salary).[23] They randomly selected 100 schools to implement performance pay at the teacher level, randomly selected another 100 schools to implement it at the school level, with the remaining 100 randomly chosen schools serving as the control group. They find that the teacher performance-pay program was effective in improving student learning: at the end of two years of the program, students in the 200 schools with incentive systems performed significantly better than those in comparison schools by 0.27 and 0.17 standard deviations (SD) in the mathematics and language tests, respectively.[24] They found a minimum average treatment effect of 0.1 SD at every percentile of the distribution of baseline test scores, suggesting broad-based gains in test scores as a result of paying teachers based on their students' performance.

The authors find no evidence of any adverse consequences as a result of the incentive programs. Students in incentive schools did significantly better not only in mathematics and language (for which there were incentives) but also in science and social studies (for which there were no incentives), suggesting positive spillover effects. The suggested channel through which the impact of the incentive scheme operates is not an increase of teacher attendance but greater teaching effort conditional on being present: teacher interviews indicate that teachers in incentive

Table 6.3 Teacher incentives

Name	Methodology	Place/date	Population	Dependant variable	Independent variable/reform/treatment	Results
Muralidharan and Sundararaman 2011	Randomized trial	India, 2005–7	Primary school teachers	Standardized math and language test scores	The program provided bonus payments to teachers based either on the average improvement in test scores of all school students (group incentives) or on the average improvement of their own students.	Students in treated schools perform 0.27*** and 0.17*** standard deviations better in math and language test, respectively. The average bonus was 3% of annual pay. Incentive schools also perform significantly better than other schools that received additional schooling inputs of a similar value.
Glewwe, Illias and Kremer 2010	Randomized trial	Kenya, 1998–99	Primary school teachers	Teacher attendance, homework assignment, pedagogy, test preparation sessions and student test scores on district exams	The program offered schools the opportunity to provide gifts to teachers if students performed well. It provided prizes to teachers in grades 4 to 8 based on the performance of the school as a whole on the district exams in each year. Prizes ranged from 21% to 43% of typical teacher monthly salaries.	Students in schools with a teacher incentive program were significantly more likely to take exams and had higher test scores in the short run. Teachers in program schools had no higher attendance rates or homework assignment rates. Pedagogy and student dropout rates were similar across schools. Teachers in program schools increased test preparation activities and encouraged students enrolled in school to take the test.
Duflo, Hanna, and Ryan 2010	Randomized trial and structural model	India, 2003–4	Rural school students	Teacher absenteeism, and students test scores	In 60 randomly chose schools out of 120, the teacher received a camera with a tramper-proof date and time function. Teachers were instructed to make one of the students take a photograph of the teacher and other students at the start and end of each school day. Each teacher was then paid according to the days worked.	Teachers' absenteeism fell by 21*** percentage points, and student's test scores increased by 0.17*** standard deviations.

Table 6.3 *(continued)*

Name	Methodology	Place/date	Population	Dependant variable	Independent variable/reform/treatment	Results
Contract teachers						
Duflo, Dupas, and Kremer 2007	Randomized trial	Kenya, 2005–7	First grade students	Student test scores, teacher absenteeism and time spent actively teaching, student attendance	70 schools out of 140 were randomly selected to receive a treatment, consisting on hiring an extra contract teacher to split the class in two, and randomly divide the students to each class.	Students randomly assigned to contract teachers score 0.23** s.d. higher and an 11% increase in grade promotion than their schoolmates assigned to civil service teachers. Contract teachers 30 p.p. more likely to be found in class teaching than civil servant teachers. This effect persists in the long run in schools where local communities where trained on how to monitor contract teachers. These schools tend to keep contract teachers after the program has ended.
Banerjee et al. 2008	Randomized trial	India, 2005–6	Primary school children	Reading and math test	NGOs trained volunteers to teach children to read and organized remedial reading camps (outside the school).	Treatment had positive impact on learning: the average child who could not read anything and attended the camp was 60%** points more likely to decipher letters after a year than a comparable child in a control village.
Banerjee et al. 2007	Randomized trial	India, 2001–3	Disadvantaged students at grades 3 and 4	Student test scores, teacher absenteeism	The program hired young women to teach students lagging behind in treated schools.	The effect was positive for all children and higher for those at the bottom third of the distribution than at for those at the top third (0.47*** s.d. versus 0.23*** s.d.).
Muralidharan and Sundararaman 2010	Randomized trial	India, 2005–7	Students at grades 1–5	Standardized math and language test scores, absenteeism rates	100 randomly chosen government-run rural schools were provided with contract teachers.	Students in schools with an extra contract teacher perform better by 0.15*** in math's and 0.9*** in language standard deviations. Contract teachers were also 9% *** less likely to be absent than civil servant teachers.
Burde and Linden 2012	Randomized trial	Afghanistan, 2007–8	Primary school students	Enrollment rate. Standardized math and language test scores	In randomly selected villages, the program provides educational material and training for locally recruited educated individuals to serve as teachers in village-based schools.	Village-based schools improved children performance. School enrollment increased by 42 %*** and test scores by 1.2*** s.d. The effect on enrollment was stronger for girls than for boys, thus alleviating the gender gap in enrollment.

Study	Method	Location	Population	Outcome	Variable	Results
Bourdon, Frolich, and Michaelowa 2006	Cross section of students; Propensity score matching	Niger, 2000–2001	Students in the second and fifth grade	Standardized math and French test scores	Dummy for contract teachers.	Contract teachers have enabled Niger to enhance enrollment, although there is some evidence of deteriorated education for contract teacher students in the 2nd grade (−5.43* points in math French test scores), the difference is small and not significant at a 10% level for fifth-grade students
Bourdon, Frolich, and Michaelowa 2010	Cross section of students; nonparametric matching estimator	Mali, 2001/2002; Niger and Togo, 2000/2001	Second- and fifth-grade students	Standardized math and French test scores	Dummy for contract teachers.	Contract teachers programs appear to have better impact for low-achieving students than high-achieving students: in Mali, students in the bottom of the ability distribution assign to contract teachers perform 14** to 33*** p.p. higher than those assigned to civil servant teachers, while there is no significant difference for high-ability students. In Niger high-ability students with contract teachers score between 19 and 25 (** to ***) p.p. lower while coefficients are not significant for low ability students. Overall, they had a positive impact when applied in a more decentralized way (in Mali) and a negative impact in centralized cases (in Niger), probably because of better monitoring from local communities.
Chaudhury, Hammer, Kremer, Muralidharan and Rogers 2006	Cross section of teachers; Matching estimates	Peru, 2002	Primary school teachers	Absence rates, measured with unannounced visits	Dummy for contract teachers.	Contract teachers 12–13%*** more likely to be absent
Goyal and Pandey 2009	Cross section of students; Propensity score matching	Madhya Pradesh, India, 2006	Teachers in grades 1 to 5	Test scores, teacher attendance and activity	Dummy for contract teachers.	Contract teachers absent 27% of the time and found teaching 37% of the time, while regular teachers absent 37% of the time and found teaching 25% of the time. These results worsen for contract teachers in second contract year but where still better than regular teachers. Difference in absenteeism and activity significant at 5% and 1% level, respectively

*, ** and *** are significance at 10%, 5% and 1% level, respectively; † = not significant at 10% level

schools were more likely to have exerted extra effort such as assigning additional homework and class work, providing practice tests, and conducting extra classes after school.

The authors of this study also compare this intervention to other interventions of similar costs that consisted of additional schooling inputs. The resource-based interventions were also effective in raising test scores, but the teacher incentive program was three times as cost effective in raising test scores.

Regarding the effect of this intervention on the distribution of test scores, the authors find that the quantile treatment effects of the treatment are positive at every percentile and increasing. However, the program also increased the variance of test scores. The authors claim that this may reflect variance in teacher responsiveness to the incentive program, as opposed to variance in student responsiveness to the treatment by initial learning levels. Last, the authors cannot study the effects on turnover because the experiment was designed so that turnover is almost ruled out (there was an agreement with the government to minimize transfers into and out of the sample schools for the duration of the study).

Another source of experimental evidence for a developing country is Glewwe, Ilias, and Kremer (2010). The authors report results from a randomized evaluation that provided primary school teachers (grades 4–8) in rural Kenya with group incentives based on test scores. They found that while test scores went up in program schools in the short run, the students did not retain the gains after the incentive program ended. Furthermore, teacher attendance did not improve, homework assignments did not increase, and pedagogy did not change, although teachers did increase their effort to raise short-run test scores by conducting more test preparation sessions. The authors of this study interpret these results as being consistent with teachers expending effort toward short-term increases in test scores but not toward long-term learning.[25]

Finally, Duflo, Hanna, and Ryan (2012) provide a valuable step in the direction of understanding incentives for teachers by combining experimental variation with the structural estimation of a model. They worked with single-teacher nonformal education centers in the rural villages of Rajasthan, India, where an NGO gave teachers in 57 randomly selected program schools a camera with a tamper-proof date and time function, to check attendance of teachers. Each teacher was then paid according to a nonlinear function of the number of valid school days for which he or she was actually present. The other 56 schools were randomly allocated to the control group. The reduced-form results of the program were positive: absenteeism by teachers fell by 21 percentage points relative to the control group. Teacher attendance increased for both low- and high-quality teachers (those scoring below and above the median test scores on the teacher skills exam conducted prior to the program).[26] Children in the program schools had more teaching days and, conditional on the school being open, teachers were found teaching during random visits (thus, the authors did not find evidence of multitasking or loss of intrinsic motivation due to the program). As a consequence of more instruction days with no apparent reduction of teacher effort, children's test scores increased by 0.17 standard deviations in treatment schools.[27] Children who could write at the time of the pretest gained the most from the program (they had mid-line test scores 0.25 standard deviations higher in treatment schools than in comparison schools), suggesting that those more advanced before the program were better equipped to benefit from it.

The authors complement these results with the estimation of a structural dynamic model of teacher labor supply to understand which component of the program affected the behavior of the teachers (monitoring or financial incentives) and assess the effect of other payment structures. They find that teachers are responsive to the financial incentives: the elasticity of labor supply with respect to the level of the financial bonus is between 0.20 and 0.30 and, when the bonus is set to zero, the model closely predicts the difference in attendance between teachers in the treatment and control schools.

6.5.3. Contract Teachers. In recent decades there has been a sharp increase in student enrollment in developing countries. One way to bring them into the education system without prohibitively expensive increases in the teacher salary budget is to arrange for local hiring of teachers on short-term contracts. We refer to the teachers under these contracts as "Contract Teachers" (De Laat and Vegas 2005). In most of these large-scale teacher recruitment programs the teachers are not employed in civil servant positions, they receive considerably lower salaries, have less tenure, and usually significantly less professional training.[28]

This policy is highly controversial. In spite of this, some economists and policymakers believe that increasing the use of contract teachers may have been one of the most efficient innovations in providing primary education in developing countries. The benefit most cited in the literature is that contract teachers face superior incentives compared to tenured civil-service teachers: they must work hard to build a reputation and eventually receive another appointment or even a civil servant position. Civil-service teacher positions are highly demanded in some countries because hiring and supervision are centrally conducted and salaries are much higher than the salaries necessary to clear the market. Because contract teachers are locally hired, it is possible that this may reduce their absenteeism through closer monitoring and better target the needs of their students—advantages associated with decentralization reform.

At the same time, many arguments have been raised against contract-teacher programs. Contracted teachers usually have less teaching experience and, due to their short-term contracts, they cannot get involved in following the progress of their students. Some authors also worry that the extrinsic incentives may crowd out the teacher's intrinsic motivation to exert teaching effort (Benabou and Tirole 2006). In a related note, providing incentives for some outcomes may end up perversely distorting the allocation of effort (Holmstrom and Milgrom 1991), as illustrated by Glewwe, Ilias, and Kremer (2010). Also, one may worry that contract teachers may de-professionalize teaching and thus impoverish the status of teaching as a profession (e.g., Bennell 2004).

Table 6.3 summarizes the main findings of the studies analyzing this intervention. Some papers exploit nonexperimental data to study the relative performance of contract teachers. For example, De Laat and Vegas (2005) compare the performance of contract teachers' students with other students in Togo; Bourdon, Frölich, and Michaelowa (2006) study contract teachers in Niger; and Bourdon, Frölich, and Michaelowa (2007) examine contract teachers in Niger, Mali, and Togo. The findings are mixed. On one hand, the findings of De Laat and Vegas (2005) suggest that students of regular teachers clearly outperform those of contract teachers, and Bourdon, Frölich, and Michaelowa (2006) argue that contract teachers may deteriorate education quality. On the other hand, Bourdon, Frölich, and Michaelowa (2007) suggest that contract teachers may have a positive impact, although they do find negative impacts when it is implemented in a more centralized manner. In addition to these studies, Goyal and Pandey (2009) report that contract teachers consistently demonstrated higher effort than regular teachers. In addition, in the Indian states they studied contract teachers were actually more educated than regular teachers. Finally, Kremer et al. (2005) report that contract teachers appear to have a rate of absenteeism similar to that of regular teachers. Likewise, Chaudhury et al. (2006) report that contract teachers in five countries are no less likely to be absent than other teachers (but not in a sixth country).

From the perspective of identification, comparing students with contract teachers to those with regular teachers can be misleading if, for example, the areas with the poorest educational outcomes may be more likely to hire contract teachers, generating a spurious negative correlation between contract teachers and student performance. Fortunately, there is an emerging literature exploiting experimental variation in the use of contract teachers. Contrary to the mixed results of the nonexperimental studies, the experimental results suggest that contract teachers tend to have positive results.

The first experimental evidence comes from the Kenyan Extra Teacher Program (Duflo, Dupas, and Kremer 2007).[29] The 210 schools in the program were randomly assigned to two groups: 140 treatment (or "ETP") schools and 70 comparison schools. In 70 of the 140 treatment schools, first-grade pupils were randomly assigned to either a newly hired contract teacher or a regular civil service teacher. Those contract teachers had the same academic qualifications as regular teachers but were paid less than one-fourth as much as the regular teachers. In treated schools, they were roughly 16 percentage points more likely to be in class and teaching than civil service teachers in comparison schools. Students assigned to contracted teachers scored 0.23 standard deviations higher and attended school 2% more often than students who had been randomly assigned to civil service teachers in program schools. Moreover, students of contract teachers were 5.5 percentage points more likely to have reached third grade in 2007 than students in treatment schools taught by civil service teachers.

Similar results are reported by Muralidharan and Sundararaman (2010), who analyze a contract teacher program conducted in India, where 100 randomly chosen government-run rural primary schools in Andhra Pradesh were provided with an extra contract teacher. After two years, students in schools with an extra contract teacher performed significantly better on academic tests than those in comparison schools, by 0.15 and 0.13 standard deviations on mathematics and language tests, respectively. While all students benefited from the program, the extra contract teacher was particularly beneficial for students in their first year of school and students in remote schools. However, these results might also be driven by the reduction in class size that resulted from adding a teacher. The authors also find, using four different nonexperimental estimation procedures, that contract teachers are no less effective in improving student learning than regular teachers who are more qualified, better trained, and paid a salary five times higher. Furthermore, contract teachers were significantly less likely to be absent from school than civil service teachers (16% vs. 27%). Finally, Banerjee and Duflo (2011) review other programs that provide indirect experimental evidence about the benefits of locally hired teachers (or volunteers) to help the more disadvantaged students.[30] For example, in a remedial education program reviewed, which hired young women to teach students lagging behind in India, they find that the intervention increased average test scores for all children in treatment schools by 0.28 standard deviations, mostly due to large gains experienced by children at the bottom of the test-score distribution.

A key goal for future research would be to disentangle the channel through which this better performance of contract teachers works. Some argue that the increase in performance is related to the fact that contract teachers perceive their temporary positions as a probation period to obtain a civil service position. For example, in the area of Kenya where the experiment by Duflo, Dupas, and Kremer (2007) was performed, 32% of the contract teachers in the program eventually obtained a civil service position. Also, in West African countries teachers' unions have made the extension of job stability to contract teachers a political goal (Bruns, Filmer, and Patrinos 2011). If it is inevitable that contract teachers will become civil servants, then we need to study whether their behavior, once they are upgraded, differs from the behavior of the teachers who started their careers as civil servants. If they do not differ, then a contract-teacher system can be viewed as a successful probation mechanism (see Gordon, Kane, and Staiger 2006), but one with effects that do not persist after teachers become civil servants.

Many of the papers advocating for contract teachers claim that the benefits arise mostly from the provision of better incentives. If this is the case, it is necessary to find the best way to provide incentives to teachers so that they engender long-lasting improvements in student learning. It is possible that this could be achieved through contract teachers or by other pay-for-performance schemes. This should be further investigated. Those benefits from better incentives could then be extended to civil service teachers, for example, by teacher union agreements to reform the tenure of the teachers to depend on performance.

As mentioned above, another aspect of education management that is involved in contract-teacher interventions is decentralization. While civil servant teachers are hired centrally—and they are supervised, promoted, and transferred in the same way—it is a local committee that is in charge of the contract teachers' appointments. It may be that contract teachers outperform tenured ones because of a better selection by the local committees, or because they are more aware of the needs of students living in their communities they can better target the needs of these children. If this is the case, decentralization of hiring and/or supervision could be enough to improve the performance of civil service teachers. In fact, Duflo, Dupas, and Kremer (2007) show that in the schools that had empowered committees to monitor teachers, civil service teachers were more likely to be in class and teaching during random visits, and their students performed better than in schools with unmonitored civil service teachers.

From the point of view of both researchers and policymakers, the biggest identification challenge that contract-teacher programs face for future research is to understand why contract teachers perform better. It is important to notice that if these programs are to be scaled up we should also consider whether there would be equilibrium effects in terms of the subsequent distribution of teacher skills.

Most obvious of all, improved evidence about these topics is crucial to assess the external validity of contract-teacher interventions. For example, the cost-effectiveness of a contract-teacher policy is likely to depend on country characteristics and the level of education involved. The experimental studies mentioned above involve contract teachers only at the primary level, where the supply of potential teachers with minimum capacity is not as likely to be constrained as at the secondary level (Bruns, Filmer, and Patrinos 2011). Also, cost-benefit evaluations will not only allow us to see whether contract teachers are preferable to regular teachers, but also to compare contract teachers to other related interventions (see chapter 8 in this volume about cost-effectiveness of educational programs).

6.6. Complementary Interventions

When we evaluate public policies—or social programs of any kind—we usually consider the effects of the program on the welfare of the affected population; this is the welfare criteria (Kaplow and Shavell 2002). An intervention that improves the welfare of at least one individual without making anyone worse off is considered desirable; this is the Pareto criteria. However, most policies cannot be ordered according to the Pareto criteria. In democratic states, the preferences of the society as a whole should be taken into account to adopt reforms. This suggests that it is convenient to have a "social welfare function" through which the different alternative policies could be compared. In spite of this, a traditional result in welfare economics shows the impossibility of aggregating preferences of diverse agents in an acceptable way (Arrow 1951).

Leaving this difficulty aside, we may act as if there exists a "correct" way to represent the preferences of the society. In the literature, different welfare functions have been postulated, implying diverse tradeoffs between the efficiency and equity objectives. Obviously, these issues are subjective, and thus controversial. Nevertheless, policymakers must make policy choices continuously due to budget constraints or to cases where the alternatives are mutually exclusive. As far as the choice of policies is concerned, if we do not consider distributional issues in principle, cost-effectiveness analysis is the best criterion available. In spite of this, distributional conflicts are always present when deciding public policy interventions.

These considerations about welfare functions and the efficiency/equity tradeoffs could be important in deciding whether a reform should be adopted. In the previous sections we reviewed different School Management interventions. Indeed, not only did we study the average effect of interventions, but also—when evidence was available—we analyzed their potential distributional effects. In the case of contract teachers there is little evidence about how heterogeneous the effects are, although some papers do report such interventions to be especially beneficial for the lowest-achieving students.[31] Instead, in the case of teacher incentives, the evidence seems to go in the opposite direction, suggesting that the most able students tend to gain more from it. Even though decentralization seems to have average positive effects, the poor do not always benefit from this type of reform, and could even be harmed. Regarding tracking, the results are more heterogeneous: most nonexperimental empirical studies report that tracking hurts the least-performing students, while the sole experimental study finds benefits for students at all skill levels.

When policies that are on average beneficial engender distributional effects, the efficiency equity tradeoff that we mentioned above is usually crucial.[32] Let's consider the following highly stylized model. Assume that there are only two groups, rich and poor, in equal proportions, denoted by subscripts r and p, respectively. There is one function mapping the common educational policy $E \in \left[\underline{E}, \bar{E} \right]$ to the incomes of the rich, $Y_r(E)$, and the incomes of the poor, $Y_p(E)$. The typical efficiency-equity tradeoff can be represented by a situation such as an increase in E produces a growth in average income, $\frac{1}{2}Y_r(E) + \frac{1}{2}Y_p(E)$, but at the same time diminishes $Y_p(E)$. Suppose there is a redistributive mechanism that can be used to transfer an amount T from rich to poor individuals. Of the income taken from the rich an amount $C(T)$ is lost, where the (increasing and convex) function $C(\cdot)$ represents the typical problems associated with distortive redistribution that are widely studied in public economics (e.g., moral hazard, distortion of relative prices). Let $U(\cdot)$ be the usual indirect utility function, strictly increasing and concave. The problem for the utilitarian government is:

$$\max_{\{T, E \in [\underline{E}, \bar{E}]\}} U(Y_r(E) - T) + U(Y_p(E) + T - C(T)) \ s.t. \ 0 \leq T \leq Y_r(E)$$

After combining the FOCs for an interior solution, we get:

$$\frac{Y_p'(E^*)}{Y_r'(E^*)} = C'(T^*) - 1$$

On the left side, we have the ratio of marginal returns from education for the rich and the poor while on the right side we have the marginal cost from redistribution. Therefore, a benevolent utilitarian government should use the marginal cost from redistribution as a rule to think about the equity-efficiency tradeoff. In the developing world this marginal cost is usually high—certainly higher than in the developed world—due to a variety of well-documented problems, such as widespread corruption, large informal sector, fiscal evasion, and lack of trust (see, e.g., Olken 2006). This would imply that the optimal educational policies in the developing world should be relatively more oriented toward equity than in the developed world.

However, instead of dismissing interventions due to inequity concerns, the policymaker could exploit complementary interventions to improve the situation of those that are harmed by the policy (i.e., seek a second instrument to achieve this desirable second goal). For example, in the case of complementary interventions to apply together with decentralization, we should think of how the educational performance of the poor could improve. According to the literature, a key point to consider is that even the best school policies may have little or no effect when students and parents fail to respond with the right actions (see, for example, the model in section 6.3). A combination of lack of information and inaccurate expectations can leave the poor trapped in poverty, given that they are unable to adopt actions that would improve their living standards considerably (e.g., Banerjee and Duflo 2011).

First, poor households may not have information about their potential returns from education. Thus, providing students/families with information—which is a relatively inexpensive policy—may push individuals toward better choices about human capital investment. Indeed, Jensen (2010) provided a random subset of schools with information on the returns to schooling (estimated from earnings data). Relative to those not provided with information, these students reported dramatically increased perceived returns when reinterviewed four to six months later, and on average completed 0.20 more years of schooling over the next four years. Nguyen (2008) also presents experimental data, in this case from Madagascar, which shows that informing fourth-grade students and their parents about the returns to schooling increased average daily attendance by 3.5 percentage points and test scores by 0.20 standard deviations after three months. And Dinkelman and Martinez (2011) show that giving/showing a DVD with information to high school students in Chile increased attendance and willingness to finance future education with government loans. Perhaps if parents and students from poor households upgrade their perceived returns to schooling with this complementary intervention, then they will better exploit the advantages of School Management reforms (e.g., by attending parent meetings).

Second, parents in poorer areas might not have information about their rights, how to demand that they be respected, and how to help the school to improve their children's education. This problem is particularly important in the context of school decentralization. In the context of the model presented in section 6.3, the value of κ_{ij}, which represents the efficiency of community ij's effort, may need to be raised. The experimental evidence shows that there is scope for improvements of this type. Banerjee et al. (2008) study the Village Education Committees (VECs) program in India, which were supposed to monitor the performance of the schools, report problems to higher authorities, hire and fire community-based teachers, and use additional resources for school improvement from a national education program.[33] Their experiments to increase participation show that citizens face substantial constraints in getting involved with the improvement of the public education system, even when they care about education and are willing to do something to improve it.[34] However, when parents are able to overcome the barriers to be involved and are also empowered, having trained school committees may prove to be a good intervention for improving students' performance.[35] Also, Gertler, Patrinos, and Rubio-Codina (2011) study a very inexpensive program in Mexico that involves parents directly managing schools located in disadvantaged rural communities.[36] They find that empowering parents reduces failure and repetition rates significantly. However, while the program was effective in poor communities, it had no effect in extremely poor communities.

A more direct strategy to provide parents with incentives to enroll their children in school is conditional cash-transfer (CCT) programs, which have been implemented in many developing countries. CCT programs provide cash transfers to finance current consumption subject to the "attainment" of certain conditions that foster human capital investments. A detailed review of CCT programs is provided by Behrman et al. in chapter 5 of this volume and also in Galiani (2008). CCT programs have had significant positive impacts on a wide range of outcomes, including educational outcomes.[37] In the context of CCTs as a complementary intervention, they seem to have a positive effect on equality: the impact on enrollment rates are generally larger for those groups that have lower baseline enrollment rates, lower transition rates from primary to secondary school, girls, or poorer households (Galiani and McEwan 2011). Also, some potential complementary interventions involve giving resources to the poor to complement other interventions that do not benefit them directly. Chapter 2 in this volume covers some examples (see also Glewwe, Kremer, and Moulin 2009). Overall, we think that it is more likely that poor communities adopt complementary interventions that are related to accountability and empowerment or giving incentives to parents rather than those involving an increase in their spending on education.

In summary, we conclude that there is an interesting menu of complementary interventions that could be combined with the School Management policies analyzed in this chapter in ways that would enhance their positive results and reduce inequality in education outcomes.

6.7. Conclusions

In this survey, we have analyzed three types of School Management interventions: school decentralization, student tracking, and teacher incentives. We cover a nonexhaustive list of empirical papers that exploit nonexperimental, quasi-experimental, and experimental identification strategies.

In our opinion, for each case, a deeper understanding of their structural mechanisms at work is a key goal for future research in this area. Given the heterogeneous effects of these policies, knowing the channels through which they operate differentially across subpopulations or settings is of high priority. This understanding will aid in designing complementary cost-effective interventions that enhance the effects of the reforms or help to extend their benefits to those that have not been reached.

Overall, we have drawn several conclusions regarding the interventions surveyed and, more important, we have raised related topics that require further exploration. Our main findings are that decentralization programs seem to be successful in increasing the average performance of students. However, the better-off communities or schools tend to profit most from this type of intervention, which increases inequality. A goal for future studies would be to understand how school autonomy differentially affects relatively poor and rich communities. Complementary interventions could then be implemented to compensate those that do not gain from decentralization; giving information to promote parental participation through school committees seems to be effective, especially in poorer communities where the decentralized resources are more likely to be diverted to other needs that do not necessarily raise welfare.

Regarding tracking, the experimental evidence suggests that tracking increases the performance of students across all skill levels. However, because there is only one experimental study, and especially because it contrasts with the nonexperimental evidence, further experimental evidence is needed. Finally, most of the teacher-incentive schemes studied proved to have positive results in terms of reducing absenteeism of teachers and improving the performance of students, although the compensation systems should be designed to discourage teaching to the test. Concerning contract teachers, the empirical evidence also shows favorable impacts on students' test scores and teachers' absenteeism. However, understanding whether this happens because of incentives, decentralization of hiring, or through other channels is key to designing better contracts for tenured civil service teachers and profiting most from the combination of the two types of teachers. Also, complementary interventions regarding monitoring of teachers by parental committees or extra hiring of contract teachers to help more disadvantaged students could be useful to increase the average and distributional benefits from this type of intervention.

Finally, School Management reforms should be accompanied by programs aimed at stimulating the demand for education of those individuals who are less likely to take advantage of the reforms. This combination of demand and supply interventions seems to be an attractive recipe for promoting and raising education outcomes, which, in turn, will promote long run economic growth in the developing world.

Acknowledgments

We thank useful comments from Jere Behrman, Paul Glewwe, Eric Hanushek, Laura Jaitman, Karthik Muralidharan, Lant Pritchett, discussants in the Conference "Education Policy in Developing Countries: What Do We Know, and What Should We Do to Understand What We

Don't Know?" as well as comments from other participants. Manuel Puente provided excellent research assistance. We acknowledge funding from the Weidenbaum Center at Washington University in St. Louis.

Appendix 6A. Solution to the Decentralized Problem

In the decentralized case, given the government education effort b_{ij}, the problem for community ij is:

$$\underset{\{a_{ij}\}}{Max} \left((\kappa_{ij} a_{ij})^{\alpha} + (\hat{\gamma}_{ij} b_{ij})^{\alpha} \right)^{\frac{1}{\alpha}} - a_{ij}$$

The first order condition for an interior solution is:

$$a_{ij}^d (b_{ij}) = b_{ij} \frac{\hat{\gamma}_{ij}}{\kappa_{ij}} \left(\kappa_{ij}^{\frac{\alpha}{\alpha-1}} - 1 \right)^{-\frac{1}{\alpha}}$$

Since there are no economies of scale, we can study the problem of the government in each particular community ij separately:

$$\underset{\{b_{ij}\}}{Max}\, \theta_{ij} \left[\left((\kappa_{ij} a_{ij}^d (b_{ij}))^{\alpha} + (\hat{\gamma}_{ij} b_{ij})^{\alpha} \right)^{\frac{1}{\alpha}} - a_{ij}^d (b_{ij}) \right] - b_{ij}^2$$

This objective function may differ in cases where the educational spending is financed in a way that may distort incentives.[38] After substituting for a_{ij}^d, the objective function becomes:

$$\underset{\{b_{ij}\}}{Max}\, \theta_{ij} b_{ij} \hat{\gamma}_{ij} \left(1 - \kappa_{ij}^{\frac{\alpha}{1-\alpha}} \right)^{\frac{\alpha-1}{\alpha}} - b_{ij}^2.$$

The first order condition for an interior solution yields:

$$b_{ij}^d = \frac{\theta_{ij} \hat{\gamma}_{ij}}{2} \left(1 - \kappa_{ij}^{\frac{\alpha}{1-\alpha}} \right)^{\frac{\alpha-1}{\alpha}}.$$

Finally, evaluating $a_{ij}^d(b_{ij})$ at b_{ij}^d we obtain:

$$a_{ij}^d = \frac{\theta_{ij} \hat{\gamma}_{ij}}{2} \left(1 - \kappa_{ij}^{\frac{\alpha}{1-\alpha}} \right)^{\frac{\alpha-2}{\alpha}} \kappa_{ij}^{\frac{\alpha}{1-\alpha}},$$

And evaluating e_{ij} (a_{ij}, b_{ij}) at b_{ij}^d and $a_{ij}^d(b_{ij}^d)$ we get the educational outcome:

$$
e_{ij}^d = \frac{\theta_{ij}\hat{\gamma}_{ij}^2}{2}\left(1 - \kappa_{ij}^{\frac{\alpha}{1-\alpha}}\right)^{\frac{\alpha-2}{\alpha}} = \frac{\theta_{ij}\hat{\gamma}_{ij}^2}{2}\lambda(\kappa_{ij}, \alpha)
$$

Notes

1. There is also the concern that the results are not robust when the experiment is scaled-up. When the policies are applied outside the controlled experiment, the behaviors of the agents may change, altering the effects previously identified. For instance, in the tracking experiments—as we review later—the allocation of teachers to sections is random, while in a nonexperimental setup there might be sorting of teachers (see Pop-Eleches and Urquiola 2011).

2. They used a cross-section of 37 countries in the TIMSS (Trends in International Mathematics and Science Study) data.

3. See also Hanushek and Woessmann (2011) for an extensive survey.

4. Only a weak relationship between spending and student outcomes has also been found in the time series variation within a given country. For example, Hanushek (2006) shows that even though the real spending per pupil in the United States rose considerably through the period 1960–2000, the performances of students showed little improvement. Gundlach and Woessmann (2001) study six Asian countries between 1980 and 1994, reaching a similar conclusion: when inputs significantly increased in that period, cognitive achievement of pupils did not change substantially.

5. According to OECD (2009), the difference between OECD and non-OECD members is 1–2 standard deviations in test scores.

6. See, e.g., Bishop 1995, 1999, 2006; Woessmann 2005; and Woessmann et al. 2009; and for a full review see Hanushek and Woessmann 2011.

7. On level of competition from private schools see, e.g., Corten and Dronkers 2006; Vandenberghe and Robin 2004; and Woessmann et al. 2009. On characteristics of the preprimary education see, e.g., Berlinski, Galiani, and Gertler 2009; Schouetz, Ursprung, and Woessmann 2008; and chapter 3 in this volume.

8. Ten percent of the World Bank's education portfolio for the period 2000–2006 supported decentralization programs (approximately 15 out of 157 projects); see Barrera-Osorio et al. 2009.

9. For example, the Program for International Student Assessment (PISA) in the 2009 Assessment Framework appraised school autonomy: "Many of the world's best-performing education systems have moved from bureaucratic 'command and control' environments towards school systems in which the people at the frontline have much more control of the way resources are used, people are deployed, the work is organized and the way in which the work gets done. They provide considerable discretion to school heads and school faculties in determining how resources are allocated, a factor which the report shows to be closely related to school performance when combined with effective accountability systems" (OECD 2009, p. 4).

10. Alesina, Baqir, and Hoxby (2004) use data on American school districts, school attendance areas, municipalities, and special districts, and find strong evidence that more heterogeneous populations (e.g., in terms of race, income) end up with more decentralized districts, thereby accentuating the inequalities in the local communities.

11. Woessmann (2003) employs micro data on 39 countries and finds that student performance correlates positively with different decentralization variables (control mechanisms and exams, school autonomy in personnel, process decisions, and the influence of teachers on teaching methods). OECD (2010) suggested that the prevalence of schools' autonomy to define and elaborate their curricula and assessments relates positively to the performance of school systems, even after accounting for national income.

12. In a similar spirit, King and Özler (2005) provide an impact evaluation of Nicaragua's school autonomy reform that started in 1993 and consisted in giving legal status and several key management tasks to school councils. The results indicate that autonomy de jure does not affect students' performance. However, higher de facto autonomy in some administrative decisions, especially in the ability to hire and fire school personnel, is correlated with higher student achievement.

13. Furthermore, he reports that the negative effects from decentralization were greater in the poorest communities.

14. The decentralization law did not change the distribution of resources among provinces. It also guaranteed that the provinces would not have to bear additional financial burden by taking on the operation of the transferred schools.

15. In the same line, Chaudhury and Parajuli (2010) study the Community School Support Project that randomized schools to an advocacy campaign and gave them a grant. Short-run estimates show significant impacts on certain schooling outcomes on disadvantaged castes although there is no evidence of improved learning outcomes.

16. The interventions at the school level, reinforced by interventions at the subdistrict and district levels, improved school attendance, reduced grade repetition, and raised test scores (particularly in Malagasy and mathematics), although the gains in learning at the end of the evaluation period were not always statistically significant. Interventions limited to the subdistrict and district levels proved largely ineffective.

17. See Salinas and Solé-Ollé 2009 for a study of the Spanish decentralization process in 1978–2005, or Barankay and Lockwood 2007 for an analysis of decentralization in the Swiss cantons.

18. Note that, depending on the equilibrium concept that one uses, students may not fully internalize the social benefits from making an effort and thus underprovide effort relative to the social optimum. However, this feature is not critical for the results that follow.

19. "School systems that seek to cater to different students' needs through a high level of differentiation in the institutions, grade levels and classes have not succeeded in producing superior overall results, and in some respects they have lower-than-average and more socially unequal performance. . . . In countries

where 15-year-olds are divided into more tracks based on their abilities, overall performance is not enhanced, and the younger the age at which selection for such tracks first occurs, the greater the differences in student performance, . . . without improved overall performance" (OECD 2010, p. 15).

20. In a similar spirit, Manning and Pischke (2006) show that controlling for baseline scores is not sufficient to eliminate the selection bias when comparing students attending comprehensive versus selective schools in the United Kingdom.

21. The fact that middle-scoring students are the group that benefits least from tracking is consistent with the model presented, when they are the only ones getting further away from the teacher target after the tracking intervention.

22. This happens in a context in which teachers have convex payoffs in student test scores.

23. The authors studied two types of teacher-performance pay (group bonuses based on school-average performance and bonuses paid to teachers based on their individual performance).

24. School-level group incentives and teacher-level individual incentives performed equally well in the first year, but the individual-incentive schools outperformed the group incentive schools after two years of the program.

25. The program was designed to offer prizes only to teachers who were already employed before the program to avoid that the entry and exit rates of teachers would be altered by the introduction of the incentives scheme.

26. The program impact on attendance was larger for below median teachers (a 24-percentage point increase versus a 15-percentage point increase for above-median teachers). However, this was due to the fact that the program brought below-median teachers to the same level of attendance as above median teachers (78%).

27. Over the 30 months in which attendance was tracked, the treatment reduced teachers' absenteeism rates (42% in control group vs. 22% in treatment group), increased students' test scores (by 0.17 standard deviations), and raised the probability of students being accepted into regular schools (by 40%).

28. See Duthilleul 2005 for a review of contract teacher programs in several countries.

29. See also Duflo, Dupas, and Kremer 2011.

30. They report the results of the remedial education program in India (Banerjee et al. 2007), which hired young women to teach students who lagged behind in basic literacy and numeric skills, with positive results. Likewise, Banerjee et al. (2008) study a reading intervention in rural India that trained community volunteers who had a tenth- or twelfth-grade education for four days to teach children how to read, which significantly improved reading achievement.

31. See Banerjee et al. 2008; Bourdon, Frölich, and Michaelowa 2007.

32. Although in some cases redistribution is actually found to be efficient (Mookherjee 2006), this tradeoff is a commonplace in the models of economists and policymakers.

33. Three different treatments were randomized. The results from the third treatment were already discussed in the section on contract teachers. In the first treatment, the NGO organized meetings in the villages, where school staff and

village local-government representatives were encouraged to share information about the structure and organization of local service delivery, including the role and activities of the VECs. The second treatment included the activities described in the first treatment, but the NGO members also demonstrated the process of creating "learning report cards" by conducting simple assessments of reading and arithmetic with the local children. The goal behind the design of the second intervention was that community members and parents become sensitized to their children's educational progress.

34. An average village of about 360 households sent about 100 people to the meetings, yet both the first and second interventions had no impact on community involvement in public schools, and no impact on teacher effort or student learning outcomes in those schools.

35. This is similar to one of the treatments in India's "Extra Teacher Program"; see Duflo, Hanna, and Ryan 2012.

36. The program finances parent associations and motivates parental participation by involving them in the management of primary school grants. They found that the program reduced grade failure by 7.4% and grade repetition by 5.5% in grades 1 through 3, although it had no effect on dropout rates.

37. For a very complete review see Fiszbein and Schady 2009.

38. For example, Kenya has a mixed educational system in which local communities are allowed to build their schools and should pay nonteacher expenditures, whereas the central government is in charge of assigning teachers to schools and paying their salaries (as well as setting the curriculum and administering national tests). This obviously introduces distortions: Kremer, Moulin, and Namunyu (2003) show that this system generates local communities with too many small schools, rather than fewer, larger schools, and where reallocating expenditures from teachers to nonteacher inputs and reducing the cost of education could improve welfare.

References

Alesina, A., R. Baqir, and C. Hoxby. 2004." Political Jurisdictions in Heterogeneous Communities." *Journal of Political Economy* 112 (2): 348–96.

Angrist, J., and V. Lavy. 1999." Using Maimonides' Rule to Estimate the Effect of Class Size on Scholastic Achievement." *Quarterly Journal of Economics* 114 (2): 533–75.

Argys, L., D. Rees, and D. Brewer. 1996. "Detracking America's Schools: Equity at Zero Cost?" *Journal of Policy Analysis and Management* 15 (4): 623–45.

Arrow, K. 1951. *Social Choice and Individual Values.* New York: John Wiley and Sons.

Banerjee, A., S. Cole, E. Duflo, and L. Linden. 2007. "Remedying Education: Evidence from Two Randomized Experiments in India." *Quarterly Journal of Economics* 122 (3): 1235–64.

Banerjee, A., and E. Duflo. 2011. *Poor Economics: A Radical Rethinking of the Way to Fight Global Poverty.* New York: Public Affairs.

Banerjee A., R. Banerji, E. Duflo, R. Glennerster, and S. Khemani. 2008. "Pitfalls of Participatory Programs: Evidence from a Randomized Evaluation in

Education in India." NBER Working Paper No. 14311. http://www.nber.org /papers/w14311.

Barankay, I., and Lockwood, B. 2007. "Decentralization and the Productive Efficiency of Government: Evidence from Swiss Cantons." *Journal of Public Economics* 91:1197–1218.

Bardhan, P., and D. Mookherjee. 2005. "Decentralizing Anti-poverty Program Delivery in Developing Countries." *Journal of Public Economics* 89 (4): 675–704.

———. 2006. "Decentralization and Accountability in Infrastructure Delivery in Developing Countries." *Economic Journal* 116 (508): 101–27.

Barrera-Osorio, F., T. Fasih, H. Patrinos, and L. Santibáñez. 2009. *Decentralized Decision-Making in Schools: The Theory and Evidence on School-Based Management.* Washington, DC: World Bank.

Barro, R., and J. Lee. 2001. "Schooling Quality in a Cross-Section of Countries." *Economica* 68 (272): 465–88.

Benabou, Roland, and Jean Tirole. 2006. "Incentives and Prosocial Behavior." *American Economic Review* 96 (5): 1652–78.

Bennell, P. 2004. "Teacher Motivation and Incentives in Sub-Saharan Africa and Asia." Knowledge and Skills for Development, Brighton. http://www.eldis .org/vfile/upload/1/document/0708/doc15160.pdf.

Benveniste, L., and J. Marshall. 2004. "School Grants and Student Performance: Evidence from the EQIP Project in Cambodia." Unpublished manuscript. Washington, DC: World Bank.

Berlinski, S., S. Galiani, and P. Gertler. 2009. "The Effect of Pre-Primary Education on Primary School Performance." *Journal of Public Economics* 93: 219–34.

Betts, Julian R., and Jamie L. Shkolnik. 2000. "The Effects of Ability Grouping on Student Achievement and Resource Allocation in Secondary Schools." *Economics of Education Review* 19 (1): 1–15.

Bird, R. M., and F. Vaillancourt, eds. 1998. *Fiscal Decentralization in Developing Countries.* Cambridge: Cambridge University Press.

Bishop, J. 1995. "The Impact of Curriculum-Based External Examinations on School Priorities and Student Learning." *International Journal of Education Research* 23 (8): 653–752.

———. 1999. "Are National Exit Examinations Important for Educational Efficiency?" *Swedish Economic Policy Review* 6 (2): 349–98.

———. 2006. "Drinking from the Fountain of Knowledge: Student Incentive to Study and Learn—Externalities, Information Problems, and Peer Pressure." In *Handbook of the Economics of Education*, vol. 2, ed. E. A. Hanushek and F. Welch, 909–44. Amsterdam: North Holland.

Bourdon, J., M. Frölich, and K. Michaelowa. 2006. "Broadening Access to Primary Education: Contract Teacher Programs and Their Impact on Education Outcomes in Africa—An Econometric Evaluation for Niger." In *Pro-Poor Growth: Issues, Policies, and Evidence*, ed. L. Menckhoff, 117–49. Berlin: Duncker and Humblot.

———. 2010. "Teacher Shortages, Teacher Contracts and Their Effect on Education in Africa." *Journal of the Royal Statistical Society: Series A (Statistics in Society)* 173 (1): 93–116.

Bruns, B., D. Filmer, and H. Patrinos. 2011. *Making Schools Work: New Evidence on Accountability Reforms.* Washington, DC: World Bank.

Burde, D., and L. L. Linden. 2012. "The Effect of Village-Based Schools: Evidence from a RCT in Afghanistan." Abdul Latif Jameel Poverty Action Lab. Available at http://www.povertyactionlab.org/publication/effect-village-based -schools-evidence-randomized-controlled-trial-afghanistan.

Burke, M. A., and T. R. Sass. 2013. "Classroom Peer Effects and Student Achievement." *Journal of Labor Economics* 31 (1): 51–82.

Chaudhury, N., J. Hammer, M. Kremer, K. Muralidharan, and F. H. Rogers. 2006. "Missing in Action: Teacher and Health Worker Absence in Developing Countries." *Journal of Economic Perspectives* 20 (1): 91–116.

Chaudhury, N., and D. Parajuli. 2010. "Giving It Back: Evaluating the Impact of Devolution of School Management to Communities in Nepal." Washington, DC: World Bank.

Corten, R., and J. Dronkers. 2006. "School Achievement of Pupils from the Lower Strata in Public, Private Government-Dependent and Private Government-Independent Schools: A Cross-National Test of the Coleman-Hoffer Thesis." *Educational Research and Evaluation* 12 (2): 179–208.

De Laat, J., and E. Vegas. 2005. "Do Differences in Teacher Contracts Affect Student Performance? Evidence from Togo." World Development Report 2004 Background Paper, 2005. http://www-wds.worldbank.org/servlet/WDS ContentServer/IW3P/IB/2003/10/24/000160016_20031024103517/Rendered /PDF/269550VegasoTeacher1contracts.pdf.

Ding, Weili, and Steven F. Lehrer. 2007. "Do Peers Affect Student Achievement in China's Secondary Schools?" *Review of Economics and Statistics* 89 (2): 300–312.

Dinkelman, Taryn, and A. Martínez. 2011. "Investing in Schooling in Chile: The Role of Information about Financial Aid for Higher Education." Working Paper no. 1296, Princeton University, Princeton, NJ. Available at http://papers .ssrn.com/sol3/papers.cfm?abstract_id=1846257.

Duflo, Esther, Pascaline Dupas, and Michael Kremer. 2007. "Peer Effects, Pupil-Teacher Ratios, and Teacher Incentives: Evidence from a Randomized Evaluation in Kenya." Mimeo. Available at http://isites.harvard.edu/fs/docs/icb .topic436657.files/ETP_Kenya_09.14.07.pdf.

———. 2011. "Peer Effects and the Impacts of Tracking: Evidence from a Randomized Evaluation in Kenya." *American Economic Review* 101 (5): 1739–74.

Duflo, E., R. Hanna, and S. P. Ryan. 2012. "Incentives Work: Getting Teachers to Come to School." *American Economic Review* 102 (4): 1241–78.

Duthilleul, Y. 2005. "Lessons Learnt in the Use of 'Contract' Teachers." International Institute for Educational Planning, UNESCO.

Faguet, Jean-Paul, and Fabio Sanchez. 2008. "Decentralization's Effects on Educational Outcomes in Bolivia and Colombia." *World Development* 36 (7): 1294–1316.

238

Figlio, David N., and Marianne E. Page. 2002. "School Choice and the Distributional Effects of Ability Tracking: Does Separation Increase Inequality?" *Journal of Urban Economics* 51 (3): 497–514.

Fiszbein, Ariel, and Norbert Schady. 2009. *Conditional Cash Transfers: Reducing Present and Future Poverty*. World Bank Policy Research Report. Washington, DC: World Bank.

Franceschelli, I., S. Galiani, and E. Gulmez. 2008. "Performance Pay and Productivity of Low- and High-Ability Workers." December. Available at SSRN: http://ssrn.com/abstract=1279189.

———. 2010. "Performance Pay and Productivity of Low- and High-Ability Workers." *Labour Economics* 17:317–22.

Fuchs, T., and L. Woessmann. 2007. "What Accounts for International Differences in Student Performance? A Re-Examination Using PISA Data." *Empirical Economics* 32 (2–3): 433–62.

Galiani, S. 2008. "Reducing Poverty in Latin America and the Caribbean." Report for the Copenhagen Consensus Center and the Inter-American Development Bank. http://www.plataformademocratica.org/Publicacoes/6827_Cached.pdf.

Galiani, S., P. Gertler, and E. Schargrodsky. 2008. "School Decentralization: Helping the Good Get Better, But Leaving the Poor Behind." *Journal of Public Economics* 92:2106–20.

Galiani, S., and P. McEwan. Forthcoming. "The Heterogeneous Impact of Conditional Cash Transfers in Honduras." *Journal of Public Economics*.

Gertler, Paul J., Harry A. Patrinos, and Marta Rubio-Codina. 2011. "Empowering Parents to Improve Education: Evidence from Rural Mexico." World Bank Policy Research Working Paper no. 3935. Available at http://papers.ssrn.com/sol3/papers.cfm?abstract_id=923242.

Glewwe, Paul, Nauman Ilias, and Michael Kremer. 2010. "Teacher Incentives." *American Economic Journal: Applied Economics* 2 (3): 205–27.

Glewwe, Paul, Michael Kremer, and Sylvie Moulin. 2009. "Many Children Left Behind? Textbooks and Test Scores in Kenya." *American Economic Journal: Applied Economics* 1 (1): 112–35.

Gordon, R., T. J. Kane, and D. O. Staiger. 2006. "Identifying Effective Teachers Using Performance on the Job." Hamilton Project Discussion Paper no. 2006-01. Available at http://www.brookings.edu/views/papers/200604hamilton_1.pdf.

Goyal, S., and P. Pandey. 2009. "Contract Teachers." South Asia Human Development Sector Report no. 28. Washington, DC: World Bank. Available at http://ddp-ext.worldbank.org/EdStats/INDwp09.pdf.

Gundlach, E., and L. Woessmann. 2001. "The Fading Productivity of Schooling in East Asia." *Journal of Asian Economies* 12 (3): 401–17.

Gunnarsson, Victoria, Peter F. Orazem, Mario A. Sánchez, and Aimee Verdisco. 2009. "Does Local School Control Raise Student Outcomes? Evidence on the Roles of School Autonomy and Parental Participation." *Economic Development and Cultural Change* 58 (1): 25–52.

Hanushek, E. 2006. "School Resources." In *Handbook of the Economics of*

Education, vol. 2, ed. E. A. Hanushek and F. Welch, 865–908. Amsterdam: North Holland.

Hanushek, E., and D. Kimko. 2000. "Schooling, Labor Force Quality, and the Growth of Nations." *American Economic Review* 90 (5): 1184–1208.

Hanushek, E., and J. Luque. 2003. "Efficiency and Equity in Schools around the World." *Economics of Education Review* 22 (5): 481–502.

Hanushek, E. A., and L. Woessmann. 2006. "Does Educational Tracking Affect Performance and Inequality? Differences-in-Differences Evidence across Countries." *Economic Journal* 116 (510): C63–C76.

———. 2011. "The Economics of International Differences in Educational Achievement." In *Handbook of the Economics of Education*, vol. 4, ed. E. A. Hanushek, S. Machin, and L. Woessmann, 89–199. Amsterdam: North Holland.

Hoffer, T. B. 1992. "Middle School Ability Grouping and Student Achievement in Science and Mathematics." *Educational Evaluation and Policy Analysis* 14:205–27.

Holmstrom, Bengt, and Paul Milgrom. 1991. "Multi-Task Principal-Agent Analyses: Linear Contracts, Asset Ownership and Job Design." *Journal of Law, Economics and Organization* 7:24–52.

Jackson, C. Kirabo. 2010. "Do Students Benefit from Attending Better Schools? Evidence from Rule-Based Student Assignments in Trinidad and Tobago." *Economic Journal* 120 (549): 1399–1429.

Jensen, Robert. 2010. "The (Perceived) Returns to Education and the Demand for Schooling." *Quarterly Journal of Economics* 125 (2): 515–48.

Jimenez, E., and Y. Sawada. 1999. "Do Community-Managed Schools Work? An Evaluation of El Salvador's EDUCO Program." *World Bank Economic Review* 13 (3): 415–41.

———. 2003. "Does Community Management Help Keep Kids in Schools? Evidence Using Panel Data from El Salvador's EDUCO Program." CIRJE F-Series CIRJE-F-236, CIRJE, Faculty of Economics, University of Tokyo.

Kaplow, L., and S. Shavell. 2002. *Fairness versus Welfare*. Cambridge, MA: Harvard University Press.

Kerckhoff, A. C. 1986. "Effects of Ability Grouping in British Secondary Schools." *American Sociological Review* 51:842–58.

King, E., and B. Özler. 2005. "What's Decentralization Got to Do with Learning? The Case of Nicaragua's School Autonomy Reform." 21COE, Interfaces for Advanced Economic Analysis, Kyoto University.

Kremer, M., S. Moulin, and R. Namunyu. 2003. "Decentralization: A Cautionary Tale." Poverty Action Lab Paper no. 10. Available at http://citeseerx.ist .psu.edu/viewdoc/download?doi=10.1.1.203.1500&rep=rep1&type=pdf.

Kremer, Michael, Karthik Muralidharan, Nazmul Chaudhury, Jeffrey Hammer, and F. Halsey Rogers. 2005. "Teacher Absence in India." *Journal of the European Economic Association* 3:658–67.

Krueger, A.B. 1999. "Experimental Estimates of Education Production Functions." *Quarterly Journal of Economics* 114 (2): 497–532.

Lassibille, G., J.-P. Tan, C. Jesse, and T. Nguyen. 2010. "Managing for Results in

Primary Education in Madagascar: Evaluating the Impact of Selected Work-flow Interventions." *World Bank Economic Review* 24 (2): 303–29.

Madeira, Ricardo. 2007. "The Effects of Decentralization on Schooling: Evidence from the Sao Paulo State Education Reform." Mimeo.

Manning, Allen, and Jörn-Steffen Pischke. 2006. "Comprehensive Versus Selective Schooling in England and Wales: What Do We Know?" Centre for the Economics of Education Working Paper no. CEEDP006. Available at http://papers.ssrn.com/sol3/papers.cfm?abstract_id=898567.

Mookherjee, D. 2006. "Poverty Persistence and the Design of Antipoverty Policies." In *Understanding Poverty*, ed. A. Banerjee, R. Benabou, and D. Mookherjee, 231–35. Oxford: Oxford University Press.

Muralidharan, Karthik, and Venkatesh Sundararaman. 2010. "Contract Teachers: Experimental Evidence from India." Mimeo. Available at http://www.fas.nus.edu.sg/ecs/events/seminar/seminar-papers/31Aug10.pdf.

———. 2011. "Teacher Performance Pay: Experimental Evidence from India." *Journal of Political Economy* 119 (1): 39–77.

Nguyen, Trang. 2008. "Information, Role Models and Perceived Returns to Education: Experimental Evidence from Madagascar." Working Paper, MIT. Available at http://www.povertyactionlab.org/sites/default/files/documents/Nguyen%202008.pdf.

Oates, W. 1972. *Fiscal Federalism*. New York: Harcourt Brace Jovanovich.

Olken, Benjamin A. 2006. "Corruption and the Costs of Redistribution: Micro Evidence from Indonesia." *Journal of Public Economics* 90:853–70.

Paes de Barros, R., and R. Mendoça. 1998. "The Impact of Three Institutional Innovations in Brazilian Education." In *Organization Matters: Agency Problems in Health and Education in Latin America*, ed. W. D. Savedoff, 75. Washington DC: Inter-American Development Bank.

OECD. 2010. *PISA 2009 Results: What Makes a School Successful? Resources, Policies and Practices*. Vol. 4. PISA, OECD Publishing. doi: 10.1787/9789264091559-en.

Pop-Eleches, C., and M. Urquiola. 2011. "Going to a Better School: Effects and Behavioral Responses." NBER Working Paper no. 16886. Available at http://www.nber.org/papers/w16886.

Pradhan, Menno, Daniel Suryadarma, Amanda Beatty, Maisy Wong, Armida Alishjabana, Arya Gaduh, and Rima Prama Artha. 2011. "Improving Educational Quality Through Enhancing Community Participation: Results from a Randomized Field Experiment in Indonesia." May. Available at SSRN: http://ssrn.com/abstract=1862143.

Rivkin, S., E. Hanushek, and J. Kain. 2005. "Teachers, Schools, and Academic Achievement." *Econometrica* 73:417–58.

Salinas, P., and A. Solé-Ollé. 2009. "Evaluating the Effects of Decentralization on Educational Outcomes in Spain." Institut d'Economia de Barcelona (IEB), Working Papers 2009/10. Available at http://www.econstor.eu/dspace/bitstream/10419/18982/1/cesifo1_wp1518.pdf.

Schouetz, G., H. W. Ursprung, and L. Woessmann. 2008. "Education Policy and Equality of Opportunity." *Kyklos* 61 (2): 279–308.

Vandenberghe, V., and S. Robin. 2004. "Evaluating the Effectiveness of Private Education across Countries: A Comparison of Methods." *Labour Economics* 11 (4): 487–506.

Woessmann, L. 2003. "Schooling Resources, Educational Institutions, and Student Performance: The International Evidence." *Oxford Bulletin of Economics and Statistics* 65 (2): 117–70.

———. 2005. "The Effect Heterogeneity of Central Examinations: Evidence from TIMSS, TIMSS-Repeat and PISA." *Education Economics* 13 (2): 143–69.

Woessmann, L., E. Luedemann, G. Schuetz, and M. R. West. 2009. *School Accountability, Autonomy, and Choice around the World.* Northampton, MA: Edward Elgar.

Zimmerman, D. 2003. "Peer Effects in Academic Outcomes: Evidence from a Natural Experiment." *Review of Economics and Statistics* 85 (1): 9–23.

7

Competition and Educational Productivity: Incentives Writ Large

W. Bentley MacLeod (Columbia University)
Miguel Urquiola (Columbia University)

1. Under-recognition of the power of what psychologists call "reinforcement" and economists call "incentives."—Well I think I've been in the top 5 percent of my age cohort all my life in understanding the power of incentives, and all my life I've underestimated it. And never a year passes but I get some surprise that pushes my limit a little farther.
Charlie Munger's first cause of human misjudgment, speech at Harvard Law School

7.1. *Introduction*

At the core of modern economics is an effort to understand how institutions shape incentives and how this affects the performance of the economy. A central institution is the market mechanism, under which firms are free to enter with new products, and consumers are free to decide whether to purchase them or not. One of the most influential proponents of this institution was Milton Friedman, who argued in his classic book *Capitalism and Freedom* (Friedman 1962) that all areas of economic activity can be enhanced with more reliance upon free markets and less reliance upon government provision of goods and services.

In the case of education, Friedman (1955, 1962) argued that allowing a greater role for private schools, and more freedom of choice for parents, would improve outcomes. He acknowledged that doing so might have distributional implications, but pointed out that these could be addressed via the distribution of vouchers, ensuring that each student received at least a minimum amount of education. This view has been influential; for example, it figures prominently in the World Bank's *World Development Report* (2004) on improving public service delivery.

In a review of the literature, Hoxby (2002) describes how these ideas have been explored theoretically and empirically. Hoxby points out that, partially due to its origins in public finance, research on school choice has emphasized questions related to distribution rather than to productivity: "School choice research has concentrated on *allocation* questions, which include: Who exercises school choice? Who chooses which school? How does choice change the allocation of resources? How does reallocation of students change peer effects?"

Hoxby argues for research to place greater emphasis on school productivity. In her definition, "a school that is more productive is one that produces higher achievement in its pupils for each dollar it spends." This definition is precise and useful, and since it concerns testing achievement, we will call it *test productivity*. Hoxby argues that competition would have large effects on test productivity, rendering distribution-related concerns less salient (i.e., it would be "a rising tide that lifted all boats").

In making these statements, our reading is that Hoxby (2002) refers to two strands of the literature. First, it is indeed the case that seminal theoretical papers (e.g., Arnott and Rowse 1987; Epple and Romano 1998) focus on peer effects and hence on how competition would affect the *distribution* of students and educational outcomes.[1] Second, a focus on productivity is quite reasonable given findings that many school systems have experienced a test productivity "collapse." For example, Hanushek (1996) describes an apparent test productivity decline in American schools, and Pritchett (2003) suggests that this development is common among OECD countries. Data restrictions make it harder to make analogous statements about developing countries, but the prima facie evidence is consistent with many of those countries also having experienced rising real expenditures in education, with at best small test score gains to show for it.

Given this background, this chapter carries out three tasks:

1. We review the empirical evidence on the effects of competition on test productivity. We do not attempt to provide an exhaustive ac-

counting of the literature; rather, we begin with a discussion of recent reviews of the voluminous US literature. We then discuss the evidence from developing countries, focusing upon Chile, Colombia, India, and Pakistan—cases where there has been important work that extends the insights from the US literature. We conclude that the impact of competition upon test productivity has proven to be more mixed and modest than would be expected given the evident success of privatization in other industries.[2]

2. We then take a step back and ask if—given the advances in the economics of industrial organization, contract theory, and asymmetric information since the 1950s—this is so surprising. We argue that in fact the literature in these areas suggests that there is no a priori reason to believe that school choice will lead to much higher test productivity. The fundamental reason is that in a rational choice framework parents and teachers care about the impact of education upon future wages, and not about test scores per se. In MacLeod and Urquiola (2012) we show that a school's reputation is a function not only of its value added, but also of its students' ability and effort. It is not always possible for the market to disentangle these three components, with the consequence that free competition may even lead to lower overall performance.

3. We conclude with a discussion of the implications of these observations for the design of education markets. In particular, effective school competition entails restricting the right of schools to select their student body (consistent with the requirement that charter schools use a lottery system for admissions under No Child Left Behind legislation in the United States). This can be combined with high-quality national exams, as suggested by Bishop (1997). As in chapter 2, our analysis suggests that the design of educational systems must carefully consider incentives.

7.2. The Empirical Evidence

The educational literature contains an expectation that competition will substantially raise school test productivity. The reviews of the literature, such as McEwan (2004) and Barrow and Rouse (2009), emphasize that the benefits of allowing private schools to enter the market, and distributing vouchers to students, would originate from three effects:

> 1. A private school productivity advantage. If private schools are more productive than public schools, then simply shifting children into the private sector increases learning.

2. A productivity-enhancing incentive for incumbents—particularly public schools—as they are forced to compete with entrants.

3. Better matching of students with specialized schools. For example, some schools may invest in high-quality arts or athletics programs, such that students with these interests are better served.

From an empirical perspective, a relevant contrast between these factors concerns the settings in which they can be studied. The first one can be analyzed in any country with a private school sector, regardless of its size. Analyzing the second requires situations in which the amount of competition observed in a given market changes substantially, for example, when a large scale voucher program results in substantial private sector growth.

In this section, we summarize the evidence on effects (1) and (2) in the United States. We then discuss four developing countries that offer settings and data that usefully complement/extend this research: Chile, Colombia, India, and Pakistan.[3]

7.2.1. The Relative Performance of Private and Public Schools.

In the vast majority of education markets, private school students on average have higher absolute test scores than public school students. This often leads to the suggestion that private schools also have higher productivity.[4] Establishing a productivity advantage in a causal sense would ideally require observing the outcomes of the same student under public and private schooling. Since this is not possible, the literature attempts to compare groups of students that are identical except with regard to the type of school they attended, with only a few (quasi-)experimental studies approximating this ideal.[5]

In the United States, such comparisons have often focused upon the impact of attending Catholic school relative to attending a public school. In general, the resulting literature does not produce evidence of a consistent and substantial advantage of private over public provision of education.[6] For example, in a recent review Neal (2009) states: "Measured solely by achievement and attainment effects, existing evidence does not support the view that private schools are generally superior to public schools in all settings." Barrow and Rouse (2009) conclude that "the best research to date finds relatively small achievement gains for students offered education vouchers, most of which are not statistically different from zero." (Table 7.1 presents a summary of the key empirical studies we discuss below.)

The studies that lead to such conclusions are often based upon a careful experimental design. For example, in 1997 New York City ran an experiment that randomly allocated school-choice vouchers to low-income students. Though the analyses of this experiment were controversial,

Table 7.1. Key empirical studies on the effects of competition on test productivity

Study	Sample	Key findings
Relative Performance of Private and Public Schools		
Neal 2009	Literature review on the effects of public versus private schooling	The empirical evidence does not suggest that private schools are always superior to public schools in terms of achievement or attainment.
Barrow and Rouse 2009	Literature review on the effects of vouchers on student achievement	Empirical studies generally find small and statistically insignificant gains in achievement for students offered vouchers.
Angrist et al. 2002	Applicants to Colombian lotteries distributing secondary school vouchers from 1992 to 1997	Lottery winners were 10 percentage points more likely to have completed eighth grade and scored 0.2 standard deviations higher on an achievement test.
Angrist, Bettinger, and Kremer 2006	Applicants to Colombian lotteries distributing secondary school vouchers from 1992 to 1997	Lottery winners were 5–7 percentage points more likely to graduate from high school and scored 0.2 standard deviations higher on a college entrance exam.
Sekhri and Rubinstein 2010	Applicants near the cutoff score for admission to public colleges in India from 1998 to 2002	There is no evidence of a difference in the performance of students attending public and private colleges on a college exit exam.
Effects of Large-Scale Competition		
Hsieh and Urquiola 2006	Chilean municipalities affected by a universal voucher scheme introduced in 1981	Municipalities with faster growth in the share of private schools exhibit greater stratification but no increase in the growth of test scores or average years of schooling.
Parents' Valuation of School Testing Performance		
Black 1999	Houses on the boundary of school districts in Massachusetts from 1993 to 1995	Parents are willing to pay 2.5% more for houses that give their children access to schools with 5% higher test scores.
Hastings and Weinstein 2008	North Carolina households receiving school test score information via natural or field experiments from 2002 to 2007	Parents who receive information on school test scores are significantly more likely to choose high-performing schools for their children.

both Mayer et al. (2002) and Krueger and Zhu (2004) agree that if one considers the entire eligible population, winning a voucher to attend a private school had a modest, statistically insignificant impact on student learning.[7]

There is increasing use of such careful evaluation techniques in developing country settings. We consider the cases of Colombia and India, where there have been several good studies.[8]

7.2.1.1. Colombia. From 1992 to 1997, Colombia operated a secondary school voucher program. A central stated goal of this initiative was to increase secondary (sixth–eleventh grade) enrollment rates, using private-sector participation to ease public-sector capacity constraints that most affected the poor. As a result, the vouchers were targeted at entering sixth-grade students who were residing in low-income neighborhoods, attending public school, and accepted at a participating private school.

The initiative was implemented at the municipal level, with the national government covering about 80% of its cost, and municipalities contributing the remainder. Resource constraints at both governmental levels resulted in excess demand in most jurisdictions. When this happened, the vouchers were generally allocated via lotteries.

These lotteries make it feasible to estimate the causal effect of winning a voucher to attend private school. A series of papers (Angrist et al. 2002; Angrist, Bettinger, and Kremer 2006; Bettinger, Kremer, and Saavedra 2008) use them to show that, in general, lottery winners have better academic and nonacademic outcomes than lottery losers. This result holds both for achievement measured using administrative data and for outcomes (such as performance in external standardized exams) that the researchers themselves measured.

This voucher program provides an excellent example of how an intervention not designed for evaluation purposes can be used to carefully measure the impact of vouchers. All the same, in terms of identifying a private test productivity advantage as defined by Hoxby (2002), the Colombian voucher experiment has a few disadvantages. First, the vouchers were renewable contingent on grade completion, and thus the program included an incentive component—voucher winners faced a stronger reward for doing well at school. Therefore, it is impossible to rule out that the superior test performance of lottery winners was due to external incentives rather than to their schools' test productivity.

Second, both lottery winners and losers tended to enroll in private schools, particularly in larger cities. Focusing on Bogota and Cali, Angrist et al. (2002) point out that while about 94% of lottery winners attended private school in the first year, so did 88% of the losers. This is not surprising to the extent that a high private enrollment rate in secondary was symptomatic of the very supply bottlenecks that the program was implemented to address. Since the reduced form estimates in these papers are based upon a comparison of lottery winners and losers, they may in some cases measure a "private with incentives versus private without incentives" effect, rather than the effect of private versus public schooling per se.

Finally, the institutional setup implies that many voucher winners (who, again, would have enrolled in private school even if they did not win the lottery) used the vouchers to "upgrade" to more expensive private schools. Specifically, Angrist et al. (2002) discuss that the maximum tuition the voucher covered was roughly equivalent to the cost of a low- to mid-price private school, and that it was common for voucher recipients to supplement this amount. Thus, part of the effect of winning a lottery could reflect the access to greater resources, as opposed to a true test productivity difference.

To summarize, these studies support the hypothesis that the Colombian voucher program enhanced student performance. However, the studies cannot distinguish between three plausible mechanisms that may explain their results: increased competition/choice, a direct effect on student incentives, and an increase in resources allocated to education.

7.2.1.2. India. The developing country literature also provides arguably causal estimates of a private/public advantage at other educational levels. For example, Sekhri and Rubinstein (2010) consider whether public universities in India have higher value added than private colleges. This raises the interesting point that while the expectation in most developing countries is that private K-12 institutions perform better than public ones, the reverse is sometimes the case for higher education.[9] This generally happens in settings in which public universities are on average older and more selective. This stacks any cross sectional comparison in their favor.

Sekhri and Rubinstein (2010) suggest that this is also the case in India, where a perception of greater productivity by public colleges has led to calls for constraining the rapid growth of the private sector. For example, they point out that in 1970, 4 out of 139 engineering colleges were private; by 2006, 1,400 out of 1,600 were private.

Sekhri and Rubinstein explore whether a true public university test productivity advantage exists by using a regression discontinuity design. Specifically, they take advantage of the fact that by regulation, private colleges must affiliate with public universities to grant degrees. They must implement the same curricula and admissions and exit examinations as the public universities they associate with. The authors compare the academic performance of students who just missed gaining admission into a selective public college—and are therefore more likely to attend a private institution—with that of individuals who just achieved it. By construction, these individuals have similar admissions exam scores, and any difference in their exit exam performance is suggestive of a public/private productivity differential. This strategy produces no evidence of such a difference.

Finally, Sekhri and Rubinstein calculate the costs of these institutions, and find average costs of 13,000 and 13,700 rupees for private and public colleges, respectively. They conclude that public colleges do not have a cost-related advantage either.

To summarize, the literature on whether there is a private test productivity advantage produces mixed results; the estimated effects do not seem to be of a regularity or magnitude such that transferring students into private schools would by itself substantially and reliably raise achievement. This finding is consistent with a broader literature on the effects of attending a higher-achieving school or class on academic performance, even when these transfers occur within a given (public or private) sector. Here again several papers find little or no effect (e.g., Abdulkadiroglu, Angrist, and Pathak 2011; Clark 2010; Cullen, Jacob, and Levitt 2005, 2006; Dobbie and Fryer 2011; Duflo, Dupas, and Kremer 2008) and some find positive effects (e.g., Jackson, 2010; Pop-Eleches and Urquiola 2013) but no uniform pattern emerges.

7.2.2. The Effects of Large-Scale Competition. Private/public comparisons essentially address a "partial equilibrium" question: how would a given student's achievement change if she transferred from a public to a private school? In contrast, studies of generalized school choice address the general equilibrium effects of competition: for example, what would be the effect of substantial private school entry into a market?

This is a relevant contrast because the magnitude of the private advantage may not be stable with respect to the private sector's market share. For example, Hsieh and Urquiola (2006) and Bettinger, Kremer, and Saavedra (2008) point out that if the private productivity advantage originates in positive peer effects, then the magnitude of this advantage may change with growth in the private sector. This in turn reflects that the composition of the students in the private and public sector is likely to change with private entry.

Tiebout choice (arising from the fact that many households can choose to settle in one of multiple school districts) provides the main opportunity to study large-scale competition in the United States. Here again, the literature produces mixed results rather than a distinct sense that greater choice raises testing outcomes (e.g., Hoxby 2000; Rothstein 2007). At the same time, there is evidence that Tiebout choice can lead to stratification (e.g., Clotfelter 1998; Urquiola 2005), which combined with causal peer effects would lead to the distributional considerations treated in models like Epple and Romano (1998).

These issues also arise in developing country settings in ways that potentially productively contribute to the literature. We begin with the case of Chile, which provides one of the central examples of the application of the principles put forth by Friedman (1962). (Several of the studies we touch upon are also discussed in chapter 5 of this volume, which discusses reforms that alter student and parent incentives.)

7.2.2.1. Chile. In 1981 Chile introduced a universal voucher scheme.[10] Prior to this reform, three types of schools were in operation: (a) public schools managed by the national government, which accounted for about 80% of enrollment; (b) unsubsidized private schools catering to upper-income students and accounting for about 6% of enrollment; and (c) subsidized private schools that did not charge tuition, received limited lump-sum subsidies, were often Catholic, and accounted for roughly 14% of enrollment.

The 1981 reform had two main components. First, it transferred public school management to municipalities, awarding them a per-student subsidy sufficient to cover their costs. Second, subsidized (or "voucher") private schools began to receive the same per-student subsidy as municipal schools.

The key elements of the reform persist to the present day, and place few restrictions on private schools. These schools can be religious and can operate for profit. They are allowed to implement admissions policies subject to few regulations, and as of 1997 can charge tuition add-ons. In contrast, public schools are not allowed to turn away students unless oversubscribed and cannot charge tuition at the primary level.

These changes resulted in substantial private school entry. By 2009, about 57% of all students attended private schools, with voucher schools alone accounting for about 50%. The latter, combined with a public share of 44% means that about 94% of all children attend effectively voucher-funded institutions.[11]

The analytical virtue of this reform is that it provides an example of a large-scale introduction of competition into an educational market. The main drawback is that the simultaneous nationwide implementation makes it difficult to establish counterfactuals. As a result, most studies have adopted quasi-experimental methodologies. Hsieh and Urquiola (2006) apply a difference-in-differences approach to municipalities for the 1982–1996 period. They find that municipalities that experienced faster growth in private sector market share show distinct signs of increasing stratification (with the higher-income students in the public sector moving to private schools), but do not display higher growth in test scores or years of schooling.

Even setting identification issues aside, these estimates do not isolate the effects of competition on school test productivity in the sense of Hoxby (2002). Many things were changing for Chilean schools during this period, including the distribution of students (and hence potential peer effects) and levels of funding.[12] Taken at face value, however, these findings suggest that competition had a modest effect on average school productivity. However, despite the use of some candidate instrumental variables, private entry into school markets is endogenous and hence there is always the possibility that the estimates are biased.

Auguste and Valenzuela (2006) and Gallego (2006) analyze cross-sectional data, using instruments for the private market share. Auguste and Valenzuela use the distance to a nearby city, and Gallego uses the density of priests per diocese (with the motivation that this lowered the costs of Catholic schools). The results from both papers differ with Hsieh and Urquiola (2006) in that both find that private entry results in higher achievement, and concur (in the case of Auguste and Valenzuela—Gallego does not analyze the issue) in finding that it also leads to stratification. Again, however, a key issue is the validity of the instrumental variables.[13]

This research must also be considered alongside aggregate trends. If there exists a substantial private productivity advantage, then one would expect Chile's relative performance on national and international tests to have improved over the years in which large numbers of children were transferred into the private sector. Furthermore, one would expect Chile to outperform other countries with similar levels of gross domestic product per capita. Neither of these predictions receives much support in the data. Other than a recent improvement in PISA test scores, national test scores in Chile have been largely stagnant even as educational spending has increased substantially.[14] Privatization has thus been associated with a decline in school test productivity.

Finally, Bravo, Mukhopadhyay, and Todd (2010) analyze the effect of Chilean reform not on test scores but on graduation rates and wages.[15] Specifically, they use retrospective survey data to estimate a dynamic model of school attendance and work decisions. The impact of the reform in this case is identified using differences in the schooling and work choices of individuals who were differentially exposed to the voucher system—that is, individuals from different cohorts were exposed to different amounts of educational competition. They find that the voucher reform increased primary and high school graduation rates by 0.6 and 3.6 percentage points respectively. They also find that it did not increase average earnings.

In short (as also discussed in chapter 5 of this volume), the research on the effect of large-scale school-choice reforms on average outcomes in Chile produces mixed results. In contrast, there is robust evidence that competition resulted in increased stratification by family background and ability. These results are consistent with the consensus within Chile (as articulated recently by the country's conservative President Piñera) that the school-choice system "perpetuates inequality" and has not done enough to raise learning. This is in marked contrast with Chile's track record of success with market-oriented reforms in many other sectors of the economy.

7.2.2.2. Pakistan. The cases of Chilean and Colombian K-12 schooling, and Indian higher education, illustrate situations in which the use of private institutions takes place in middle-income settings and with significant state subsidies. However, developing countries also provide settings in which private schools enter and compete unaided in low-income markets. These cases are frequently more challenging to study, if only because the necessary data are not as readily available.

Andrabi, Das, and Khwaja (2008) document substantial growth in private enrollment in four large provinces in Pakistan during the 1990s. For example, they find that private enrollment grew from 4% to 6% in Balochistan, and from 15% to 30% in Punjab. This expansion took place in both urban and rural areas. The result is that "by the end of the 1990s, nearly all rich Pakistani children in urban areas, almost a third of the richer rural children, and close to 10% of children in the poorest deciles nationally were studying in private schools."[16]

Andrabi, Das, and Khwaja (2008) emphasize that this growth is not due to an expansion of religious schools (e.g., Madrasas), but rather reflects an expansion in for-profit institutions that charge very low fees—a typical village private school in these provinces charges about 18 dollars per year.[17] These schools achieve extremely low costs by hiring young, single, untrained local women as teachers and paying them much less than the trained men more common in public schools.[18]

These observations imply that Pakistan could in fact buy education for much lower cost if it further shifted enrollments to the private sector. Would these savings come at a cost of lower educational attainment? "Not necessarily," according to Andrabi, Das, and Khwaja. First, they note evidence by Das, Pandey, and Zajonc (2006) suggesting that an estimated private school test advantage persists in Pakistan even after controlling for child, household, and community characteristics. Andrabi, Das, and Khwaja point out, however, that this result relies on less solid empirical identification than, for example, the studies on Colombia reviewed above.

In summary, Pakistan illustrates that in much of the developing world, private schools can enter and provide competition even without state support. As in the case of Chile, private entry is associated with significant stratification (as suggested by the authors' broad description of the users of these schools, cited above) but need not result in lower achievement. Andrabi, Das, and Khwaja (2008) also highlight the potential limits to such expansion. A notable one is that private entry has mostly occurred at the primary level. Secondary education would require for-profit private schools to hire trained teachers, driving their costs up significantly.

To summarize the contents of this section thus far, the evidence from developing countries suggests that large scale expansions of the private school sector lead to stratification, but there is less evidence that they lead to substantial gains in average school productivity.[19] This is consistent with the lack of a systematic private school advantage, and additionally suggests that the introduction of competition may not by itself have a large impact on public school productivity.

7.2.3. Other Pieces of the Puzzle. Overall, the evidence is, perhaps surprisingly, not strongly supportive of Friedman's hypothesis that parental concern for school quality, combined with schools' concern for their reputation, implies that increased competition would produce substantial improvements in school productivity.

This result is even more surprising given the usual expectation that parents value school testing performance. For example, Black (1999) uses US data and quasi-experimental methods to show that households are willing to pay more for houses that give them access to schools with higher test scores.[20] In an experimental setting, Hastings and Weinstein (2008) show that parents react to information on school performance by requesting higher-scoring schools. While the developing country literature does not provide such direct evidence, households in many countries (including Chile, Colombia, and Pakistan, as discussed above) are willing to leave the public sector to move into private schools with higher absolute outcomes, often at substantial cost to themselves.

This willingness to pay for schools with higher absolute achievement—combined with the evidence reviewed earlier—suggests that in many cases parents prefer such schools even if they do not provide higher value added (e.g., Abdulkadiroglu, Angrist, and Pathak 2011). The question, then, is why are parents so eager to access selective schools given the paucity of evidence that they provide higher test productivity? As emphasized by Hoxby (2002), the standard explanation has centered on peer effects. Positive human capital spillovers would warrant a preference for higher performing schools even if these do not supply higher value added. Two problems immediately arise with this explanation, however.

The first is simple but often not appreciated. It is that human capital spillovers are conceptually and empirically part of a school's value added. When papers like Cullen, Jacob, and Levitt (2005), Clark (2010), and Sekhri and Rubinstein (2010) produce a reduced form estimate that suggests no benefit to attending a higher-achievement school, this estimate includes peer effects. If academic peer effects are truly positive, then these schools may have even lower value added than the lower absolute achievement schools that families so eagerly pay to escape. Since the higher-achievement schools are often more expensive, they could be of substantially lower productivity.

Second, the direct evidence on the significance and magnitude of peer effects is rather mixed and suggests these are small (Angrist and Lang 2004; Katz, Kling, and Liebman 2006; Oreopoulos 2003). In a recent study Carrell, Sacerdote, and West (2010) directly control classroom composition as a function of student performance. They find no reliable effect of peer group composition on student performance. In conclusion, when studies are better able to control for selection based upon ability, they find modest peer effects.

7.2.4. Where Is Empirical Research 50 Years after Friedman? Five decades after Friedman's seminal 1962 work on school choice, economists do not have a full understanding of the impact of private participation and competition on the performance of educational markets. The evidence

thus far is mixed. When it comes to policy in developing countries, this stands in stark contrast to our more successful policy interventions, such as, in many cases, using privatization to enhance the performance of the telecommunications sector.

Another way of seeing that competition has not produced the desired results is by taking stock of where empirical economic research on education is today. Two topics receiving a great deal of attention are:

1. Randomized evaluations of educational interventions, and
2. The design and implementation of methodologies to identify and reward/terminate especially effective/ineffective teachers.

Neither of these approaches is particularly consistent with Friedman's market and incentive-centered approach. Underlying Friedman's idea is the theme that bureaucrats (and perhaps researchers) might not be able to discover how to improve education, but that given the right incentives, market actors would do so. Hanushek (1995) articulates this view: "My own interpretation of the existing evidence . . . is that schools differ in important ways, but we cannot describe what causes these differences very well." Given this perspective, Hanushek argues for providing incentives and letting market actors figure out the production function:

> Performance-based policies are those that reward accomplishment—such as good reading skills or adequate numeracy skills. These policies would specify end goals, provide carrots and sticks related to them, and harness the energies of the actors in the system, but they would not specify how individual schools would achieve these goals.

In contrast, in his review of approach (1), Banerjee (2007) calls for economists to "step into the machine"—to enter schools and discover the specifics of the educational production function. In advocating for this planning approach, Banerjee explicitly criticizes Friedman's market and incentive-centered approach: "To those who believe in it, the word 'incentives' is an abstraction, a metonymy for faith in the power of the market. They do not claim to know how exactly the market will achieve the promised miracle, but it will do it (indeed for them this unpredictability is part of the appeal)." To summarize, by calling for economists themselves to use randomization to discover the educational production function, Banerjee suggests an approach manifestly distinct from letting markets figure out the best course of action.

Similarly, in presenting explicit recipes regarding when/how teachers should be hired and fired, Hanushek (2011) differs from an approach that would leave such decisions to incentivized principals or private-school owners. This is obviously not how other competitive markets are designed. For example, it would be considered heavy-handed for government to dictate when/how restaurants should fire line cooks.

It might be the case that the focus on randomization and teacher hiring/firing is in response to the difficulty of implementing competition, due to political and other constraints. Yet, at least in the case of Chile, randomization and teacher accountability remain central to the current academic/policy discussion, despite massive privatization. Thus, we conclude that the continued interest by economists in carrying out randomized evaluations and teacher-related interventions reflects that simply liberalizing the market has proven to be disappointing.

7.3. Incomplete Markets, Incomplete Contracts, and Incomplete Knowledge

In this section we trace the intellectual history of some important ideas in modern economics that are necessary for building a sound economic theory of the market for education. We shall show that, in light of these ideas, Friedman's case for free markets cannot be directly justified by an appeal to economic theory. Rather, we suggest that the theory is consistent with the desirability of a regime of managed competition, a ubiquitous feature of all complex markets in advanced market economies.

Our story begins with some foundational contributions dating as far back as the 1950s. These include:

> General equilibrium theory (Arrow and Debreu 1954; Debreu 1959)
> Game theory (Luce and Raiffa 1957; Nash 1951)
> Decision theory (Savage 1954).

This work is technical and, to many, even esoteric. However, the ideas from these contributions are the foundation of modern graduate economics training, and even if not always acknowledged, form the intellectual framework within which economists view the world.[21]

We show that if one takes this research seriously, then there is little reason to expect school choice to enhance school test productivity—in the end it comes down to Charlie Munger's observation (in the quote opening this chapter) that we continually underestimate the power of incentives. Specifically, in this section we review each of these three contributions, discussing how it might suggest that the empirical findings discussed above are not surprising. In Section 4, we describe a model that brings these ideas together, and show that it is consistent with much of the evidence we have discussed.

7.3.1. What Is a Commodity?

Let us begin with general equilibrium theory. The first welfare theorem states that when markets are complete, a competitive equilibrium is efficient. This result does not deal explicitly with the problem of distribution. This is addressed in the second welfare theorem: If markets are complete, and the production technology is "convex," then every efficient allocation can be achieved as a competitive equilibrium after the appropriate redistribution of resources. In principle, there is no tension between efficiency and equity.

One can see immediately that Friedman's idea of introducing competition via vouchers has its root in the second welfare theorem—school vouchers can be used to appropriately redistribute income, while the market efficiently supplies education services. These results explicitly depend upon the existence of complete markets and a convex technology (essentially, there are no economies of scale or other frictions). Education services do not even come close to satisfying either precondition.

First, consider the complete markets assumption carefully defined in chapter 2 of Debreu (1959). At a minimum, it must be possible to price every commodity that is in the market. Technically, a commodity is a good or service that is delivered at a specific time and place, and conditional upon the state of the world at that time (the model is sufficiently rich to deal with uncertain future events).

The first question is what exactly "education" is—what is being supplied to the buyer? In labor economics, education is measured by the number of years of consumption of this service. Yet in practice education consists of many distinct services and goods, including listening to lectures, making presentations, working on assignments, receiving grades as a function of performance, and so on. If one were to use the Arrow-Debreu model (and apply the associated welfare theorems), then each of these various components would have to be measured and priced.

One might argue that these are details for technical nitpicking; however, parents *do* care about such details, and the fact that they are not priced explains many observed behaviors. For example, parents who use a given school often form a preference regarding specific teachers and sometimes lobby to get their children assigned to them. If a teacher's performance is lacking, then parents may file a complaint with the principal. If the market were truly competitive, each teacher-class combination would be priced, and there would be an equilibrium where the teacher-class price would be set so parents were indifferent between the available options.[22]

The fact that there is politicking and lobbying is a natural consequence of market incompleteness. Williamson (1975) makes this point explicitly, and uses the general term "transactions cost" to denote the reason why organizations such as firms and schools use nonmarket mechanisms to allocate resources. One may view the move toward more school choice as an attempt to make the market more complete, which one might expect to lead to enhanced performance. This is not generally correct, however. As shown in Hart (1975), not only is a competitive equilibrium with incomplete markets not necessarily efficient, but making the market more complete by allowing ex post trading can make things worse.

The second welfare theorem also supposes that the technology of production is "convex"—essentially there are no economies of scale. In practice, education is rife with fixed adjustment costs—costs that Williamson (1975) has identified with large potential market failures. In a paradigmatic competitive market, consumers can easily change their choices over time. This is not the case with schools. For starters, the best schools ration supply. Moreover, if one month into the academic year a student discovers that his school is substandard, he might have to wait until the end of the year to switch. Changing schools mid-year is costly, and not feasible for many parents.

To summarize, the welfare theorems show that if markets are complete, then one can use the market mechanism to achieve an efficient and equitable allocation of resources. However, not only are markets in general incomplete, there is no known result—either theoretical or empirical—that proves that making a market *more* complete by allowing free entry and reducing price controls will *necessarily* improve performance.

7.3.2. What Is the School's Obligation? Friedman (1962) anticipated many of the observations we have made regarding the fact that the market for education is incomplete. What he claimed was that free entry and competition would still enhance outcomes because schools would develop reputations for quality that would discipline their behavior. However, a reputation is nothing more than the market's belief regarding the quality of the good that a school is producing. A necessary condition for the efficient operation of a market is that parties can enter into a contract with a well-specified performance obligation, the breach of which leads to a loss in reputation or damages (MacLeod 2007).

Hoxby (2002) introduces a clear definition of a school obligation—namely, producing an increase in test scores at an agreed-upon cost. More productive schools either have better test score performance at the same cost, or the same performance at a lower cost. If test score gains are indeed the output that parents wish to achieve, then the natural way to do this is to have a contract with the school that sets test score gains as an explicit product that the school is expected to deliver. The contract would specify damages for failing to meet this obligation, and at the end of the year the school would simply pay out to parents whose children did not achieve the agreed upon improvements.

Such a contract would lead to obvious incentives to game the system. At the end of a year, parents would have a financial interest in having their children perform poorly in exams, regardless of their actual learning during the year. Further, test scores are noisy and only imperfectly controlled by schools (e.g., Chay, McEwan, and Urquiola 2005; Kane and Staiger 2002). One can create systems that control for this behavior and improve the precision of test scores, but one cannot escape from the fundamental problem that any school performance measure that is not *directly controlled* by the school can be gamed.

More generally, as MacLeod (2007) emphasizes, a well-designed contract imposes obligations that are easy to observe and under the control of the agent who has the obligation. In the case of education, the school can control the curriculum, the qualifications of teachers, school hours, amount of homework, and so on.[23] Many jurisdictions, such as New York City, have experimented with systems that reward test score productivity, ignoring these other measures. Yet there is little evidence that these experiments have been successful. This finding is consistent with the more than 100 years of evidence on compensation systems, as we discuss next.

7.3.3. Strategic Behavior. When markets are incomplete, firms/schools have incentives to make strategic product choices. The industrial organization literature, having long recognized this point, contains an extensive literature on product differentiation. This research builds upon the second theme from the 1950s—the use of Nash equilibrium to model choice behavior.[24] This approach yields several insights.

Suppose schools competing with each other choose the bundle of services to sell taking as given the bundles provided by other schools. The literature identifies two strategies they might follow, both of which complicate the link between free entry/competition and increased productivity.

The first is horizontal differentiation. This involves characteristics over which parents are not unanimous in their preferences. For example, some schools may emphasize sports, while others focus on academics or music. A particularly important characteristic in education is location—parents often prefer schools that are close to their homes. Spence (1973) and Dixit and Stiglitz (1977) introduce a model of "Chamberlinian competition" and show that with strategic product choice there may be too few or too many products in the market. Another example is the popular model of product choice on a line due to Hotelling (1929). An interesting feature of this model is that if the world has well-defined boundaries, and firms can choose price and location, then in some cases firms all crowd in the middle of the market, leaving students away from the center poorly served.[25]

Second, there is vertical differentiation, where firms sort in terms of quality (Gabszewicz and Thisse 1979). Below we will describe a model we have developed (MacLeod and Urquiola 2012), which shows that when schools can vertically differentiate through their admissions policies, then a competitive equilibrium need not be efficient. Moreover, increasing private participation may have ambiguous consequences on skill accumulation. Before turning to that illustration, we discuss a few more points related to strategic behavior.

7.3.4. Expectations and Hope. Let us now move from the issue of the supply of educational services to the issue of student demand. In general, education is a multi-product good, of which test-score performance is only one dimension. Parents also care about the physical attributes of the school, dress codes, athletic programs, and so on. This implies that expanding school choice might raise parents' and students' welfare because they obtain more of a commodity they desire; it does not imply that test scores will necessarily increase.

Further, a test score is merely a signal that many parents hope is correlated with future labor market success, as emphasized in the labor economics literature. In this case, parents, and perhaps policymakers, should focus on schools' *wage* as opposed to *test* productivity. It is difficult to measure wage productivity, but we are seeing some progress.

Bravo, Mukhopadhyay, and Todd (2010) examine the impact of the Chilean school reform on wages and find that while the reform slightly reduced inequality, it had little effect upon lifetime earnings.

To illustrate the notion of wage productivity, let $\hat{w}_A(x, A)$ be the average wage of a person of age A, with x years of schooling. Then the return to an additional year of schooling is $r(x,A) = \dfrac{\hat{w}_A(x+1, A) - \hat{w}_A(x,A)}{\hat{w}_A}$. From this the *wage productivity* would be:[26]

(1) $$WP(x, K, A) = \frac{r(x, K)\hat{w}_A}{K} = \frac{\hat{w}_A(x+1, A) - \hat{w}_A(x, A)}{K},$$

where K is the cost of the additional year of schooling. This is the increase in income due to an additional year of schooling, divided by its cost.

Despite the work of Bravo, Mukhopadhyay, and Todd (2010) and studies like Card and Krueger (1992), measuring a concept like wage productivity at the level of individual schools (a precondition if parents are to evaluate schools based on such a measure) is very difficult. This point is emphasized by Speakman and Welch (2006), who review attempts to measure the relationship between school quality and future wages. They conclude that there are serious problems associated with establishing such a link, and hence parents and students have no reliable way to assess the causal impact of school quality on future labor market outcomes. If so, how can students and parents rationally choose a school?

This is where the third major contribution from the 1950s is relevant. Savage (1954) introduced the idea that the first step when making a rational choice is to build a model of the future. In particular, even if there is little evidence, rational individuals will form subjective probability assessments that link current actions to future outcomes. Without such beliefs, decisions would just be noise.

In the context of education: How should a parent evaluate the consequences of attending a particular school? The algorithm that many parents (at least the authors of this chapter) use is to see how the previous graduates of a given school performed: Did they go to college? Are they now "successful"? Do they exhibit "good" behavior? This is rough and ready, but it is nonetheless based upon concrete evidence. As a result, parents and students may place weight upon tangible evidence that comes from peer success at a school. Given that there is no easy way to relate marginal test-score performance to future "hopes and dreams," they are unlikely to respond to such signals.

Notice that employers are likely to use similar algorithms—for example, college recruiting firms explicitly target campuses where they have had previous success. In section 7.4 we describe research (MacLeod and Urquiola 2012) that makes these ideas more precise and, again, shows that if competitive firms use the reputation of a school an employee attended to assess her quality, then competition may not necessarily raise test score levels.

There is an important caveat. Here we have assumed that test scores are merely a measure of student learning. In some countries, there are real labor-market consequences to test-score performance. For example, China, France, Romania, Singapore, and Turkey have national exams whose results are published and have real consequences for higher-education and labor-market outcomes. Both Bishop (1997) and Woessmann (2007) suggest that these jurisdictions outperform others in terms of test-score productivity, although making causal assertions in this area is difficult.

These observations are consistent with the hypothesis that what is driving school demand are expectations regarding future outcomes. When test scores and future labor-market outcomes are more tightly linked, then individuals respond. When they are not linked, then individuals respond to other measures of future performance, such as the past outcomes of peers at one's school.[27] It is these expectations writ large, balanced against the many other amenities supplied by schools, that drive school demand.

Consider some empirical motivation relevant to developing countries. Figure 7.1 is based on IPUMS (Integrated Public Use Microdata Series) information and shows the proportion of individuals who are not working ("not in the universe" for area of work in the IPUMS terminology) as a function of their level of schooling. For a benchmark, the top segment refers to the United States, and the lower two segments refer to Tanzania and Ghana.

A first observation is that among people with very low levels of schooling (no schooling or only primary completed), a large fraction does not work in the United States. This is not surprising as this is a highly selected sample in high-income settings (e.g., disabled individuals). The more notable fact for our purposes is that that while the fraction not working descends significantly and consistently with schooling in the United States, that is not as much the case in Tanzania or Ghana. In these two countries it displays a more gradual descent with occasional increases as one moves to higher-education categories. The implication is that if one of the objectives individuals have in pursuing schooling is avoiding unemployment, then the incentives to study will be lower in Tanzania and Ghana than in the United States.

Fraction of Population Not in Labor Force

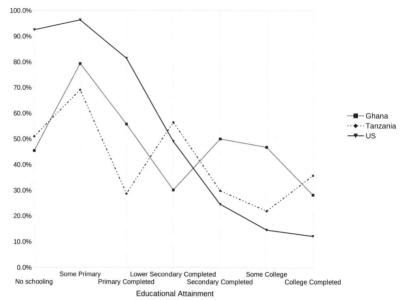

FIGURE 7.1 Fraction of population not in labor force.

7.3.5. Compensation Policies. Before proceeding to an illustration of these ideas we touch upon compensation policies. Taylor (1911) is often regarded as the father of modern management science. He observed closely the behavior of manufacturing workers and found that in many cases employment was inefficient. By this he meant that the firm would like to pay the workers more for higher output, and at the same time the workers themselves would agree to work harder for the increased compensation. These findings suggested that a pay-for-performance system would be Pareto-improving.

Implementing performance-pay systems has proven to be extraordinarily difficult. The fundamental issue is that mechanical performance-pay systems are almost always subject to some form of gaming. In what has become a business school classic, Kerr (1975) documents several examples of failed incentives systems. The problem is not that individuals do not respond to incentives—quite the contrary—they respond too readily. Thus, Kerr points out that many organizations claim, or hope, to be rewarding B when in fact they are rewarding A.

For example, universities often stress the importance of teaching. Yet, compensation is typically linked to a person's outside opportunities, which, for most academics, is more closely related to research rather than teaching performance. To the extent that compensation is linked to teaching performance, this is achieved via teaching evaluations. Having sat on faculty promotion committees, we can attest to the fact that teaching evaluations do have some weight in faculty evaluation. Yet, as Arum and Roksa (2011) observe, these evaluations sometimes result in faculty making courses easier so that their student/clients are happier, rather than in necessarily improving their future job prospects.

In a recent analogous example, Reback (2008) documents that schools strategically respond to accountability systems that specify minimum competency requirements (e.g., systems that measure the proportion of students who pass a given statewide test). Schools focus their effort on students who are close to the passing score, diverting it away from, for example, students who will clearly score above it.

More generally, there has been extensive research on pay-for-performance systems in the hope of reducing the inefficiencies that Taylor (1911) noted. The National Academy sponsored a study in 1991 (Milkovich and Wigdor 1991) that explored the extent to which performance pay could be used to enhance government. They concluded:

> The search for a high degree of precision in measurement does not appear to be economically viable in most applied settings; many believe that there is little to be gained from such a level of precision. The committee concludes that federal policy makers would not be well served by a commitment of vast human and financial resources to job analysis and the development of performance appraisal instruments and systems that can meet the strictest challenges of measurement science. The committee further concludes that, for most personnel management decisions, including annual pay decisions, the goal of a performance appraisal system should be to support and encourage informed managerial judgment, not to aspire to the degree of standardization, precision and empirical support that would be required of, for example, selection tests.

Despite this skepticism, there has been increased interest in implementing performance-pay systems for teachers. For example, the US Department of Education has introduced a fund to encourage states to measure and reward teacher performance (the Race to the Top Fund).[28] Recently, the National Academy returned to the issue of performance pay with particular attention to teacher compensation (Hout and Elliott 2011). The conclusion:

> Our review of the evidence uncovered reasons to expect positive results from incentive programs and reasons to be skeptical of apparent gains. Our recommendations, accordingly, call for policy makers to support experimentation with rigorous evaluation and to allow mid-course correction of policies when evaluation suggests such correction is needed.

This nuanced view is consistent with a century of experimentation with performance pay systems. MacLeod and Parent (1999) document the use of performance pay in the US economy, finding that performance pay is explicitly used in about 30% of jobs. Its use is highly correlated with job characteristics: the incidence of performance pay is much higher for jobs for which there is a clean, unambiguous measure of performance. This is particularly evident in sales, where revenue is often a good measure of a salesperson's productivity.

If there are significant subjective elements to employee performance, then explicit performance pay is not a silver bullet. Holmström and Milgrom (1991) highlight the fact that if one can measure only a single dimension of individual performance, then rewarding only that element can distort behavior away from the efficient solution. If there are differences of opinion regarding what constitutes good performance, then the optimal contract is flat or there is increased conflict between management and employees as one increases the link between measured performance and pay (MacLeod 2003).

In the case of education, one should keep in mind that test scores are diagnostics, and not goals in and of themselves. They measure a student's command of information that is correlated with the ultimate goal—namely, obtaining meaningful employment in the future. The fact that many educators focus upon test scores, while students care about future employment, helps explain why educators and students/parents may not always agree on the way forward.

7.4. An Illustration

In recent work we attempt to provide a concrete illustration of the ideas raised in section 7.3. To do so, we add elements of industrial organization and labor economics to the more public finance–focused theory of school choice. Specifically, in MacLeod and Urquiola (2012) we construct a model in which students go to school, acquire skills, and then work in a competitive labor market.

7.4.1. Setup. Relative to the existing literature the model has three key novel ingredients:

1. *Students have to exert effort to accumulate skill.* Although student effort has not been a focus of the literature, Bishop (2006) has emphasized its importance; student learning is a joint product of school and student inputs. Moreover, it is clear from cross-country evidence that societal levels of educational effort display wide variation. Dang and Rogers (2008) illustrate such variation in their review of evidence on private tutoring industries that exist in many countries. For example, Korean households spend 2.9% of GDP on private tutoring, which approaches the 3.4% the public sector allocates to education. In Turkey, private spending similarly approaches the public effort. Tutoring expenditures have been growing quickly in Canada, Kenya, and Vietnam.[29] Finally, there is growing empirical research on interventions to elicit effort (see, e.g., Angrist, Lang, and Oreopoulos 2009; Kremer, Miguel, and Thornton 2009).

2. *Schools have reputations given by their graduates' expected skill.* Since Spence (1973), the idea that an individual's years of schooling can signal her ability has been standard in labor economics. We introduce school reputation to capture the idea that *conditional* on years of schooling, the identity of the school a person attended can provide the market with information regarding her ability. This is consistent with research on Colombia (Saavedra 2009) and the United States (Hoekstra 2009) that uses regression discontinuity designs to show that school identity/ prestige has a positive effect on wages—upon entry into the labor market and about five years later, respectively.[30]

3. *The school sector is perfectly competitive in that private schools with selective admissions and different levels of value added are free to enter.* We assume educational systems consist of a continuum of schools, each of which contains a continuum of students. We thus abstract from small numbers problems, which differentiates our model from earlier work on school choice, such as Epple and Romano (1998). These models focus on monopolistic competition where there is an efficient scale for schools, and hence each school has some market power. Conceptually, such a setup supposes that the number of schools is fixed in the short run, and that students select into schools (see Nechyba 2006 for a general discussion of this class of models). Our concern, rather, is with

understanding the implications of perfect competition in the presence of reputation effects. Thus, the model incorporates elements of test productivity, wage productivity, school reputation, and parental demand, factors that are central concerns of the literature we have reviewed.

The model has two periods. In the first, student *innate ability* is realized when individuals are born, but it is not directly observed. Ability can be revealed only after an individual learns and engages with the world. When this happens, individuals, schools, and the labor market observe signals that lead them to update their beliefs regarding individual ability.

One such signal is *family background*, which is observed by all agents.[31] Another is an *admissions test* observed by individuals and schools prior to enrollment. This measure is soft information that is not verifiable by employers.

Schools select admissions policies that, to different extents, exploit the admissions test and family background; these policies are public information. Schools also set their value added. Students then choose among the set of schools that have offered them admission. They also make consumption choices and decide how much effort to allocate to study. Finally, student skill is realized as a function of three factors: student innate ability, student effort, and school value added.

In the second period, students graduate and enter the labor market. The market observes two signals of individual skill:

1. The *identity/reputation* of the school attended by each student; when schools are selective, this provides a signal of the student's innate ability. We assume that no given individual can (through his own effort) affect his school's reputation. Intuitively, this reflects that in reality a school's reputation is based on the characteristics of multiple cohorts of graduates, and no single person can easily manipulate such a measure.

2. An individual-specific measure of skill we term a *graduation test*. As its name indicates, this measure can be motivated using the highly publicized standardized high school graduation or college entry exams in countries such as Germany, Romania, South Korea, and Turkey. Other individual-specific measures are seen in other settings and educational levels. For example, in the United States college graduates distribute letters of recommendation and lists of honors received, while economics PhD students distribute "job market papers." Finally, in contrast to her inability to affect her school's reputation, we assume that through her effort a student can directly affect her graduation assessment.

The labor market sets wages equal to expected skill given these two signals. To summarize, we situate an analysis of school system test productivity (how much learning is produced for a given level of resources) in a context in which individuals and schools respond to incentives.

In this setup we have focused upon signals of ability that follow from family background, an assessment that takes place before students apply to school, and an assessment given immediately upon graduation. In practice, the evaluation of an individual's ability is an ongoing process. What is important, and we feel realistic, is that no test or assessment is perfectly predictive of future ability.

For example, the background of American presidential candidates is carefully scrutinized, yet there still seems to be a great deal that one learns about their abilities after they get the job. Our economics department has an analogous discussion during each graduate admissions round—we have plenty of information on individuals' test scores, but these signals are only imperfectly correlated with a student's future ability for research.

Our graduate students realize this, and so even if they do not have the top test scores, they can still hope to make significant contributions to research. However, they cannot do so if they do not get admitted to graduate school. Moreover, getting into a more prestigious graduate program means that they will have a step up in the job market. This in turn means that they *do* care about a program's reputation, and all else equal would want admission to the most prestigious department possible. We now turn to the implications of these observations for school choice.

7.4.2. Implications: The Anti-Lemons Effect. The first result from our setup is that parents/students will prefer schools with better reputations—they will value selectivity and better peers per se. Due to signaling concerns, students will prefer schools with higher achievement even if this advantage does not originate in higher value added or positive peer effects (indeed, our model does not even feature the latter).

This result can reconcile three observations highlighted in section 2: (a) there is clear evidence that parents prefer higher achieving schools; (b) the evidence on whether higher achieving schools produce higher *value added* is mixed; and (c) the evidence on the significance and magnitude of peer effects is also mixed. Note that in our model the concern for peer quality emerges *endogenously*—students will wish to attend schools whose graduates have been successful in the past. As previewed above, this highlights a contrast with earlier theoretical work on school competition by Benabou (1996) and Nechyba (2000), which also predicts stratification; in these models sorting originates in unpriced peer externalities.

A second set of results concerns the impact of private entry and competition on the system's performance. These follow from an *anti-lemons* effect that arises when firms (schools) can influence their reputation by positively selecting their buyers (students). Specifically, in MacLeod and Urquiola (2012) we show that:

1. All else equal, competition will raise school productivity, capturing Friedman's (1962) intuition. However, this need not always be the case. In some situations, students will prefer a school with lower value added, provided its reputation (due to an outstanding peer group) is strong enough. In such settings, increasing choice and competition may actually lower average school productivity.[32]

2. Private entry may have detrimental effects on effort, and therefore on skill accumulation. Suppose there is a system that originally consists of nonselective public schools (i.e., of schools that essentially admit applicants at random). Now consider the entry of selective private schools (i.e., schools that admit based on students' performance in the admissions assessment) into this setting. This will tend to lower student effort among the students who attend such schools. This is a straightforward application of Holmström (1999). The intuition is that as selectivity increases, school reputation provides a more precise signal of student skill. As a result, the extent to which an individual is able to affect the market's assessment of his skill through the one signal he can affect—the graduation test—falls, and hence so does the incentive to study. This implies, for example, that if the introduction of school choice results in stratification, then it might not result in large academic achievement gains. The prediction that school selectivity lowers effort is also consistent with anecdotal and circumstantial evidence on student behavior. For example, students in Japan work very hard to get admitted to elite schools like the University of Tokyo, yet those who are successful are said to dramatically lower their effort once there. In the United States, Hoxby (2009) shows that the selectivity of colleges has increased over the past decades, while Babcock and Marks (2010) document that during this same period, the amount of time spent studying declined from 40 to 27 hours per week.

3. The entry of private selective schools has adverse effects on the effort of students who remain in the nonselective sector[33]—an illustration of the effect of stratification on student hope and aspirations.[34] The intuition is that the students left behind in these schools are revealed to the labor market as being of lower ability. By a logic similar to that in the previous point, they therefore have a lower incentive to signal their

skill via the graduation test. Individuals left behind in the nonselective public schools find that their peers are less successful than the students from more selective schools, and this lowers their motivation. This result is a natural consequence of a Bayesian framework in the spirit of Savage (1954). Note also that social learning research indicates that peer success is salient for individuals when forming beliefs regarding their future (Bandura 1986).

These predictions are consistent with cases in which independent schools are subsidized and allowed to be selective. As described above, in 1981 Chile implemented school choice in a manner that fits our framework. Consistent with our predictions, private schools entered by cream-skimming, enrolling the wealthiest children. Further, the private sector itself is highly stratified. For instance, Mizala, Romaguera, and Urquiola (2007) show that the identity of the school a child attends is a good predictor of her household income. Meanwhile, the market share of the private sector has grown—particularly in urban areas, the public sector accounts for a distinct minority (20–30% of enrollments in some cases), and is composed primarily of the lowest-income students.

More generally, our model implies that educational markets will display a strong tendency toward stratification—in fact there is no equilibrium to the simple framework described above if only nonselective private entry is allowed. This suggests that schools will rationally try to engage in some kind of selection as a means of securing a market niche. Consistent with this notion, even in cases in which selection by independent schools is not allowed, one sees that it emerges in different ways.

For example, in the United States most states require that charter schools select by lottery if oversubscribed. But even in this context, there is anecdotal evidence that some charter schools (potentially for quite understandable reasons) engage in selection within the constraints imposed by the law. For instance, the well-known KIPP academies require that parents and students sign certain participation commitments to apply (e.g., students may have to commit to attend schools on Saturdays, or parents to take part in PTA meetings). The result is that at least in terms of motivation these schools are not equivalent to the public ones they compete with. Similarly, in the case of Sweden, independent voucher schools operate under similar selection restrictions as US voucher schools. Yet Bjorklund et al. (2005) conclude that their entry increases segregation across schools, as immigrants and children with highly educated parents are more likely to enroll in them.

This analysis suggests that selection/stratification may be a central feature of stable education markets. For example, the US higher-education market features substantial private participation, and also substantial stability; the group of institutions that comprise the top 20 universities or colleges changes little over time.

Finally, one way to mitigate the negative impact of private entry—and more generally raise educational systems' performance—is by raising the precision of individual-specific measures of skill, as emphasized by Bishop (2006). Consistent with this idea, Woessmann (2007) points to a country-level correlation of standardized graduation or college admissions exams and international test performance. In anecdotal evidence, few observers disagree that such high-stakes examinations result in high levels of student and parental effort. Additionally, casual observation suggests that the presence of such examinations may be one of the driving factors behind the large private tutoring industries studied by Dang and Rogers (2008).

7.5. Conclusion

Given the fall of communism and the success of the deregulation movement over the last 40 years, it is widely agreed that free markets have the potential to dramatically improve the quality and lower the cost of many goods and services. At the same time, this period has seen increased dissatisfaction with the public provision of education, leading to calls for more choice and competition in the market for education. This view is illustrated in the introduction to the World Bank's (2004) *World Development Report* on public service delivery:

> Poor people—as patients in clinics, students in schools, travelers on buses, consumers of water—are the clients of services. They have a relationship with the frontline providers, with schoolteachers, doctors, bus drivers, water companies. Poor people have a similar relationship when they buy something in the market, such as a sandwich (or a samosa, a salteña, a shoo-mai). In a competitive-market transaction, they get the "service" because they can hold the provider accountable. That is, the consumer pays the provider directly; he can observe whether or not he has received the sandwich; and if he is dissatisfied, he has power over the provider with repeat business or, in the case of fraud, with legal or social sanctions. For the services considered here—such as

health, education, water, electricity, and sanitation—there is no
direct accountability of the provider to the consumer.

The implication, as the report goes on to discuss, is that introducing
greater choice and competition in these services would produce greater
accountability and enhance outcomes.

We have discussed a large literature on the effectiveness of this approach, finding that increased competition has had mixed success in
raising school test productivity. The key insight we use to explain this
finding is that education is not a commodity in the normal sense of the
term—in other words, education is *not* like a sandwich or a samosa.

For instance, in many ways education can be better understood as
an employment relationship. Students are in some sense "employed" by
teachers who must encourage, coach, and otherwise cajole their flock
into acquiring a set of skills that is beneficial to them in the distant future. Most economists would be surprised if a particular industry was
required to perform well while not having the right to choose its employees. Yet, we expect (at least public) schools to "employ" all students and
to successfully engage them. In a sense, schools are students' first and
last opportunity to be treated in this way. Upon graduation, they face a
labor market where employers have no obligation to employ them or to
keep them if hired.

Accordingly, we have discussed a model of education that builds
upon the employment model of Holmström (1999) to capture some of
the ways in which education is a complex commodity. These include
(a) several of its key outputs are difficult to contract upon; (b) from a
consumer's perspective, many of its key products (e.g., long-term job-
market outcomes) are observed significantly after the transaction between student and school has taken place; (c) education requires significant relationship-specific investments that imply that it is costly for
students to switch schools; (d) schools' productivity is extremely difficult
to disentangle from their student composition (hence the reason for the
whole private/public comparison literature), and so reputations can be
durably built on student composition; and (e) unlike policymakers, parents and students do not care about test scores per se—they care about
the opportunities that attending a particular school will offer them in the
future, and perhaps also about what consumption the school's amenities
allow them in the present.[35]

These and other such considerations suggest that "competition plus
reputation" is not sufficient to improve school productivity. It is worth

highlighting the fact that in a modern market economy, free competition is really a fiction. All markets for sophisticated goods rely upon a complex legal and regulatory framework operating in the background. In the case of transportation, there are safety regulations that must be respected. New drugs must pass regulatory approval before entering the market place. In China recent experiences with tainted food products are likely to lead to greater food-industry regulation.

Since education is also a complex good, the issue is not really one of private versus public provision, but one of market design, and what might be better called "managed competition."[36] Our analysis has highlighted that one key design issue is the link between education and future rewards. In an environment where the labor market cannot easily observe individual productivity, then it will rely upon other signals such as school reputation. This leads to an anti-lemons effect that adversely affects the least able students.

This again reflects that the challenge facing education is similar to an employment relationship, where the firm confronts the problem of motivating its marginal workers. Successful individuals continually receive positive feedback and hence are encouraged to work hard to get more rewards. It is harder to provide rewards to effort for less-able individuals. We have argued that the evidence is consistent with the hypothesis that unfettered competition in the market for schools, combined with imperfect information about ability, leads to a stratified school system and an anti-lemons affect—less-able individuals are negatively selected when young. These individuals may not expect to receive significantly higher rewards in the future, regardless of how hard they work. Given this prospect, many young people rationally work less hard, perpetuating the cycle of inequality.

To overcome the anti-lemons effect, countries that want to raise their testing performance might choose to make their test scores more meaningful in terms of determining individuals' outcomes. China is an example of such a design, since in its case doing well in national tests has been a route to success for hundreds of years. In short, our point is that if the goal is to improve testing performance to Shanghai levels, this might be very hard to achieve merely by introducing private or charter schools. Rather, the structure of the educational system might have to be changed significantly, such that parents and students are able to see clear links between their effort and the outcomes they care about. For example, a system that allows free entry by schools but restricts their ability to select students, combined with high-quality individual performance measures, may perform better than a pure *laissez-faire* system.

In terms of dealing with the lower tail of the distribution, a solution may lie in an observation made by Holmström and Milgrom (1987) regarding the design of incentives in a complex dynamic environment. They show that optimal rewards should be designed so that, regardless of one's past performance, one is always rewarded for improved effort. In the context of education, it is important to avoid reward systems with the feature that students who fall below a certain performance level view engaging in noneducational activities as more rewarding. A similar principle applies to teacher rewards—weak teachers should face positive rewards for incremental improvements in performance. The current trend to threaten them with dismissal may simply lead to low morale and worse performance until the day of judgment arrives. In the meantime, both students and society pay the costs. This is just the theory. Putting effective solutions into practice is much harder and will require more research.

Acknowledgments

We thank Lorne Carmichael, Sebastian Galiani, Paul Glewwe, Patrick McEwan, and workshop participants for helpful comments. For excellent research assistance we thank Wilfredo Lim and Evan Riehl. We are grateful for funding from the International Growth Center and the Russell Sage Foundation. All opinions and remaining errors are our own.

Notes

1. Later versions of such models do feature reduced-form productivity effects from competition, see, e.g., Epple and Romano 2008.

2. For instance, The World Bank (2004, chapter 9) provides examples of success stories in utility privatization.

3. Due to space constraints we do not focus on point (3).

4. For example, in a recent World Bank report, Patrinos, Barrera-Osorio, and Guaqueta (2009) open their review of the literature by stating that "the existing evidence from around the world shows that the correlation between private provision of education and indicators of educational quality is positive, which suggests that the private sector can deliver high quality education at low cost."

5. Holland (1986) calls this—not being able to observe the outcomes of the same student under public and private schooling—the fundamental problem of causal inference.

6. In this literature the focus is mainly on determining if private schools have an advantage in terms of value added as opposed to cost-effectiveness. Chapter 8 in this volume describes a general framework for evaluating cost-effectiveness in

the context of developing country education policy. For a general discussion on cost-effectiveness issues in education, see Levin and McEwan 2001.

7. The controversy surrounds the effects on subgroups—the conclusion for these varies with how subgroups are defined.

8. There is of course a large literature on private/public comparisons in developing countries, one that extends beyond these two cases. As is the case in the United States, papers meet with varying success in terms of establishing credible control groups; some implement cross-sectional analyses only, others look for explicit sources of exogenous variation. For a review of several countries, see Patrinos, Barrera-Osorio, and Guaqueta 2009. For reviews on Latin America, see Somers, McEwan, and Willms 2004. For reviews on Chile see Bellei 2007 and McEwan, Urquiola, and Vegas 2008. For work on India see Kingdon 1996; on Indonesia, Newhouse and Beegle 2006; and on Pakistan, Das, Pandey, and Zajonc 2006.

9. Brazil and Chile are relevant examples. Newhouse and Beegle (2006) suggest that Indonesian public schools benefit from positive selection even at the primary level.

10. For further institutional details see McEwan and Carnoy 2000 and Urquiola and Verhoogen 2009.

11. The "elite" unsubsidized private schools account for about 6% of enrollments.

12. The value of the school voucher fell significantly during the 1980s and grew substantially during the 1990s.

13. It is possible, for example, that more motivated parents migrate toward cities in search of better schools, or that priests were allocated to communities in a manner correlated with characteristics (e.g., population density) that might affect educational achievement.

14. This improvement in PISA test scores is observed in reading and not in math, and it is concentrated among low-income children, who predominantly attend public schools. Given the numerous reforms that have occurred in Chile over the past two decades (e.g., compensatory funding for schools with low-income students, accountability initiatives, teacher pay reform, early childhood programs, and so on) it is difficult to attribute this change to a particular intervention, let alone to the introduction of school choice three decades back.

15. The latter is an outcome we focus on below; we cite the results here but return to this aspect of the study below.

16. This is certainly not the only case of large-scale unsubsidized private school entry in low-income areas. For instance, Kremer and Muralidharan (2006) point out that about 25% of children in rural India have access to fee-charging private schools. There is less data on such low-cost private schools in Latin America, but the anecdotal evidence is certainly consistent with a significant role for them, particularly in poor urban neighborhoods.

17. See also Alderman, Orazem, and Paterno 2001.

18. Andrabi, Das, and Khwaja (2008) note that the fact that these women are often high school graduates from public schools is one way in which the public sector indirectly supports the private sector.

19. For other examples of school market liberalization leading to stratification see Bjorklund et al. 2005 and Mbiti and Lucas 2009 for the cases of Sweden and Kenya, respectively.

20. See also Fack and Grenet 2010.

21. Even many economists may not be familiar with the formal details of these contributions. This work shows that the concepts that are used daily in economics, such as free markets, opportunity cost, the irrelevance of sunk costs for current decisions, market equilibrium, risk, rational expectations, and so on can be placed into a coherent and unified mathematical framework. This, we suggest, explains in part why the economic mode of reasoning has been so powerful in policy debates.

22. In addition, parents and students consume a collection of other goods that are packaged with the education services, including afterschool programs, the quality of the physical plant, and so on. In a competitive market, each of these would be priced.

23. A nice example of an enforceable contract that produces skill acquisition is the apprenticeship contract. See Malcomson, Maw, and McCormick 2003 on how this contract is designed to achieve an efficient skill acquisition.

24. See Tirole's (1988) classic text for an illustration of the power of game theory for understanding market structure.

25. D'Aspremont, Gabszewicz, and Thisse (1979) showed that for such a model there does not exist a Nash equilibrium in prices (a result that Mac-Leod [1985] generalized to the multiproduct case that is particularly relevant for schools). Existence would be restored if schools could collude on prices, in which case the market equilibrium would be characterized by schools moving to the center of the preference distribution and earning rents, leaving students with specialized needs underserved.

26. It is worth observing that we are measuring productivity only with regards to the pecuniary cost of education. A more complete measure would also include the disutility/cost of attending school, as in Spence 1973. Even though individual effort does play a role in the theory, since it is not easily measured it plays no role in traditional measures of school performance.

27. See also recent work suggesting that the schooling choices of individuals in developing countries respond to changes in the perceived wage returns to schooling, e.g., Jensen 2010 and Oster and Millett 2010.

28. See http://www2.ed.gov/programs/racetothetop/index.html.

29. For other work on how the presence of a private tutoring industry affects incentives in the public sector, see Jayachandran 2008.

30. Dale and Krueger (2002) find no effect of school selectivity on wages about 20 years after graduation. Note, however, that all three studies could be consistent with an impact of school selectivity on *starting* wages, since a Bayesian framework would predict this effect would become attenuated over time as the market gained more information on individuals' ability—this is in fact the prediction of the model we describe below.

31. There is evidence that family background provides some information regarding a person's likely future ability (Almond and Currie 2011).

32. For example, this case can arise if the government constrains the number of schools, as happens in many jurisdictions.

33. In MacLeod and Urquiola 2012 we show an equilibrium exists where selective private and nonselective public schools coexist.

34. Coate and Loury (1993) make a similar point about the negative effect of racial stereotypes. Austen-Smith and Fryer (2005) show that behaviors, such as "acting white," can be viewed as signaling phenomena.

35. The World Bank (2004) arrives at conclusions distinct from ours precisely because it assumes education is like a conventional good. For example, implicit in its arguments is that parents can easily evaluate a school's wage productivity, when as discussed by Speakman and Welch (2006), this might be close to impossible.

36. Chapter 6 in this volume also highlights the importance of market design for education policy in the context of School Management interventions.

References

Abdulkadiroglu, A., J. Angrist, and P. Pathak. 2011. "The Elite Illusion: Achievement Effects at Boston and New York Exam Schools." National Bureau of Economic Research Working Paper No. 17264. Available at http://www.nber.org/papers/w17264.

Alderman, H., P. Orazem, and E. Paterno. 2001. "School Quality, School Cost, and the Public/Private School Choices of Low-Income Households in Pakistan." *Journal of Human Resources* 36 (2): 304–26.

Almond, D., and J. M. Currie. 2011. "Human Capital Development before Five." In *Handbook of Labor Economics*, vol. 4, ed. O. Ashenfelter and D. Card, 1315–1486. San Diego, CA: North Holland.

Andrabi, T., J. Das, and A. Khwaja. 2008. "Students Today, Teachers Tomorrow: Identifying Constraints on the Provision of Education." Mimeo, World Bank. Available at http://www.cgdev.org/doc/event%20docs/MADS/ADK_PriSchools_Feb06.pdf.

Angrist, J., E. Bettinger, E. Bloom, M. Kremer, and E. King. 2002. "The Effect of School Vouchers on Students: Evidence from Colombia." *American Economic Review* 92 (5): 1535–58.

Angrist, J., E. Bettinger, and M. Kremer. 2006. "Long-Term Educational Consequences of Secondary School Vouchers: Evidence from Administrative Records in Colombia." *American Economic Review* 96 (3): 847–62.

Angrist, J. D., and K. Lang. 2004. "Does School Integration Generate Peer Effects? Evidence from Boston's Metco Program." *American Economic Review* 94 (5): 1613–34.

Angrist, J., D. Lang, and P. Oreopoulos. 2009. "Incentives and Services for College Achievement: Evidence from a Randomized Trial." *American Economic Journal: Applied Economics* 1 (1): 136–63.

Arnott, R., and J. G. Rowse. 1987. "Peer Group Effects and Educational Attainment." *Journal of Public Economics* 32 (3): 287–305.

Arrow, K. J., and G. Debreu. 1954. "Existence of an Equilibrium for a Competitive Economy." *Econometrica* 22 (3): 265–90.

Arum, R., and J. Roksa. 2011. *Academically Adrift*. Chicago: University of Chicago Press.

Auguste, S., and J. P. Valenzuela. 2006. "Is It Just Cream Skimming? School Vouchers in Chile." Mimeo, Fundacion de Investigaciones Economicas Latinoamericanas.

Austen-Smith, D., and R. Fryer. 2005. "An Economic Analysis of 'Acting White.'" *Quarterly Journal of Economics* 120 (2): 551–83.

Babcock, P. S., and M. Marks. 2010. "The Falling Time Cost of College: Evidence from Half a Century of Time Use Data." NBER Working Paper 15954. Available at http://www.nber.org/papers/w15954.

Bandura, A. 1986. *Social Foundations of Thought and Action*. Englewood Cliffs, NJ: Prentice-Hall.

Banerjee, A. 2007. "Inside the Machine: Toward a New Development Economics." *Boston Review* 32 (2): 12–18.

Barrow, L., and C. Rouse. 2009. "School Vouchers and Student Achievement: Recent Evidence and Remaining Questions." *Annual Review of Economics* (January): 17–42.

Bellei, C. 2007. "The Private-Public School Controversy: The Case of Chile." Working paper, Harvard PEPG Working Paper 05-13. Available at http://www.periglobal.org/sites/periglobal.org/files/BELLEI%20-PEPG-05-13%20 Private%20Public%20in%20Chile.pdf.

Benabou, R. 1996. "Heterogeneity, Stratification, and Growth: Macroeconomic Implications of Community Structure and School Finance." *American Economic Review* 86 (3): 584–609.

Bettinger, E., M. Kremer, and J. E. Saavedra. 2008. "Are Educational Vouchers Only Redistributive?" *Economic Journal* 120 (546): F204–F228.

Bishop, J. H. 1997. "The Effect of National Standards and Curriculum-Based Exams on Achievement." *American Economic Review* 87 (2): 260–64.

———. 2006. "Drinking from the Fountain of Knowledge: Student Incentive to Study and Learn." In *Handbook of the Economics of Education*, vol. 2, ed. E. A. Hanushek and F. Welch, 909–44. Amsterdam: Elsevier B.V.

Bjorklund, A., M. Clark, P.-A. Edin, P. Frederiksson, and A. Krueger. 2005. *The Market Comes to Education in Sweden*. New York: Russell Sage Foundation.

Black, S. 1999. "Do Better Schools Matter? Parental Valuation of Elementary Education." *Quarterly Journal of Economics* 114 (2): 577–99.

Bravo, D., S. Mukhopadhyay, and P. Todd. 2010. "Effects of School Reform on Education and Labor Market Performance: Evidence from Chile's Universal Voucher System." *Quantitative Economics* 1 (2): 47–95.

Card, D., and A. B. Krueger. 1992. "Does School Quality Matter—Returns to Education and the Characteristics of Public-Schools in the United States." *Journal of Political Economy* 100 (1): 1–40.

Carrell, S. E., B. I. Sacerdote, and J. E. West. 2010. "Beware of Economists Bearing Reduced Forms? An Experiment in How Not to Improve Student Outcomes." NBER Summer Institute 2010. Available at http://www.nber.org/papers/w16865.ack.

Chay, K., P. McEwan, and M. Urquiola. 2005. "The Central Role of Noise in Evaluating Interventions That Use Test Scores to Rank Schools." *American Economic Review* 95 (4): 1237–58.

Clark, D. 2010. "Selective Schools and Academic Achievement." *B.E. Journal of Economic Analysis and Policy: Advances* 10 (1): 9.

Clotfelter, C. 1998. "Public School Segregation in Metropolitan Areas." Mimeo, National Bureau of Economic Research Working Paper no. 6779. Available at http://www.nber.org/papers/w6779.

Coate, S., and G. Loury. 1993. "Will Affirmative-Action Policies Eliminate Negative Stereotypes?" *American Economic Review* 85 (5): 1220–40.

Cullen, J., B. Jacob, and S. Levitt. 2005. "The Effect of School Choice on Student Outcomes: An Analysis of the Chicago Public Schools." *Journal of Public Economics* 89 (5–6): 729–60.

———. 2006. "The Effect of School Choice on Student Outcomes: Evidence from Randomized Lotteries." *Econometrica* 74 (5): 1191–1230.

D'Aspremont, C., J. Gabszewicz, and J. Thisse. 1979. "Hotelling's Stability in Competition." *Econometrica* 47 (5): 1145–50.

Dale, S. B., and A. B. Krueger. 2002. "Estimating the Payoff to Attending a More Selective College: An Application of Selection on Observables and Unobservables." *Quarterly Journal of Economics* 117 (4): 1491–1527.

Dang, H.-A., and H. Rogers. 2008. "The Growing Phenomenon of Private Tutoring: Does It Deepen Human Capital, Widen Inequalities, or Waste Resources?" *World Bank Research Observer* 23 (2): 161–200.

Das, J., P. Pandey, and T. Zajonc. 2006. "Learning Levels and Gaps in Pakistan." Working paper, World Bank Policy Research Working Paper no. 4067. Washington, DC: World Bank.

Debreu, G. 1959. *Theory of Value.* New Haven, CT: Yale University Press.

Dixit, A., and J. Stiglitz. 1977. "Monopolistic Competition and Optimal Product Diversity." *American Economic Review* 67:217–35.

Dobbie, W., and R. Fryer. 2011. "Exam High Schools and Academic Achievement: Evidence from New York City." NBER Working Paper no. 17286. Available at http://www.nber.org/papers/w17286.

Duflo, E., P. Dupas, and M. Kremer. 2008. "Peer Effects, Teacher Incentives, and the Impact of Tracking: Evidence from a Randomized Evaluation in Kenya." NBER Working Paper no. 14475. Available at http://www.nber.org/papers/w14475.

Epple, D., and R. E. Romano. 1998. "Competition between Private and Public Schools, Vouchers, and Peer-Group Effects." *American Economic Review* 88 (1): 33–62.

———. 2008. "Education Vouchers and Cream Skimming." *International Economic Review* 49:1395–1435.

Fack, G., and J. Grenet. 2010. "When Do Better Schools Raise Housing Prices? Evidence from Paris Public and Private Schools." *Journal of Public Economics* 94 (1–2): 59–77.

Friedman, M. 1955. "The Role of Government in Education." In *Economics and the Public Interest,* ed. R. Solo. New Brunswick, NJ: Trustees of Rutgers College.

Friedman, M., with the assistance of Rose D. Friedman. 1962. *Capitalism and Freedom.* Chicago: University of Chicago Press.

Gabszewicz, J., and J. Thisse. 1979. "Price-Competition, Quality and Income Disparities." *Journal of Economic Theory* 20 (3): 340–59.

Gallego, F. 2006. "Voucher School Competition, Incentives, and Outcomes: Evidence from Chile." Mimeo. MIT, Cambridge, MA. Available at http://laje-ce.org/economia_puc/images/stories/profesores_jornada_completa/fgallego/vouchers.pdf.

Hanushek, E. 1995. "Interpreting Recent Research on Schooling in Developing Countries." *World Bank Research Observer* (August).

———. 1996. "The Productivity Collapse in Schools." In *Developments in School Finance*, ed. W. Fowler, 183–95. Washington, DC: National Center for Education Statistics.

———. 2011. "The Economic Value of Teacher Quality." *Economics of Education Review* 30 (3): 466–79.

Hart, O. 1975. "On the Optimality of Equilibrium When the Market Structure Is Incomplete." *Journal of Economics Theory* 11 (3): 418–43.

Hastings, J., and J. Weinstein. 2008. "Information, School Choice, and Academic Achievement: Evidence from Two Experiments." *Quarterly Journal of Economics* 123 (4): 1373–1414.

Hoekstra, M. 2009. "The Effect of Attending the Flagship State University on Earning: A Discontinuity Approach." *Review of Economics and Statistics* 91 (4): 717–24.

Holland, P. W. 1986. "Statistics and Causal Inference." *Journal of the American Statistical Association* 81 (396): 945–60.

Holmström, B. 1999. "Managerial Incentive Problems: A Dynamic Perspective." *Review of Economic Studies* 66 (1): 169–82.

Holmström, B., and P. Milgrom. 1987. "Aggregation and Linearity in the Provision of Intertemporal Incentives." *Econometrica* 55:303–28.

———. 1991. "Multi-Task Principal-Agent Analyses: Incentive Contracts, Asset Ownership, and Job Design." *Journal of Law, Economics, and Organization* 7:24–52.

Hotelling, H. 1929. "Stability in Competition." *Economic Journal* 39 (153): 41–57.

Hout, M., and S. W. Elliott, eds. 2011. *Incentives and Test-Based Accountability in Education*. Washington, DC: National Academies Press.

Hoxby, C. 2000. "Does Competition among Public Schools Benefit Students and Taxpayers?" *American Economic Review* 90 (5): 1209–38.

———. 2002. "School Choice and School Productivity (Or Could School Choice Be a Tide That Lifts All Boats?)." NBER Working Paper no. 8873. Available at http://www.nber.org/papers/w8873.

———. 2009. "The Changing Selectivity of American Colleges." *Journal of Economic Perspectives* 23 (4): 95–118.

Hsieh, C.-T., and M. Urquiola. 2006. "The Effects of Generalized School Choice on Achievement and Stratification: Evidence from Chile's School Voucher Program." *Journal of Public Economics* 90:1477–1503.

Jackson, C. K. 2010. "Do Students Benefit from Attending Better Schools?: Evidence from Rule-Based Student Assignments in Trinidad and Tobago." *Economic Journal* 120 (549): 1399–1429.

Jayachandran, S. 2008. "Incentives to Teach Badly? After School Tutoring in Developing Countries." Mimeo, Stanford University, Stanford, CA.

Jensen, R. 2010. "The Perceived Returns to Education and the Demand for Schooling." *Quarterly Journal of Economics* 125 (2): 515–48.

Kane, T. J., and D. O. Staiger. 2002. "The Promise and Pitfalls of Using Imprecise School Accountability Measures." *Journal of Economic Perspectives* 16 (4): 91–114.

Katz, L., J. Kling, and J. Liebman. 2006. "Experimental Analysis of Neighborhood Effects." *Econometrica* 75 (1): 83–119.

Kerr, S. 1975. "On the Folly of Rewarding A, While Hoping for B." *Academy of Management Journal* 18 (4): 769–83.

Kingdon, G. 1996. "The Quality and Efficiency of Private and Public Education: A Case Study of Urban India." *Oxford Bulletin of Economics and Statistics* 58 (1): 57–82.

Kremer, M., E. Miguel, and R. Thornton. 2009. "Incentives to Learn." *Review of Economics and Statistics* 91 (3): 437–56.

Kremer, M., and K. Muralidharan. 2006. "Public and Private Schools in Rural India." Mimeo, Harvard University, Cambridge, MA.

Krueger, A., and P. Zhu. 2004. "Another Look at the New York City Voucher Experiment." *Behavioral Scientist* (January): 658–98.

Levin, H., and P. McEwan. 2001. *Cost Effectiveness Analysis*. Thousand Oaks, CA: Sage Publications.

Luce, R. D., and H. Raiffa. 1957. *Games and Decisions*. New York: Dover Publications.

MacLeod, W. B. 1985. "On the Non-Existence of Equilibria in Differentiated Product Models." *Regional Science and Urban Economics* 15 (2): 245–62.

———. 2003. "Optimal Contracting with Subjective Evaluation." *American Economic Review* 93 (1): 216–40.

———. 2007. "Reputations, Relationships and Contract Enforcement." *Journal of Economics Literature* 45:597–630.

MacLeod, W. B., and D. Parent. 1999. "Job Characteristics and the Form of Compensation." *Research in Labor Economics* 18:177–242.

MacLeod, W. B., and M. Urquiola. 2012. "Anti-Lemons: School Reputation and Educational Quality." Technical Report 6805, Institute for the Study of Labor (IZA).

Malcomson, J., J. Maw, and B. McCormick. 2003. "General Training by Firms, Apprentice Contracts, and Public Policy." *European Economic Review* 47 (2): 197–227.

Mayer, D., P. Peterson, D. Myers, C. Tuttle, and W. Howell. 2002. "School Choice in New York City after Three Years: An Evaluation of the School Choice Scholarships Program: Final Report." Technical report, Mathematica Policy Research, Inc., Princeton, NJ.

Mbiti, I., and A. Lucas. 2009. "Access, Sorting, and Achievement: The Short-Run Effects of Free Primary Education in Kenya." Technical report, Southern Methodist University, Dallas, TX.

McEwan, P. 2004. "The Potential Impact of Vouchers." *Peabody Journal of Education* 79 (3): 57–80.

McEwan, P., and M. Carnoy. 2000. "The Effectiveness and Efficiency of Private Schools in Chile's Voucher System." *Educational Evaluation and Policy Analysis* 22 (3): 213–39.

McEwan, P., M. Urquiola, and E. Vegas. 2008. "School Choice, Stratification, and Information on School Performance: Lessons from Chile." *Economia* 8 (2): 1–27.

Milkovich, G. T., and A. K. Wigdor. 1991. *Pay for Performance: Evaluating Performance and Appraisal Merit Pay.* Washington, DC: National Academies Press.

Mizala, A., P. Romaguera, and M. Urquiola. 2007. "Socioeconomic Status or Noise? Tradeoffs in the Generation of School Quality Information." *Journal of Development Economics* 84:61–75.

Nash, J. F. 1951. "Non-Cooperative Games." *Annals of Mathematics* 54: 286–95.

Neal, D. 2009. "Private Schools in Education Markets." In *Handbook of Research on School Choice*, ed. M. Berends, M. Springer, D. Balou, and H. Walberg, 447–60. New York: Routledge.

Nechyba, T. J. 2000. "Mobility, Targeting, and Private-School Vouchers." *American Economic Review* 90 (1): 130–46.

———. 2006. "Income and Peer Quality Sorting in Public and Private Schools." In *Handbook of the Economics of Education*, vol. 2, ed. E. A. Hanushek and F. Welch, 1327–68. Amsterdam: Elsevier.

Newhouse, D., and K. Beegle. 2006. "The Effect of School Type on Academic Achievement: Evidence from Indonesia." *Journal of Human Resources* 46 (2): 529–57.

Oreopoulos, P. 2003. "The Long-Run Consequences of Living in a Poor Neighborhood." *Quarterly Journal of Economics* 118 (4): 1533–75.

Oster, E., and B. Millett. 2010. "Do Call Centers Promote Enrollment? Evidence from India." Discussion Paper, University of Chicago.

Patrinos, H., F. Barrera-Osorio, and J. Guaqueta. 2009. *The Role of and Impact of Public-Private Partnerships in Education.* Washington, DC: World Bank.

Pop-Eleches, C., and M. Urquiola. 2013. "Going to a Better School: Effects and Behavioral Responses." *American Economic Review* 103 (4): 1289–1324.

Pritchett, L. 2003. "Educational Quality and Costs: A Big Puzzle and Five Possible Pieces." Mimeo, Harvard University, Cambridge, MA.

Reback, R. 2008. "Teaching to the Rating: School Accountability and the Distribution of Student Achievement." *Journal of Public Economics* 92:1394–1415.

Rothstein, J. 2007. "Does Competition among Public Schools Benefit Students and Taxpayers? Comment." *American Economic Review* 95 (5): 2026–37.

Saavedra, J. 2009. "The Learning and Early Labor Market Effects of College Quality: A Regression Discontinuity Analysis." Mimeo, Harvard University, Cambridge, MA.

Savage, L. J. 1954. *The Foundations of Statistics.* New York: Wiley.

Sekhri, S., and Y. Rubinstein. 2010. "Do Public Colleges in Developing Countries Provide Better Education Than Private Ones? Evidence from General Education Sector in India." Mimeo, University of Virginia, Charlottesville.

Somers, M.-A., P. McEwan, and D. Willms. 2004. "How Effective Are Private Schools in Latin America?" *Comparative Education Review* 48 (1): 48–69.

Speakman, R., and F. Welch. 2006. "Using Wages to Infer School Quality." In *Handbook of the Economics of Education*, vol. 2, ed. E. A. Hanushek and F. Welch, 813–64. Amsterdam: Elsevier.

Spence, M. 1973. "Job Market Signaling." *Quarterly Journal of Economics* 87 (3): 355–74.

Taylor, F. W. 1911. *The Principles of Scientific Management*. New York: Harper.

Tirole, J. 1988. *The Theory of Industrial Organization*. Cambridge, MA: MIT Press.

Urquiola, M. 2005. "Does School Choice Lead to Sorting? Evidence from Tiebout Variation." *American Economic Review* 95 (4): 1310–1326.

Urquiola, M., and E. Verhoogen. 2009. "Class-Size Caps, Sorting, and the Regression Discontinuity Design." *American Economic Review* 99 (1): 179–215.

Williamson, O. E. 1975. *Markets and Hierarchies: Analysis and Antitrust Implications*. New York: Free Press.

Woessmann, L. 2007. "International Evidence on School Competition, Autonomy, and Accountability: A Review." *Peabody Journal of Education* 82 (2–3): 473–97.

World Bank. 2004. *World Development Report 2004: Making Services Work for Poor People*. Washington, DC: World Bank.

8

Comparative Cost-Effectiveness Analysis to Inform Policy in Developing Countries: A General Framework with Applications for Education

Iqbal Dhaliwal (Abdul Latif Jameel Poverty Action Lab [J-PAL])
Esther Duflo (MIT and J-PAL)
Rachel Glennerster (J-PAL)
Caitlin Tulloch (J-PAL)

8.1. Introduction to Cost-Effectiveness Analysis

In the last 15 years there has been a sharp increase in the number of rigorous evaluations of the impact of development programs in a host of fields including education, health, environment, agriculture, finance, and governance. One of the major objectives of such studies is to provide evidence to policymakers on what works and does not work in the fight against poverty, so they can use scientific evidence to determine which policies and programs to adopt and invest in.[1] But it can be very difficult for policymakers to compare results from different programs and their evaluations, performed in different countries, in different years, and that use different instruments to achieve the same outcome. For instance, studies have evaluated the impact on years of schooling of a deworming program in Kenya, conditional cash transfers in Mexico, providing free uniforms in Kenya, and providing information to parents in Madagascar. Faced with a growing body of evidence from field research and given their time and resource constraints, policymakers can find it very hard to analyze and interpret the results of multiple studies, most of which are published in technical or academic journals. As a result, policymakers may decide to ignore such evidence altogether and go back to relying on their instincts on what works or does not work, or selectively choose studies that support their instincts or predetermined choices.

One way to encourage policymakers to use the scientific evidence from these rigorous evaluations in their decisionmaking is to present evidence in the form of a cost-effectiveness analysis, which compares the impacts and costs of various programs run in different countries and years that aimed at achieving the same objective. Some earlier work has attempted to compare the relative cost effectiveness of different education programs within a particular context. For example, Kremer, Miguel, and Thornton (2009) show the relative cost effectiveness of different programs carried out by International Child Support in Kenya; while Banerjee et al. (2007) compare education programs run by the NGO Pratham in India. Limiting an analysis to programs carried out by the same organization in the same country makes it easier to ensure that costs and impacts are calculated using the same methodology, but it restricts the range of interventions that can be compared. Drawing comparisons across projects performed in different countries, by different organizations, and in different years, as we discuss in this chapter, raises many more questions about how to ensure comparability, but it also holds the promise of being a more useful tool for policymakers. Examples exist of this kind of analysis, such as Carnoy (1975), although they seem to be infrequent in the literature. A major challenge in this kind of analysis is to strike the right balance in the tradeoff between the need for policymakers to see comparisons in a form that is intuitive and easy to understand and the need to present enough information to help them appreciate the finer nuances of the programs, including the programs' sensitivity to various factors such as population density or certain large input costs. We believe that the value of promoting the use of scientific evidence in policymaking is sufficiently high that it is valuable for researchers to create such analyses, while explicitly stating their assumptions and clearly acknowledging the limitations.

Cost-effectiveness analysis by itself does not provide enough information for a policymaker to make an investment decision, but such analysis does provide a very useful starting point for researchers and policymakers to collaborate in assessing the efficacy of the different programs and their relevance to a particular situation. Cost-effectiveness analysis results, with detailed information on underlying costs and impacts, combined with an understanding of the problem being addressed and of other contextual factors such as current input prices and local institutions, can provide important insights into which programs are likely to provide the greatest value for money in a particular situation, and to identify the key factors to which these outcomes are most sensitive. When cost-effectiveness analyses have been done with data at a highly disaggregated level, where assumptions about key factors such as program take-up or unit costs are made explicit, it is much easier to perform sensitivity analysis. This sort of sensitivity analysis gives policymakers an idea of how cost effective a similar program might be in their situation by varying key assumptions to reflect their context.

There is a substantial literature on how to conduct cost-effectiveness and cost-benefit analyses, much of which has been written for the assessment of domestic policies in the United States or other developed countries (Levin and McEwan 2001; US Department of Health and Human Services 1996). But there is no single right methodology—the appropriate assumptions to make usually depend on the precise question being asked or how the analysis will be used. For example, whether to include user costs as a cost of the program will depend on whether the objective of the policymaker or implementer is to maximize cost effectiveness of the implementer or of society as a whole. This chapter examines many of these questions by presenting a standardized approach to applying cost-effectiveness analysis to inform educational policymaking in developing countries.

In this chapter we discuss various alternative assumptions and methodologies, which of these are most appropriate in what situation, and why J-PAL as an organization has chosen the particular approach that we use in constructing comparative cost-effectiveness analyses. We illustrate our discussion of cost-effectiveness methodology with an analysis of programs that seek to increase student attendance in different countries. Because we recognize that different policymakers may have different perspectives, we also show how sensitive these results are to different assumptions or approaches, and throughout our analysis we place an emphasis on transparency so that users can understand the various components of the analysis and how it should, and should not, be interpreted. We also suggest some ways to illustrate sensitivities in a way that can be reasonably easy to interpret and include examples of user-friendly sensitivity data throughout the chapter, as well as in appendix 8A. However, it is impossible to include every alternative way of showing the results in one chart, and eventually decisions based on tradeoffs between various alternatives have to be made so that a useful picture of relative cost effectiveness emerges.

Such cost-effectiveness analysis requires detailed underlying cost and impact data. Currently, most published articles evaluating social-sector programs in developing countries, including education, do not provide enough specific cost data to undertake a good cost-effectiveness analysis (Levin 2001). For an excellent listing of the existing articles that do focus on educational cost-effectiveness analyses in the developing world, see the bibliography of Levin and McEwan's (2001) book *Cost-Effectiveness Analysis*. One of our objectives moving forward is to encourage researchers to record detailed cost and impact data (ideally on a standardized basis) and make underlying calculations publicly available so that more, and more complex and rigorous, cost-effectiveness analyses can be done in the future.

8.1.1. Goals of Cost-Effectiveness Analysis. Cost-effectiveness analysis, in the simplest terms, calculates the ratio of the amount of "effect" a program achieves for a given amount of cost incurred or, conversely, the amount of cost required to achieve a given impact. For program evaluation, this means measuring the impact of a program in achieving a given policy goal (e.g., the extra years of schooling induced) against the cost of the program. This ratio, when calculated for a range of alternative programs addressing the same policy goal, conveys the relative impacts and costs of these programs in an easily understandable and intuitive way. However, relatively few studies published in academic journals include cost data on the programs they are evaluating, and what data are available are presented in a wide variety of formats that does not allow for easy comparison between programs. Moreover, what exactly is meant by "costs" and "impacts" is itself subject to considerable debate, depending on the perspective from which the analysis is being undertaken. Are the costs to all stakeholders relevant, or only those that accrue to the implementing organization? Can multiple effects on a number of outcomes be included in the measure of "effectiveness"? To think about these questions, it is important to first explicitly state the goals of cost-effectiveness analysis.

The value of cost-effectiveness analysis is twofold: first, its ability to summarize a complex program in terms of an illustrative ratio of effects to costs, and second, the ability to use this common measure to compare multiple programs evaluated in different contexts and in different years. The first requires technical correctness with respect to the program's actual costs and impacts as they were evaluated, while the second requires adherence to a common methodology for estimating costs and effects across various studies. For cost-effectiveness analysis to be useful and informative, it must maximize the comparability of estimates for different programs without straying from a correct and complete representation of the costs and effects of each program as it was actually evaluated. When done correctly, such analysis can be a useful tool for decisionmakers in organizations that fund or implement education and other social programs in developing countries, allowing them to compare the results of alternative programs when deciding how to allocate resources. This includes funders (such as foundations and international development organizations), and governments and NGOs that both fund and implement programs.

8.1.2. Why Cost-Effectiveness Analysis Rather than Cost-Benefit Analysis?

Cost-effectiveness analysis shows the amount of "effect" a program achieves on one outcome measure for a given cost, while cost-benefit analysis combines all the different benefits of a program onto one scale (usually a monetary scale) and shows the ratio of the combined benefits to cost. The advantage of cost-benefit analysis is that it makes it easier to assess a program with multiple outcomes. Additionally, putting both costs and benefits onto the same scale delivers not just a relative but an absolute judgment: whether or not a program is worth the investment, and which program among several yields the best rate of return. A good example of where cost-benefit analysis is most useful is a program that involves an up-front investment (say, the building of a new hospital) that will generate a stream of benefits (e.g., reduced maintenance costs) in the future. Apply the cost of capital as the discount rate and the result will tell you whether the investment is worthwhile.

The downside of using cost-benefit analysis is that it requires a number of assumptions about the monetary value of benefits on which different organizations may have very different views. When an organization's value of statistical life or years of education is known, then cost-benefit gives very concrete answers. But from a general perspective, where readers may place very different values on outcome measures, a single cost-benefit analysis may not be generally applicable. In the calculation of disability adjusted life years (DALYs), for example, there is disagreement about whether to give different weights to the health of people of different ages (Anand and Hanson 1997), and even once the improvement in the

number of DALYs has been calculated for a program, there is no standard monetary value per DALY. In the case of education in developing
countries, cost-benefit analysis would require, among other things, estimating the increase in productivity achieved as a result of an increase in
school quality or quantity. A monetary valuation of any improvement
in health, intergenerational benefits, and the pure consumption benefits
of education could also be included. However, there are few commonly
agreed-upon monetary values for outcomes such as years of life or increases in test scores, making it difficult to create a single cost-benefit
analysis that would be useful for a wide range of organizations. Cost-
effectiveness analysis, on the other hand, allows users to apply their own
judgment about the value of the benefits. The analysis tells the users
what can be achieved for what cost and leaves it to the user to decide
whether that benefit is worth the cost.

8.1.3. Cost-Effectiveness Analysis in Education. For cost-effectiveness analysis to be a useful alternative to cost-benefit analysis, however, it is necessary to agree on an outcome measure that would be the "key objective"
of many different programs and policymakers. In the field of education
there are a few obvious contenders. Two of the Millennium Development Goals focus on children's school enrollment. Although time spent
in school is an imperfect measure of the increase in education, it does
provide a useful approximation, particularly given the recent focus on
increasing primary school enrollment and attendance. Similarly, there
is increased attention on the need to reduce provider absenteeism, and
standard methods of measuring teacher absenteeism are emerging.
J-PAL recognizes that these are both important aspects of improving
education and is undertaking cost-effectiveness analyses of both of
these outcome measures. For the purposes of this chapter, we will use
the cost-effectiveness analysis for student attendance and enrollment
to illustrate key issues. This analysis includes 13 programs from eight
countries, all of which were assessed using a randomized evaluation.[2] Table 8.1 provides short descriptions of each of the 13 programs.

The analysis, which is summarized in figure 8.1, shows that the cost
effectiveness of programs to increase children's time in school varies
widely, with informational campaigns in Madagascar and school-based
deworming in Kenya providing the greatest value for money among the
programs examined here. Both of these programs can be delivered inex-
pensively and cause large increases in student attendance and enrollment.
Programs that reduce the costs of schooling through subsidies or provide

Table 8.1 Programs included in cost-effectiveness analysis of student attendance and enrollment

	Project	Base Year	Country	Publication
1	Information session on returns to education, for parents	2006	Madagascar	Nguyen 2008
2	Deworming through primary schools	1999	Kenya	Miguel and Kremer 2004
3	Free primary school uniforms	2002	Kenya	Evans, Kremer, and Ngatia 2009
4	Merit scholarships for girls	2001	Kenya	Kremer, Miguel, and Thornton 2009
5	Cash transfers for secondary school girls	2008	Malawi	Baird, McIntosh, and Özler 2011
6	Iron fortification and deworming in preschools	2002	India	Bobonis, Miguel, and Puri-Sharma 2006
7	Building village-based schools	2007	Afghanistan	Burde and Linden 2012
8	Camera monitoring of teachers' attendance	2003	India	Duflo, Hanna, and Ryan 2012
9	Computer-assisted learning curriculum	2001	India	Banerjee et al. 2007
10	Remedial tutoring by community volunteers	2001	India	Banerjee et al. 2007
11	Menstrual cups for teenage girls	2006	Nepal	Oster and Thornton 2011
12	Information session on return to education, for boys	2001	Dominican Republic	Jensen 2010
13	Cash transfers conditional on attendance at primary school	1997	Mexico	Schultz 2000, 2004

incentives conditional on attendance also increase time in school, but at a higher cost, and conditional cash-transfer programs are not as cost effective as a program to increase time in school. As we discuss below, it is important to think about context and the sensitivity of these results to other factors when drawing conclusions for new programs based on these numbers.

A more challenging question for cost-effectiveness analysis is how to appropriately measure the quality of learning in a comparable way across studies. Some educationists believe that test score measures fail to capture some important aspects of learning. We will not engage in that discussion here. Instead we are concerned with how to appropriately compare gains in test scores in one context with such gains in another context. For instance, how do you compare a 7-year-old boy in India learning to recognize letters with a 13-year-old girl in Colombia learning the chemical composition of water? There are internationally standardized tests available that could be used, such as the Program for International Student Assessment Test (PISA), but these are often at too advanced a level to detect changes in test scores in poor countries. The NGO Pratham's rapid assessment tests are a useful tool for testing literacy and basic math skills across countries and have been widely used

COST-EFFECTIVENESS: ADDITIONAL YEARS OF STUDENT PARTICIPATION PER $100

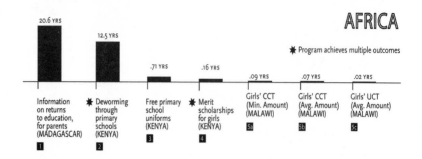

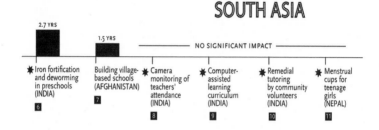

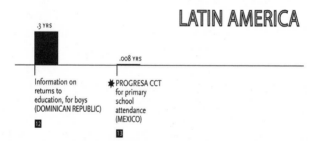

FIGURE 8.1 Cost effectiveness: Additional years of student participation per $100.

in India, Pakistan, Tanzania, Kenya, and Morocco. Most education programs, however, are affecting learning in between these two extremes, and the majority of education evaluations in developing countries therefore use tests that are tailored to the specific context to measure learning outcomes. One practical approach is to use the standard deviation of scores in the control group as the scale against which impact is measured, as is quite common in the education literature.[3] This is the approach that J-PAL is taking in measuring the cost effectiveness of programs aimed at increasing learning. The results of this analysis are not presented here, as it is still ongoing.

8.1.4. Defining the Perspective of Users of Cost-Effectiveness Analyses.

As discussed above, the appropriate methodology to use when doing a cost-effectiveness analysis usually depends on the perspective of the policy-maker who will use it. The methodology that is adopted in the examples given here (and by J-PAL as an organization) is intended for an audience of policymakers in governments, foundations, international development agencies, and NGOs that have a particular policy objective in mind and are trying to decide between a range of different options for achieving that policy objective. We are not trying to help the prime minister of a country or the chairman of a foundation to decide whether to put money into education versus health. In our view, we do not have enough information to help them make that decision, which should reflect the specific social preferences in that country or the mission of that foundation. Instead we are taking the perspective of, for example, the minister of education of a state in India, or an education program officer in a foundation, who aims to maximize the impact on a particular objective such as student attendance within a budget constraint. We assume that the policymakers care not just about their own budgetary costs, but also about the costs that a particular program will impose on the beneficiaries—they are presumably involved in these decisions because they wish to help the beneficiaries of their programs. This perspective influences a number of judgments we make in this chapter.

8.1.5. The Challenge of "Comparative" Analyses.

Because cost-effectiveness analysis is intended as "an input into resource allocation decisions concerning a wide spectrum of alternative programs" (US Department of Health and Human Services 1996), it is necessary to provide comparable figures for programs whose costs and impacts were accrued in different countries, years, and institutional contexts. For example, programs may have been paid for in different currencies (e.g., 2008 dollars versus 1999 pesos) and evaluated with slightly different outcome measures (i.e., percentage change in student attendance versus number of days of schooling gained). But cost-effectiveness analysis requires that these units be harmonized so that the cost-effectiveness ratios for all programs in an analysis are expressed in the same units. There are two primary challenges in arriving at comparable estimates: applying a common methodology to varying sets of data, and making appropriate adjustments to reflect different time, currency, and inflation rates. The rest of the chapter addresses these two issues and is organized as follows: Section 8.2 discusses methods of quantifying program impacts in a standard manner, including spillover and secondary effects. Section 8.3 reviews which costs should be included based on the perspective outlined above and how to assemble accurate cost data from available resources. Section 8.4 discusses the standardization of both costs and benefits into "standard units," accounting for inflation, exchange rates, and varying streams of costs and benefits. Finally, section 8.5 reviews some more general issues with cost-effectiveness analysis, including the generalizability of costs and effects and a discussion of partial and long-term equilibrium effects.

8.2. Quantifying Impacts

In this section we discuss a number of issues related to the calculation of impact.

8.2.1. Sources of Impact Estimates. Many reports and studies attempt to assess the impact of education programs in developing countries. These range in quality from the anecdotal to the highly rigorous. In the examples presented here, we have chosen to include only randomized evaluations. This is not because we think that only randomized evaluations are rigorous or that there is nothing to be learned from nonquantitative studies. However, this cost-effectiveness work has been undertaken under the auspices of J-PAL, which applies randomized evaluations to social programs to understand what works or does not work in the fight against poverty, and randomization provides a transparent criterion for selection of studies. As a result we have excluded some rigorous nonrandomized studies (including some done by the authors), but we believe that this is compensated for in the resulting transparency of the selection process. By being transparent in our methodology, we make it possible for others to add more programs to our comparisons.

8.2.2. Programs Achieving Multiple Impacts. Cost-effectiveness analysis, by definition, focuses on the ratio of costs a program incurs to progress it causes in *one* outcome measure, but antipoverty programs often have multiple impacts on the lives of the poor (see, e.g., chapter 5). This means that, in some cases, the chosen outcome measure may not reflect the full set of impacts of the program being analyzed. Giving children free school meals increases attendance at preschools, and its cost effectiveness can be expressed in terms of cost per additional years of attendance. But school meals may also improve children's nutritional status, an additional impact that is "bought" with the same dollars as the increased attendance (Kremer and Vermeersch 2004).

This is an issue that cannot be easily resolved within the framework of cost-effectiveness analysis, which deliberately focuses on a single-outcome measure of compelling interest to policymakers. As discussed above, cost-benefit analysis may be more suited to comparing programs with multiple outcomes, although it does so at a cost of reduced transparency. In some cases it may be possible to separate out the proportions of a program's costs that are "responsible" for different impacts. An example might be a conditional cash-transfer program that offers incentives for both school attendance and regular doctor appointments for children. If the incentives are given separately, the impacts on education could be assumed to be mainly from the education subsidy rather than the health subsidy (unless one believed that improved health contributed significantly to increased school attendance). In this case it might be appropriate to include only the costs of the education subsidy in the cost-effectiveness analysis for education outcomes, and only the costs of the health incentive in the cost-effectiveness analysis for health outcomes. On the other hand, separating out the costs of overhead and administration can be much harder.

An alternative approach, which some researchers are experimenting with, does not attempt to allocate costs by outcome, but accepts that a program is a package and should be assessed as such. In this case, if it is possible to allocate total costs between outcome measures in such a way that the effect-to-cost ratio for all the different outcome measures is superior to the best alternative method of reaching the outcome, the program is clearly cost effective. Take deworming as an example: deworming achieves both health and education outcomes (Miguel and Kremer 2004; see also chapter 4). If we split the costs of deworming and allocate half to student attendance and half to child health, it would be possible to calculate the cost per additional year of schooling and the cost per DALY saved. As both of these figures would indicate a highly cost-effective program for the outcome in question, we could conclude that the program was cost effective as a package.

As is usually the case, the appropriate methodology depends on the perspective of the user of the cost-effectiveness information, or the precise question being asked. For example, an education minister with a fixed budget and an objective of reaching the Millennium Development Goal of universal primary education would want to know the cost effectiveness of deworming with all the costs allocated against the student attendance objective. Similarly, the most relevant analysis for the Global Alliance for Vaccines Initiative (GAVI), which has an objective of increasing coverage of childhood immunizations, would be the full cost of various programs against the single-outcome measure of increased immunization. Instituting a conditional cash-transfer program that pays beneficiaries for regular visits to health clinics would be a relatively expensive way for GAVI to achieve its objective. In contrast, the Mexican government, which has a multiplicity of objectives including health, education, and income redistribution, would probably not want to make a judgment on whether to continue with a conditional cash-transfer program based on a cost-effectiveness analysis of PROGRESA that considers only a single outcome. Where we have evidence that a program achieves multiple outcomes beyond the one addressed in the cost-effectiveness estimation, we flag that study as "achieving multiple outcomes" on the cost-effectiveness graph. And if it is possible to clearly separate program costs between multiple outcomes as discussed above, we attempt to do so.

8.2.3. Imprecision in the Estimation of Impact. Estimates of impact can be measured only with a limited level of precision. Depending on the power of the underlying evaluation, different impact estimates will be measured more or less precisely. The point estimate of impact is typically used to calculate cost effectiveness, at least where the impact is found to be significantly different from zero. However, comparative analyses are concerned with the *relative* cost effectiveness of different programs, and it is quite possible that while one program may appear more cost effective than another using point estimates of impact, the two may not be significantly different from each other if the variance around the two point estimates is taken into account.

The first question this raises is what level of significance is an acceptable criterion for the program to be included in the cost-effectiveness analysis. Programs whose impact is significant at 10% or better are included in J-PAL analyses. Having chosen a cutoff level of significance, there is a further question about what to do with insignificant impacts. Insignificance could represent one of two things: an estimate that is quite precisely measured and is close to zero, or one that is very imprecisely measured and where a moderate or large impact cannot be ruled out. For these two kinds of insignificant results, it is not immediately clear whether to include such programs in an analysis, and what point estimate of impact, if any, to use in calculations of their cost effectiveness.

If a point estimate is insignificantly different from zero and precisely estimated, we often say that the estimated impact is zero ("the program did not work"), even though it is rarely the case that the point estimate is exactly zero. We believe that it is important to disseminate information about which programs *do not* work, as well as those that do; thus, we have chosen to include studies that show precisely estimated insignificant impacts on our graphs. However, rather than showing a bar calculated with the insignificant point estimate, we include a space for the program on the graph with a label indicating that the program had no *significant* impact. In addition to technical clarity, there are practical reasons for labeling these programs as "no significant impact," rather than including cost-effectiveness estimates for them. This approach avoids including cost-effectiveness calculations with insignificant negative impacts or displaying very large bars in the chart if cost effectiveness is calculated as cost per unit of impact.

It is more complicated to consider results that are not statistically different from zero but that have wide confidence intervals including large positive or negative values for the point estimates. Because they are imprecisely estimated, we have less evidence as to the actual impact of the program. For this reason, we have chosen to exclude imprecisely estimated zero-impact programs from our analyses.

One way to examine the sensitivity of cost-effectiveness estimates to significance level is as follows. Rank the programs based on their relative cost effectiveness using the point estimate of their impact and then recompute the cost effectiveness using the lower and upper bounds of the impact estimate. If this results in a program's cost effectiveness changing drastically (for instance, moving from the top quartile to the bottom quartile of cost effectiveness), then that cost-effectiveness estimate cannot be reported with as much confidence. This kind of check may be difficult to perform, however, in cases where only a few programs have sufficient data to be included in an analysis, making the range of cost-effectiveness estimates quite small.

Depending on the audience, it may be possible to include a confidence interval for cost effectiveness based on some chosen level of significance, giving a sense of the precision of the estimation as well as the size of the impact. However, including a discussion of statistical power in the primary results to a nonresearch audience can obscure the main message of the analysis and make it harder for that audience to understand. It can also provide a false sense of precision. The true error bands around a cost-effectiveness calculation stem not just from imprecision on the estimated impact of the program, but also on estimates of costs and how

Table 8.2 Confidence intervals of cost-effectiveness: Additional years of education per $100 spent

	Program	Country	Lower bound	Point estimate	Upper bound
1	Information session on returns to education, for parents	Madagascar	1.0	20.6	40.2
2	Deworming through primary schools	Kenya	5.1	12.5	19.9
3	Free primary school uniforms	Kenya	0.33	0.71	1.09
4	Merit scholarships for girls	Kenya	0.07	0.16	0.24
5a	Conditional cash transfers for girls (minimum transfer amount)	Malawi	0.03	0.09	0.16
5b	Conditional cash transfers for girls (average transfer amount)	Malawi	0.03	0.07	0.12
5c	Unconditional cash transfers for girls	Malawi	0.00	0.02	0.04
6	Iron fortification and deworming in preschools	India	0.10	2.7	5.4
7	Building village-based schools	Afghanistan	1.0	1.5	3.0
8	Camera monitoring of teachers' attendance	India		*No significant impact*	
9	Computer-assisted learning curriculum	India		*No significant impact*	
10	Remedial tutoring by community volunteers	India		*No significant impact*	
11	Menstrual cups for teenage girls	Nepal		*No significant impact*	
12	Information session on return to education, for boys	Dominican Republic	0.08	0.24	0.40

Note: Ranges based on 90% confidence interval of program impact.

they could vary between contexts. In some cases the uncertainty in cost-effectiveness analysis may stem more from the cost side than from the impact side, and it may be more appropriate to use error whiskers on the cost-effectiveness bar graph to highlight this variability than to focus on impact uncertainty. However, attempting to include error bands both for impact and costs is likely to be too confusing to be useful for many policymakers. It is straightforward to include information about the precision of estimates of impact at a secondary level for the more sophisticated reader, an approach J-PAL is starting to adopt on our website, where we will report confidence intervals of cost-effectiveness estimates based on the 90% confidence intervals around the impact estimate for each evaluation included. An example is included in table 8.2.

8.2.4. Spillovers. In many cases, the effects of a program may spill over onto the untreated population, as in the provision of deworming drugs to schoolchildren to promote school attendance in Kenya (Miguel and Kremer 2004). Intestinal worms are spread through skin or oral contact with soil or water contaminated with infected fecal matter, and reducing the overall number of community members infected with worms has positive externalities in reducing local disease transmission to untreated children. Even though the program did not directly treat them, the untreated children are still more likely to attend school as a result of the overall decrease in the transmission of worm infections. In the case of school-based deworming in Kenya, there were two kinds of spill-over effects: the worm burden was reduced among children in treatment schools who chose not to take deworming drugs and also among children in nearby control schools that did not receive drugs that year.

In deciding whether to include the effect of spillovers in a cost-effectiveness analysis, one must assess whether spillovers would take place even when a program is scaled up. In the case of deworming, it is reasonable to think that not all children would be at school on the day of a large-scale deworming campaign or some others may not agree to take the pill, yet both groups would benefit from the within-school spillovers that would still occur due to the lower overall infection rate. Therefore, if a scale-up is likely to have imperfect coverage within the target population, then it is reasonable to include spillover effects that accrued to un-treated targeted children in the original evaluation. However, a scale-up would probably attempt to reach all schools in an area, so spillovers to control schools would not be included in the calculation of benefits. In short, spillover effects should be included only when they are carefully measured and would also occur when the program is scaled up.

8.2.5. Aggregating Impacts. In its simplest form, calculating the total impact of a program follows this formula:

Total Impact of Program = Impact (per sample unit) × Sample Size × Program Duration

This calculation produces a figure for the total impact that a program had (time discounting is discussed in a later section). When there were differential impacts on different proportions of the population and those impacts occurred at different times, then this calculation requires more work. Any impact estimate used in calculations must correspond to the sample by which it is being multiplied, and particular care must be taken when separating Treatment on the Treated (ToT) and Intention to Treat (ITT) effects. So long as the effect is multiplied by the correct sample, then ITT and ToT coefficients should give the same estimates of aggregate impacts, but it is important that no matter which estimate is used, the costs must always be aggregated over the entire population that was targeted.[4]

Another issue is that of proximal versus final impact of programs. The aim of impact analyses is to show not just the relative costs of different channels of distributing goods or services to the poor, but how those goods and services translate into impacts, and what the impact is for a given expenditure. We therefore make a distinction between the proximal "success" of a program (immediate outcomes) and its final "impact" (effects on problems such as low learning and disease), resulting from immediate outcomes, which is a result of that proximal success. While most studies report final impact numbers, some only report proximal impacts. For example, studies that promote chlorination of water to prevent diarrheal disease may measure success in terms of the number of additional households with chlorinated water (proximal success), but the ultimate objective of the program is to reduce diarrheal disease (final impact). If there is relevant evidence from other rigorous studies, especially meta-studies, to link the proximal impacts to final impacts, then this can help translate proximal effects into calculations of their final impact.

8.3. Quantifying Costs

Quantifying the costs of a program can appear deceptively simple, particularly when only aggregate cost data (such as the entire budgetary total) are reported in academic papers without a full explanation of what that budget includes and for what time period. But in order to ensure comparability across studies, it is necessary to obtain far more detailed cost data, to better understand the actual structure of the program and how its costs were distributed across beneficiaries and over time. To calculate the costs of many programs on a comparable basis, a number of judgments need to be made about what constitutes a "cost to the program." What should be included will depend on what the cost-effectiveness analysis will be used for, and by whom, but we will focus on a general principle for cost analysis given the perspective we have described—that of a policymaker allocating resources between different programs. In general we have taken the position that it is most useful to assess the incremental cost of adding a new education program, assuming that many of the fixed costs of running a school system will be incurred with or without the program (i.e., there is a "comparator case" against which the program is being compared).

8.3.1. Gathering Cost Data. Very few evaluations report comprehensive cost estimates, so cost data can be surprisingly difficult to obtain. Budget information tends to be incomplete and, in some cases, inaccurate (Levin and McEwan 2001). The Ingredients Method is a useful way of making sure that all the appropriate costs have been included. Specifying all the ingredients necessary to replicate the program and then gathering unit cost information helps to ensure that a complete picture of the program's costs is included and guarantees comparability between programs. The academic papers on the relevant evaluation are usually a good starting point for the specification of ingredients, since they tend to provide an extensive description of the program itself. However, it is nearly always necessary to go back to the authors of the original evaluation and field staff to get clarifications on costs, how they were calculated, and how they broke down into different categories, as well as to get data on additional costs that were not listed in the academic paper. We are currently developing a general worksheet for researchers to use as a template for collecting cost data as they run evaluations. This will not only make it much easier to perform future cost-effectiveness analyses, but will also help improve comparisons of the different programs as part of cost-effectiveness analysis. The current iteration of J-PAL's worksheet is available in appendix 8C, and we hope to refine it based on feedback from researchers and practitioners.

8.3.2. Modeling Program Costs at the Margin. When adding up the gathered ingredients costs, one must have a clear concept of what is meant by "the program" and the context in which it is assumed that this program will be replicated. Many evaluations examine different variations of an existing program, or evaluate a completely new one, so it is important to be cognizant of the starting situation against which the new cost model is being compared (the "comparator case"). Take, for example, an analysis of a computer assisted learning program in a school that already had computer facilities (Banerjee et al. 2007). In the case of this evaluation, it was not necessary to pay for computers since they were already present in the school. However, if the program were to be scaled up to schools without computers, the cost of the program would have to include the cost of setting up a computer lab. Alternatively, a school could have a lab that was unable to accommodate additional users, necessitating the purchase of more computers. In essence, these issues boil down to estimating the marginal costs of lumpy inputs such as hours of teacher time or computer use in the presence of discontinuous marginal cost functions.

This situation exemplifies how the right approach depends on the precise question being asked. The head of a school district that had underused computers would want to know the cost effectiveness without including the cost of computers, while the head of a school district without any computers at all would want to have their costs included in the estimate. Without knowing precisely who is going to use our analysis we have to make an assumption about who is most likely to use the information. In this case, most schools in poorer regions of developing countries still do not have computers, and because the policy question that is often asked is whether or not computers should be provided, we include the costs of computers in our analysis.

On the other hand, take the example of a program providing merit scholarships to public school students based on standardized tests (Kremer, Miguel, and Thornton 2009). In this case, the verification of test scores and selection of winners may be undertaken by school administrators whose salaries would have been paid even if the program had not taken place, and because the additional work is not very time-consuming it seems likely that most government schools in which this program would be replicated would have the administrative capacity to select the top 15% of tests. It therefore seems reasonable to ignore the cost of administrators (but not of computers) because the analysis assumes that administrators (but not a computer lab) would already be present in most contexts in which a similar program would be replicated.

This point about what is reasonable to assume in a replication context is, in essence, another way of specifying the assumed situation into which a marginal program is being introduced (the comparator case). Cost-effectiveness analyses are not comparing the implementation of merit scholarships to doing nothing at all; if that were the case then every single cost associated with running the school in which scholarships were provided could be attributed to this program. The cost effectiveness of a program is calculated as the *incremental change* in test scores (for example) as a result of the program, divided by the *incremental change* in costs because the program was implemented.

$$\text{Cost-Effectiveness Ratio} = \frac{[\text{Test Scores with Program}] - [\text{Test Scores without Program}]}{[\text{Costs with Program}] - [\text{Costs without Program}]}$$

Underlying all cost-effectiveness calculations is an implied basic level of costs (e.g., teacher salaries, classroom supplies) and achievement (e.g., student attendance, test scores) that would exist even in the absence of the program. We call this the "comparator case" for cost-effectiveness analysis. Within this framework, the choice to "ignore" the cost of teachers who would still be paid in the absence of the new program is another way of saying that this cost appears in both terms of the denominator of the cost-effectiveness ratio above ("cost with program" and the comparator case of "costs without program") and thus cancels out of the calculation. The context in which one assumes that replications would be implemented is merely another way of expressing the comparator program against which the new program is being evaluated, or the existing situation onto which this marginal program is being added.

Because of the important role that this comparator case plays in cost-effectiveness calculations, it is extremely important that it be well specified. We cannot assume different comparator cases for different programs in the same cost-effectiveness analysis. An example of this is the evaluation of a contract teacher program in Kenya (Duflo, Dupas, and Kremer 2011). This program gave funds to schools to hire a contract teacher, allowing them to split their first-grade classes into two, one taught by the contract teacher and the other by the regular civil service teacher. In practice, this program involved both decreasing class size and introducing a contract teacher who was accountable to the local parents, but the evaluation also allowed for comparison between contract and civil service teachers independent of class size (since both taught smaller classes).

Accordingly, one could estimate the costs of this program as the cost of hiring a contract teacher to allow for two first-grade classes, or as the costs of replacing civil service teachers with contract teachers. This choice has a significant impact on the outcome of cost-effectiveness analysis. The additional cost of adding one new contract teacher to a school while keeping everything else the same would include the new teacher's wages and training as well as any materials necessary to supply and oversee an additional classroom. But if a contract teacher were hired in place of a civil service teacher, the marginal cost of this new program would include the wages of the new contract teacher, net of the saved money that no longer needs to be paid to the old one. And because contract teachers have far lower wages than their civil service counterparts, the cost of replacing one government teacher with a contract teacher would actually be negative, resulting in negative cost effectiveness (money saved per standard deviation increase in test scores). It is plausible to calculate cost effectiveness for either (or both) of these programs, but it is important to be explicit about the structure of the program and the situation to which it is being compared.

Many development programs also require certain survey data during their implementation, but it is not necessarily the case that similar survey data would be available if the program were to be scaled up or replicated in a different context. For example, a program giving families information about returns to education relies on local wages for various education levels, and conditional cash-transfer programs often use detailed data from proxy means testing to identify beneficiaries. Even if an evaluated program were able to take advantage of existing information about the returns to education in a particular context, or an existing survey of the poorest households in a community, and thereby not incur additional survey costs, it is still necessary to consider whether such information would exist in a typical context where such a program could be replicated. It is possible to do cost-effectiveness calculations either way—with or without the costs of collecting such underlying information that is critical for program implementation—but it is important to be explicit about what the program components are, and be consistent about the survey data that are assumed to be available in the context where the program may be replicated.

8.3.3. Goods and Services Procured at No Cost. In some evaluations, certain goods and services are provided at no cost to the program implementers—for example, members of a community may donate their labor to a project, or an outside organization may donate an input such as textbooks or deworming medicines. If the object of a cost-effectiveness analysis is to look at costs to society as a whole, the market cost of such free goods and services should be included. And even from the perspective of a particular implementing agency, inputs that were available for free on a smaller-scale project may not be available at no cost if the program is scaled up elsewhere, suggesting that the market costs of these free goods and services should be included. This process is relatively straightforward for material inputs that are necessary for the intervention (such as donated textbooks) for which the standard ingredients method can be applied using a market cost for the ingredient. In cases where services, such as labor for water-source improvement projects, were provided at no cost by beneficiaries, the cost can be estimated as what it would have cost to get the same work done by a paid laborer.

8.3.4. Costs to Beneficiaries. In many cases, programs also require beneficiaries to spend time contributing to the program—for instance, when parents must attend meetings to get information about the returns to education or give consent for the administration of deworming drugs. Some donors and policymakers may not be concerned with the costs of this time because it does not constitute an accounting cost to them. But because this time is a requirement of the program and represents a real cost to the user, we have chosen to include such costs wherever programs required users to commit their time. Where user costs are not a direct requirement of the program (for instance, in the girls' merit scholarship

COST-EFFECTIVENESS: SENSITIVITY TO BENEFICIARY'S COSTS
(Additional years of education per $100 spent)

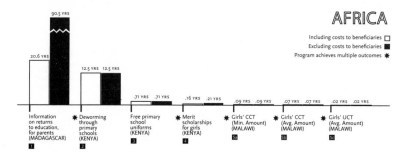

AFRICA

Including costs to beneficiaries □
Excluding costs to beneficiaries ■
Program achieves multiple outcomes ✳

90.5 YRS

20.6 YRS

12.5 YRS   12.5 YRS

.71 YRS   .71 YRS

.16 YRS   .21 YRS

.09 YRS   .09 YRS

.07 YRS   .07 YRS

.02 YRS   .02 YRS

| Information on returns to education, for parents (MADAGASCAR) 1 | ✳ Deworming through primary schools (KENYA) 2 | Free primary school uniforms (KENYA) 3 | ✳ Merit scholarships for girls (KENYA) 4 | ✳ Girls' CCT (Min. Amount) (MALAWI) 5a | ✳ Girls' CCT (Avg. Amount) (MALAWI) 5b | ✳ Girls' UCT (Avg. Amount) (MALAWI) 5c |

SOUTH ASIA

2.7 YRS   2.7 YRS

1.5 YRS   1.5 YRS

———— NO SIGNIFICANT IMPACT ————

| ✳ Iron fortification and deworming in preschools (INDIA) 8 | Building village-based schools (AFGHANISTAN) 7 | ✳ Camera monitoring of teachers' attendance (INDIA) 8 | ✳ Computer-assisted learning curriculum (INDIA) 9 | ✳ Remedial tutoring by community volunteers (INDIA) 10 | ✳ Menstrual cups for teenage girls (NEPAL) 11 |

LATIN AMERICA

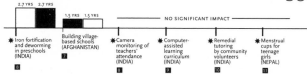

.3 YRS   .3 YRS

.008 YRS   .008 YRS

| Information on returns to education, for boys (DOMINICAN REPUBLIC) 12 | ✳ PROGRESA CCT for primary school attendance (MEXICO) 13 |

FIGURE 8.2 Cost effectiveness: Sensitivity to beneficiary's costs.
Note: Additional years of education per $100 spent.

program in which parents were invited but not required to attend an awards ceremony) we do not include them as costs of the program.

Most evaluations report the average household income of the treatment and comparison group and we use this data to estimate the cost of users' time spent on the project. Because the average local wage rate for the poor in developing countries is quite low compared to total program costs, the relative ranking of the various programs in our cost-effectiveness analysis for student attendance does not change under differing assumed costs of foregone labor, as can be seen from the charts in figure 8.2. However, the magnitude of estimated cost effectiveness of some programs does change, especially those such as the information campaign in Madagascar, that had relatively low costs of implementation before including users' costs (see figure 8.2).

8.3.5. Ingredients with Overlapping Uses. Many educational interventions require inputs such as teacher time, use of facilities, or administrative overhead. These ingredients are clearly necessary components of the program (it would be hard to adopt a new curriculum without a teacher to teach it), but there are sometimes reasons not to include every possible ingredient cost into an estimation of the cost effectiveness of a program. In the earlier example of administering girls' merit scholarships in Kenya, we concluded that it was not reasonable to include the cost of administrators' time because it overlapped so heavily with the basic functioning of the school.

On the other hand, it is also possible that other, future programs could piggyback onto the program one is examining now. For example, a significant proportion of the costs of PROGRESA come from the "targeting activities," where the poorest areas and households are identified for inclusion into the program. The information gained from these targeting surveys can be used by other programs in the future to identify beneficiaries, or even as simple demographic information to guide policymaking. Because there is no way to identify which of these costs may be distributed among other programs in the future, and because they still represent an accounting cost to the organization implementing the program at the time when the original program is run, we have not attempted to exclude such costs that may overlap with other programs in the future. Further, if a program such as PROGRESA is replicated in other countries where a targeting survey has already been conducted for other reasons, and/or the intended beneficiaries have already been identified, such survey costs would not be incurred. But again, since it is impossible for us to know this a priori, we have included these costs. When reviewing whether to replicate a program, implementers will be able to easily redo the cost-effectiveness analysis by excluding these costs if such a survey already exists.

A special case of the problem of "overlapping uses" concerns inputs that are not completely used up in a year, such as school buildings or teaching materials that can be used for a longer period of time than is modeled in the cost-effectiveness analysis. If a program's impact is only measured over one or two years, but costs are included for goods that can actually continue to be used over many more years, it can result in an underestimation of the cost effectiveness of the program. Consider a program that incurs large initial costs of procuring textbooks. The evaluation runs for one year, while the textbooks last for three years. If the full cost of the textbooks is attributed to only one year of impact, then the program's cost effectiveness could suffer relative to another program that requires lower initial investment but has higher variable costs. One way to deal with this problem is simply to use the rental cost for any goods that could be rented rather than purchased. However, it may not be possible to find rental costs for particular goods, such as investments in improving a building, in which case the cost of the input can be amortized over the assumed life of that good.

8.3.6. Transfers. Transfers, where money or goods are redistributed from one person or organization to another, represent an accounting cost to the government or organization undertaking the program, but not to the society as a whole. If we are concerned with costs and benefits to society as a whole, we should not include transfers as a cost. However, another way to look at the issue is that transfers are an example of a multiple-outcome program where one of the benefits is increased cash for the poor. If cost-effectiveness analysis focuses on one outcome only and ignores all other outcomes, why should cash outcomes be treated differently from, say, nutritional benefits? We will examine this question in some depth.

Mexico's PROGRESA program, where the government transferred money to families conditional on their children's attendance at school and healthcare checkups, is a well-known example of cash transfers. The government's costs in this case can be divided into administrative costs (e.g., the costs of targeting poor households, monitoring whether children are attending school, and organizing the distribution of funds) and transfer costs (the amount of money that is actually transferred to families who have complied with the conditions of the program). Administrative costs are a resource cost—real resources are used up by the program.

Transfer costs are not a resource cost: the total resources in the economy do not go down, they simply get redistributed from one person to another. If we want to include PROGRESA in a cost-effectiveness analysis of alternative approaches to increasing attendance at school, should we include transfer costs or not?

If we were doing a cost-benefit analysis this would not be an issue. We would include all the costs to the implementer, including the transfers, as a cost but the cash received by the family would be included as a benefit, and the two would cancel each other out. (To be fully accurate we would want to include the deadweight cost of raising taxes to fund the subsidy, but we will ignore this as there are few good estimates of the deadweight cost of taxation in developing countries, and these are likely to vary considerably between countries with different tax systems.)

Within the context of a cost-effectiveness analysis, however, there are two ways to see this question, and they point to different answers. If we are interested in assessing cost effectiveness to society as a whole, then transfers should not be considered a cost as they are not a cost to the society (except the deadweight cost of taxation). It could be argued, however, that a transfer is a cost to the implementer and a benefit to the beneficiary. Conditional cash transfers achieve more than one outcome—for example, they increase school attendance and they redistribute cash to the poor. Through this lens, it becomes difficult to see why we should adjust for the benefits of cash transfers when we don't adjust for other outcomes—from the nutritional benefits of school meals, for example, or to the health benefits of deworming. We argued that we did not want to put a monetary value on these benefits as they will vary across contexts, and cost-effectiveness estimates are likely to be sensitive to the choice of values. What is the monetary value of a child receiving a free meal at school? Is it the full value of the meal? It is probable that the child's family would not value it at the full cost of the meal. If given the cash equivalent of the meal they would probably not spend it all on food for the child. One reason to give in-kind benefits is because one thinks that the implementer has a different valuation of benefits than the recipient and one wants to skew his or her own spending in a particular direction, in this case towards child nutrition. That said, the family would undoubtedly put a positive value on the meal (Kremer and Vermeersch [2004] actually attempt to back out families' implicit valuation of the meals). Indeed, the majority of programs included in the cost-effectiveness analysis of school enrollment and attendance include multiple benefits, and some of them are monetary. Assessing the appropriate valuation of all these benefits, however, is highly problematic, and in our view makes the

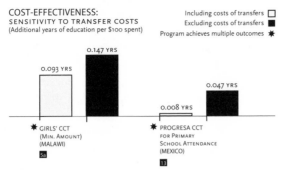

FIGURE 8.3 Cost effectiveness: Sensitivity to transfer costs.
Note: Additional years of education per $100 spent.

analysis extremely opaque. An assessment of the cost effectiveness of the school meal program, for example, would be very sensitive to exactly how much one thought people valued the meal.

Our conclusion is that a cash benefit is another case of a multi-outcome program, but it is a special one because it is easier to estimate its value. However, even in the case of cash transfers it is not necessarily true that the marginal benefit of $1 to a poor household is equal to the marginal value of $1 to a wealthier household. Therefore, we attempt to clearly show what proportion of costs is due to transfers and sometimes show cost effectiveness without transfers. Figure 8.3 illustrates the impact of excluding cash transfers on the cost effectiveness of PROGRESA. To compute the cost of transfers, we used the disaggregated transfer amounts that are linked only to primary school attendance and not transfers associated with either secondary school or health outcomes.

A practical point to keep in mind when deciding whether to include transfers as costs is that while funders do care about costs incurred and benefits received by beneficiaries, they also have budget constraints that require accounting for both administrative costs and transfer costs. They may want to know how much "bang" they can "get for their buck" in terms of impact on a narrow outcome, such as school attendance, from different programs—including conditional cash transfers, and netting out transfers makes it hard for them to do this calculation. We therefore provide a version of the cost-effectiveness analysis with transfers included as a cost because funders do face budget constraints and because other programs also have multiple outcomes.

8.3.7. High-Level Management Overhead. One of the most difficult cost items to incorporate in cost-effectiveness analysis is the incremental cost of indirect overhead. This is because the additional time, effort, and cost of high-level administration and oversight that is incurred by the organization due to a new program is rarely tracked or quantified. This section is not meant to revisit the previous category of costs of a new program that overlap with the basic functioning of a school or local administration (such as paying for facilities or electricity). Rather, it will focus on the costs of higher-level overhead, such as additional administration time needed to process the payroll of new employees, or the time an existing civil servant spends overseeing the implementation of the program. These additional costs are almost never reported, especially at the pilot or research stage when they represent a small amount in a (likely) much larger organizational budget. As such, they are almost impossible to observe and any estimations by us would be extremely imprecise. In many cases, the costs of such high-level overhead are likely to be relatively small compared to the other costs of the program, and are also likely to be similar across the various programs being compared. This suggests that, in most cases, they can be netted out of calculations without biasing the relative cost-effectiveness estimates.

If there were a reason to believe that programs within an analysis had drastically different costs of indirect overhead (for instance, because a program would require protracted renegotiation of union contracts by very senior management, such as some of the programs described in chapter 6), then it could be possible to put together some estimate of the indirect overhead costs. Assuming that the indirect overhead costs are a function of the amount of personnel costs, one could assume an additional 10% or 15% of cost for the indirect overhead of administration. However, the choice of an overhead "rate" would be extremely arbitrary, and we do not make these assumptions in our analysis.

8.3.8. Experimental versus Scalable Modes. The costs of a program evaluated in its pilot phase may be different from the actual costs if one were to massively scale up the program. This is because there may be advantages to working on a larger scale, such as purchasing supplies in bulk, which have the potential to increase the cost effectiveness of programs. On the other hand, there may be disadvantages to working at scale, such as the increased difficulty of administering a program over a wide area or the cost of hiring new senior management to administer the scaled program, which may affect both costs and impacts. The ratio of fixed to variable costs can also impact how cost effective a program looks at pilot versus at scale. When this ratio is high, a pilot program will not look as cost effective because the fixed cost is spread over only a small number of beneficiaries. But a program with high fixed costs relative to its variable costs may be more cost effective at scale, when the fixed cost is spread over a larger number of beneficiaries. When scale economies are very obvious and guaranteed to be realized, these may be used to estimate the cost of a program.

For example, in performing a cost-effectiveness analysis of a program that supplies flipcharts to schools in Kenya, the budget would report the cost of flipcharts based on their purchase through retail outlets. If this program were to be adopted across an entire state, flipcharts could be purchased in bulk, and so bulk costs should be applied to this ingredient. This can be particularly important in programs where the majority of the costs come from goods or services that are particularly sensitive to scale. However, it is important to be cautious in the application of "scale economies" to the ingredients in the program. If a program has not been tested at scale there may be a concern that while the costs would go down with scale, so might the quality of monitoring or delivery, and hence the impact. Without good reason, it is often better to stick with the actual costs and actual benefits of the program as it was evaluated.

For this reason, wherever changes have been made to an original program design in its scaled-up version, it may be useful to conduct an evaluation of a pilot to verify the program's impact. Similarly, if there is reason to believe that the costs of the scale-up are likely to be different from the original evaluation, it is advisable to perform a detailed survey of local costs before choosing to expand the program. This is what J-PAL advises policymakers who are looking to expand or replicate programs found to be successful in evaluations. As more and more piloted evaluations are scaled up in the next few years, there will be a better understanding among researchers and policymakers about how individual costs of goods and services in evaluations translate into costs in large scale-ups.

8.4. Using Common Units

One of the unseen challenges of cost-effectiveness analysis, beyond the selection of an appropriate outcome measure and the inclusion of the appropriate costs, is converting all costs and impacts into "common units" adjusting consistently for inflation, exchange rates, and year of implementation. For the sake of clarity, it is useful to define two terms at the beginning of any analysis:

Year of Analysis: The year in which a cost-effectiveness analysis is undertaken or the choice between the various programs is made. The year of analysis must be consistent for all programs in an analysis. If the year of analysis is 2010, all final cost figures should be inflated to 2010 dollars.

Base Year: The year in which the program being evaluated was launched. Before inflating forward to the year of analysis, costs and benefits are discounted back to the base year of the program so that inflation is compounded over the correct number of years.

It is necessary to define a single year of analysis that is used for all programs in a given analysis. If this is not done, and the base years of each individual program are used as the effective year of analysis (i.e., costs are reported in terms of that year's currency), then differences in costs may be driven by inflation between the different years of analysis. When adjusting for common units, costs are first converted into a common currency (usually the US dollar), then converted to prices in terms of base year dollars, and thereafter the present value of these cost flows in the base year is computed. Costs are then inflated forward to their value in the year of analysis using a common inflation rate.

8.4.1. Adjusting for the Base Year of the Program. When a program's costs and impacts are distributed across time, it is necessary to discount them back to their present value in the base year of the program to account for an organization's time preference for both costs and benefits. There is no universally applicable real discount rate in the literature, and in practice there are significant variations in public discount rates applied by different countries. Developing countries tend to apply higher social discount rates (8–15%) than developed countries (3–7%) (Zhuang et al. 2007). The "correct" discount rate depends on who is making the investment: different decisionmakers will use different methods to estimate their discount rate.

The discounting of costs is representative of the choice a funder faces between incurring costs this year, or deferring expenditures to invest for a year and then incurring costs the next year. An organization or government's discount rate is usually calculated as the social opportunity cost of capital (SOC). This rate varies across countries and organizations, but there seems to be a higher variance in the public, rather than private, cost of capital.

The discounting of benefits, on the other hand, represents how an end user of the program would trade off between the uses of the services this year versus next year. The appropriate discount rate for such a cal-

Table 8.3 Survey of social discount rates

Country	Discount rate	Theoretical basis
Germany	3%	Based on federal refinancing rate
Norway	3.5%	Unknown
United Kingdom	3.5%	SOC until early 80s, SRTP after
France	4%	SRTP approach
Spain	4–6%	SRTP approach
Italy	5%	SRTP approach
United States (OMB)	7%	Unknown
People's Republic of China	8%a	Weighted average approach
Canada	10%	SOC approach
New Zealand (Treasury)	10%	SOC approach
Asian Development Bank	10–12%	Unknown
India	12%	SOC approach
Pakistan	12%	SOC approach
Philippines	15%	SOC approach

ª For short- and medium- term projects

culation is the social rate of time preference (SRTP), or the rate at which users would trade off one unit of consumption today versus one unit of consumption tomorrow. There is relatively little information on the time preferences of people in poorer countries, and the fact that variations will depend upon the intended user of the program, rather than the implementer, makes it difficult to choose one rate which would be applicable in a variety of cases.

If an organization were performing a cost-effectiveness analysis of programs that they run in particular countries, then it would be possible to use the SOC to discount their costs knowing their own cost of capital and use the SRTP of the country in which beneficiaries live to discount effects. However, in performing general cost-effectiveness analysis that is likely to be used by policymakers in different organizations and countries, one is unlikely to have such specific information about users, and so it is practical to choose a single discount rate. Because of the high variance and scarce empirical data on time preferences in the developing world, the SRTP is not a practical option. This suggests that the SOC may be the best available discount rate, but the question remains as to which country or organization's SOC should be used. International aid tends to come from the developed world (even when it is channeled through local governments), and so the opportunity cost of devoting capital to a given program is most often based on the foregone return or cost of borrowing on the developed country capital markets. For a list of discount rates used by various governments and organizations, see table 8.3. One of the most striking features of this table is the relative

Table 8.4 Sensitivity of cost-effectiveness to discount rate

	Program	Country	Time frame (years)	Discount rate		
				5%	10%	15%
1	Information session on returns to education, for parents	Madagascar	1	20.6	20.6	20.6
2	Deworming through primary schools	Kenya	1	12.5	12.5	12.5
3	Free primary school uniforms	Kenya	1	0.71	0.71	0.71
4	Merit scholarships for girls	Kenya	3	0.16	0.16	0.16
5a	Conditional cash transfers for girls (minimum transfer amount)	Malawi	2	0.09	0.09	0.09
5b	Conditional cash transfers for girls (average transfer amount)	Malawi	2	0.07	0.07	0.07
5c	Unconditional cash transfers for girls	Malawi	2	0.02	0.02	0.02
6	Iron fortification and deworming in preschools	India	1	2.7	2.7	2.7
7	Building village-based schools	Afghanistan	1	1.5	1.5	1.5
8	Camera monitoring of teachers' attendance	India	—	No significant impact		
9	Computer-assisted learning curriculum	India	—	No significant impact		
10	Remedial tutoring by community volunteers	India	—	No significant impact		
11	Menstrual cups for teenage girls	Nepal	—	No significant impact		
12	Information session on return to education, for boys	Dominican Republic	4	0.26	0.24	0.23
13	Cash transfers conditional on attendance at primary school	Mexico	4	0.008	0.008	0.008

Note: Additional years of schooling per $100 spent.

similarity of rates across organizations using the SOC to calculate their discount rate. Looking at the median rate of countries using the SOC methodology suggests that 10% is a reasonable rate for discounting the costs and benefits of educational programs in developing countries.

Many of the programs included in our examples of analysis were run and evaluated over a relatively short time frame.. Except in cases where there are large one-time start-up costs, most of these programs can be examined over a one- or two-year time frame, and so their comparative cost effectiveness is not particularly sensitive to the choice of a discount rate. The relative insensitivity of this kind of estimate to changes in the discount rate is shown in table 8.4. In cases where there are large one-time costs, such as targeting activities or construction of new buildings, but benefits that accrue over a longer time frame, the cost-effectiveness estimates would be more sensitive to the choice of discount rates.

8.4.2. Adjusting for Inflation. When performing cost-effectiveness analysis based on the results of an impact evaluation, ingredient costs are frequently taken from the costs incurred in the evaluation itself, which in many cases are reported in terms of their nominal amounts in the year in which they were incurred. Depending on how costs are reported, this can necessitate up to two adjustments for inflation. First, any costs that were reported in terms of the year in which they were incurred (e.g., 2004, 2005, and 2006 US dollars [USD]) must be deflated back to their real value in base year dollars (2004 USD), to account for the fact that inflated prices may make later costs appear larger even if they are identical in real terms. Second, once the present value of the cost stream has been calculated from the perspective of the base year, it is usually necessary to inflate this figure forward to reflect what it would cost in the year of analysis (in our student attendance example, this is 2011 USD). For both of these calculations it is preferable to use the average GDP deflators rather than consumer price indices as the measures of inflation, since they cover a wider range of goods and services of the kind used in most antipoverty programs.

On average there should be no difference between converting to dollars and applying the US inflation rate versus applying the local inflation rate and then exchanging currencies, but in practice distorted exchange rates may not always capture inflation adequately. For this reason we have chosen to convert to dollars and then use the US inflation rate. We follow the same methodology consistently in all J-PAL cost-effectiveness analyses.

8.4.3. Currency and Exchange Rates. Many evaluations report program costs in US dollars, but some also report costs in local currencies, and where costs are gathered from a number of sources there may even be a mixture of units. It is obvious that all programs being evaluated must have their costs exchanged into a single currency, but the choice of an exchange rate has significant implications for the interpretation of the results.

When standard (i.e., market) exchange rates are used, the resulting estimates represent the cost effectiveness of that program assuming the relative price levels for different goods in the country in which it was originally implemented. The difficulty in using standard exchange rates is that there are significant differences in the relative prices of different goods across countries. Purchasing Power Parity (PPP) exchange rates adjust somewhat for the different price *levels* in different countries, which are driven by the higher prices of nontradables in wealthier countries. But since PPP is based on a standard basket of goods and services, it does not completely adjust for the different relative prices of the goods and services used in a particular program across countries, because of the variations in factor endowments across countries. For example, skilled

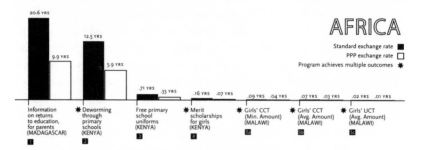

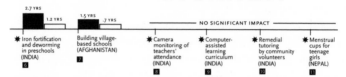

FIGURE 8.4 Cost effectiveness: Sensitivity to exchange rates
Note: Additional years of education per $100 spent.

labor is far cheaper in India than in Mexico, so if a program that is more intensive in skilled labor is piloted in Mexico, it will look less cost effective than a similar program piloted in India. But there is a danger that some readers may not appreciate this fact and will assume that the relative prices of different categories of goods have been completely adjusted in the PPP version.

Moreover, because PPP exchange rates effectively adjust to what a program would cost in the United States ($1 PPP = $1 USD), the cost-effectiveness estimates for all of the programs will decrease significantly in absolute size, potentially giving an inaccurate estimate of what could be achieved with a given expenditure in a developing country. This could be resolved if readers were first converting from PPP back into standard US dollars using the conversion factor for each program's country of origin, but it is almost certain that this kind of mental calculation will be done straight from PPP to a policymaker's domestic currency using standard rates, while US-based policymakers might miss the conversion altogether. Therefore the default presentation of our cost-effectiveness results uses standard exchange rates, but whenever possible, we will also present a version with PPP rates to show that the relative cost effectiveness of the programs does not change (see, e.g., fig. 8.4). Given that relative prices do differ across countries, it is useful before launching a large program to do an assessment of costs in the intended location, especially when costs in the original program were driven mostly by a particular factor cost, such as wages. Again, providing the underlying calculations should enable policymakers to make such adjustments.

8.4.4. Order of Operations. For simplicity's sake, we keep track of the units for costs and impacts, including currency, year, and whether present value has been applied. Table 8.5 specifies the order of operations that J-PAL uses to harmonize cost units for the most complex program in our example: a program for which there are cost data reported in the prices of the years in which the costs were incurred, in local currency. This particular order of operations is not necessarily better than any other, the important thing is that an order be selected and consistently applied to all programs in an analysis.

8.5. General Issues with Cost-Effectiveness Analysis

8.5.1. Partial versus General Equilibrium. Randomized evaluations provide a snapshot view of what the partial equilibrium effects of a program will

Table 8.5 Order of operations

Step	Operation	Unit of currency (e.g.)
1	Gather cost data	2004, 2005, and 2006 pesos
2	Exchange value in US dollars using the year-specific exchange rates.	2004, 2005, 2006 USD
3	Deflate nominal costs back to real value in base year (2004) using average annual US inflation rate over time elapsed between base year and incurrence of costs.	2004 USD (incurred in 2004, 2005, and 2006)
4	Take the present value of this cost stream using a 10% real discount rate.	PV of the cost stream in 2004, in 2004 USD
5	Inflate forward to year of analysis (2010) using average annual US inflation rate over time elapsed between base year and year of analysis.	PV of the cost stream in 2010, in 2010 USD

be. Some randomized evaluations are designed to pick up the long-term impacts of a program, but many only attempt to measure shorter-run effects. Even when an evaluation is designed to pick up long-run effects for a particular cohort, it is possible that people will change their response to a program as it becomes more established—that is, later cohorts may respond differently—or the benefits of the program will change as the program is scaled up. For example, graduates of a vocational education program in a rural area could be expected to see high returns at the outset, since they are the only ones with specialized knowledge. But as time goes by and more people graduate from the vocational education program, the supply of educated workers would increase and the returns to vocational education could decrease as a result of excess supply. Spillovers may also decline as programs become universal, as discussed earlier. On the other hand, benefits sometimes become larger as programs are scaled up and behavior change is reinforced by seeing peers undergo the same behavior change. The marginal benefits of education can also increase as more people become educated and there are complementarities between skilled workers. It is difficult to precisely estimate the extent to which general equilibrium impacts may be different from partial ones, although individual studies often discuss the issues in a particular context. The level at which general equilibrium effects will be observed can vary in different situations and can only be determined empirically, although it may be possible to make reasonable estimates of how a program will perform at scale based on the design of the program and the size of the target population. It is not practical to attempt to include general equilibrium effects in our cost-effectiveness analyses, although we will attempt to flag the most problematic ones.

8.5.2. Initial Levels of Underlying Problems. Different countries or regions will have different intensities of the underlying problems that programs are seeking to address. For example, there is far higher baseline attendance in Mexico than in Kenya. Because of this, they may be at different points on the "marginal benefit curve" of intervention, which can result in variations in the cost-effectiveness figures for the same program piloted in different regions. For instance, a deworming pill should be equally effective at killing intestinal worms in Africa or in Asia, but there is declining marginal benefit to more deworming, and so the number of school days gained as a result of a deworming program depends on the pre-existing intensity of infection in any particular place. Thus deworming might buy five additional days of schooling in western Kenya, where worm prevalence is very high, but fewer additional days of schooling in Andhra Pradesh state in India, where the worm prevalence is lower. Similarly, intuition tells us that the "last-mile problems" would make it harder to increase school enrollment from 90% to 95% than from 50% to 55%. But whether this is the case, and to what extent, is an empirical question that is very hard to resolve a priori. In some cases, especially among education interventions, we have used impacts (such as an increase in test scores) reported in terms of standard deviations to mitigate some of the issues associated with the initial level of the underlying problem that the programs seek to address.

When considering the baseline rates of the initial problem that a given program tries to address, there are two separate issues: putting programs on more similar footing, and producing accurate estimates of what a program's impact would be where a user wanted to implement it. Our goal in comparative analysis is to generate good estimates of the relative cost effectiveness of different programs, but these estimates will always be representative of programs as they were piloted in a particular context. Providing policymakers with the underlying calculations for cost-effectiveness analysis can allow them to run sensitivity analysis by adjusting factors that are important for their context, such as population density. However, given that most pilots are tested in areas where the underlying problem is severe (for instance, where parents systematically underestimate the returns to primary education) and programs are likely to be scaled up or replicated only in areas where that problem is also salient, it is unlikely that baseline levels in pilot areas will be significantly different from baseline levels in the replication context.

Another way to minimize the bias in comparisons across different contexts is to group programs by the region or type of country in which they were piloted. Programs in similar regions or national income brackets are more likely to have common elements in terms of the baseline rates of the underlying problems. Thus policymakers may be able to study the programs that were piloted in their region, or in countries facing similar problems and that are at a similar stage of development to compare cost effectiveness. For example, we have grouped our student attendance graph by the region in which the program took place.

While grouping programs by the region or income group of the country in which they were piloted reduces the bias in comparisons across regions, it can also make comparisons difficult when there are only a few programs in a particular region. Our student attendance and enrollment analysis is not yet complete, and more programs will be added to allow for better comparisons within regions.

8.5.3. Generalizability of Costs. In cost-effectiveness analysis, it is necessary to incorporate some features of individual programs as assumptions about the general implementation of the program. While normalizing the assumed pre-existing levels of absence or disease can help to ensure the comparability of impact figures, there are other location-specific parameters that can influence the cost effectiveness of a program. For example, in the area of India where the Balsakhi remedial tutoring program was tested, there were sufficient volunteers available with a high enough education level to take advantage of the pedagogical materials provided and use them to provide out-of-school tutoring for local children. In another state in India where education levels are lower, it might be harder to find a volunteer to teach in every village, and so the fixed cost of developing the pedagogical materials would be spread among a smaller pool of villages. These costs can vary across different contexts, even within the same country, due to demographic factors. For example, the number of schools an administrator can visit in a day may vary depending on school size, transportation infrastructure, and so on.

Similarly, some other contextual factors, such as population density in the area in which a program is piloted, can influence estimates of cost effectiveness. Many programs will cost more, and be less cost effective, when the population is sparsely settled compared to more densely populated regions. But it should be relatively easy to adjust cost estimates based on expected population density if the amount of goods and services necessary per household or individual is known. If all programs within a given analysis are piloted in areas with similar population density, then population density should not present any problems for their relative cost effectiveness. If, however, different programs are piloted in areas with dramatically different population densities, policymakers may be interested in substituting the population density for the region of interest to them.

In addition to its complicating effect on comparisons, the sensitivity of cost-effectiveness estimates to certain parameters complicates the presentation of cost-effectiveness results. Simple bar graphs that cannot include information on all sensitivities can create the misleading impression that if a program were to be implemented in *any* area, the cost per impact would be the same as in a cost-effectiveness analysis of the pilot program. While cost-effectiveness analyses are intended to provide a means of comparison between different programs if they were implemented by the policymaker, they are not intended to reflect exactly what a particular program would cost to implement in any setting. To reflect the way that costs per impact can be expected to vary as a function of certain parameters, it can be useful to select the most relevant variable for a given program and show how the cost effectiveness of that program would change with that variable over a reasonable range. Using the example of a remedial education tutoring program, one can present the point estimate of how much it would cost to increase test scores by one standard deviation if the actual (observed) proportion of villages in the study (say, 75%) found a tutor and implemented the program, as well as a range around this point estimate of cost per unit increase in standard deviations of test score if 70% of villages implemented the program and if 80% of villages implemented it. For educational interventions, the largest cost item is often wages, which vary widely across contexts, and so it can be instructive to include an interval of cost effectiveness under a reasonable range of wages.

As J-PAL performs cost-effectiveness analyses, more detailed spreadsheets will be made available to help those wishing to scale up and implement programs for which cost-effectiveness results are given in different contexts. Such dissemination of underlying calculations, thoroughly cited and explained, will allow other organizations to examine the underlying calculations and modify various parameters based on their situation. For example, a detailed analysis can be tailored to include revised cost estimates taken from local knowledge of the costs in specific contexts and country-specific prevalence rates and to generally adapt the figures shown in original analyses to the needs of different users.

8.6. Conclusion

Cost-effectiveness comparisons can be a powerful tool to inform the debate about how best to improve education in developing countries.

By placing program costs and impacts on a similar basis these analyses can make comparisons of different programs very salient. But a number of judgments need to be made in the process of undertaking cost-effectiveness analyses, for example, what is the appropriate discount rate or exchange rate to use, and should transfers be included as costs or not? In this chapter we have set out a particular set of assumptions or judgments that we believe provide a useful basis for comparing education programs in developing countries. As we have pointed out throughout the chapter, determining which assumption is best depends on the precise question or context to which the analysis will be applied. In some cases the cost-effectiveness calculations are not very sensitive to changes in the assumptions within reasonable ranges. This is the case for discount rates, for example. In other cases the absolute values change with different assumptions but the relative ranking of programs does not change (this is true for market exchange rates versus purchasing power parity, for example). Wherever the results are highly sensitive to a particular assumption we highlight this fact.

A cost-effectiveness analysis should be taken as one input into a decision about which programs to fund, along with other considerations, and not the only factor. While costs and impacts may vary between settings, by making available the underlying data and calculations that go into the analysis, we hope to provide a framework for funders and implementers to think through what results they might expect in their particular context. We have found this useful for working with funding organizations to assess the likely cost effectiveness of scale-ups in new contexts by adapting the inputs and methodology set out here.

None of this work is possible without detailed data on costs and impacts. The process of doing more and higher quality comparative cost-effectiveness work will be greatly enhanced if researchers record detailed cost information during their field research. We hope this chapter helps develop standard ways to collect data on costs and impacts. If a consensus emerges about the best way to measure education quality and quantity, it will make comparisons much more useful. In some subject areas J-PAL is attempting to coordinate with researchers on agreed standardized outcome and cost measures, but in education, as with other sectors, there is still more work to be done.

With all the assumptions and imperfections involved in undertaking comparative cost-effectiveness analyses, some may argue that they should not be undertaken. In our view, policymakers will always make comparisons across programs about cost effectiveness—they have to, given limited resources and the large number of programs aimed at similar outcomes that compete for those resources. Providing policymakers with tools that are clear about the assumptions being made and that can be easily adapted makes the process more transparent, less ad hoc and is likely to increase the use of rigorous research evidence in policymaking.

Appendix 8A

COST-EFFECTIVENESS OF DIARRHEAL DISEASE INTERVENTIONS
Sensitivity to population density

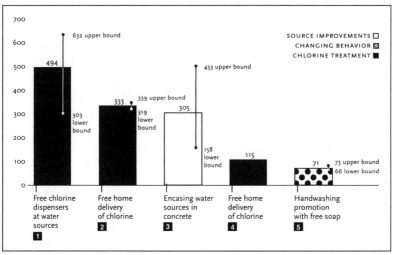

FIGURE 8A.1 Cost-effectiveness of diarrheal disease interventions: Sensitivity to population density.

Appendix 8B. Example of Cost-Effectiveness Calculations

The calculations below illustrate how the assumptions and decisions discussed above are put into practice in an actual cost-effectiveness analysis, using as an example a Malawian program of conditional cash transfers targeted at adolescent girls in Malawi and evaluated by Baird, McIntosh, and Özler (2011). We wish to gratefully acknowledge the contributions of Berk Özler, Sarah Baird, and Craig McIntosh in providing us with original cost data about the Zomba Cash Transfer Program, and in working with us to develop the cost-effectiveness model. A more complete discussion of the lessons of this cost-effectiveness calculation, including sensitivity analysis, will be available in the J-PAL bulletin on increasing student attendance and enrollment.

In this evaluation, enumeration areas (EAs) were randomly assigned into a control group or one of two treatments: conditional cash transfers or unconditional cash transfers. Girls who were still enrolled in school ("baseline schoolgirls") as well as girls who had dropped out before the program began ("baseline dropouts") were eligible for the transfers. Within the conditional cash-transfer (CCT) treatment group, the transfer that families received was randomly varied between $5 and $15 per month, to study the effect of differing transfer amounts on education and health outcomes. To measure potential spillover effects of the program, a randomly selected percentage (33%, 66%, or 100%) of baseline schoolgirls in each treatment EA were selected to be eligible for cash transfers. The program was run over two school years.

Below we walk through an example of calculating the cost effectiveness of one of the two treatments in this evaluation (the CCT program) at increasing years of schooling. We list all the costs separately and model the setup of the program and the number of participants to calculate the total cost of the program, and then we divide that total cost by the total impact, which is modeled by scaling up the impact per person by the total number of participants. When an evaluation has multiple treatments, as this one does, each treatment arm requires its own cost-effectiveness calculation. Thus, the following example focuses only on the costs and impacts of the CCT treatment group, and the cost-effectiveness analysis for the second treatment (unconditional cash transfers—UCT) is not shown.

8B.1. Demographics

To estimate the cost effectiveness of the CCT program at increasing years of schooling, we first start with the basic number of students in each group so that we can later multiply the costs and impacts of the program in the correct way. We look at the 46 enumeration areas (fig. 8B.1, cell B11) that received the CCT program, out of the total 176 EAs (cell B12). Each of these EAs has an average of 16.5 baseline schoolgirls in it who are eligible for the program (cell B13).[5] For the evaluation, a randomly selected percentage of baseline schoolgirls within each EA were chosen to participate in the program. However, we assume that all eligible girls in an EA will participate, since a scaled-up program would be extremely unlikely to withhold transfers from eligible girls within the program area. (This assumption affects how we will later calculate the cost per student. For example, if there are fixed costs for serving an EA or a school, these costs will now be spread across all the students in the school.) This gives a total of 759 baseline schoolgirls (cell B16) across the CCT EAs. Of these, 33% (cell B15) are in secondary school and will

	A	B	C
1	**Study Title**	"Cash or Condition? Evidence from a Cash Transfer Experiment"	
2	Authors	Sarah Baird, Craig McIntosh, Berk Ozler	
3	Publication Date	Nov. 2011 The Quarterly Journal of Economics (2011) 126 (4): 1709-1753	
4	Location	Zomba District, Malawi	
5	Base Year	2008	
6	Year of Analysus	2010	
7	Outcome Measure	Additional years of education induced, per US $100 spent	
8	Treatment Arm	Conditional Cash Transfer, Minimum Transfer Amount	

	A	B (Number)	C (Unit)
10	**Demographics**	Number	Unit
11	Number of treatment enumeration areas (EAs)-CCT arm	46	EAs
12	Total number of EAs (UCT, CCT, and control arms)	176	EAs
13	Number of baseline schoolgirls per EA	16.5	schoolgirls
14	Baseline schoolgirls, as % of eligible population	87%	
15	Proportion of eligible girls in secondary school	33%	
16	Total baseline schoolgirls eligible for CCTransfers	759	schoolgirls
17			
18	Parent time spent at initial meeting (travel & meeting)	3.5	hours
19	Parent time to pick up transfer, per month	2.5	hours
20	Program duration	2	years
21	Average # of months transfers actually given, per year	7.05	months
22	Number of school terms per year	3	terms
23			
24	US annual inflation, base year to 2009	2.18%	
25	Avg US annual inflation, base year to year of analysis	2.00%	
26	Time elapsed between base year and year of analysis	2	years
27	Discount rate	10%	
28	Base year standard exchange rate	140.52	MWK/USD
29	Year of analysis standard exchange rate	140.52	MWK/USD
30	Year of analysis PPP exchange rate	48.95	MWK/USD

Item	J	K
Enrollment and Attendance, Baseline & Impacts		
Comparison group enrollment rate	79.9%	
Percentage point change in enrollment, treatment	9.5%	
Treatment group enrollment rate	89.4%	
Comparison group attendance rate	81.0%	
Percentage point change in attendance, treatment	8.0%	
Treatment group attendance rate	89.0%	
Opportunity Cost of Parent Time		
Average daily wage, MWK	87.5	2009 MWK
Average daily wage, USD	0.62	2009 USD
Average monthly wage, USD	0.08	2009 USD
Administration Costs		
Total variable admin cost of program, Year 2	$70,000	2008 USD
Total fixed admin cost of program, Year 2	$10,000	2008 USD
% of variable costs spent on transfer distribution, CCT and UCT	33%	
% of variable costs spent on gathering attendance data, CCT and UCT	67%	
Total costs of transfer distribution, baseline schoolgirls in CCT arm	$12,792	2008 USD
Admin costs of gathering attendance data, CCT arm	$40,600	2008 USD
Fixed admin costs, CCT arm	$6,301	2008 USD
Total cost of census, in evaluation for UCT and CCT arm	$100,000	2008 USD

FIGURE 8B.1

	Ingredient	Unit Cost	Currency (Location & Yr)	Units Req'd (per year)	Years Req'd	Total Cost/Yr, Local Currency	Total Cost/Yr, Yr Incurred USD	Total Cost/Yr, Base Year USD	PV of Cost Stream, Base Yr USD	Total Cost Yr of Analysis USD	Cost Incurred By
		B	C	D	E	F	G	H	I	J	K
34											
35	Census to identify eligible girls in CCT EAs	$26,136	2008 USD	1	1		$26,136	$26,136	$26,136	$27,193	Implementer
36	Admin costs of transfer distribution, per year	$12,792	2008 USD	1	2		$12,792	$12,792	$24,421	$25,408	Implementer
37	Admin costs of gathering attendance data, per year	$40,600	2008 USD	1	2		$40,600	$40,600	$77,509	$80,642	Implementer
38	Fixed costs of admin, per year	$6,301	2008 USD	1	2		$6,301	$6,301	$12,030	$12,516	Implementer
39	Parents' foregone hourly wage to attend meeting	$0.08	2009 USD	2657	1		$207	$202	$202	$211	Beneficiaries
40	Monthly transfer per girl meeting criteria (parents)	$4.00	2008 USD	5351	2		$21,404	$21,404	$40,862	$42,513	Implementer
41	Monthly transfer per girl meeting criteria (schoolgirls)	$1.00	2008 USD	5351	2		$5,351	$5,351	$10,215	$10,628	Implementer
42	Per term secondary school fees, per schoolgirl	3,000	2008 MWK	759	2	2,277,000	$16,204	$16,204	$30,935	$32,185	Implementer
43	Parents' foregone hourly wage to collect transfers	$0.08	2009 USD	13377	2		$1,041	$1,019	$1,945	$2,024	Beneficiaries
44											
45											

	Impacts	# Eligible Girls	Enrollment Rate	Attendance (Conditional on Enrollment)	Total Years of Schooling Achieved
46					
47	Years of schooling achieved per year, comparison girls	759	79.9%	81.0%	491
48	Years of schooling achieved per year, treatment girls	759	89.4%	89.0%	604
49					
50	Additional years of schooling from treatment				113
51	Present value of additional years of schooling				216

FIGURE 8B.1 (*continued*)

	A	B	C	D	E	F	G	H	I	J	K
54	Cost-Effectiveness	Standard	PPP					Assumptions - All eligible girls, not randomly assigned proportion, (as in the evaluation) can receive transfer			
55	Total Cost	$233,319	$669,811	2009 USD							
56	Total cost to implementer	$231,084	$663,396	2009 USD				- Average daily wage data is taken from the mean of the 10th and 90th percentiles of wage distribution in a survey in central Malawi, rather than the median			
57	Total cost to beneficiaries	$2,235	$6,415	2009 USD							
58	Cost-Effectiveness										
59	Cost per additional year of schooling, to implementer	$1,082	$3,108	per year							
60	Cost per additional year of schooling, to beneficiaries	$10	$30	per year							

FIGURE 8B.1 (*continued*)

also have their secondary school fees paid, if they meet the attendance cutoff.

Next, because we include the cost of beneficiary time to participate in the program, we estimate the time that families spend on different aspects of the program. Under the demographics section, we record that the authors estimate that it will take the average parent 3.5 hours (cell B18) to travel to and attend the initial meeting that informs them about this program. Each month in which they pick up transfers, the authors estimate that they will spend another 2.5 hours (cell B19) traveling round-trip. The program was run over two years (cell B20) and the average girl met the eligibility criteria for the CCTs 7.05 (cell B21) of the 10 months they were available. There are three school terms (cell B22) each year.

8B.2. Inflation and Exchange Rates

In order to bring all cost and impact calculations in terms of present value in USD for a standard year of analysis (the same year of analysis we use for all other programs in this cost-effectiveness analysis) we must use a few outside pieces of information. As we have some costs in terms of 2009 USD, and some in terms of 2008 USD, we will need to know the average annual inflation rates between 2009 and 2010 (cell B24) and between 2008 and 2010 (cell B25). As discussed above, we use GDP deflator inflation rates for this analysis. We also note the discount rate that we will assume for this analysis (cell B27), which is around the median discount rate used by countries employing the SOC (see table 8.3 above), and the standard and PPP exchange rates for both the base year and the year of analysis (cells B28–B31).

8B.3. Enrollment and Attendance Impacts

Enrollment in the comparison group was approximately 79.9% (cell J11). Over the six terms of observation, the minimum transfer amount caused an additional 0.572 terms of enrollment, translating into a 9.5 percentage point (cell J12) change each term. There was no additional impact from giving more money beyond the minimum transfer amount, and so we will use the impact estimate based on the minimum transfer amount. (This decision also affects how costs are calculated—to match the assumption about impact, we will also estimate costs as though all girls received the minimum transfer amount.) This means that the enrollment in treatment group was on average 89.4% (cell J13).

Attendance in the comparison group was approximately 81% (cell J15). Overall in 2009 (the year over which attendance was observed) the average transfer amounts caused an 8 percentage point (cell J16) increase in attendance, conditional on being enrolled. Data are not currently available for the effect of the minimum transfer amount on student attendance (the sample size is too small to precisely measure effects among this group) so we assume that the minimum and average transfer sizes have the same effect on attendance. This means that the conditional attendance in the treatment group was on average 89% (cell J17).

8B.4. Opportunity Cost of Parent Time

To estimate the costs that families faced in participating in this program, we need to know the opportunity cost of their time, in addition to how much time they spent participating, which was recorded above. This evaluation did not gather information on average daily wages in the study area; nor were we able to find district-level data on daily wages. Using information from Jessica Goldberg's (2011) paper "Kwacha gonna do?" we estimate a rural Malawian daily wage of 87.5 MWK (cell J20), or approximately 62 cents (cell J21). This translates into an hourly opportunity cost of parent time of around 8 cents (cell J22).

8B.5. Administration Costs

We also need to estimate how much was spent on the administration of the program. Because the CCT treatment was implemented alongside the UCT treatment, administrative costs were only available in aggregate, and so we had to estimate how much of those total administrative costs were attributable to the CCT arm. The authors estimated that the total administration costs in year 2 were approximately $80,000, split between $10,000 of fixed costs (cell J26) and $70,000 of variable costs (cell J25). Approximately 33% (cell J27) of these variable costs were spent on the distribution of transfers in all treatment EAs, while 67% (cell J28) were spent on gathering attendance data to verify conditionality in the CCT EAs.

It should be noted that these administration costs covered both baseline schoolgirls and baseline dropouts, so if we are restricting our estimate of the impacts to baseline schoolgirls, we must include only the costs of administration needed to include the baseline schoolgirls in the program. And when we calculate the costs for "the CCT program," we need to exclude the costs that were spent on administration on the other treatment, unconditional cash transfers. This can be done by assuming that the cost of transfer distribution was the same across EAs, and so the cost of transfer distribution within one treatment arm was simply equal to (for instance) the number of CCT EAs as a proportion of all of the treatment EAs (46/(46 + 27)) = 63%. Based on these considerations, we separate out three types of administrative costs:

- Administrative costs of transfer distribution, spent just on baseline schoolgirls in CCT EAs (cell J29) = $70,000 * 33% of administrative costs spent on distribution * 63% of distribution costs spent in CCT EAs
- Administrative costs of verifying attendance, spent just on baseline schoolgirls in CCT EAs (cell J30) = $70,000 * 67% of administrative costs spent on verification * 87% of verification done for baseline schoolgirls
- Fixed administrative costs, proportion attributable to CCT EAs (cell J31) = $10,000 * 63% of fixed administrative costs spent in CCT EAs

These costs, as well as others based on the demographics and program characteristics outlined above, are brought together in the ingredients section below.

8B.6. Ingredients Section

The information above provides all of the necessary details on the costs of this program, but it is necessary to make sure that all of these costs are expressed in the same currency, from the perspective of the same year, and taking into account the present value of the cost stream (discounting).

a. *Listing Ingredients.* The total cost of the initial census for all EAs (CCT, UCT, and control) was $100,000 (cell J32). We have distributed this proportionally to each EA by multiplying $100,000 times 26.1% (46/176) and included the fraction of the initial census for the CCT arm of the program (row 35). We then bring in the administrative costs of transfer distribution, gathering attendance, and the fixed administrative costs in rows 36–38, and the opportunity cost of parents' time to attend informational sessions in row 39. As we are modeling the cost effectiveness of the minimum transfer amount, we assume that each girl gets a total of $5/month for all months for which transfers are given (rows 40–41). For each eligible girl in secondary school, the program must pay 3,000 MWK per term of the school year to pay for her secondary school fees, included in row 42. Last, we include the opportunity cost of parents' time to pick up transfers each month in row 43.

Next, in moving from left to right in the spreadsheet, we follow a number of steps to bring all the costs that we have now listed into a common currency and a common year, and discounted to reflect the present value stream of costs. This same order of steps is used for all the programs included in our larger cost-effectiveness analysis on student participation.

b. *Currency Exchange.* The only ingredient whose cost is not reported in USD is the secondary school fees for girls (row 42), therefore this must be converted using the exchange rate noted above in cell B28. Now, all costs are expressed in terms of the same country's currency (column G).

c. *Deflation to Base Year.* The opportunity cost of parents' time was available only in terms of 2009 currency, and so it is necessary to deflate this back to the base year (2008) using the inflation rate noted above in cell B24. Now, all costs are expressed in terms of the same country's currency, in the same year (column H).

d. *Present Value of Cost Streams.* This was a two-year program, and many of the ingredients must be purchased over both years of the program. For all ingredients for which this is true (everything except rows 35 and 39), it is necessary to calculate the present value of the cost stream using the discount rate identified above in the Demographics section (cell B27). Now, all costs are expressed as the present value of the cost stream in terms of the same country's currency, in the same year (column I).

e. *Inflation to Year of Analysis.* The costs in column I are still expressed in terms of the present value in the base year of the actual program (2008), and so it is necessary to inflate them forward to the year of analysis (2010) using the inflation rate noted above in cell B25. Now, all costs are expressed as the present value of the cost stream in terms of the same country's currency, in the year of analysis (column J).

The total cost of the program can now be calculated as the sum of all of these present value streams (see the "Total Cost" cell in the "Cost-effectiveness box below: cell B55).

8B.7. Aggregating Impacts

We also need to calculate the total impact for the entire group for which we just totaled the costs. To calculate total impacts, we calculate the total years of schooling achieved in the treatment (row 57) and comparison (row 56) EAs, and subtract. We calculate the total years of schooling achieved by multiplying the enrollment rate (cell C47) times the conditional attendance rate (cell D47) and then multiplying by the number of eligible girls (cell B47). Note that we do not use the actual number of baseline schoolgirls in comparison EAs to calculate the total impacts in the "comparison group" — this is because we are not calculating the total years of education that would occur in the 88 comparison EAs, but rather the total years of education that would occur if the 46 treatment EAs has not experienced the program. So, we take the level of enrollment and attendance experienced in the comparison group, and then scale that up by the number of girls in the treatment we are analyzing. We estimate that girls in treatment EAs experience a total of 113 additional years of schooling over one year of the program (cell F50), and at a 10% discount rate this works out to be 216 additional years of schooling over the two-year life of the program (cell F51).

8B.8. Cost Effectiveness

The final cost per additional year of schooling (cell B58) is calculated as the total cost (cell B55) divided by the total impact over the life of the program (cell F51).

Appendix 8C

Table 8C.1 Worksheet for gathering costs

1. Study Information

Study title

Authors

Location

Base year (year in which program launched)

2. Demographics

	Number	Unit
Intervention duration		
Number of individuals/Schools/Communities in treatment		
Number of individuals per school/Class/Community		
Exchange rate used (if costs already in USD)		
Local daily wage (i.e., opportunity cost of time)		

3. Cost Data

Please bring together all of the costs of running the project you're evaluating (distinct from the costs of actually evaluating it) and fill out information on all cost items that apply to this program. The goal of this information is to get an idea of how much it would cost a government or NGO to replicate the program, so it's important to consider whether the project had any cost categories covered for you (i.e., by piggybacking on existing NGO infrastructure) that a scaled-up model of your program would have to pay for. One useful way to think about this cost-gathering exercise is as though you were writing a recipe for the intervention you are testing, and you need to come up with a list of all ingredients.

- What is every single ingredient necessary for this program to have the observed impact?
  - How much of each ingredient is needed?
  - How much does one unit of this ingredient cost?
  - When is this ingredient used?

The categories listed are intended as ideas for the kinds of costs you might incur. Please add your own categories and items as necessary.

Exchange → Deflation → Present value → Inflation

				Total cost per year				
Costs of administration and training	Unit cost	Currency (location and year)	Units required (per year)	Years required	Year incurred local currency	Year incurred USD	Base year USD	PV of cost stream, base year USD	Total cost, year of analysis USD
Hourly wages, surveyors for targeting survey?									
Transportation per diem for surveyors?									
Hourly wages, data entry staff?									
[Insert your own cost items]									
[Insert your own cost items]									

Exchange → Deflation → Present value → Inflation

				Total cost per year				
Costs of marketing and education	Unit cost	Currency (location and year)	Units required (per year)	Years required	Year incurred local currency	Year incurred USD	Base year USD	PV of cost stream, base year USD	Total cost, year of analysis USD
Development of outreach leaflets?									
Printing of outreach leaflets?									
Hourly wages of trainers, for marketing training?									
Per diems of trainers, for marketing training?									
Hourly wages of marketers?									
[Insert your own cost items]									
[Insert your own cost items]									

Exchange → Deflation → Present value → Inflation

	Unit cost	Currency (location and year)	Units required (per year)	Years required	Total cost per year				
					Year incurred local currency	Year incurred USD	Base year USD	PV of cost stream, base year USD	Total cost, year of analysis USD
Costs of materials and productive assets									
Procuring productive assets?									
Productive asset (per client)?									
Transportation fee (per asset)?									
Cash subsidy (per client per month)?									
[Insert your own cost items]									
[Insert your own cost items]									

Exchange → Deflation → Present value → Inflation

	Unit cost	Currency (location and year)	Units required (per year)	Years required	Total cost per year				
					Year incurred local currency	Year incurred USD	Base year USD	PV of cost stream, base year USD	Total cost, year of analysis USD
Costs to clients									
Hourly wage of incorporating new technology?									
Subsidies for clients (negative cost of cash subsidy)?									
[Insert your own cost items]									
[Insert your own cost items]									

Exchange → Deflation → Present value → Inflation

	Unit cost	Currency (location and year)	Units required (per year)	Years required	Total cost per year				
					Year incurred local currency	Year incurred USD	Base year USD	PV of cost stream, base year USD	Total cost, year of analysis USD
[Insert your own category here]									
[Insert your own cost items]									
[Insert your own cost items]									

Acknowledgments

We are grateful to Abhijit Banerjee, Paul Glewwe, Jere Behrman, Miguel Urquiola, and Patrick McEwan for valuable discussion and feedback. We also thank participants at the Minnesota conference on "Education Policy in Developing Countries" for their comments and many colleagues at J-PAL including Mary Ann Bates, Cristobal Marshall, Leah Horgan, Dina Grossman, Anna Yalouris, and Shawn Powers.

Notes

1. We use the term "policymakers" to refer not only to civil servants in governments, but also to decision makers in foundations, international development organizations and nongovernmental organizations (NGOs) who make decisions regularly on how to allocate resources between competing programs that try to achieve the same objective.

2. These programs were analyzed from the perspective of 2010 in USD. The discount rate used was 10%, all exchange rates were standard, and inflation was calculated using GDP deflators.

3. See, e.g., Burde and Linden 2012; Glewwe, Ilias, and Kremer 2010; Lassibille et al. 2010; and Linden 2008.

4. Often cost-effectiveness is obtained by calculating the cost per beneficiary and then dividing this by the impact per beneficiary to get a cost-effectiveness ratio per beneficiary, without aggregating total impacts or costs. While mechanically this should give the same result as first aggregating costs and impacts across all beneficiaries and then dividing out those totals, we have chosen to begin with aggregate estimates, as it allows us to spell out the assumptions explicitly. For instance, if a remedial education program that cost $15 per child per year increased test scores by 0.15 standard deviations per child, it would appear relatively simple to divide these out. But if the impact per child had been measured after two years of the program, while the costs were incurred in both years, then the time frames would not match. And if the cost per child had been simply summed up, then divided by the number of children, then the costs from the second year of implementation would have been implicitly assigned a 0% discount rate. While aggregating impacts and costs and then dividing them out cannot prevent errors or accidental assumptions of this kind, the process of aggregation makes these issues more visible and provides a convenient opportunity to address them.

5. Note that we are not including impacts on baseline dropouts as they did not receive the conditionality experiment. Given that the program did have an impact on the reenrollment of baseline dropouts, this means that the calculations produce an underestimate of the cost-effectiveness of a population-based CCT like the one studied (rather than a commonly used school-based CCT).

Bibliography

Anand, Sudhir, and Kara Hanson. 1997. "Disability-Adjusted Life Years: A Critical Review." *Journal of Health Economics* 16 (6): 685–702. doi: 10.1016/S0167-6296(97)00005-2.

Baird, Sarah, Craig McIntosh, and Berk Özler. 2011. "Cash or Condition? Evidence from a Cash Transfer Experiment." *Quarterly Journal of Economics* 126 (4): 1709–53. doi: 10.1093/qje/qjr032.

Banerjee, Abhijit V., Shawn Cole, Esther Duflo, and Leigh Linden. 2007. "Remedying Education: Evidence from Two Randomized Experiments in India." *Quarterly Journal of Economics* 122 (3): 1235–64. doi:10.1162/qjec.122.3.1235.

Bobonis, Gustavo, Edward Miguel, and Charu Puri-Sharma. 2006. "Anemia and School Participation." *Journal of Human Resources* 41 (4): 692–722. doi:10.3368/jhr.XLI.4.692.

Burde, Dana, and Leigh Linden. 2012. "The Effect of Village-Based Schools: Evidence from a Randomized Controlled Trial in Afghanistan." NBER Working Paper No. 18039, National Bureau of Economic Research, Cambridge, MA. http://www.nber.org/papers/w18039.

Carnoy, Martin. 1975. "The Economic Costs and Returns to Educational Television." *Economic Development and Cultural Change* 23 (2): 207–48.

Duflo, Esther, Pascaline Dupas, and Michael Kremer. 2011. "Peer Effects, Teacher Incentives, and the Impact of Tracking: Evidence from a Randomized Evaluation in Kenya." *American Economic Review* 101 (5): 1739-74. doi:10.1257/aer.101.5.1739.

Duflo, Esther, Rema Hanna, and Stephen P. Ryan. 2012. "Incentives to Work: Getting Teachers to Come to School." *American Economic Review* 102 (4): 1241-78. doi:10.1257/aer.102.4.1241.

Evans, David, Michael Kremer, and M thoni Ngatia. 2009. "The Impact of Distributing School Uniforms on Children's Education in Kenya." Working paper. Washington, DC: World Bank. http://www.povertyactionlab.org/publication/impact-distributing-school-uniforms-childrens-education-kenya.

Glewwe, Paul, Nauman Ilias, and Michael Kremer. 2010. "Teacher Incentives." *American Economic Journal: Applied Economics* 2 (3): 205–27. doi:10.1257/app.2.3.205.

Goldberg, Jessica. 2011. "Kwacha Gonna Do? Experimental Evidence about Labor Supply in Rural Malawi." Working paper, University of Michigan, Ann Arbor, MI. http://www-personal.umich.edu/~jegoldbe/docs/goldberg_ganyu.pdf.

Jensen, Robert. 2010. "The (Perceived) Returns to Education and the Demand for Schooling." *Quarterly Journal of Economics* 125 (2): 515-48. doi: 10.1162/qjec.2010.125.2.515.

Kremer, Michael, Edward Miguel, and Rebecca Thornton. 2009. "Incentives to Learn." *Review of Economics and Statistics* 91 (3): 437–56. http://www.mitpressjournals.org/doi/pdf/10.1162/rest.91.3.437.

Kremer, Michael, and Christel Vermeersch. 2004. "School Meals, Educational Achievement, and School Competition: Evidence from a Randomized Evaluation." World Bank Policy Research Working Paper No. 3523. Washington, DC: World Bank. http://papers.ssrn.com/sol3/papers.cfm?abstract_id =667881.

Lassibille, Gérard, Jee-Peng Tan, Cornelia Jesse, and Trang Van Nguyen. 2010. "Managing for Results in Primary Education in Madagascar: Evaluating the Impact of Selected Workflow Interventions." *World Bank Economic Review* 24 (2): 303-29. http://wber.oxfordjournals.org/content/early/2010/08/06 /wber.lhq009.full.

Levin, Henry M. 2001. "Waiting for Godot: Cost-Effectiveness Analysis in Education." *New Directions for Evaluation* 90: 55–68. doi:10.1002/ev.12.

Levin, Henry M., and Patrick J. McEwan. 2001. *Cost-Effectiveness Analysis*, 2nd ed. Thousand Oaks, CA: Sage Publications.

Linden, Leigh. 2008. "Complement or Substitute? The Effect of Technology on Student Achievement in India." Working paper, Colombia University, New York, NY. http://www.povertyactionlab.org/publication/complement -substitute-effect-technology-student-achievement-india.

Miguel, Edward, and Michael Kremer. 2004. "Worms: Identifying Impacts on Education and Health in the Presence of Externalities." Econometrica 72 (1): 159-217. doi: 10.1111/j.1468-0262.2004.00481.x.

Nguyen, Trang. 2008. "Information, Role Models, and Perceived Returns to Education: Experimental Evidence from Madagascar." Job market paper, MIT, Cambridge, MA. http://www.povertyactionlab.org/sites/default/files /documents/Nguyen%202008.pdf.

Oster, Emily and Rebecca Thornton. 2011. "Menstruation, Sanitary Products, and School Attendance: Evidence from a Randomized Evaluation." *American Economic Journal: Applied Economics* 3 (1): 91-100. doi: 10.1257 /app.3.1.91.

Schultz, T. Paul. 2000. *Final Report: The Impact of PROGRESA on School Enrollments*. International Food Policy Research Institute, Washington, DC. http://www.ifpri.org/publication/impact-progresa-school-enrollments.

———. 2004. "School Subsidies for the Poor: Evaluating the Mexican PROGRESA Program." *Journal of Development Economics* 74 (1): 199–250. doi: 10.1016/j.jdeveco.2003.12.009.

US Department of Health and Human Services. 1996. *Cost-Effectiveness in Health and Medicine: Report to the U.S. Public Health Service by the Panel on Cost-Effectiveness in Health and Medicine*. United States: U.S. Department of Health and Human Services, Office of Public Health and Science, Office of Disease Prevention and Health Promotion.

Zhuang, Juzhong, Zhihong Liang, Tun Lin, and Franklin De Guzman. 2007. "Theory and Practice in the Choice of a Social Discount Rate for Cost-Benefit Analysis." ERD Working Paper No. 94, Asian Development Bank, Manila. http://www.adb.org/publications/theory-and-practice-choice-social -discount-rate-cost-benefit-analysis-survey.

Index